The person charging this book is
responsible for its return to the
Learning Resources Center (LRC)
Richland Community College
One College Park
Decatur, IL 62521-8512
on or before the latest date
stamped below.

To renew, call
Circulation Department of the
LRC, 875-7211, Ext. 303

Due Date	Due Date

Refugees in a Global Era

Refugees in a Global Era

Philip Marfleet

First published in 2006 by
PALGRAVE MACMILLAN
Houndmills, Basingstoke, Hampshire RG21 6XS and
175 Fifth Avenue, New York, N.Y. 10010
Companies and representatives throughout the world.

PALGRAVE MACMILLAN is the global academic imprint of the Palgrave Macmillan division of St. Martin's Press, LLC and of Palgrave Macmillan Ltd. Macmillan® is a registered trademark in the United States, United Kingdom and other countries. Palgrave is a registered trademark in the European Union and other countries.

ISBN-13: 978–0–333–77783–1 hardback
ISBN-10: 0–333–77783–2   hardback
ISBN-13: 978–0–333–77784–8 paperback
ISBN-10: 0–333–77784–0   paperback

This book is printed on paper suitable for recycling and made from fully managed and sustained forest sources.

A catalogue record for this book is available from the British Library.

Library of Congress Cataloging-in-Publication Data

Marfleet, Philip, 1948–
    Refugees in a global era / Philip Marfleet.
        p. cm.
    Includes bibliographical references and index.
    ISBN 0–333–77783–2 (cloth)—ISBN 0–333–77784–0 (pbk.)
        1. Refugees. 2. Forced migration. 3. Emigration and immigration.
    4. Globalization. I. Title.

HV640.M333 2006
305.9′06914—dc22   2005056102

10 9 8 7 6 5 4 3 2 1
15 14 13 12 11 10 09 08 07 06

Printed in China

This book is dedicated to my loving and much-loved parents, Gwyneth and Gerry Marfleet, who never stopped encouraging all their children; and to my daughter Ellie, with big apologies for all those hours at the computer

Contents

Foreword

I first visited a refugee camp in 1977. It had been home to several thousand Palestinians but had already disappeared from official maps, having been bombed so effectively that only the shells of houses and the walls of a school and a clinic remained. Still there was evidence among the weeds and flowers of those who had lived there: battered cooking utensils, old boots, shreds of newspaper and pages of school-books. It was an awful scene in a beautiful setting: Nabatiyeh camp in Southern Lebanon had been blown out of existence. Who were the people of the camp? How had they got there? What had happened to them? Did anyone record their experiences? Did anyone care?

The inhabitants of the camp had originated in Galilee, fleeing north in 1948 during conflicts which brought the state of Israel into being. Like many refugees they had expected to return soon: their homes were not far away and they had been promised that all would be well. They were still in Nabatiyeh more than 25 years later when the bombers came and they faced displacement for a second time. Many years after my first visit I met an old woman in Beirut who had lived in Nabatiyeh and who related her life in Palestine and in the camp. I asked about the others who had lived there: they were 'all gone' she said. After the destruction most had moved to other camps in Lebanon where they had faced repeated conflict. Recently many had left for the United States and Canada – displaced for a third or fourth time they had 'gone far away, to look for a new life'.

I had thought at first that the experiences of the Palestinians must be unusual. The refugees I knew about in Britain had come mainly from states on the other side of the Iron Curtain and occasionally from Africa or Latin America. They travelled individually or in small groups, seeking protection from persecution: most seemed to have been welcomed and some had celebrity status. The idea of repeated mass displacement was new but the more I investigated, the more evidence there was of similar experiences. Eventually I worked for Amnesty International, at which there was a wealth of material on refugee movements. More and more people were facing multiple displacements: forced from their places of origin, they too were moving from camps and holding centres to the cities of Africa, Asia, Latin America and beyond. Sometimes they undertook long journeys to seek asylum in the West; sometimes they were caught up in war zones or local conflicts and moved back and forth en masse. Few seemed to return to their original homes, or to do so under circumstances of their choosing. It was a complex and puzzling picture.

In 1989 I went to work in Cairo, where the situation started to become clearer. Here there were a number of large refugee communities, most originating in the Horn of Africa. Each day people arrived to join them, fleeing the war zones but finding only a brief respite – most were compelled to live in extreme hardship, marginals in a city in which the mass of the population had only a precarious existence. A small group of researchers, notably the late Derek Cooper, had made it their business to bring to light the circumstances under which the refugees were living. They revealed much about the complex journeys of those who had reached Cairo, the communities which were in formation, and the pressures which compelled refugees to move on in the search for security. Their work also provided disturbing insights into the workings of the asylum system, and hints of the way in which exclusionary activities of Western states and transnational agencies were to develop. It needed to be taken further – but who was investigating refugees and their experiences?

In the late 1980s the Stalinist states of the Eastern Bloc finally collapsed and there were trumpetings of a New World Order. These included assertions that with Communism dead conflicts worldwide would subside and forced migration would diminish. But the 'new' world was volatile, disordered and productive of repeated crises of mass displacement. It was clear that conflicts were continuing and intensifying, and that the number of refugees was increasing rapidly. As more sought security in the West there were panic reactions in Europe and North America. A new discourse of the refugee, which had been emerging throughout the 1980s, had hardened into an official ideology of extreme hostility towards forced migrants. Now refugees were to be feared: they were an unhealthy, even malign influence. They had nothing in common with those earlier invited to seek sanctuary: on the contrary, they should be kept far from countries in which they hoped for asylum. The questions were mounting: why had yesterday's deserving refugees become the menacing and unwelcome aliens of today? Why did so many become 'illegal' immigrants, and why were they harassed so relentlessly? Had the migrants changed, or had politicians, officials and those who wrote increasingly hostile newspaper editorials, transformed their own agendas?

The new field of Refugee Studies was in an early phase of development and its small core of researchers was faced with an enormous deficit between growing official interest in forced migration, coloured by increasing hostility to refugees, and investigations which could be carried out in a non-prejudicial atmosphere and with some concern for the fate of migrants. In 1995 I was fortunate to meet two colleagues at the University of East London (UEL), Patricia Tuitt and Alice Bloch, who had similar concerns. When we initiated a postgraduate programme in Refugee Studies at UEL, some answers started to appear. The course drew in many students, including refugees from every part of the world. Over the years a huge range of experiences was represented, and by means of discussion and debate with individuals and groups light has been thrown upon many difficult questions. At the same time there has been an enormous increase in the literature on forced migration. Stimulated by the exchanges at UEL and by the new research I have attempted in this book to look in detail at the issues that seemed so perplexing at Nabatiyeh, in Cairo and later in London, and which are often addressed much too hesitantly in the key academic fields concerned with migration.

States and borders

I have not attempted to address the whole refugee agenda. I have not tackled issues of refugee settlement, of return or repatriation – the final stages of the refugee 'cycle'. Nor have I taken up directly matters of integration, or of refugee well-being in the context of psychosocial perspectives. Some of the suggestions I have made will meet with a mixed response. Two arguments in particular may seem controversial: that relating to the conduct of states in relation to migrants, and that which sets out the case for open borders. I have suggested that the historical record shows a high level of cynicism of states vis-à-vis refugees: that states have taken a calculated and instrumental approach to people who are vulnerable and often defenceless, and that this must be put on the record and challenged. I have also proposed that states cannot be left with responsibility for refugees: a suggestion that for some is at odds with an international legal regime based upon the duties of states in relation to those who merit protection. But states themselves are abandoning their responsibilities: the most wealthy, powerful and stable states take the most calculating approach towards refugees, who may be punished again and again simply because they have been displaced, they are poor, and they are vulnerable. It falls to those concerned with the fate of migrants to examine other means of assuring security: to hold to account the partisans of globalisation, with their formal commitment to a world of free movement, and to advance the argument for open borders.

Ideas about world development and international affairs are dominated by neo-liberalism and by theories of global politics which emanate from the US foreign policy establishment. They are often endorsed by academics for whom they have become foundational statements about world order, and about which it is implausible or even unthinkable to produce a systematic critique. But even among those most committed to neo-liberal orthodoxy some feel compelled to address its failures. Joseph Stiglitz, former chief economist at the World Bank, observes that contradictions in neo-liberal globalisation are so glaring that they demand to be confronted (Stiglitz 2002: x). Academics must be prepared to take on these hallowed ideas, he maintains. He quotes Pierre Bourdieu, who asked for politicians to behave more like academics, engaging in scientific research based on fact and evidence. Stiglitz continues: 'Regrettably the opposite happens too often, when academics involved in making policy recommendations become politicized and start to bend the evidence to fit the ideas of those in charge' (ibid). This has been all too evident in the area of migration, where some academics and researchers have accommodated their work to the agendas of states hostile to the interests of most migrants. The outcome is work which does less to reveal the patterns and dynamics of migratory movements than to confirm prejudices and ultimately to damage the interests of the displaced and of the wider society.

Acknowledgements

I want to acknowledge first the editors at Palgrave, Catherine Grey and Emily Salz, who have shown great patience over a book that has taken far too long to write. Thanks also to colleagues who have read various drafts: Adrian Budd of London South Bank University, John Molyneux of Portsmouth University and Giorgia Dona of UEL. Particular thanks to the Refugee Studies team at UEL: Giorgia Dona, Anita Fabos, Maja Korac, Siraj Sait and Helen Taylor, who have developed a series of innovative approaches to refugee issues, and with whom it has been a pleasure to work. Thanks too to friends who over years have provided all manner of materials, opportunities, insights and support, in particular to Tony Cliff, Nigel Harris, John Rose, Simon Assaf, Anne Alexander, Eli Rostami Povey, Mike Grewcock, Penny Green, John Nassari, Clare Walter, Pedro Trespadarne Fernandez, Mireia Cano Vinas, Nicola Ravden, Richard Payne, Fran Cetti, Lynne Hubbard, Kim Thomas, Barbara Harrell-Bond, Derek Cooper, Enid Hill, Kasia Grabska, Denis Cattell, Pat Ellis, Patricia Tuitt, Alice Bloch, Fred Bemak, Rita Chi-Yung Chung, Sameh Neguib, Ashraf Dabbah, Mohamed Abu Zeineh, Miriyam Aouragh, Mohamed Maragha and Aida Seif al-Dawla. I hope that no one will feel implicated in the errors and omissions – they are all my own. Finally my thanks to the students of the MA programme in Refugee Studies at UEL for the profound experiences they have been willing to share.

Introduction

Refugees – the pressing questions

In 1995 police in Hungary found 18 Sri Lankans dead in a road trailer near the town of Gyor. It was the end of a journey that had begun months earlier when each responded to advertisements in their home country offering entry to Western Europe. Most had sold all their possessions, paying migration agents to move them to Russia. Here they joined a larger group of migrants which moved on through Ukraine, Moldova and Romania to Bulgaria, where the Sri Lankans made further payments to a trucker to transport them in two trailers to Germany. After several days the occupants of one trailer were told that they had arrived at their destination. They soon discovered that they were in Hungary – and that all their compatriots in the other trailer had already died of suffocation. Most of the survivors applied for asylum in Hungary: they were refused refugee status and were soon deported.[1] Over the next ten years the Sri Lankans' tragedy was to become a familiar story. Thousands of migrants perished attempting to enter Western Europe, while many more met their deaths in efforts to reach North America and Australia. Meanwhile among those whose journeys were successful tens of thousands were seized and imprisoned, and many were forcibly repatriated. A very large number were refugees – forced migrants seeking to escape repression, war, civil conflict, and a host of economic and environmental crises. A generation earlier they might have been offered sanctuary; by the 1990s, however, most were refused on principle. This book asks about their circumstances: about the causes of their migration, their journeys and attempts to find security, and about the attitudes of states increasingly inclined to reject them. It considers a number of questions:

- Why is the world producing so many refugees?
- How are they displaced?
- Where and by what means do they travel?
- Why are so many compelled to enter illegal networks, and what are the results?

1

- What are asylum rights and why has their implementation become so problematic?
- Why are refugees the object of increased hostility in states of the West?
- Why have attitudes to refugees changed so radically, and what does this tell us about forced migrants and about host societies?
- In a climate of increased suspicion of migrants, what is the future for refugees?

Globalisation

The context for such enquiries is that of a 'globalising' world. For almost 20 years there have been loud declarations that a new era of world integration is bringing increased prosperity and harmony. As part of the process of globalisation, it is said, obstacles to the movement of capital, information and people are being radically reduced. The liberating powers of the market are bringing benefits for all – there is a general advance of economy and society, and reduction of political tension and of conflict. The old polarities – the First World against the Third World, the North against the South – are becoming less and less relevant. On this view, the dominant, neo-liberal account of globalisation, mass displacement of people is likely to become less significant and the refugee tragedies of the twentieth century will be remembered as a mark of the tortured decades that preceded a new era. For the *Financial Times*, a journal which ardently supports such views, globalisation is 'the most effective tool we have to make the world not just more prosperous, but also a freer and more peaceful place.'[2] For its chief economist Martin Wolf the challenge is to spread the opportunities presented by market integration: 'The world needs more globalization, not less' (Wolf 2005: ix and 320).

This vision of integration and harmony is at odds with the lived experience of billions of people. Falk (2002: 64) comments that 'apologists for capitalism, with their facile assumptions of an "invisible hand" and "trickle down" benefits of economic growth, are ideologically removed from the existential reality of human suffering.' The contemporary world is one of continued poverty and of greatly increased inequality; it is also the context for systemic conflict – the decade of the 1990s witnessed a host of disputes, notably local inter-ethnic struggles, followed by wars in Afghanistan and Iraq involving the world's dominant state. Very large areas of Africa, Asia and Latin America operate under conditions of 'low-intensity democracy', in which weak states experience repeated political upheavals and crises of mass displacement, producing large numbers of refugees. Driven from the zones of conflict, they have found it increasingly difficult to find security. More and more have become long-distance migrants, seeking asylum in the relatively stable societies of Europe and North America. Here, however, hostility to refugees has reached levels unseen since the 1930s. Then, argued Arendt (1986: 267) refugees were repudiated: homeless, stateless and rightless, they had become 'the scum of the earth'. Today refugees are the focus of new punitive policies which echo the tragedies of the mid-twentieth century.

During the 1980s and 1990s a series of alarmist books and articles predicted inundation of North America by refugees from the Third World. Among these was Kaplan's warning of 'The Coming Anarchy'. In the dislocation of life in West Africa, Kaplan saw an inability of local society to manage its affairs and a warning to the world at large:

> West Africa is becoming the symbol of worldwide demographic, environmental and societal stress, in which the criminal emerges as the real 'strategic' danger. Disease, overpopulation, unprovoked crime, scarcity of resources, refugee migrations, the increasing erosion of nation-states and international borders and the empowerment of private armies, security firms and international drug cartels are now most tellingly demonstrated through a West African prism. (Kaplan [1994] 2000: 36)

For Kaplan (2000: 45) world integration was under threat from such regions and their 'Juju Warriors' (sic). In support he summoned the work of Samuel Huntington, whose theory of the 'clash of civilisations' pitched much of the world's population against societies of North America and Western Europe. Huntington (1993) predicted confrontation between a series of cultural blocs, most importantly between the West and the Islamic world. Kaplan endorsed this thesis, adding only that the threat posed by migration should not be underestimated. Refugees and rural–urban migrants, he maintained, would transform the world's cities: 'uneducated but newly empowered millions' would replace the sophistication of urban life with the crudities of 'culture and tribe' (Kaplan 2000: 45). Despite new laws to regulate migration, refugees would find ways to crash official borders, 'bringing their passions with them, meaning that Europe and the United States will be weakened by cultural disputes' (Kaplan 2000: 46). Soon 'our civilization' would be under the influence of the malign elements on view in Africa and other regions of the non-Western world (ibid). An effective strategy, he concluded, *must* contain migrants within the zones of crisis.

Zolberg (2001: 5) testifies to the 'electrifying impact' of these shrill warnings on foreign affairs and defence officials in the United States. They also had their effect in Europe, where the notion of civilisational conflict developed wide currency among leading politicians and

Eurocrats, so that by the mid-1990s the idea of sealing the European Union (EU) against people from hostile 'cultural blocs' had become a key part of discussions on exclusion of immigrants (Delanty 1995, Marfleet 2003). Official hostility towards migrants appeared to have a dual purpose. With the end of the Cold War, foreign policy strategists of the Western states struggled to identify a new agenda for their traditional security concerns: as Huntington himself observed frankly: 'How will we know who we are if we don't know who we are against?'[3] A number of new enemies came into focus: Islam, terrorism, international crime – and refugees. The latter also served a specific ideological function. By the mid-1990s it was clear that much of the Third World had failed to conform to the globalist model of development. Many regions of Africa, Asia and Latin America remained stubbornly poor and increasingly afflicted by conflicts apparently rooted in differences of religion, sect, language or tradition. The response in Western thinktanks and ministries was to identify large areas of the world as dysfunctional and as threatening to the global good. Forced migrants were depicted as evidence of such dysfunction – of the inability of non-Western society to conform to the market model. A new discourse of the refugee took shape in which forced migrants bore the same base and threatening qualities said to produce instability and disorder in their places of origin. They were associated directly with the alleged criminality of regions such as West Africa – Kaplan's 'real "strategic" danger' – or with the base character Huntington imputed to people of the Islamic world. Zolberg (2001: 5) notes that these highly coloured and prejudicial accounts were not limited to the media and to official circles: academic literature evolved in parallel, albeit 'in a more moderate vein'.

As the pace of forced migration increased, immigrant communities within societies of the West were treated more and more as a threatening presence. A document prepared for the EU asserted that 'every other migrant in the "first world" ' should be assumed to be irregular and hence inauthentic.[4] By 2000 the personal details of 1.3 million people were being held on the EU's largest computer database, the Schengen information system (*Guardian*, 18 December 2000). A minority of cases involved criminal convictions; the majority were migrants whose presence on the database was taken to imply criminal activity and for whom entry to member states was to be inhibited.[5] Morrison and Crosland (2001: 93) comment on the development of a myth of migrant criminality across the European Union, 'reinforced by offialdom helping to entrench the perception of refugees as uninvited guests or deviants'. Demands for exclusion of refugees have recently become more insistent. Hundreds of detention centres have been opened in EU states and scores of thousands of applicants for asylum have been incarcerated and deported. Meanwhile in Australia all informal migrants are imprisoned, as politicians raise the spectre of invasion by refugees whose presence is said to threaten the health of the nation (see Chapters 11 and 12). The more that the world system fails to conform to the model of growth and global harmony the more eager are those in authority to displace responsibility onto the victims of conflict and social breakdown. Refugees are reviled and rejected, becoming the focal point of campaigns through which they are made to carry more and more of the historic burden of racism.

Crisis and exclusion

This book examines the theory of globalisation and its implications for patterns of forced migration. It looks at the yawning gap between developmental models prescribed by globalist theory and the reality experienced by billions of people worldwide, among whom more and more undergo the experience of displacement. It argues that forced migrants face a regime of exclusion that is itself associated with globalising processes. Economic and political changes at a world level have not diminished obstacles to free movement, rather they have prompted the construction of new physical and cultural barriers.

These developments should be understood as part of the history of the nation-state. Migration has long been driven by the forces of the market but at the same time it has been integral to the development of the state, which for over 500 years has variously encouraged and discouraged migratory movements. Those in authority in the modern state have often supported or even initiated *anticipatory* journeys: those of traders, merchants and craftsmen who have been part of historic trading networks; those of military leaders and their armies; those of voyages of discovery; those of settlers involved in colonisation and colonial rule; those of contracted workers and those of refugees whom states have sometimes welcomed and sometimes solicited. Other journeys have been *coerced*: these include the journeys of many rural migrants; those who have been victims of slavery and systems of indentured labour; those displaced by war and conflict; those transported and deported and those sent into internal exile, to prison camps and to death camps. These journeys have been part of complex migratory patterns: the transportation of vast numbers of slaves from Africa, for example, was organised initially by European traders and by settler communities which had themselves been implanted by colonial powers. More recently migration has been strictly controlled or even prohibited, as during the period between the two world wars of the twentieth century when most states erected barriers against entry, declaring that immigration threatened the integrity of the nation. Global patterns of migration have been intimately associated with the changing agendas of the state.

Periods of relatively free movement have sometimes been seen as a golden age for migration but these phases have also been associated with specific strategies of states and those they represent. They have often ended abruptly, with mass expulsions and deportations. These changes of policy have usually been linked to increased pressure on minorities within the host society, so that regulation of entry has been inseparable from an internal regime in which specific communities have been targeted, sometimes with fatal consequences. The global era has not modified this pattern – both exclusion and internal discrimination are affecting unprecedented numbers of people. Today the process of global integration by means of economic liberalisation is accompanied by intensified border control and rigorous policing of aliens. It also embraces a paradox which is seldom addressed by those who examine migratory movements. Since the late 1970s there have been sustained attempts in the West to remove restrictions on corporate business, to erode welfare provision, to weaken the power of labour and to reduce wages. One means of achieving these changes has been to import the most vulnerable form of labour, that of the informal – 'illegal' – migrant. The unofficial policy of most states of North America and Western Europe has been to maintain inward movement of such migrants through various 'back doors' and 'side doors' within the system of exclusion (see Chapter 8). In the case of Europe most of those who enter by these means are forced migrants who find that they are both reviled *and* tacitly accepted by states in which they hope to find security. Driven from the zones of crisis in Africa, Asia and Latin America, they have become objects of intense hostility and, at the same time, an integral part of efforts to restructure Western economies. Among the special features of migration in the global era is an unprecedented level of exploitation of displaced people in 'free' markets, linked to ideological efforts aimed at their social, cultural and political exclusion.

With the exception of some writers in the field of International Relations most work on migration has ignored the state or greatly underplayed its role. Hollifield (2000: 138) is right to argue that now is the time 'to bring the state back in'. But how should we view the state? Hollifield and others such as Weiner (1995), Sassen (1999) and most recently Gibney (2004) are concerned primarily with the liberal-democratic tradition: here the state is viewed as a body which mediates between competing interests within national communities, guaranteeing legal structures based upon well-established rights and interacting with other states to pursue the concerns of citizens.[6] Such an approach does not, however, provide explanations for state involvement in shaping patterns of migration; in particular, it does not account for the instrumental conduct of states in relation to migrants, and for the many sharp and often contradictory turns in policy. A more critical standpoint is required, one which allows that the modern state is part of the structure of power relations which operates within national societies and across the global system. This book raises questions about the character of the liberal state: Can it represent the interests of citizens as an integrated national community? Is it benign in relation to society as a whole? Does it mediate among contending parties or in fact champion particular interests? What is the role of politicians and state officials in making migration strategy? Why do they mislead or even deceive their publics about the reality and the outcome of such policies?

Disciplinary perspectives

There is an intense, sometimes obsessive interest in refugees among politicians and the media in the West. At the same time there is a dearth of systematic work on forced migration – a huge gap between ill-informed and often highly charged official discourses of the refugee, and research and analysis carried out without prejudice and which can be the basis for a considered approach to refugee issues. Although Refugee Studies has grown rapidly over the past ten years it remains a very small field in which researchers struggle to make good the deficit. There is a further problem: even within Refugee Studies there have been very few attempts to consider forced migration as a global phenomenon. This is understandable: migration is a notoriously difficult field in which, Harris (2002: vii) observes, 'The issues are both simple and very complicated.' The wider perspective on migration, especially forced migration, requires an approach which draws on many disciplines, and this may be one reason why, since the pioneering work of Zolberg, Suhrke and Aguayo (1989) there has been little analysis of refugee issues in the context of international/transnational developments. The present book attempts such an analysis by examining both the dynamics of forced migration and some key areas of the refugee experience. It adopts a global framework but focuses upon refugee movements to the West, both because these are becoming more significant and because they have become central to official concerns and fantasies of inundation, threat and cultural pollution.

Refugees are *produced* by a complex of factors: economic, political, social, cultural and environmental. Their lives are shaped by formal political and legal structures, and by both official and popular ideas of nation and nationalism, citizen and alien, 'race' and ethnicity. A broad frame of analysis is required – one which draws on insights from a number of disciplines and attempts to integrate these around refugees as the focus of enquiry. This book begins by using perspectives from Development Studies and International Political Economy, going on to borrow from the insights of Anthropology, Sociology, Political Science, Migration Studies, Cultural Studies and Critical Legal Theory. It also attempts to introduce matters of history – a vital and often neglected dimension of Refugee Studies. Few writers in the field of forced migration have addressed historical issues directly – there seems indeed to be an aversion to approaches which take a longer view of refugee matters, especially of relationships between forced migrants and states (perhaps because of the disturbing questions which arise over the conduct of the latter). At the same time few historians have viewed the socio-political and cultural aspects of international migration as an appropriate area for study, a situation explained in part by the nation-centred and national character of much historical writing. Although refugees do appear in some specific historical accounts there have been very few analyses of comparative issues or of conceptual matters.[7] This book therefore attempts to introduce key historical issues, beginning with developments in seventeenth-century Europe (Chapter 3), and considering attitudes and practices of the Classical and Medieval periods, of the nineteenth century, and – crucially – the troubled and ultimately tragic record of the twentieth century.

The book is arranged in three parts:

Part I – Disordered World looks at globalisation and migration. It examines the globalisation thesis and the realities of economic and political change worldwide. It considers the impact of global forces on local states and survival systems, and the pressures which produce mass displacement. It considers the early history of migration and the nation-state, and the implications for refugees. It looks at patterns of migration over the past 50 years, especially at developments which have produced unprecedented numbers of refugees.

Part II – Rights looks at the notion of universal rights, especially at the idea of the right to asylum. It examines the idea of the refugee and the ways in which this has been defined and redefined over the past three centuries. It considers how changing practices of states have presented refugees variously as heroes and as villains. It considers the refugee tragedies of the mid-twentieth century and what they can tell us about the status of aliens in modern society. It looks at patterns of migration, legal and 'illegal', and ways in which the changing policies of states have affected the status of refugees today.

Part III – Journeys and Destinations examines the circumstances of displacement and flight. It considers how social inequality and gender relations affect the displaced and shape their initial experiences of exile. It looks at refugees in camps and in urban settings, and at relationships within transnational networks. It considers the experiences of those in flight from regimes of terror and from war and intense social conflict. Finally it looks at responses in the West to the predicaments of the displaced.

Borders

This book advocates a policy of open borders. For most politicians, media people and academics in the West this means, in Harris's words, 'Thinking the Unthinkable' (Harris 2002). The modern nation-state has always prioritised control of population movement: in one sense such states have been largely about the regulation of people within national borders. In the same way international affairs has been concerned with relations among states and about the regulation of movements between them – national frontiers have been a key measure of difference and a basis upon which conflicts have been justified and often initiated. But they have always marked imagined boundaries, dividing people linked over millennia by intimate relationships, in trade and commerce and in all manner of socio-cultural and political relationships. There is therefore a glimmer of virtue in the utopian vision of globalists such as Ohmae (1989), with his 'borderless world'. But most partisans of neo-liberal globalisation have contradictory views on freedom of movement: free movement of capital (or capital of a specific origin) is to be desired, free movement of people is another matter. One of the paradoxes of the global era has been that the determination of states of the West to implement neo-liberal policies world-wide has been accompanied (at least officially) by frenetic efforts to exclude people displaced by the consequences.

The question of borders goes to the heart of contradictions in the political arrangements of contemporary capitalism. Leading politicians and diplomats, men and women of the military, corporate executives, senior academics, tourists of certain origins and highly skilled workers in certain categories move relatively freely – these are the world travellers of the global era. Almost everyone else is forbidden to cross borders unless under specific arrangements such as those which regulate contract labour. Yet the rules may be subject to sudden change. When states decide that certain migrants are desirable restrictions may be lifted, only to be reimposed when large numbers of people are en route. The result is that today's 'economic migrant' becomes tomorrow's undesirable alien. Nowhere are the contradictions clearer than in the area of asylum rights. Certain categories of refugee may be welcomed by host states and even solicited by politicians for whom they have an instrumental value. When the latters' agendas change, people who have undergone similar experiences in the very same countries of origin may be repudiated and refused asylum, so that today's refugee becomes tomorrow's 'bogus' asylum-seeker.

The focus on border control is ostensibly to do with refusing admission to non-citizens. It also has an impact on minority communities *within* the wider society, for concern with territorial borders invariably directs attention to internal cultural boundaries, encouraging nationalist and racist discourse and putting in danger people judged to differ from the national cultural norm. This process operates even when national borders are replaced by transnational frontiers – hence the creation of a passport-free area within the European Union has heightened concern among European governments about the presence of migrants in countries of the Union. Here a supranational entity mimics the exclusionary obsessions of the nation-state.

The policy of open borders has until recently been viewed with scepticism by most politicians of the mainstream and by most academics. Migration control is usually seen as necessary for the very functioning of the state system and as a good in itself. Miller (1999: 20) spells out a typical view:

> The regulation of international migration is not inherently morally objectionable. The maintenance of public order is the first obligation of every government, and effective immigration regulation is important to the achievement of a host of valued goals and objectives.

Here the relationship between immigration control and domestic politics is explicit. What is moral is that which ensures the stability of domestic society: threats to order, which apparently include immigration, must therefore be contained. This approach is common to most versions of what Gibney (2004) terms 'partial' accounts of the state in the context of migration. But the arbitrary character of controls and the instrumental intent behind state policies is becoming more widely recognised. Global changes are throwing into relief the inconsistency of controls, especially in relation to mass 'illegal' migration. Although officially 'illegal' movements are not tolerated, in practice they are encouraged, both pushing and pulling millions of migrants into the informal networks – as in the case of the Sri Lankans whose long and tortuous journey to Germany ended tragically in Hungary. Immigration policy is in fact an area of gross opportunism and extreme injustice in which the practice of states is being questioned more and more by citizens for whom it is indeed morally objectionable.

The case against immigration control is receiving a wider hearing, especially from a new and mainly youthful audience. From the late

1990s movements pursuing the strategy of globalisation 'from below', what Mittelman (2004: xi) calls 'alter globalisation', have identified strongly with refugees and migrant communities. For millions of people who have grown up in an era of globalist rhetoric the old frontiers, external and internal, seem unnecessary and their implications appear unjust. This changing climate is reflected in sustained arguments against the present regimes of control advanced in books such as those by Hayter (2000), Harding (2000), Dummett (2001), Harris (2002),[8] Cohen, Humphries and Mynott (2002), and Cohen (2003). The present book seeks to provide further support for the case to open the borders. It does not pursue in detail arguments undertaken by those who wish to endorse close control of migrants by the state (for a comprehensive account see Gibney 2004, ch 1). Rather it attempts to demonstrate that both history and contemporary practice reveal how exclusion damages migrants and host societies alike, and that there is now a compelling case for free movement – as Dummett (2001: 72) suggests, this should become less a remote aspiration and more a principle recognised as the norm.

Asylum rights

The argument for open borders is being advanced as some states prepare to narrow even the limited rights to asylum enshrined in international law. In 1951 the Geneva Convention emerged as the first coherent international statement on refugees. It defined the refugee in strictly limited terms: refugeehood, the formal status associated with the forced migrant, was reduced to a single legal definition – an expression of the priorities of Western governments then deeply involved in the ideological struggles of the Cold War. The Convention viewed refugees solely as victims of specific forms of political persecution (see Chapter 6) but it was soon clear that this did not allow for the main phenomena productive of forced migration worldwide, and the Convention was modified by regional agreements which recognised 'de facto refugees'. The most significant of these, that drawn up by the Organisation for African Unity (OAU – now the African Union), recognised the right to asylum of all those displaced by war, occupation and 'events seriously disturbing public order', allowing for some of the multiple causes of mass displacement. Even these more liberal approaches have, however, proved inadequate in a world in which scores of millions of people are being displaced. As the United Nations High Commissioner for Refugees (UNHCR) has observed, people may flee because of specific forms of persecution but also because their circumstances make it impossible to remain: hence refugees include those who flee poverty and 'wretched conditions' associated with marginalisation and prejudice (UNHCR 1995: 198). Since these comments were made in the mid-1990s the circumstances of the mass of people in vulnerable regions have worsened, prompting more to flee as a means of survival. The response of governments in desired regions of asylum has been to interpret the 1951 Convention more narrowly. In 1995 the UNHCR noted the practice whereby 'a movement that was once perceived by the receiving countries as a refugee flow is redefined as a movement of economic migrants. ... The refugee/migrant distinction is ... subject to changing interpretations by countries of asylum' (ibid). This practice has become more and more general, so that today those who apply for asylum in the West are routinely assumed to be illegitimate. Most are denied asylum rights by politicians and officials who interpret the Convention in increasingly narrow terms, with the result, suggests Tuitt (1996: 20), that we are witnessing 'the death of the refugee'. The combined effect of these measures has been to weaken ideas about asylum throughout the world, so that even countries which hitherto accommodated refugees without difficulty have become much more reluctant to do so. Human Rights Watch (1999) has suggested that the 'increasingly hostile and xenophobic' attitude of Western states is being adopted elsewhere as states close their borders and sometimes endorse or even initiate attacks upon long-established refugee communities.

States which were authors of the 1951 agreement are now attempting to rewrite it. The key principles recognised in the Convention should be supported against this attack. The only satisfactory answer for those who experience displacement is a policy of open borders but until such time as there is greater freedom of movement it is necessary to endorse the premise which underlies ideas of asylum rights and is recognised in part in the Convention – that displaced people have good reason to seek security and that it is in the interests of all that they should be accommodated.

Definitions

Western states exclude most forced migrants because the latter are said to lack authenticity: their claims for asylum do not satisfy the definition of the refugee. Who then is a refugee? Papademitriou has commented on an obvious problem:

> increasingly, both pure refugees and purely economic migrants are ideal constructs rarely found in real life; many among those who routinely meet the refugee definition are clearly fleeing both political oppression and economic dislocation. (Papademitriou 1993: 212–13)

There is no 'pure' refugee who can be distinguished from the opportunists and dissemblers said to make most applications for asylum in the West today. After over 40 years of work in the field of forced migration the UNHCR (1995: 197) concluded that global movements had become so complex that 'facile distinctions' between refugees and other migrants were less and less meaningful. A UN report reached a similar conclusion, suggesting that the mixture of 'fears, hopes and aspirations' which prompt migrants to leave their homes can be impossible to unravel.[9] Researchers at the Centre on Migration, Policy and Society (Compas) have argued that the causes of today's migratory movements, which are usually depicted as either voluntary or involuntary, are increasingly closely related and that the practice of differentiating between migrants is unsustainable.[10] The category 'refugee' has always been mutable: for over 300 years the term has been defined and redefined by politicians and officials. Their approaches have always been contingent – the outcome of calculations as to the value and/or acceptability of incomers under particular circumstances. These usually relate to the stability of the state and the perceived need to emphasise ideas of national identification which may be served by policies of inclusion or exclusion – the official refugee has been shaped and reshaped by states and political interest groups to serve changing purposes. As Shacknove (1991: 518) has observed, states are strongly orientated upon their own interests, and 'State interests are a term of art'.

For Cottret (1991: 11) 'refugee status is by definition transitory and depends upon social recognition'. Formal recognition can be short-lived, especially when states adopt various and changing approaches to immigration. During the late 1940s the British government recruited large numbers of European Voluntary Workers (EVWs). They were forced migrants and viewed themselves as such: Kay and Miles (1992: 7) comment that 'they had a clear conception of themselves as refugees'. The government defined them officially as labour migrants but represented them in public in terms which served contingent interests: 'official emphasis on the EVWs as either "refugees" or "workers" shifted according to the context and audience' (ibid). When a formal definition of the refugee emerged in international law a few years later some states adopted a similar approach, moving migrants in and out of the refugee category at will. The Geneva Convention of 1951 was endorsed by most Western states but paradoxically not by the United States, which had been the chief architect of the agreement. American politicians preferred to write a new definition of the refugee which they enshrined in domestic law; soon, however, this was also abandoned in favour of a modified Convention (see Chapter 7). Over the course of a few years the American state had taken three distinct positions vis-à-vis the refugee. Migrants had variously been welcomed, rejected or – in some cases – welcomed and then rejected en route to their desired place of sanctuary. The international legal regime on asylum was born in controversy and, with a brief interlude, has continued to be a highly contentious area of policy and of law-making which has proved increasingly unfavourable to the displaced.

The problem of numbers

Mass displacement is the outcome of a complex of economic, political, environmental and socio-cultural pressures. As we shall see (Chapters 1 and 2) the instabilities of the world economy have made many regions vulnerable. Across the Third World, survival systems – means of assuring food, shelter and basic security – are being seriously weakened, sometimes to the point of collapse. In this situation all manner of local factors can be the trigger for displacement. These include repression by states, militias and political factions; wars and civil conflicts; environmental changes; and intense economic pressures. The dominant discourse of the refugee in the West uses the 1951 Convention to insist that most of those who seek security in the face of such problems are illegitimate: they cannot be refugees and must be viewed as opportunists who seek to manipulate international agreements on asylum to advance their own interests. This is implausible. People do not willingly undertake long and dangerous journeys to unknown or uncertain destinations, abandoning their material, social, cultural and other resources, unless they are under extreme pressure. Given the scale of crisis in many regions the determination to remain *at home* is a measure of the extreme distress of those who are obliged to flee. As the UNHCR (1995: 229) has observed, despite the pressures which have built up in many countries, 'the surprising thing is not how many migrate but how few'.

The question of refugee numbers is a vexed issue. At the lower end of the scale figures provided by the UNHCR suggest that the global total peaked in the mid-1990s at 27 million and has since fallen sharply, so that by 2003 some 10 million people were listed as refugees, with a further 5 million 'of concern' to the agency (UNHCR 2004). At the other end of the scale Harris (1996: 120) suggested that in the mid-1990s there were up to 70 million Internally Displaced People (IDPs) and a further 70 million refugees 'proper', while the Global IDP Survey (1998: xvi) proposed that numbers of all displaced people had reached 100 million. Sorensen *et al.* (2002) took evidence from all the leading migration agencies, concluding that between 1992 and 2000 the number of refugees fell from 18 million to 13.3 million but that the number of IDPs increased from 18 million to 22.5 million. The refugee agenda is so highly charged that all such numbers have their own ideological significance. In general, politicians and officials of the dominant states wish to see falling figures. This serves their wish to depict a world of harmony – one in which the strategies of neo-liberalism deliver prosperity and peace. It also assists domestic political strategies, in particular efforts to convince certain political constituencies that migration controls have discouraged applications for refugee status.[11] But statistics showing increased numbers of refugees may also serve a political interest, especially when it is convenient to stress the repressive character of rival states or political factions, or the need for intervention – part of what Stedman and Tanner (2003: 6) see as a pattern of 'refugee manipulation'. In addition, it would not do for refugees to become insignificant – they perform an important function as an imagined threat to good order and to the health of Western societies (see Chapter 12). And for some states in refugee-producing regions it may be helpful to overstate the scale of displacement in order to obtain aid, arms or military assistance.

Statistical issues are a minefield. What is certain, however, is that UNHCR figures, usually the benchmark for calculations by agencies and academics, are an underestimate of the total of forced migrants. Millions of displaced people who live in the cities of Africa, Asia and Latin America go completely unrecorded – 'invisible' to governments and to agencies reluctant to identify urbanites as legitimate refugees (see Chapter 10). In addition millions of IDPs are excluded from the category of refugees 'proper'. Thus those displaced in Darfur in 2004 and 2005 who did not cross the border from Sudan into neighbouring Chad could not be counted officially as refugees. So too with the hundreds of thousands forced from their homes in Ivory Coast in 2002 and 2004, or those displaced in Myanmar, Colombia or Indonesia during conflicts which have persisted for decades. The global total of IDPs has continued to rise, partly as the result of changed patterns of conflict worldwide but also because of the determination of dominant states to inhibit movements of the displaced – to confine them within national borders in order that they do not make a claim for refugee status as Convention refugees (see Chapter 9). Meanwhile very large numbers of people evicted from their lands and homes by intense economic and environmental pressures are excluded from all consideration. Although often viewed informally by media, agencies and politicians as refugees, their claims for asylum are usually dismissed out of hand.

It is likely that there are many scores of millions of forced migrants and that their numbers are increasing. This book argues that to make 'facile distinctions' among them merely contributes to the ideological fog which envelopes refugee issues and that until such time as there is free movement *all* such migrants should be viewed as refugees. Can we ask states to offer asylum and, at the same time, require them to abandon border control? Can we, in effect, invoke the obligations of states to protect refugees *and* propose an end to measures often seen as integral to the state itself? The argument advanced here is that the increasingly negative response of states to the predicament of refugees amounts to a crisis in which radical changes of approach are required. Policies of exclusion not only penalise migrants but inflict serious damage upon 'host' societies: to paraphrase Kaplan, they are a 'real strategic danger' at the global level. They should be modified in order to accommodate the many migrants now denied entry; at the same time we need to re-examine historic relations between states and migrants and their implications for a policy of open borders.

The crisis of migration policy is intimately related to the posture of denial adopted by Western governments in relation to chronic instabilities within the global system. Unwilling to accept a share of responsibility for economic and political collapse they treat its victims as dissemblers. Across Europe, North America and Australasia immigration services operate a culture of disbelief within which officials are directed to treat migrants' testimonies with extreme scepticism. This leaves unanswered key questions associated with the experience of forced migration. What causes people to leave their homes? Why do some undertake long and dangerous journeys? How do they choose destinations, routes and means of travel? What is the lived experience of flight and of exile? In 1999 Crisp observed that there was a serious dearth of research on asylum seekers themselves – the 'purposive actors' at the centre of the drama of forced migration (Crisp 1999: 5). The culture of disbelief has since narrowed discussion further, inhibiting understanding of a phenomenon of increasing importance. If the refugee tragedies of the twentieth century are not to be repeated, a different approach is necessary: one which asks critically about processes of global change, and about displacement, flight and the search for security, and which views refugees as people with experiences and struggles which have much to tell us about the global order.

Notes

1. For an account of the events in Hungary see: http://www.hri.org/news/balkans/bta/1995/95-11-22.bta.html#06
2. Quoted in Mittelman 2004: 48.
3. Quoted in O'Hagan 1995: 28.
4. Quoted in Harding 2000: 13.
5. According to the British human rights organisation Justice, 89 per cent of entries on the system involved immigration cases. Justice identified serious

deficiencies with the system, including poor quality of data and obstacles placed in the way of those who wished to correct mistakes (*Guardian*, 18 December 2000).

6. In a novel and wide-ranging review of the relationship between contemporary liberal democracies and migrants, Gibney (2004) treats the state primarily as a representative of national communities with collective interests. He has little to say about states as power structures and as actors in socio-political conflicts within the domestic arena, considerations which bear directly upon matters of migration.

7. In the case of American historians of migration, suggests Diner (2000: 29), there is a 'fundamental disinterest in theory'.

8. Harris's eclectic approach combines opposition to migration control and racism with a commitment to the market system as agent of global change. Some of his arguments draw upon traditions of internationalism and can be seen as a contribution to the wider argument for open borders.

9. UNFPA report quoted by Crisp 1999: 4.

10. 'The Migration and Asylum Nexus – definitions and dimensions', a paper presented by Stephen Castles and Nick van Hear of Compas to the 9th Conference of the International Association for the Study of Forced Migration, Sao Paulo, Brazil, January 2005.

11. See for example the statement by British minister Des Browne on falling numbers of applications for asylum in the United Kingdom. When applications declined by almost 30 per cent in the third quarter of 2004 he declared that the British government's 'achievements' in the area of immigration control showed the continuing success of efforts to 'modernise and strengthen our border controls'. ('Asylum statistics: year on year fall continues', Home Office statement 354/2004, London, 16 November 2004).

Part I

Disordered World

Part I looks at globalisation and migration. It examines the globalisation thesis and its impact upon those who study forced migration. It considers the realities of economic and political change worldwide, especially the effects upon vulnerable regions of Africa, Asia and Latin America. It considers the impact of global forces upon the local state and on survival systems, and the pressures which produce mass displacement. It examines the early history of migration within and between Europe and the Americas, the relationship between migrants and the nation-state, and the implications for refugees. It looks at patterns of migration to the West over the past 60 years, especially at developments which have produced unprecedented numbers of refugees.

1

Globalisation and Forced Migration

Globalisation

Forced migration takes place under specific circumstances and to understand the experiences of displacement and flight each refugee movement must be treated concretely. Such an approach is becoming more important, for refugee crises are triggered by an increasingly wide range of events. But forced migration is also more *general*: crises of forced migration are more common and are impelled by developments that have common underlying features. Of these the most important are failures of basic survival systems and the weakening or collapse of social and political structures, often structures of the local state. These crises are associated directly with economic and political changes at a world level: understanding of forced migration therefore requires an understanding of processes of world development. This chapter considers key patterns of development, especially the economic changes said to be producing a new global environment. It looks at myths and realities of globalisation, focusing on movements of capital which play an increasingly important role in destabilising many vulnerable regions.

Forced migration is related to systemic changes at a world level: it has a *global* dimension. But most accounts of refugee movements place them in a different context: that of *globalisation* and of 'globalising' processes.[1] Migratory movements in general are seen as one expression of the powerful forces said to be reshaping world affairs – part of new networks through which move capital, data and people. These are said to be so important that any attempt to understand economic and socio-political developments must take account of their influence. Spybey (1996: 9), for example, argues that globalisation is encompassing: 'political, economic and cultural institutions have been globalized. Today there is virtually no one on the planet who can participate in social life without reference to globalized institutions'. Failure to engage with this reality is often viewed as naïve or even as perverse, so that Gray (1998: 67) comments of 'globalization sceptics' that they are 'trading in illusions'. But the theory of globalisation is flawed. As Weiss observes, it is 'a big idea resting on slim foundations' (Weiss 1998: 212). There is mounting evidence to suggest that core theories of globalisation *conceal* much of the reality of economic and political relations worldwide, including the processes which stimulate forced migration.

Ideas about globalisation are notoriously diverse and often elusive. There are a number of core contentions, however, among which one is of critical importance: the idea that world-spanning economic networks have brought into being unprecedented forms of world integration. This is at the heart of what Mittelman (2004: xi) calls the 'ascendent paradigm' of globalisation – a powerful intellectual force embodied in a system of knowledge, propagated by specific institutional authorities, and manifested in neo-liberal ideology. It has exerted a strong influence upon those who study forced migration. Analysing the implications of globalisation for refugee movements, Collinson (1999: 2) asserts that, 'globalisation of financial, commercial and other international relations is bringing about enormous and significant changes in the broader political, economic and social context in which cross-border migration takes place'. It is these changes, she suggests, that affect national, regional and international political structures, and the international refugee regime. For Adelman (1999: 87), also focusing on contemporary refugee movements, 'most commonly ... globalization refers to the current dramatic changes in the world economy'.

> Globalization is characterized by the total abstraction of capital in the form of instantly transferable 'money' through electronic means anywhere around the world, so that investment capital can shift readily and rapidly to whichever location will show the best return on capital. The rationality of the market is opposed to any artificial boundaries of currency controls, tariffs, duties etc. which impede the flow of capital, services or goods around the world. The world of global capital is totally divorced from both nature and history, where value depends primarily on the faith in the global system itself. (ibid)

Such certainty about the impact of globalising processes is typical of most literature on contemporary world affairs, including that on forced migration. It is misplaced. Movements of capital are far more complex and contradictory than allowed by the globalist orthodoxy. They do not produce a world system integrated by the 'rationality of the market' but one in which crisis is more general and in which dislocation and conflict are more widespread – but with impacts that vary according to the resilience of local economic and political systems and the vulnerability of specific social groups. It is this world of increasingly *uneven development* that gives rise to repeated crisis of mass displacement.

New world order

Giddens (1999: 9) comments of globalisation sceptics that they view the theory as 'an ideology put about by free-marketeers'. It is indeed difficult to distinguish between neo-liberalism and the idea of a globalising world. During the early 1990s leading Western politicians declared the beginning of a new age of world harmony and prosperity. Their language was often highly coloured: US President George Bush senior identified changes of 'biblical proportions', announcing 'a new world order – where diverse nations are drawn together in a common cause, to achieve the universal aspirations of mankind'.[2] Bush's Secretary of State, James Baker, welcomed 'an era full of promise, one of those rare transforming moments in world history'.[3] For his successor in the Clinton administration there were heroic possibilities: Warren Christopher declared, 'We stand on the brink of shaping a new world of extraordinary hope and opportunity'.[4] This enthusiasm was fired by conviction that the new order had been enabled by victory secured by the West at the expense of the Soviet bloc. The promise of a new world was linked to an assertion of values of the old order, especially to the principles of free-market economics and liberal democracy seen as the hallmark of American capitalism. The very possibility of positive change at a global level was viewed as a manifestation of Western, principally American, superiority. For Fukuyama (1989: 3) the twentieth century – which had begun 'full of self-confidence in the ultimate triumph of Western liberal democracy' – was ending where it started, with 'the unabashed victory of economic and political liberalism [and] the total exhaustion of viable systematic alternatives to Western liberalism'. These claims were shared by many academics, analysts and media people. Writing in 1994, Chomsky observed that the collective view seemed to crowd out all other perspectives, being heard '[on and] on endlessly in the ideological institutions – the media, scholarship, the intellectual community generally – in a chorus of self-adulation scarcely troubled by the odd discordant note far at the periphery' (Chomsky 1994: 7).

Theories of globalisation became current during the early 1990s as these visions of world order became widespread. The key idea at work was that capital, liberated from political constraints, was already bringing a novel and beneficial integration of economic and political structures worldwide. If the free market was allowed to operate unhindered, it was argued, it would achieve a balance or equilibrium which was itself conducive to productive activity. Under these circumstances the sum of the world's material wealth would be greater and, in the absence of conflicts among states and between the superstates, opportunities to distribute wealth would also increase. According to the pioneer theorist of globalisation, Kenichi Ohmae, there would be universal benefits: 'prosperity and improved quality of life for the people of the global economy' (Ohmae 1995: 149). The agenda for radical economic and political change would become largely meaningless and, with the sub-versive activities of the Soviet Union and the Communist movement long past, conflict in general would subside. Upheavals like those which had disfigured the world during the twentieth century, producing regional and world wars, and stimulating mass forced migration, would be only memories.

Such perspectives had their impact on analyses of forced migration. Suhrke (1997: 234) argued that with the end of the Cold War refugee movements in general had become less problematic. She observed that in the 1980s superpower rivalry had intensified local political conflict and increased refugee flows worldwide, whereas in the 1990s refugee movements were related primarily to local humanitarian crises.

> These [recent] conflicts may all produce major refugee flows, but since they are not structurally related the probability that they will occur simultane-ously is rather low. Hence, the sense of crisis that struck the international refugee regime in the late 1970s and lasted into the 1980s and was generated by the simultaneous wars of the Cold War, is not likely to be repeated. Since the international refugee regime is less likely to be overwhelmed if refugee flows are diverse and spread out over time, there is reason to conclude that a global refugee crisis – which implies inability to respond – is an improbable scenario for the post-Cold War world. (ibid)

Adelman (1999) too argued that the crumbling of the Soviet Empire and the emergence of new zones of economic growth, such as the Asian 'Tiger' economies, had had the effect of easing refugee crises worldwide.

By the late 1990s, however, globalist optimism was under challenge. The vision of a stable, expanding world market under enlightened leadership had been shaken by successive economic crises, numerous political upheavals, and accumulation of evidence that hundreds of millions of people remained at the margin of survival. Even the most partisan globalists expressed anxiety about the volatility of the market and increased political instability. Reflecting a widespread millennial gloom, *The Financial Times* suggested that arguments about globalisa-tion had shifted to new ground, being less about freedoms of the market than about 'how to harness the animal spirits of capitalism'

(*Financial Times*, 1 January 2000). *The Economist*, an ardent promoter of free market formulas, observed that although 'this has been the millennium of the West' and of a triumphant capitalism, 'nothing proves the triumph will endure' (*The Economist*, 1 January 2000). The 'global' era had not brought stability and harmony; rather it gave evidence of a continuing crisis of world development.

The global system: myth and reality

Those who subscribe to the core thesis of globalisation see *positive* integration of the world system. In this view, freely flowing capital is dispersing material wealth and accelerating social development. Old boundaries are disappearing and it is necessary to think of world affairs on the basis of supranational networks. This is the perspective advanced by early theorists of globalisation such as Ohmae (1990), for whom integration has been driven by expansion of the market to make a 'borderless world'. On this account, the globalised economy is the outcome of innovative activity by financiers, traders and entrepreneurs worldwide. Acting on the principle of rational self-interest they have made countless individual investment decisions, prompting movements of capital across continents and producing a world-embracing network of business relations. During the 1990s this perspective was absorbed by many business people. In a typical observation from the viewpoint of corporate capital, Niall Fitzgerald, vice-chairman of Unilever, one of the largest European corporations, commented that globalisation should be accepted as 'a fact of life' (Fitzgerald 1997: 741). He maintained that all people now lived in a 'global village' of diminished borders, internationalism and free trade, in which companies no longer debated the existence of global circumstances but focused upon 'responding to its effects'. Similar views were incorporated into academic perspectives, so that in a critical review of the literature on globalisation, Hirst and Thompson (1996: 195) observed that 'unquestioning certainty about the existence of a truly global economy' underlay most analyses. Even the most powerful transnational corporations are in fact aware that the world in which they operate is more complex than this vision allows. Flows of capital are shaped by many influences, including by states and transnational bodies such as financial and commercial institutions: Gray (1998: 76) comments that no one except 'a few Utopians in the business community' expects the world to become a single market in which nation-states have withered away. But executives of corporations, international organisations, governments and the media often speak *as if* they are operating within this context. A theme of corporate propaganda is the need to achieve 'global' status;

likewise, companies and governments routinely attempt to discipline a local workforce or even an entire national labour force by reference to the alleged 'portability' of jobs across the global market place – what Garrett (2000: 112) calls 'the exit threat'. Hoogvelt suggests that a defining characteristic of the contemporary world is the global market *principle* – the assumption made by key actors on the international stage that they should rationalise their actions on the basis of specific 'global' standards (Hoogvelt 1997: 123). Research into corporate management practice reveals that many attempts to articulate and implement a global 'strategic vision' fail utterly (Roberts 2003); such attempts continue, however, 'whether or not the pretensions of management to be able to manage the world are defensible, the consequences of the belief that they *are* remains an irreducible fact' (emphasis in original).[5]

This is a different view of globalisation – as a change in the way that major institutions think and operate: 'their ways of conceptualising their mission ... their basic rules and decision-making procedures and routines' (Biersteker 2000: 150). This notion of a global *principle* – a global 'logic' – is indeed the key to understanding the main principles of the globalisation thesis. The *idea* of a global system which can discipline certain states, institutions and collectives (such as a workforce) is congenial to many governments and to those who operate the multinational enterprises (MNEs) which are often seen as the chief agents of globalisation. It is at the heart of the Washington consensus – the set of neo-liberal economic principles which emerged in the 1980s and have been adopted by most Western governments and by institutions such as the International Monetary Fund (IMF) and the World Bank. On this basis, governments in Africa, Asia and Latin America have been constrained to accept 'entry' to the world market, securing what Biersteker (2000: 156) calls the 'apparent "triumph" of neoclassical economic thinking throughout the developing world'.

But this picture of an integrated world economy operating on free-market principles is no more than a model. It does not describe contemporary realities; rather, it is an account of the world as ideologues of neo-liberalism *wish it to be* – one which is indeed inseparable from the doctrine of free-market economics advanced as the basis of a New World Order. There has been no 'transforming moment' in world history, ushering in a prospect of global prosperity. The 1990s saw acceleration of certain trends long evident within the world economy. Among these *is* a trend to integration: of equal importance, however, are contrary trends, especially the tendency to greater inequality within the world system, manifested in wider differences of social class and polarisation of rich and poor regions. These contradictory tendencies have increased the volatility of the world system as a whole, creating circumstances under which local and regional economies are seriously weakened, and social and political structures rapidly destabilised. Under these circumstances some states have collapsed. Others, however, including the dominant states of the world system, have remained strong. Indeed such states have in general become stronger in relation to many increasingly frail states of the Third World.

The key criticism of globalisation theory is not simply that it provides rationales for 'a new mode of Western imperialism' (McGrew 2000: 350). The world *has* changed – but in ways that have intensified contradiction, with global integration accompanied by disintegration, economic dynamism paralleled by decay and by political collapse. In a world of increasingly uneven development the net outcome is a more unstable system in which many more people face an acute struggle for survival. This is the context within which all manner of specific factors, including political repression, social conflict, and climatic and environmental crises, more readily trigger forced migration.

Poverty

Until the late 1990s most analyses of world affairs accepted the globalisation thesis. Then the financial 'meltdowns' in South-East Asia and Russia gave pause for thought. Commenting upon growing anxiety among academics, analysts and investors, *The Economist* (5 September 1998) observed that 'panic' was abroad, together with the dangerous idea 'that it is not merely the international capital market but the basic principles of capitalist economics that need to be questioned'. These reflections were an echo of anxieties already voiced by academics and activists in vulnerable regions. Egyptian writer Mohamed Sid-Ahmed, for example, had warned

> [T]he assumption that markets can be beneficial to all is widely questioned in the Third World, where many see the interplay of market forces as deepening discrepancies rather than levelling them out. In their eyes, markets are more likely to make the rich richer and the poor poorer than the opposite ... not everybody in the new globalist world is equal. (*Ahram Weekly*, 20 March 1997)

In Egypt Sid-Ahmed had witnessed a striking increase in poverty. In the mid-1970s the Sadat regime had been a pioneer of market reform, dismantling state controls with a speed which brought approbation in the West and the blessings of the IMF, which provided a series of loans. The mass of Egyptians found it difficult to discern the benefits: in the late 1970s it was estimated that 23 per cent of the population lived below the poverty line; over the next 15 years the figure rose to over

40 per cent (El-Ghomeny 1998: 231). As we shall see (Chapter 9) poverty as such is seldom the key factor in crises of forced migration. But increased poverty is invariably associated with widening inequality and with increased social and political conflict; it is often an expression of the weakening or breakdown of survival systems, and is an important index of instability.

Questions about poverty and income distribution are contentious and go to the heart of debates about globalisation. Partisans of neo-liberalism claim that over the past two decades both world poverty and world inequality have fallen for the first time in over 150 years. This historic change, they argue, is attributable to activities of the market in an era of economic integration. James Wolfensohn, former president of the World Bank, maintains that during the 1980s and 1990s some 200 million people moved out of absolute poverty, rising above the income level of US$1 a day.[6] A number of economists, some associated with the Bank, make a similar case.[7] Against this, a series of analyses – mostly by critics of the globalisation thesis – suggest increases in poverty and inequality. Mazur (2000), for example, maintains that sharp increases in both are attributable to the same market mechanisms lauded by Wolfensohn. Wade (2004) has attempted to unravel the statistical complexities. Weighing data and arguments on both sides he concludes that, although poverty indices are arbitrary and probably provide a mis-leading picture of global trends, it is just possible that the proportion of people worldwide living in absolute poverty *may* have declined over the past 20 years. On the subject of income inequality he is much more con-fident. 'World income inequality has been rising', he maintains, 'absolute income gaps are widening and will continue to do so for decades' (Wade 2004: 16). On the poverty/inequality argument as a whole, he observes: 'The balance of probability is that – like global warming – the world is moving in the wrong direction' (ibid).

Within this debate special attention must be given to access to resources at the local level. Milanovic has studied household incomes: he concludes that while per capita income worldwide increased by 5.7 per cent between 1988 and 1993, inequality measured at the household level increased by some 5 per cent. All the gains went to the top 20 per cent, while income of the bottom 5 per cent declined by 25 per cent.[8] By the mid-1990s the vast majority of the world's people – 84 per cent – had access to just 16 per cent of global income; the richest 10 per cent received 114 times the income of the poorest 10 per cent.[9] The widening of global inequalities has been accompanied by exagger-ation of class differences at the local level. In Egypt, the rise in poverty witnessed by Sid-Ahmed was linked with very rapid enrichment of a small minority. The same pattern has been evident in Brazil, where during the 1960s the poorest 50 per cent of people received 18 per cent of national income; by the mid-1990s their share had fallen to 11.6 per cent (UNDP 1998: 30). By 2000 the poorest 20 per cent of the Brazilian population – over 30 million people – had access to just 2.5 per cent of national income (UNDP 2000a: 169). Scores of countries show a similar pattern of increased inequality. This includes those presented as models of neo-liberal practice in which the mass of the population had been expected to benefit from aggressive free-market policies. In Thailand by 1976 the richest 20 per cent of the population received 49 per cent of national wealth; by 1988 their share had risen to 55 per cent. Over the same period, the share of the poorest 20 per cent fell from 6 per cent to 4.5 per cent (Hewison 1996: 146). George and Sabelli (1994: 148) comment of the global pattern that 'the breach lies not just between the North and South but also between rich and poor, the "ins" and the "outs", the consuming classes and the excluded *within* the developing world'.[10]

Movements of capital

What *is* happening in the world economy and what are the implications for migratory movements?

There have been changes in the world system – but not those lauded by the partisans of globalism. This becomes clear when the latters' core contentions are examined. Most globalisers assume that economic forces which make for world integration operate similarly, even that they are unitary. Giddens, for example, identifies expansion of trade, finance and capital investment as motors of globalisation, assuming that each has behaved according to a common principle (Giddens 1999: 9). Among analysts of forced migration, Adelman also suggests that globalisation is characterised by a 'pure abstraction of capital', which allows money to be converted freely into investment capital and dispersed worldwide. In fact, movements of capital across the world system are strikingly dissimilar. It is the *difference* in such patterns that explains much of the increased instability of the world system, the tendency to crisis and even collapse of local socio-political structures, and the immiseration of people in the most vulnerable regions.

Finance capital

In providing evidence for an integrated world, theorists of globalisation make much of the transnationalisation of finance. The increase in volume of financial transfers is very striking: between 1976 and 1993 borrowing on international capital markets increased from less than

US$100 billion to US$818 billion (Hirst and Thompson 1996: 40). By 2000 the *daily* volume of transfers on world currency markets had reached US$1.5 trillion – a figure more than the annual domestic product of all but three national economies (UNDP 2000b: 46). The change in scale of activity has been accompanied by a change in means and speed of transfer. In the 1970s there was still a system of national financial centres linked by a relatively small number of operators who bought and sold credit. By the 1980s this had been replaced by a global network of dealers linked by digital communications systems. In the new context, comment Stopford and Strange, physically separate national markets were able to function 'as if they were all in the same place' (Stopford and Strange 1991: 40). This is often seen as testimony to the development of a globalised system in which 'elimination of space has accomplished the conquest of time' (Waters 1995: 88).

The changes are indeed very significant. They are associated with introduction into world networks of a large number of local financial markets in Africa, Asia and Latin America which were hitherto relatively isolated. Local banking centres established during the colonial era, such as Shanghai, Hong Kong, Sao Paulo, Cairo, Istanbul, Beirut, Johannesburg and Jakarta have been given increased importance. At the same time, a large number of new equity markets have been established, the role of which is to conduct business within the global networks. These include disparate and physically distant cities – Harare, Nairobi, Abidjan, Lima, Quito, San Jose, Kingston, Karachi, Dacca and many others. Their emergence is often taken as evidence that all economies may now participate fully in the world system. There is also a widespread assumption that the technology associated with such change is itself constructing a globalised world: Cerny (1993: 18) suggests that the power of new technology and the financial flows it facilitates mean that today 'the world order follows the financial order'. But greater interconnectedness has not produced a uniform pattern of integration. Most financial activity continues to take place within and between established centres of world finance in North America, Europe and Japan. Activities which do involve the new financial centres are often predatory ventures – plays upon local currencies or tradeable securities undertaken by Western banks and finance houses which are able to move vast amounts of money in search of quick speculative gains. The 1997 'meltdown' in East/South-East Asia was the outcome of rapid inflows of capital followed by a crisis of confidence in which, comment Tussie and Woods (2000: 60), 'short-term investors fled more quickly than they had arrived'. Joseph Stiglitz, former chief economist at the World Bank, describes this episode as a crisis of 'excessive exuberance' – a 'bubble' produced by hot speculative money (Stiglitz 2002: 198). Interconnectedness of markets has transmitted such crises with great speed: the 'Tequila effect' identified after the collapse of the Mexican *peso* in 1994 also caused destabilisation of currencies across a whole continent. Later meltdowns in South East Asia provided further evidence of how local crises are generalised, precipitating headlong falls in currencies and securities and a widespread collapse in investment. The effect of the 1997 events in South-East Asia, for example, was to halve inflows to the ten largest capital importers across the Third World (*Financial Times*, 11 April 2000).

In much of the Third World local currencies are highly volatile, and in an increasing number of countries they are being displaced, usually by the US dollar. In Lebanon and Cambodia, for example, prices have for years been quoted in both the currencies. Several countries have taken the step to 'dollarisation': when El Salvador abandoned its *colon* for the dollar in 2001 the president of the country's central bank described the move as a strategic step into a 'bullet proof' currency (*Financial Times*, 29 December 2000). Some economists suggest that by 2010 many small currencies will have become unviable and will vanish as governments adopt the dollar, the euro or the yen. On such a perspective, large areas of the Third World will be integrated formally into the United States, European or Japanese financial systems. These developments *do* suggest that flows of finance are productive of integration at a world level. Integration is not, however, accompanied by the positive outcomes celebrated in globalism; rather it emphasises the extreme unevenness of the world system.

Commercial capital

Such difficulties are much more pronounced in the areas of trade and of investment. The neo-liberal agenda for trade, aggressively pursued by the IMF, the World Bank and the WTO, insists upon deregulation as the catalyst for economic growth, especially in countries in which there have been strong state-centred development policies. Hoogvelt comments that for 20 years from the 1970s, the Bank and the IMF targeted the 'development state' as 'the real cause of Third World poverty and underdevelopment' (Hoogvelt 1997: 169). Under immense pressure from these institutions, governments in Africa, Asia and Latin America dismantled trade controls and protectionist measures. But after a generation of reform most Third World countries were placed *less* advantageously within the world system. Although world trade has grown steadily – sometimes spectacularly – since the 1960s, the proportion associated with all developing countries has declined. In 1970, countries of the Organisation for Economic Co-operation and Development (OECD) enjoyed 81 per cent of world trade; by 1990 this had increased to 84 per cent (Garrett 2000: 115). The Third World had been further marginalised, a process made even more stark by the fate of the least developed countries (LDCs): in 1990 they accounted for just 0.6 per cent of world exports; by 1995 this had declined to 0.5 per cent and by 1998 to 0.4 per cent (UNDP 2000a: 82).

The change is wholly at odds with globalists' formal expectations. It is partly the result of the tendency of dominant states to trade more with each other and, since the end of the colonial era, less with regions which were formerly their colonies. It is also explained by the trend among such states to trade more in capital-intensive goods than in the raw materials, which earlier constituted a large part of world trade. Tussie and Woods (2000: 56) observe that over the past 30 years this pattern has reflected the needs of a small group of Western industrialised countries, working against the interests of most developing countries. Decades of intensive activity by the General Agreement on Tariffs and Trade (Gatt) and later by the WTO have reduced tariff barriers between states exchanging mainly manufactured goods. Between the 1940s and the 1980s, the average OECD tariff level fell from 40 per cent to 5 per cent, but tariffs on raw materials and agricultural products – produced primarily in the Third World – remained high. The LDCs still face tariffs 30 per cent higher than the world average, and developing countries as a group face tariffs 10 per cent higher than the average (all figures from Tussie and Woods 2000: 58).[11] The promise of prosperity through liberalised trade, which was at the heart of the globalist vision, has proved illusory. Poorer states have been locked out of the network of intensified trade exchanges: among Eastern European states, for example, the initial enthusiasm for liberalisation 'has been replaced by a bitter recognition that the trade practices of most large industrialized countries are protectionist and restrictive, even though they are within GATT/WTO rules' (Tussie and Woods 2000: 69).

Industrialised economies have clustered in trade blocs, of which the most significant are the European Union and the North American Free Trade Agreement (Nafta). Of the latter, Judis comments that 'Nafta is not really about free trade'; rather, he argues

> [it] is a prudent step towards creating a regional trading bloc that could withstand the devolution of Western Europe and Asia into rival blocs. The treaty's free trade proponents would never admit this, but Nafta's underlying thrust is towards managed trade and investment. (Kegley and Wittkopf 1995: 247)

Such alliances ostensibly link national economies for mutual advantage. In fact they have usually served the interests of dominant local states. In the case of Nafta, the United States set out to build a hemispheric free-trade zone stretching from Alaska to Tierra del Fuego, the first stage being to incorporate Mexico to the advantage of American corporations (see Chapter 4). Meanwhile EU states intensified trading activity within the European bloc: in 1991, 23 per cent of exports of EU countries were within the Union; by 1997 the figure had reached 36 per cent (Tussie and Woods 2000: 69).

Two American economists who have been deeply involved in making US government policy on trade recognise the long-term difficulties for states of the Global South. Spero and Hart (1997: 224) comment that the problems of commodity trade are numerous: price fluctuations that affect foreign exchange earnings; Northern protectionism and discriminatory tax policies; and competition from synthetics and substitutes. They note that between 1965 and 1992, the period identified by many theorists of globalisation as the key period of world integration, the trading status of developing countries worsened dramatically: for countries defined by the World Bank as 'low income', the overall index for terms of trade almost halved (Spero and Hart 1997: 219). By 2001 the situation had worsened, following the steepest decline in commodity prices for 20 years.

Such trends have not inhibited the dominant or 'Northern' governments, which have worked aggressively through Gatt and the WTO to dictate patterns of world trade. The WTO is dominated by the 'Quad' – the United States, the European Union, Canada and Japan – which effectively write the organisation's rulebook and decide the outcomes of debates and disputes. Following the Gatt agreements of the mid-1990s it was estimated that global income would increase by up to $510 billion while there would be a net loss of $600 billion for the LDCs and of $1.2 billion annually for sub-Saharan Africa (UNDP 2000a: 83). Even leading proponents of free trade warned that if this trend continued it would bring outcomes uncongenial to Western governments: in 1997 the *Financial Times* declared that, 'Corporate self-interest lies at the heart of both world trade and the organisation [WTO] that settles disputes between participants. ... Prepare for tears' (*Financial Times*, 1 November 1997). These comments proved prophetic: in 1999 talks at the WTO Seattle conference, at which Western states sought to gain further advantage, collapsed in what one newspaper called 'a hail of public execration' (*Observer*, 5 December 1999).

Trade has *not* contributed to a universal developmental interest. On the contrary, trade relations as an expression of world inequalities speak of greater asymmetry within the global system. In 2002, after over 20 years of trade liberalisation, Stiglitz commented that relentless pressures on Third World countries to lower trade barriers had had the effect of making them more vulnerable. In a reassessment of global trade battles he observed: 'It is clear to almost everyone that something has gone horribly wrong' (Stiglitz 2002: 4).

Investment capital

Such extreme unevenness of development is even clearer in investment in production. Cross-border investment, also known as Foreign Direct Investment (FDI) is often viewed as the motor of globalisation. FDI is the primarily the work of MNEs, which are therefore regarded as agents of globalisation *par excellence*.

During the 1980s FDI grew five times faster than world trade (Hirst and Thompson 1996: 55): by 2000 the annual total had reached $1.3 trillion (UNCTAD 2001: 1). Over this period some MNEs moved towards alliances of 'networked' companies able to operate from a number of nation-states and to move capital relatively freely across national economic frontiers. Like developments in finance, such activity has mesmerised many economists and corporate strategists, prompting assertions that an embracing globalisation has already been accomplished. Harman (1996: 7) comments that it has enabled the globalist orthodoxy 'to paint a picture of capital flowing evenly across the face of the earth, ceaselessly shifting from one spot to another in search of lower wages and higher profits, with a tendency to the sprinkling of production facilities uniformly across all five continents'. Some of those who contest free-market principles have been sufficiently impressed by MNE activity to accept this picture. Robinson (1996: 15) sees the internationalisation of capital as a 'juggernaut' driven by 'globalisation of the process of production itself'. Sivanandan (1998: 8) identifies a new capitalism – 'its assembly lines are global, its plant is movable, its workforce is flexible'. But capital movements have been much more restrained than these accounts suggest. Investment in factories and machinery, and in infrastructure including railways, docks, airports and communications systems, cannot be moved freely, as in a speculative operation involving currencies or commodities. As Harman (1996: 14) observes, 'These [fixed investments] take years to build up and cannot be simply be picked up and carted away. ... Productive capital simply cannot be footloose.' Although MNEs in specific areas of production are able to select from a wider range of potential production sites, most do not do so: 'Obviously [MNEs] cannot close a plant in one country and open a new one in a foreign location instantaneously, nor can they "exit" without incurring significant start-up costs' (Garrett 2000: 111).

Capital mobilised through FDI is directed to remarkably few destinations: in 2000 over 95 per cent of such investment went to just 30 countries (UNCTAD 2001: 5). The pattern had long been evident to those who looked beyond globalist rhetoric: in 1995 Ruigrok and van Tulder had presented detailed evidence that MNEs invest primarily within quite limited territories. Cross-border activity is overwhelmingly of a *regional* character and often amounts to no more than investment in a country or countries adjacent to the nation-state of origin – as with many of the most prominent European corporations. By this means MNEs hope to take advantage of 'clustering', securing access to local networks based on new technology, advanced means of distribution, and specific markets – all of which are to be found primarily in the industrialised regions. On the basis that most world investment takes place within (and to a lesser extent between) the 'Triad' of North America, the European Union and Japan, Ruigrok and van Tulder argue for a notion of regionalisation or 'Triadisation', rather than of globalisation. By 2001 this process had become even more marked, so that UNCTAD (2001: 13) noted that 'mobile factors [of production] only go and "stick" in places where effective complementary factors exist'.

During the 1980s and the early 1990s the proportion of FDI invested outside the Triad increased sharply, peaking at 41 per cent in 1994 (UNCTAD 2001: 1). Ninety per cent of this total was, however, directed towards just nine countries already classified as Newly Industrialising Countries (NICs), with a very marked increase in movements to interest in India and China. When the flow to developing countries fell away – halving by 2000 – the inequality in distribution was even more marked (UNCTAD 2001: 1). NICs continued to receive the lion's share while the LDCs together attracted just 0.3 per cent of the global total (ibid). When FDI collapsed further, falling by 60 per cent in two years, the LDCs were effectively abandoned by investors (UNCTAD 2004: 33). The emergence of India and China as pace-setting NICs has emphasised the trend, as clustering of new enterprises leaves most regions bereft of meaningful investment. These figures suggest that transnational capital is in general *avoiding* the very low wage economies, contrary to the assumptions of many globalists and to the approach of most corporate executives, with their talk of the 'portability' of production. The pattern of FDI does not suggest world-embracing investment activity: rather, it testifies to a pattern of unevenness in which capital *bypasses* most states, which it finds lacking in stability, infrastructure, skills and interconnectedness with key zones of world economic activity. Investors continue to ignore most of Africa, Asia, Latin America: 'the world system is not integrating the Third World, it is marginalising it' (Kiely 1998: 112).[12]

The much vaunted MNEs are less agents of capital dispersal than networks of accumulation based in the centres of global wealth. Of the top 100 non-financial MNEs in 2001, 90 were headquartered in the Triad; just three were based in developing countries (UNCTAD 2004: 5). The largest MNEs in these states, including widely known manufacturers such as Samsung and Daewoo of Korea, were minnows in comparison with global leaders like General Electric, ExxonMobil, Royal Dutch/Shell, General Motors and Ford. In the case of General

Motors, corporate sales were almost equal to the GDP of the world's fourth most populous nation, Indonesia, and were greater than the combined GDP of Malaysia, Venezuela and Nigeria. Combined annual sales of the top five corporations amounted to 3.5 times the GDP of the whole of sub-Saharan Africa, with its 500 million people; they were twice the combined GDP of South Asia with its 1.3 billion people, over a fifth of all humanity (ibid) Each was firmly anchored within its region of origin (UNCTAD 2001: 6–7).

Contradiction

Globalist theory maintains that dualisms such as those which distinguish 'First' and 'Third' worlds are outdated – relics of an earlier era during which the market was constrained by the irrationalities of state structures. But world markets are not constructed upon even flows of capital which have the capacity to equalise processes of development; rather they are based upon powerful relationships of inequality. Over the past 30 years capital movements have emphasised such relationships, with the result that global differences have been *intensified*. Many countries in Africa and Asia which have seen less and less of FDI have all but disappeared from the global investment schedule. The human cost is enormous. During the 1980s the UNDP's Human Development Index (HDI) measured falls in general well-being in four countries: during the 1990s the number with negative ratings increased to 21 (UNDP 2003: 41). The organisation commented that 'when the HDI falls, it indicates crisis, with nations depleting their basis for development – people, their real wealth' (ibid). Even management analysts, long associated with theories of globalisation, have been compelled to address the very striking difference between globalist rhetoric and reality. According to Jeffrey Garten of the Yale School of Management, 'The fact is that ... millions of people in emerging markets [*sic*] have suffered horribly'.[13] The doctrine of prosperity has concealed increased immiseration in the most vulnerable regions, together with wider inequality and more general world crisis. This is the context in which the phenomenon of forced migration must be assessed.

Notes

1. Suhrke (1997: 217), for example, comments on 'the globalization of the refugee phenomenon'. Collinson (1999: 2) explains that migration is invariably associated with changing international, political and strategic environments, 'associated very broadly with globalisation'. King sees migration as 'intimately linked' to globalisation (1995: 7) and Cohen (1997a: 157)

identifies migratory flows as among the defining features of a 'globalised' world. See also Horsmann and Marshall (1994) Sassen (1998) and Gungwu (1997).

2. Quoted in Kegley and Wittkopf 1995: 5.
3. Quoted in Chomsky 1994: 7.
4. Quoted in Kegley and Wittkopf 1995: 551.
5. Grey and French, quoted in Roberts 2003: 32.
6. Quoted in Wade 2004: 5–6.
7. See, for example, Sala-i-Martin (2002).
8. Quoted in Wade 2004: 11.
9. Ibid.
10. Meanwhile inequality within the world's dominant economies had also intensified. Measures of deprivation adopted by the Organisation for Economic Co-operation and Development (OECD) show that an average 15 per cent of the population in the United States was in poverty during the early 1990s; in Britain the figure was 20 per cent (*The Guardian,* 12 January 2000). In 1995, 53 million people across the European Union were viewed as 'impoverished' – receiving less than half average per capita income – a 40 per cent rise over levels 20 years earlier (Leontidou and Afouxenidis 1999: 259). By 2000, wealth in the United States was concentrated in an unprecedentedly small group: 40 per cent of all private assets was in the hands of some 0.1 per cent of the population (*New York Times,* 15 June 2000).
11. There are many examples of the devastating consequences of tariff reform. Haiti is the poorest state in the western hemisphere. By 2002, reported Oxfam, its rural economy was being profoundly changed as corn and rice production collapsed in the face of subsidised US exports (*Financial Times,* 12 April 2002).
12. UNCTAD (2001: 11) shows that if the index for inward FDI is set at 1.0, figures for regional performance include: Western Europe 3.0, North America 2.3, East and South Asia 0.6, and Africa 0.4.
13. Jeffrey Garten, Dean of the Yale School of Management, quoted in *The Independent,* 13 September 1999.

2
Crisis of the State

States and migrants

The vast majority of forced migrants originate in zones of economic and political crisis located in vulnerable regions of the Third World. In 1999 over 80 per cent of those recorded by the UNHCR as refugees came from these areas (UNHCR 2000: 310). Their predicaments are associated with increased instability of local economic and political structures, especially of the local state. Most forced migrants are in fact produced by events in which economic or environmental collapse, conflict or war, are intimately linked with crises of the state; they go on to enter a legal system regulated by other states, those of the West, which dominate the international legal regime. If they attempt long-distance migration they confront structures of exclusion established and regulated by such states. The whole experience of displacement, flight and exile is shaped by institutions of the nation-state, above all by the wish of those in authority in states to *control* migration.

Globalist theory insists that the nation-state is less and less significant in world affairs. Analysing the relationship between globalisation and refugee movements, Collinson (1999: 4) suggests that states in general face a crisis of 'deterritorialisation'. Capital movements are said to proceed on the basis of detachment from territory, she notes, taking place simultaneously and instantaneously across vast distances, so that the world must be viewed as a single place in which the state struggles for its existence (ibid). But as we have seen, capital does not behave according to formulae set out in such theories. Some movements of capital show much greater fluidity worldwide; others reveal a tendency for close association with specific territories, and for a *closer* relationship with certain states and regions at the expense of others. The nation-state remains an enormously significant feature of the modern world. As Harman (1991: 45) pointed out at an early stage in debates over globalisation, there is a difference between neo-liberal ideology, with its hostility to state intervention and economic regulation, and the reality of a capitalist system which *requires* state structures. He observes that capitalism needs states: to maintain local monopolies of armed forces that prevent some capitals using direct, Mafia-style violence against others; to impose regulations that prevent some capitalists defrauding others; to organise labour markets and to prevent recession turning into economic collapse. He comments

> The world may no longer be made up of capitals fused one hundred per cent to states. But it is not, and cannot be, a world in which capitals float free of states ... This is a world in which capitals look both to economic competition and political influence for obtaining the resources for accumulation. It is a world in which the jostling for position between capitals involves not only peaceful competition for markets but also the carving out of political alliances, not only arguments over trading arrangements but also the reinforcement of these arguments through the deployment of military force. (Harman 1991: 50)

The relationship between the state and the world system is changing because the internationalisation of capital is a reality. But the state is not disappearing; rather states exist in changed circumstances in which movements of capital may transcend state borders but continue to depend upon them. Sassen (1999: 150) suggests that in regions in which economic linkages are most advanced, territorial borders should be seen less as sites at which states exercise control and more as 'transmitting membranes' guaranteeing flows of goods, capital and information. But even here, she adds, 'neither the old border wall nor the nation state has disappeared' (Sassen 1999: 151). The global pattern is one in which states *and* supra-national movements of capital are accommodated by the world system – a system of structured inequality in which recent developments have served to emphasise unevenness, especially the strength of dominant states in relation to those in vulnerable regions. Weiss (1998: 212) comments that one of the biggest problems with the discourse of globalisation is that it has 'obfuscated some of the more fundamental processes whereby "strong" states themselves have altered the rule of the game'. Former US Secretary of State Henry Kissinger makes the point more tersely, insisting: 'Globalisation is only another word for US domination'.[1]

'New' emergencies – old problems

During the 1970s and 1980s refugee movements in the Third World increased very rapidly in number and in scale. This has often been attributed to the involvement of the superpowers in local conflicts, to the extent that refugee movements are said to have been shaped by 'the logic of the Cold War' (Suhrke 1997: 225). This understates the extent to which such movements were associated with the legacy of colonialism, with crises of the world economy, and with the policies of dominant states towards others that were weaker and more vulnerable.

Cold War rivalries had an impact on many conflicts but in general they did not precipitate them. In the 1960s the majority of the world's refugees were in Africa. Displacement was usually associated with struggles against colonial rule, most importantly in Angola, Mozambique, Guinea-Bissau and Rhodesia, and against the rulers of apartheid South Africa. In other cases refugees were produced by conflicts rooted in the crisis of the post-colonial state, as in Congo, Rwanda, Sudan and Chad. By the 1970s most refugees across the continent had been displaced during remaining struggles against the colonial powers, notably against Portugal, or by further problems in newly independent states, as in the Central African Republic, Uganda, Equatorial Guinea and the 'Spanish' Sahara. Elsewhere conflicts such as those in Indochina, often viewed as examples of 'hot spots' in the Cold War, were more profoundly affected by the superpowers. But these were also matters of unfinished business of the colonial era: interventions by the United States and the Soviet Union altered the trajectory of conflicts but did not usually change their basic character. So too in other regions of intense superpower competition such as West Asia and Central America, where Washington and Moscow competed to supply arms and win ideological influence. Here refugees were often important as populations within which Washington and Moscow attempted to organise directly. In Afghanistan, invaded by the Soviet Union in 1979, the United States armed the Mujahidin resistance; in Central America, where a series of insurgencies was directed against regimes allied to the US, the latter launched movements of exiled 'freedom fighters' such as the Nicaraguan Contras (see Chapter 10); and in South-East Asia it backed the much-reviled Khmer Rouge guerrillas. Meanwhile the Soviet Union and its Eastern European allies intermittently supported, among others, factions of the Palestine Liberation Organisation. Loescher (1993: 88) comments that in these and other cases external support to warring parties 'altered the balance of forces in the field, and so made a decisive resolution even more difficult to achieve'.

The superpowers had a role in precipitating specific crises of forced migration but they did not 'shape' refugee movements worldwide. Rather there was continuity in patterns of displacement across the Cold War era and the succeeding period. In the mid-1990s the UNHCR (1995: 34) observed that the end of the Cold War had generated a sense of optimism about the international refugee situation:

> With the rivalry of the superpowers over, it was thought, many conflicts would be resolved, large numbers of refugees would be able to go back to their homes, and resources being used for relief could be moved to rehabilitation and development.
>
> In the event, precisely the opposite has happened. Relatively successful ... peace settlements ... now appear to be the exception rather than the norm,

and they have been overshadowed by a crop of new and very large humanitarian emergencies:

These emergencies have been associated with a different pattern of conflict. Between 1989 and 1994 there were 94 conflicts in 64 locations across the world, of which only four were confrontations between states – the 'Clausewitzian' military encounters viewed as traditional wars (Bennet 1998: 16). The rest were 'internal' conflicts of the type often identified as 'new' wars – disputes focused on claims for specific rights and representation or on communal concerns, and involving militias, paramilitary groups and informal means of support (Kaldor and Vashee 1997). Such conflicts were in fact less novel than some accounts have maintained, for a number had their roots in movements for independence from the colonial powers and had been under way since the 1940s. They were concentrated in the Third World, overwhelmingly in economically marginal regions: by the mid-1990s Miall *et al.* (1999: 25–7) counted major armed conflicts within 44 states, of which 29 were in Africa or Asia, and only five in Europe. In some of these states, such as India, there were multiple major conflicts (many 'minor' conflicts, with fewer than 1000 deaths, were not recorded). The great majority were associated with refugee movements: Schmeidl (2001: 77) notes that among 60 intrastate wars which took place during the 1990s only three did not coincide with crises of mass displacement.

Two developments were of importance in generating the 'new' conflicts.[2] The end of the Cold War exposed rulers of some states who had depended upon support from one or other of the superpowers, or sometimes upon both: at the same time it affected opposition groups and others tied to Washington or Moscow, or who exploited the latters' rivalries. This sometimes changed the local balance of power and prompted new struggles for control of resources or of the state itself. It was less significant, however, than pressures brought to bear by changes in the world economy and by the imposition of reform policies championed by the transnational financial organisations. These were targeted at the weakest and most vulnerable states of the Third World: those which, faced by intense economic pressures, lobbied for loans and concessions and were least able to resist demands for change.

In Africa, Asia and the Middle East such states had their origins in political structures developed by colonial entrepreneurs and colonising powers.[3] Colonial states were centralised and highly authoritarian, using differentiation by religion, language, 'race' or ethnic group (usually interpreted by metropolitan strategists as 'tribalism') as the basis for administration, and exploiting local differences to facilitate centralised control.[4] The strategy of France in the Arab East was typical: Kirk (1948: 163) describes it bluntly as 'an unashamed policy of "divide-and-rule" '. Limited authority was sometimes vested in groups deemed to possess special rights on account of their status within pre-colonial society; where no arrangements could be constructed on existing affiliations, 'traditions' were frequently invented and imposed, providing new candidates to mediate relations with the colonial power.[5] Struggles for independence within these states often unified diverse peoples, marking both the success of colonialism in creating 'national consciousness' and the determination of local populations to rid themselves of occupation forces, notwithstanding problems of identification with the new state. In other cases, however, the state produced lethal inter-communal conflicts which inhibited the anti-colonial movement and left a very strong mark upon the independent state.

Such states did not have long to consolidate. In the 1970s the 'long boom' of the world economic system which had followed the Second World War came to an end. Local rulers faced rising levels of popular resistance as it became clear that expectations of a bright post-colonial future were not to be fulfilled. An early expression of such frustration came in Egypt, where the Free Officers regime under Gamal Abdel Nasser symbolised the efforts of many independent states to achieve economic and social advance on the basis of self-reliance. As one of the leaders of the Non-Aligned Movement of countries in Africa, Asia and Latin America, Nasser was the subject of immense hopes for radical change. By the late 1960s his experiment with modernisation directed by the army seemed at an end as a mood of hostility towards the regime spread widely in Egyptian society. Abdel-Malik (1968: 366) argued that the mass of Egyptians had been discarded by their government, which had become 'a devouring bureaucracy ... let loose with the immunity of autocracy'. Now 'it was the state, ruled ... by the military apparatus which determined the objectives and modes of national action: the task of the people was to supply the manpower' (ibid). He predicted confrontation as the mass of the population sought its place in the post-colonial order.

From reforms to riots

From the early 1970s problems experienced by the Egyptian regime became general among rulers of Third World states. Many governments had come to power on promises of radical change. Guided by the model of the development state and influenced by experiences in the Soviet Union, Eastern Europe and China, they had adventurous plans for economic independence, in particular to replace expensive imports from the West with domestic products. There were also projects for infrastructural support – for electrification, dams, canals, roads and railways. These required investment capital, which was in short supply, especially as foreign earnings of most Third World states were falling. Many economies had long performed the function of producing one or two key mineral or agricultural products for the metropolitan centre, and when prices of such commodities fell, foreign earnings plummeted. During the 1970s commodity prices became more volatile, with huge, sudden movements, and terms of trade in general moved sharply against most non-oil producing countries. In addition, crises of food availability became more general. During the 1960s food production per capita for the Third World as a whole had grown at 0.3 per cent a year; between 1970 and 1975 it fell by 0.1 per cent a year, and in Africa by 2 per cent a year (Harrison 1993: 274).

Many states now required loans to fund development programmes and to secure food stocks. In 1970 the total of long-term debt of developing countries stood at £62 billion: by the end of the decade it was US$481 billion (Chossudovsky 1997: 45). The move into debt was welcomed by Western institutions, especially by banks eager to operate through the new 'Euromarkets' in which large volumes of currency circulated outside their countries of origin – an early expression of the internationalisation of finance capital that was to come. Slump in the industrialised economies made them uncongenial territory for lending: Third World states, however, had urgent need of funds and banking executives pursued the opportunity aggressively, developing the notion of 'borrowing for prosperity' – the idea that states should embrace debt, navigating immediate problems in the expectation of growth (Sampson 1981). By 1977 most major US banks were making more than half their profits from overseas lending, the bulk to countries of Latin America judged a good risk because of their mineral resources and/or large volumes of agricultural exports. Many other countries received smaller amounts which nonetheless had an enormous impact upon their finances as more and more government income went to debt servicing. In the early 1980s the world economy took another sharp turn downwards. Between 1980 and 1982 commodity prices fell by 30 per cent, putting immense pressure on Third World borrowers to accept further loans on very disadvantageous terms. By the mid-1980s such countries were net exporters of capital to the West, with total interest payments more each year than the sum of incoming loans, foreign investment and aid.[6]

Third World governments were in a vice – under pressure from Western bankers and from their own populations, which were being made to bear the impact of the crisis. As a rule, governments accepted the discipline of the lending institutions and reacted to popular protests with campaigns of repression. From the mid-1970s numerous states in Africa, Asia and Latin America witnessed mass protests against food price rises

and cuts in subsidies. Many coincided with the imposition of programmes designed by international financial institutions which stipulated
the changes as a condition for loans or re-scheduling packages: the
protests were soon dubbed 'IMF riots'. Walton and Seddon (1994:
39–40) note that between 1976 and 1992 there were almost 150 such
events, many the scene of very violent confrontations between protesters
and forces of the state. They remark on the significance of the protests:

> an international wave of price riots, strikes and political demonstrations has
> swept across the developing world in a pattern at once historically unprece-
> dented and reminiscent of classical food riots best documented in European
> social history. (Walton and Seddon 1994: 23)

Transnational agencies were unmoved: imposition of 'reform' policies
continued, as did the protests, which took many forms. In Latin
America several regimes faced mass opposition, some under religious
influence – as in Brazil, where the Liberation Theology movement
grew with great speed. In the Middle East there were upheavals in
Egypt, Syria, Lebanon, Iraq and in Iran, where in 1979 a mass movement, also under religious influence, removed the monarchy. In Africa,
conflicts in a score of states intensified as post-colonial regimes faced
general crises of development.

The IMF 'menu'

In most independent states local rulers continued to operate within
political frameworks put in place during colonial rule. National boundaries had not changed – in most cases they had been frozen at the
moment of independence – and internal political structures largely
remained intact. Almost invariably power was monopolised by a specific
ethnic group or clan, by people of a particular region or religion, and/
or a specific social/political status – as in the case of army officers and
senior bureaucrats who dominated many nationalist regimes. The new
rulers often viewed socio-cultural differences institutionalised by the
colonial state as a means of perpetuating their own rule. Although they
emphasised national identification, at the same time notions of religious, sectarian or ethnic affiliation were exaggerated or suppressed
according to changing circumstances. Until the 1970s the fragility of
these structures was concealed by modest but real growth achieved
within most economies, allowing governments to provide welfare
reforms, and in some cases to subsidise staples or accumulate stocks as
means to deal with crises of food availability. But as Zolberg (1989: 40)
observes, 'states do not exist in a vacuum; their fate depends substantially on the international environment. Thus the weakest of states may

survive if this environment is supportive ... But the other side of the coin is that stronger states may collapse if the international environment invites destructive processes.' During the 1970s, general economic crisis created a far less favourable environment for Third World states, while Western institutions and states took measures which invited 'destructive processes'.

In 1979 the World Bank formally introduced the idea of structural adjustment. This amounted to a set of conditions to be imposed on all states which requested finance, and which were applied by all major lending institutions, notably by the IMF. Chossudovsky describes how the 'IMF menu' of budgetary austerity, devaluation, trade liberalisation and privatisation was implemented:

> Debtor nations forgo economic sovereignty and control over fiscal and monetary policy, the Central Bank and the Ministry of Finance are reorganised (often with the complicity of the local bureaucracies), state institutions are undone and an 'economic tutelage' is installed. A 'parallel government' which bypasses civil society is established by the international financial institutions (IFIs). Countries which do not conform to the IMF's performance targets are blacklisted. (Chossudovsky 1997: 35)

Partisans of structural adjustment such as the US development agency USAID saw the strategy as 'the most important way to help the poor'.[7] Other assessments saw what George and Sabelli (1994: 59) call 'an unmitigated social and ecological disaster'. In 1990, after a decade of structural adjustment plans (SAPs), the stock of debt owed by developing countries had risen to US$1.4 trillion; by 1997 it was US$21.17 trillion (*Guardian*, 11 May 1998). Throughout the 1990s, Western banks received far more from Third World countries in debt repayments than in profits extracted by MNEs; in 1998 such countries paid out US$717 million in debt service every day (ibid).[8] Governments which questioned IMF terms received blunt warnings: in the case of Tanzania, said former President Nyerere, 'When we reject IMF conditions we hear the threatening whisper, "Without accepting our conditions ... you will get no other money" '.[9]

More borrowing and rescheduling of debt meant more 'liberal' reform – especially higher food and fuel prices – and more widespread distress. This produced an increased level of resistance in the form of mass protest, so that riots which had begun in the mid-1970s shortly after the introduction of the first SAP-style package in Peru tracked the imposition of austerity programmes across the continents. As Walton and Seddon (1994: 5) observe,

> growth of popular struggles and protest [became] a distinctive political development ... involving an exceptionally wide range of social forces, both

responding to, and itself shaping, the process of structural adjustment that has accompanied a global crisis.

These protests were not only an expression of the cost of neo-liberal policies to the mass of people but also evidence of the dislocation likely to occur in the face of continued economic reform. The IMF, the World Bank and Western banks nonetheless maintained their demands for austerity in creditor states, 'with little heed for the social, and even political implications' (Seddon 1989: 130).

Evidence was mounting that policies of market reform greatly increased the vulnerability of local economies and state structures. Dominant states and transnational financial institutions insisted, however, that liberalisation must continue at a faster pace. In 1997, a leading American official told African leaders that the United States would never abandon neo-liberal principles. According to Charlene Barshevsky, the core premises of the American plan for world development were aggressive growth-oriented economic policies based upon an 'opening' to the world market (*Guardian*, 8 October 1998). There were to be no concessions, even to the most vulnerable economies and even in relation to debt – the area in which they might most easily be offered. The Highly Indebted Poor Countries initiative (HIPC), launched in 1996, aimed formally to relax debt repayment. But HIPC set out strict conditions, including rigorous implementation of measures to open local economies to foreign capital. Even after five years the scheme had failed to produce tangible results for any of the countries involved. Commenting on the British government's contribution to the HIPC – a debt 'write-off' to 41 countries of some £640 million – *The Economist* suggested that the 'lavish promise' was merely one of the 'soft-focus millennial visions' aimed more to bring popularity among the domestic electorate than to secure benefits for the mass of people in poor countries (*Economist*, 1 December 2000). The journal asked readers who might take debt forgiveness at face value: 'Do you believe in fairies?' (ibid).[10] Others expressed the relationship between debtor and creditor more pithily: Reno (1998: 50) quotes a contractor in West Africa who argued that, 'little shit countries cannot be allowed to show the rest that irresponsibility is rewarded with debt cancellation'.

Imposition of reform

Sen (1993: 41) writes of the importance of human 'capability' – the ability to achieve 'certain crucially important functionings up to certain minimally adequate levels'. When capability cannot be achieved, survival is threatened. The protest movements of the 1970s and 1980s were an index of the distress of hundreds of millions of people whose minimal requirements were not being met. They were often associated with the weakening or collapse of local survival systems and with general breakdown of social and economic networks, with intense conflict, and with mass displacement. These were the 'very large humanitarian emergencies' identified by the UNHCR, affecting tens of millions of people, including large numbers who were not counted as refugees because as IDPs they had not crossed borders of a nation-state. By the late 1990s there were at least 22 million such people in countries of the Third World, in the Russian Federation and in Eastern Europe (Global IDP Survey 1998: xiii). The incidence of such crises increased as the internationalisation of capital accelerated, leaving many states chronically weak. During the 1990s movements of finance capital cut a speculative swathe through weak currencies; at the same time, in the least developed regions productive investment declined so sharply that some local economies in effect fell out of the world economy, becoming what Hoogvelt (1997: 176) calls 'a structural irrelevance'. In the early 1990s the Horn of Africa (Ethiopia, Eritrea, Djibouti, Somalia, Sudan) experienced just such a regional collapse; by the end of the decade the crisis of sub-Saharan Africa was much more advanced and Central Africa (Congo–Rwanda–Burundi) and West Central Africa (Liberia–Sierra Leone–Guinea–Ivory Coast) were also marked by economic regression, systemic conflict and extreme insecurity. It was in these regions that some states collapsed, becoming the 'failed' states identified in Kaplan's dystopic vision of West Africa.

The IMF and the World Bank were nonetheless determined to redirect economic activity in conformity with their model of the efficient local economy. The main concern was to break down relations of patronage said to inhibit rational business activity in much of the Third World, and the main target was the state – in particular the corrupt and unproductive clientist networks identified with 'cronyism', 'mafias' and 'warlord capitalism' (Reno 1998). The preferred method was to attack the state directly by use of radical methods of privatisation – the formal aim being to transfer state services to new businesses focused on profit rather than upon privileged access to resources. This approach was applied widely: when it proved ineffectual in the short term, and/or stimulated protests and general instability, the medicine was often repeated. Stiglitz (2002: 47–8) comments that the dogma was plainly counterproductive:

> If policies imposed by lenders induce riots, as has happened in country after country, then economic conditions worsen, as capital flees and businesses worry about investing more of their money. Such policies are not a recipe either for successful development or for economic stability.

In very weak and vulnerable states the strategy has proved particularly destructive. As resources are directed away from the state, disrupting food supplies and local economic networks and producing job losses, and governments begin to lose legitimacy among the mass of people. Protests are met by repression, further undermining central authority and encouraging factionalism on the basis of regional, religious, sectarian or other differences. The apparatus of state – the police, the army and civil administration – itself becomes an arena for conflict as rival leaders compete for influence. Factional conflict becomes general and the armed forces may collapse or retreat to portions of the territory formally under their control. Large numbers of people may flee ahead of armed groups and militias, or may be purposefully displaced by them. They leave the countryside for cities in which the state has concentrated resources; in other cases, urban populations seek sanctuary in the countryside. It is in such circumstances that millions seek an 'exit from the state' (Zolberg 1989: 44). For many people choices have run out: they are forced to become migrants.

Each crisis of displacement has its own distinctive features. Many recent crises, however, share certain characteristics, of which the most important is the imposition and re-imposition of neo-liberal reforms. Examples from four continents demonstrate how unrelenting pressure from the IMF, the World Bank, and creditor states and institutions has been a key factor in the mass production of refugees.

Crisis and mass displacement

Somalia

The collapse of the Somali state in the early 1990s took place in association with one of Africa's most traumatic crises of mass displacement. It has been seen mainly as an expression of 'warlordism' – a simplistic explanation which locates responsibility for the events in Somali political traditions and in local cultural practice.

In the nineteenth century the region of Somalia was the subject of intense colonial competition and was divided between neighbouring Ethiopia and three European powers – Britain, France and Italy. Each imposed its own system of centralised control upon traditional social structures, creating new networks of privilege which cut across existing solidarities. Samater suggests that this experience 'rather than Somali society or traditions ... represents the genesis of contemporary Somali dictatorship and warlordism'.[11] The colonial powers made little attempt to gain direct economic benefit from areas under their control. British and French possessions were primarily of strategic importance; the

Italian occupation amounted to little more than 'shopkeeper' colonialism. When the British and Italian territories were unified at independence in 1960 the economy of the new state was among the most fragile in Africa. Its main source of revenue was from livestock supplied to the booming Gulf states: in 1978 this accounted for 90 per cent of export earnings (Laitin and Samater 1984: 70). Political structures were marked strongly by the colonial experience, so that throughout the first decade of independence rival groups based on clan affiliation struggled for influence. By 1969 a coup had brought Siad Barre to power. The new president's unsuccessful war with Ethiopia over the disputed Ogaden region was followed by a decade of manoeuvres between the superpowers, during which the regime accumulated arms and aid. This was accompanied by a domestic policy of divide-and-rule which borrowed much from the colonial manual. What soon produced crisis and disintegration was the relentless pressure brought to bear by the IMF and the World Bank. In the early 1980s a devaluation of the Somali shilling, together with an austerity programme, were conditions for loans to service interest on debts to the Paris Club of Western creditors, and there were steep rises in the cost of food staples and of fuel. At the same time Somalia was becoming dependent on imported grain: between the mid-1970s and mid-1980s food aid increased by 1500 per cent (Chossudovsky 1997: 102). Bulk imports of rice and wheat brought a change in consumption patterns, with producers of local grains increasingly marginalised. These developments were applauded by the IMF, which reported that: 'Somalia has been able to achieve, within a short space of time, substantial improvement in its economic conditions' (Laitin and Samater 1984: 71). A series of privatisation measures aimed at the livestock sector now caused a decline in production and in 1984, Saudi Arabia – the main customer for Somali exports – turned to Western suppliers offering subsidised meat. At a stroke Somalia's main source of foreign currency was cut off and soon debt-service obligations represented almost twice export earnings (Chossudovsky 1998: 102). At this point, comments Horst (2003: 57), 'internationally ordained economic policies' appear to have increased poverty and destroyed many livelihoods. The economy was in a parlous condition and structures of central government began to break up – in many areas the education system, for example, ceased to function. When the World Bank proposed emergency measures it nevertheless insisted upon mass sackings of state employees. Even this was not enough: in 1989 both the IMF and the World Bank cancelled loan agreements.

The end of the Cold War exposed the Barre regime, which could no longer use Somalia's strategic location as a means to bargain with the superpowers for arms and aid. The economy was already chronically weak and now became much weaker, as economic networks associated with pastoralism and production of grain started to disintegrate and hunger became general in many rural areas. The Barre faction was involved in fierce conflict with rival groups, especially with the opposition movement of the north. The state ceased to exist as an agency associated with public functions and Barre retreated towards defence of his remaining influence. By early 1990, his attacks on the northern region had displaced almost a million people and groups from the southern and central regions had mobilised against him. By 1991 the apparatus of state had collapsed entirely and organisations in the north, which was now under opposition control, declared for secession. Clan groups became the focus of mass loyalties, not least because they appeared to provide a minimum of physical security and access to basic resources. In many areas survival systems gave way and at least 300,000 people died of starvation. Amnesty International (1993: 258) attributed the loss of life to 'fighting, breakdown of government, famine, and obstruction of the flow of international relief aid'. Almost a quarter of the population of 6 million became refugees, crossing into Kenya, Ethiopia and Djibouti. Vast numbers of people were also internally displaced. The state had imploded and, alarmed at the political vacuum, Western governments attempted to put in place a proxy structure. In 1993, 28,000 US troops occupied Somalia as part of the UN-sanctioned Operation Restore Hope – an imposition by strong states of means of political authority in a region which their own strategies had made 'stateless'. It was described by the Global IDP Survey (1998: 82) as 'an unprecedented fiasco … leaving Somalia in perhaps an even worse state of anarchy'. In 1995 the UNHCR (1995: 251) estimated that there were at least 535,000 Somali refugees; in 1997 the UN estimated that there were still some 1.2 million people internally displaced (Global IDP Survey 1998: 84).

Yugoslavia

In the early 1990s the state of Yugoslavia disintegrated. A series of violent upheavals was accompanied by repeated mass displacement, causing the biggest refugee crisis in Europe for 50 years. The Yugoslav Federation had been formed after the First World War as an attempt to satisfy the aspirations of a complex of ethnic groups for various forms of autonomy and independence (see Chapter 6). The Federation was inherently unstable, collapsing during the Second World War but recovering strongly in the 1940s, largely thanks to US aid and to the strategies of its president, Josip Tito, who exploited Cold War antagonisms to steer a path between Washington and Moscow. At the same time Tito developed a domestic political system which combined centralised bureaucratic rule with a significant level of local autonomy, establishing complex networks of interest among federal officials and local groups. These arrangements came under pressure in the 1970s, when Yugoslavia was badly affected by repeated crises of the world economy, and by the early 1980s the Federation was heavily in debt to Western banks. In common with a host of states it now came under the discipline of the major transnational financial organisations. The IMF insisted on economic reforms, including cuts in state spending: most subsidies were withdrawn and the cost of transport and of essential goods including fuel and food rose sharply. Meanwhile a programme of privatisation was initiated, with enormous consequences for the Titoist system of interlocking interest groups. Andor and Summers (1998: 23) comment that these measures were imposed 'without any consideration of the consequences for the creeping disintegration of the federal state'.

By the late 1980s austerity programmes were in force and there had been a sharp deterioration in living standards; industrial production had fallen by 10 per cent and GDP by 7.5 per cent (Hudson 2003: 57). IMF pressure nonetheless continued, together with encouragement from the United States and Western European governments to the more stable republics to cease supporting weaker units within the Federation and to seek entry to the European Community. In 1990 a policy of 'economic shock therapy' was imposed, also under IMF direction, hugely increasing tensions (ibid). This abolished the self-managed and 'socially owned' enterprises which had been the hallmark of the Yugoslav system, replacing them with private enterprises. There were mass closures and some 600,000 workers were laid off by bankrupt firms (Chossudovsky 1997: 169). The economic and political networks which had bound together the Federation now began to break up. The two richest republics, Slovenia and Croatia, declared independence in 1991, and a series of wars began which were to last for almost a decade. Each saw intense conflict involving ethnically based militias and units of the former national army, and campaigns of terror aimed at removing specific sections of the local population – 'ethnic cleansing'. Vast numbers of people were displaced, including 300,000 from each of Croatia and Bosnia, and some 460,000 within and from Kosovo (Hudson 2003: 90; van Selm 2000: 5). Hundreds of thousands of people fled to 'safe' areas or to neighbouring states and many were accepted as refugees in Western Europe (most on a temporary basis).

Many interpretations of these events have sought to attribute them in their entirety to local communal rivalries. Stubbs (1999: 4–5) comments on the use of 'one-line explanations referring to such things as "the Balkan mentality", "endemic ethnic conflict", "the death of Tito", "nationalism after communism" and such like'. The leading Eurocrat Jacques Attali has drawn on the discourse of colonialism: echoing Kaplan's warning of contamination of the West by base Third World influences, he has ascribed the events to 'Balkan tribalism' – a contagion which, he feared, would threaten the whole of European society.[12] The events were, however, the immediate outcome of very rapid economic collapse in which transnational financial organisations were deeply implicated. Andor and Summers (1998: 135) suggest that implosion of the Federation was associated directly with pressure from external agencies: economic crisis had been exacerbated 'by ill-thought out, ideologically driven markets reforms', leading to 'total social and economic breakdown'. In this respect the Yugoslav events were little different from those which had taken place in the Horn of Africa.

Indonesia

Throughout the 1970s and 1980s Indonesia was lauded as a 'Dragon' economy – a candidate to join the elite of NICs. President Suharto had seized power in 1965 in a coup accompanied by slaughter of political radicals and the elimination of the communist party. In 1967 Richard Nixon, soon to be US president, described Indonesia under the new regime as 'the greatest prize in South East Asia'.[13] During the 1970s and 1980s it was the scene of feverish activity by MNEs eager to exploit mineral and agricultural products (oil, gold, tin, copper and rubber) and a labour force regulated by Suharto's militarised state. Many factories were opened, largely in light manufacturing, and between 1979 and 1996 GDP doubled (Robison 1996: 79). During this period Western governments and the transnational financial organisations ignored the continuing violence of the regime, the nepotistic networks constructed around Suharto, and growing extremes of inequality. In 1989 the World Bank (1989: 104) endorsed Suharto's policies of financial deregulation; in 1992 the IMF (1992: 19) noted an increase in GDP of over 7 per cent annually and recorded Indonesia's status among the seven fastest-growing economies in Asia. Less attention was paid to the yawning gap between rich and poor: even official figures showed that the ratio between receipts of the highest and lowest income groups almost doubled between 1985 and 1993 (Fermont 1998: 10).

In the late 1990s the Suharto era came to an abrupt end. The financial meltdown of 1997, which had begun in Thailand, spread quickly to Indonesia and the local currency and the stock exchange went into free fall. A rescue package organised by the IMF offered US$37 billion but at the usual cost: the regime was to dismantle all state monopolies and restrictive trade practices. In effect the cost to MNEs of payoffs to Suharto and his networks, said to amount to a third of the cost of many projects (ibid), was now judged excessive. Over six months the *rupiah* was devalued by 500 per cent and most local companies became technically bankrupt. Meanwhile household consumption was plummeting: during the crisis it fell by almost a quarter (Harris 2003: 204). Despite strikes and demonstrations of protest across the country the IMF's offer of a further US$43 billion loan was conditional on more cuts in fuel subsidies – a direct threat to the mass of Indonesians. In May 1998 there were huge increases in the cost of electricity, water and fertiliser, producing a further round of riots: 'the beginning of the end for Suharto' (Fermont 1998: 17). In May 1998 the president resigned, to be replaced by his associate B. J. Habibie, and a series of events familiar in other continents now began to unfold. Habibie was committed to the IMF programme and implemented further cuts in food subsidies. Protests spread throughout the archipelago, encouraging separatist and secessionist movements. The apparatus of state began to fracture, with sections of the army command acting independently to protect their own interests. The legacy bequeathed by Dutch colonialism had been of a state founded on unstable alliances of regional elites; as they came under pressure from millions of desperate people factional conflicts were initiated by those fearful of losing their power and privilege. As in Yugoslavia, 'economic crisis, exacerbated by ill-thought out, ideologically driven market reforms' was leading to social and economic breakdown.

The army played a leading role, initiating attacks on the independence movement in East Timor and on minority religious and ethnic groups elsewhere. Communal conflict spread – by mid-2000, hundreds of thousands of people were in flight across the archipelago, especially in and from Aceh, Sulawesi and the Moluccas, and many were lost at sea in a series of tragedies in which overcrowded boats sank or were attacked. Still the IMF insisted on driving through further reforms. In a state with over 100 million officially poor people the agency demanded removal of subsidies on kerosene – widely used for cooking – and on other fuels. There were further riots and interventions by the army. Again ethnic conflict spread, this time to Kalimantan in Indonesian Borneo and to Irian Jaya. The world's fourth most populous state had become less a Dragon than another candidate for Balkanisation.

Argentina

In the 1990s Argentina was the developmental model for Latin America. With a relatively diverse and robust economy, and a government prepared to accept principles of liberalisation, its politicians won praise from economic strategists in the West. They radically reduced public spending, encouraged foreign investment and began a programme of privatisation of core state activities. Argentina became the IMF's star pupil – its president was invited to address boards of governors at both the Fund and the World Bank. But in the late 1990s the economy suffered badly from the South-East Asia meltdown and the trade deficit ballooned. In order to finance these debts and payments on long-standing foreign loans the government negotiated a new deal with the IMF. In 2001 the organisation abruptly reneged on the agreement – the loan facility was withdrawn and the economy collapsed. Thousands of businesses now failed, producing a huge rise in unemployment and serious food shortages. A nationwide movement of protest erupted, targeting local politicians and external agencies. These were in effect 'IMF riots' on a vast scale – the country had become ungovernable and appeared to be on the edge of revolutionary upheaval. Stiglitz (2002: 18) comments that given the unbearable pressures upon most Argentinians, 'the wonder is not that the citizens eventually rioted, but that they suffered so quietly for so long.'

By mid-2002, the government estimated, one person was falling under the poverty line every four seconds – at this stage 61 per cent of the population of 36 million was officially 'poor' or 'extremely poor' (Levy 2004: 13). Many sought to escape the crisis by emigrating: 60 per cent of young people declared that they wished to leave (*Observer*, 19 May 2002). Huge queues formed outside consulates in Buenos Aires as Argentinians applied for passports from European states. Between January and July 2002 some 300,000 of the 10 million Argentinians of Italian origin applied for Italian passports (*Guardian*, 12 August 2002). Those who could not enter Europe by formal means used other methods: by 2004 Argentinians formed one of the largest groups of irregular workers in Spain (Pajares 2004: 12). A state constructed upon immigration had become a source of new migrants – people convinced that for reasons of survival they must flee the crisis.

In 2001 at least 23 countries witnessed civil conflicts in response to policies initiated by the IMF. Levy (2004: 52) asks whether the agency's presence on the scene was coincidental: 'One economic meltdown might be forgivable, two rather careless, but the string of social and economic disasters while the IMF was chief economic advisor suggests that there is a logic to this consistent undermining of developing economies.' Stiglitz (2002: 18), who for years worked closely with the architects of neo-liberal reform, also believes that there is clear pattern, arguing that the IMF imposes models likely to stimulate both local crisis and systemic problems at a global level: 'The IMF has made mistakes in all the areas it has been involved in: development, crisis management, and in countries making the transition from communism to capitalism.' The explanation, he maintains, lies in the interests of those who control the agencies – the wealthiest industrial countries and the commercial and financial interests within them.

He concludes that they have advanced a vision of globalisation which benefits the few at the expense of the many, the well off at the expense of the poor. For the mass of people the strategy seems to be 'an unmitigated disaster' (Stiglitz 2002: 20). This outcome is not only a matter of failures of economic development, however. Neo-liberal globalisation supports an environment in which the strong are encouraged to attack the weak, in which dominant states further marginalise weak states, and those with authority use their powers against those who are most vulnerable.

In 1989 Cohen and Joly reviewed the policies of European governments towards refugees arriving from Africa, Asia and Latin America. It was already clear, they argued, that the sole means of avoiding repeated crises of forced migration was a massive injection of aid to the Third World (Cohen and Joly 1989: 16). This would require emergency assistance, resolution of the debt problem and lifting of controls on commodity prices. But a major package might be insufficient: ultimately the whole relationship between industrialised and Third World countries would have to be reassessed and 'there is simply no evidence that European governments have grasped, or wish to grasp, the scale and complexity of the problem' (ibid). Instead, mainstream political parties had bowed to internal right-wing pressures, focusing on detention and deportation of asylum-seekers, so that the European Community had taken on the appearance of 'a gilded cage with the Ministers of the Interior bracing and painting the bars' (Cohen and Joly 1989: 17). Fifteen years later Castles (2004) made a similar diagnosis. Dominant states had failed to address root causes of mass displacement, he suggested. In the case of the European Union, despite a strong formal commitment to tackle mass emigration by addressing problems in the regions of crisis, interventions had been ineffectual. In 1999 the Union had drawn up a series of Action Plans for countries producing large numbers of migrants (Albania, Afghanistan, Iraq, Morocco, Somalia and Sri Lanka), undertaking to develop a comprehensive and coherent approach to relations with these countries. In fact little attention had been paid to fundamental issues such as sustainable development, poverty reduction or conflict resolution; rather, the Union had focused on exporting techniques of migration control such as extra-territorial policing and agreements for the readmission of undesired migrants. 'As a result the Action Plans did not amount to programmes to effectively prevent human rights violations, or combat the root causes of forced migration' (Castles 2004: 220). These failures have long been general among dominant states: despite rhetorical commitments to address deep-lying problems of the world's most vulnerable regions they prefer to target migrants. Rather than take responsibility for the legacy of colonialism and the failures of global development they target *the displaced themselves* as the cause of problems associated

with migration and with domestic instability. This practice comple-
ments the efforts of those committed to structural reform of the world
economy: it is one of the 'disasters' of neo-liberal globalisation.

Notes

1. Quoted in *Ahram Weekly*, 30 December 1999.
2. Analyses within international relations, conflict studies and peace studies
   have advanced various typologies of the 'new' wars. For a comprehensive
   account of contending approaches see Miall *et al.* 1999, chapters 2 and 3.
3. There are rare exceptions where historic borders of empires survived the
   colonial experience more or less intact. Examples include Iran, Sri Lanka,
   Thailand, Japan and China. There are no such examples in Latin America,
   and in sub-Saharan Africa only Ethiopia – ancient Abyssinia – recalls the
   state of the pre-colonial era.
4. The pattern was somewhat different in Latin America. In South America
   colonial occupation was followed by struggles for independence, led principally by *mestizo* elites, which resulted in the formation of independent
   states by the mid-nineteenth century. In Central America the pattern was
   somewhat closer to that in South Asia, Africa and the Middle East.
5. Colonial powers invariably exacerbated or even generated conflict within
   indigenous populations, often alongside campaigns to implant new ideas in
   the form of 'traditions': see Hobsbawm and Ranger 1983.
6. For a concise account of these developments see Chossudovsky 1997.
7. Quoted in George and Sabelli 1994: 59.
8. In Africa by the late 1990s every inhabitant of the continent was indebted
   at a level of US$370 (*Guardian*, 11 May 1998).
9. Quoted in Reno 1998: 50.
10. Meanwhile speculators who bought Third World debt on the open market
    at knock-down prices were supported in efforts to enforce payment at full
    face value. In the case of companies which bought Latin American govern-
    ment debt the courts have been used to compel payment on the penalty of
    loss of all holdings in the United States. By such means in 2002 one New
    York-based hedge fund made US$65 million in a single claim against the
    Peruvian state (*Guardian*, 19 October 2000).
11. Samater, quoted in Deng 1993: 55.
12. Quoted in Burgess 1997: 60.
13. Quoted in Fermont 1998: 7.

3
Migrants Old and New

Migration and inequality

Recent events in Somalia, Yugoslavia, Indonesia and Argentina illustrate many of the characteristics of historic crises of forced migration, most important the involvement of poor and vulnerable people, and the central role of the state. These have been evident since the first migrations of the modern era.

For centuries migration has been shaped by the demands of capitalism – a system rooted in relations of inequality. The first major forced migrations of the modern age took place during the earliest phases of capitalist development.[1] This was the era of primitive accumulation – the seizure by commercial capitalists of wealth which was later mobilised to launch industrial production. In Europe and elsewhere the process was dependent upon mass movements of population. These first took place on a large scale in England, where from the sixteenth century landowners began to seize common lands, displacing the peasantry. Over the next 300 years these clearances accelerated as land came into the hands of agrarian capitalists supported by an increasingly centralised state. The aim was to exploit the land by producing for the market and at the same time to create a new, 'free' labour force which could be recruited to urban industry. This form of primitive accumulation, argued Marx (1957: 813), 'cleared the ground for capitalist agriculture, made the land part and parcel of capital, while providing for the needs of urban industry and the requisite supplies of masterless proletarians'. By the late eighteenth century, the enclosures in Britain had produced immiseration of many rural communities. Thompson (1968: 217) records 'years of wholesale enclosure, in which, in village after village, common rights are lost, and the landless and ... pauperized labourer is left to support the tenant-farmer, the landowner, and the tithes of the Church'. Under these pressures former peasants and craft workers moved en masse to towns and cities. Those reluctant to leave their homes met further measures of compulsion directed by the state: by the nineteenth century the Poor Law aimed to make life so intolerable for the rural poor that they would move to any jobs offered.[2]

For the emerging capitalist classes these developments were necessary if economic and social advance was to be accomplished. Hobsbawm (1962: 184) comments on a consensus across Europe that the bulk of the rural population must be encouraged to move:

> surplus population[s] ... had to be torn away from their roots and allowed to move freely. Only thus would they migrate into the towns where their muscles were increasingly needed. In other words the peasants had to leave their land together with their other bonds.

These migrant labourers were formally 'free': unlike various forms of tied labour they had certain rights in law and notionally they had freedom of movement and choice of employer. In fact they were coerced to migrate and compelled to move into the urban economy as unskilled labour in an insecure environment. By the early nineteenth century, most governments in Western and Northern Europe had initiated land reforms which facilitated these movements. Within 30 years, the process was largely complete and change was accelerating in Eastern and Southern Europe. Everywhere the state intervened aggressively to promote migration and to feed growth of industry. Scores of millions of people were compelled to seek new lives in the cities.

Colonies and slaves

These developments took place alongside a different but complementary form of migration – the mass movements organised by European colonialism:

> The discovery of gold and silver in America, the extirpation of the indigenes in some instances, their enslavement or entombment in mines in others; the beginning of the conquest and looting of the East Indies; the transformation of Africa into a precinct for the supply of negroes who were the raw material of the slave trade – these were the incidents that characterised the rosy dawn of the era of capitalist production. (Marx 1957: 832)

The expansion from Europe of commercial or mercantile capitalism was inseparable from a new mass migration – that of the slave trade, a business encouraged and supported by the state. The first voyages to the Americas of Columbus and his fellow adventurers were financed by the kingdom of Spain to serve both commercial interests and the Spanish Treasury. Their main aim was to seize bullion – gold and silver – although they also hoped to pillage the Americas for human resources. At first vast numbers of indigenous people were slaughtered but as the expeditions of the *conquistadores* lasted longer, becoming a process of settlement, colonisers began to view the population as a source of labour to be exploited locally. Slavery became important as a means of facilitating colonisation proper: in mining, construction, growing and processing food, and in providing services for the Europeans. The colonisers, migrants themselves, were soon organising mass forced migration of the communities they controlled.

There were precedents for slavery in Europe but in the Iberian states all people had been formally 'freeborn'. The benefits to be gained from enslavement of indigenous people in the colonies induced the Spanish monarchy to change the law, so that all native Americans who opposed occupying forces, and specifically those who opposed Christianisation, could be enslaved. Many people in the colonies of Central and South America and the Caribbean were seized and taken on forced marches to mines and farms on which they were to work. Slavery was abolished in 1511 but new laws allowed the commitment of indigenous people to lifelong labour – they were slaves in all but title. To facilitate forced labour in agriculture, the Spanish Crown assigned native Americans to specific *conquistadores* under the system of the *encomienda*. Formally the Americans were free, although they were also vassals of the king, who could allocate them to favoured subjects among whom the right to command labour was inheritable. Simpson comments that the arrangement was 'a subterfuge for slavery'.[3] Initially the *encomienda* also provided labour for the mines; when the supply proved insufficient the *mita* was introduced – a system of raising labour by obliging communities in mining regions to provide specific numbers of labourers. These and other similar systems mobilised American populations that had survived the early massacres. They often involved long-distance migration at huge cost in terms of loss of life – they were the earliest form of long-distance transportation endorsed by European states and had the aim of serving commerce and the state itself.[4] Although there were repeated conflicts between *conquistadore* communities and the metropolitan state, each required a structure for exploitation of labour. Potts (1990: 16) comments

> Whereas [the colonists] were interested in the private deployment and control of the labour force and short-term profits, the Crown, not least in order to counteract the conquistadors' attempts at gaining independence, had an interest in state control of the labour force and in the long-term maintenance of this source of wealth, ie, in the reproduction of labour power.

Commerce and the state had forged an alliance in organising the first large-scale system of slavery in the history of capitalism.

Elimination of most of the indigenous American population by mass murder, disease, death during transportation and through forced labour, brought a new enslavement – that of the African peoples. The trade was initiated by Portuguese merchants who first transported Africans to Europe to act as domestic labour and later began to supply the sugar plantations of Brazil. From the early eighteenth century the leading participants were British merchants, who pioneered the 'triangular trade', bringing together human cargo with the movement of cotton and manufactured goods between Africa, the colonies and the metropolitan centre – a system of transactions that was a key element in commercial activities intimately associated with the rise of industrial capital.[5] Contemporary observers of the Atlantic trade were certain as to its immense importance to the European economies. In 1729 the British merchant Joshua Gee observed that, 'All this great increase in our treasure proceeds chiefly from the labour of negroes in the plantations'.[6] Estimates of the total number of Africans imported into the Americas over 250 years until abolition in the mid-19th century range up to 20 million (Potts 1990: 41).

Slave traders and slave owners operated for private gain but did so in the context of specific strategies of the state. In Europe, a process of 'nationalisation' of economic forces was under way, in which acquisition of colonies and command of the slave trade were increasingly important.[7] The more that the colonies demanded slaves the more profitable the transatlantic trade became and the more urgently European powers competed to secure it. In England the state both stimulated and regulated trade, financing voyages of 'discovery' which aimed to secure uncolonised territories before they fell into the hands of rival powers. As early as the mid-sixteenth century, the Merchant Adventurers of England received endorsement from the Crown for the discovery of 'regions, territories, islands, possessions and domains unknown and not frequently visited by sea or by navigation'.[8] A generation later commercial capital had greatly advanced its status and Walter Raleigh, described by Ferro (1997: 47) as 'the theoretician of a sort of maritime imperialism', set out a formula for competitive expansion of the English state: 'Whoever rules the waves rules commerce; whoever rules commerce rules the wealth of the world, and consequently the world itself' (ibid). Although merchants of the period were described as 'adventurers', with the implication that their activities were independent of state control, they operated as part of the new national strategies for colonisation. Senior figures of the state were guided by the doctrine of mercantilism, in particular by the belief that for a successful struggle vis-à-vis national rivals it was necessary to dominate the widest territories, repatriating wealth from the colonies and at the same time denying it to enemies abroad. The European powers competed increasingly fiercely, especially in the Americas where colonies often changed hands, and in Africa where weaker states such as Portugal were compelled to operate in regions more and more distant from Europe. It is significant that by the mid-eighteenth century, when Britain was becoming the first industrial power, its merchants had become dominant in the Atlantic slave trade and British colonies in the Americas had become immensely productive.[9] The mass migrations of slavery were inextricably linked to the full emergence of capitalism and of the nation-state.[10]

Structures of the state were integral to the operation of the colonies and to slavery as a business. Slaves were non-persons: they were bought and sold as property and disposed of by their owners at will. They had no independent status and did not appear in law as legally capable. The matter of slavery was, however, the subject of much law-making. Ghai (1997: 154) comments that, 'a great deal of jurisprudence was built on the need of society to subordinate slaves ... the state had of course a general interest in maintaining the institution and incidence of slavery, as central to the well-being of powerful classes'. The colonising powers also developed elaborate codes of ownership and means of regulating disputes among traders and slave-owners. Core structures of the state which had emerged in Europe – centralised legal systems, judicial institutions and means of enforcement – were reproduced in the colonies as mechanisms which both guaranteed rights in property (including in slaves) and which mediated relations among property owners. Slavery was not merely the outcome of market activities initiated by voracious European merchants but of the implantation of social and political structures that were integral to capitalism at home and abroad.[11]

Indenture

Following a series of slave rebellions, and in the context of growing support in Europe for emancipation, slavery was formally abolished by all the major powers by the 1830s. Although it continued at a reduced level for many decades[12] a new migrant stream was now organised: that of indentured labour. This was operated mainly by British and Dutch contractors who recruited in India, China, Japan and Malaya, and shipped their cargoes initially to colonies in the Caribbean, South and East Africa, South East Asia and the Pacific islands, and later to the United States, Canada, Australia, New Zealand and Peru. Potts (1990: 67 and 73) estimates that over the course of 100 years, 40 countries imported indentured labour and that by the mid-twentieth century some 37 million people had been transported.

By the early nineteenth century some regions under colonisation had experienced changes like those which had earlier occurred in Europe: millions of people had been driven from the land and lived in precarious circumstances, 'freeing' them to be recruited as contracted labour. China, forcibly opened to the world market by Britain, offered the greatest resources. Here indentured labourers were often bound into their contracts by force, being 'shanghaied' – seized like the Chinese peasants who visited the city of Shanghai to sell their produce. Unlike slaves indentured labourers were paid, although they received token wages and worked under conditions which differed little from slave regimes. Everywhere the legal system operated to endorse the activities of planters and labour contractors: in the case of Indian labourers working in Mauritius, even a British Government report remarked on 'the extreme deference' shown by the courts to the wishes of the masters.[13] The level of exploitation was such that indentured labourers were often used to undercut the wages of 'free' workers, among whom in the Americas many were former slaves.

Although European states benefited greatly from slavery, specific initiatives to seize, transport and exploit slave labour had been taken primarily by private capitalists. In the case of indentured labour the state was more intimately involved. This reflected the character of the international system of states and empires that had emerged by the mid-nineteenth century. When movements of indentured labour took place within imperial systems they were regulated by laws and by agencies of the metropolitan state. The role of the British was especially important – indentured labour effectively began with a law of 1837 written to facilitate recruitment in India. When contractors recruited there on behalf of planters and entrepreneurs elsewhere in the British empire they were subject to regulations established within the British legal system. Meanwhile movements of labourers between territories controlled by rival European states involved formal bilateral treaties. Ghai (1997: 158) comments that such dealings were of enormous significance: bilateral treaties, which even today play a key role in international migration, had their roots in the regulation of indentured labour. The system came to an end after the First World War – less as a result of reform than through rapid contraction of the world economy and reduced demand for labour. Like slavery it had arisen under circumstances of rapid growth of commercial capitalism – in this sense it had been shaped by forces of the market. But like slavery it was also dependent upon specific socio-political structures which facilitated the exploitation of labour: in the case of slavery, the system had relied upon application of extreme violence to the victims; in the case of contracted labour, the worker was formally free but subject to overwhelming force. The state was the means by which the minority of entrepreneurs (planters, mine owners, construction bosses) sustained their control over vast populations of labourers. This relationship – between the market (the drive for profit) and the state – was to remain integral to international migration, shaping the journeys of migrants of all types, including forced migrants.

There was a further legacy of slavery and of indentured labour. Each required the elaboration of specific rationales which turned upon notions of essential European superiority. Racism developed as part of the project of colonisation and specifically of slavery and other forms of forced mobilisation of labour.[14] It was not only a justification for violence and exploitation in the colonies but was also integral to the domestic agendas of the new ruling classes of Europe. Here the emerging bourgeoisies attempted to bind people of 'their' territories by elaboration of ideas of nation defined vis-à-vis other European states and/or against 'internal' enemies depicted as alien to the national group (see Chapter 5). At the same time, they pursued general initiatives against peoples of the colonial world – an arena in which they competed against and collaborated with other European states. An essential element in this venture was the notion of inherent European superiority vis-à-vis people of Africa, Asia and Latin America. Delanty (1995: 46) comments that, 'It was Europe's mastery of the Atlantic ... that signalled the arrival of a new age and a new European identity.' This was described in various ways: in terms of religious rights and obligations, of 'civilisational' superiority, and eventually in theories of 'scientific' racism. These ideas were ideological in the strict sense: they were false accounts of the social order, concealing extremes of inequality and justifying activities of those with a direct interest in exploitation of peoples of the colonial world. Ghai (1997: 157) comments that with slavery and the consolidation of ideas about inferiority of Black African people, 'the seeds of racism were effectively sown and a rich harvest was garnered'. When slavery eventually ended, racism remained: 'The ending of slavery did not ... mark any great watershed for its dominant assumptions and many of its practices were continued in new legal forms and ideologies' (ibid). Racism was to remain an integral element in activities of the state through the twentieth century and into the third millennium. Ideas which emerged together with the first forced migrations of the modern era were to have a profound effect upon many generations of migrants.

Migrants and the state in Europe

In pre-capitalist Europe immigrants were usually viewed by political authorities as an asset. Most were urbanites – displaced peasants almost invariably returned to the land – and often came from merchant or artisan communities. The former moved through complex family and commercial networks, the latter as communities of production, with their tools and equipment. Braudel (1972: 433) describes craft workers of southern Europe in the sixteenth century as 'an itinerant labour force ... made up of many races, rarely native to the area'. They could be induced to move by offers of investment from merchants or from political authorities in distant regions: 'industry followed the merchants, or rather their capital' (Braudel 1972: 434). As early as the thirteenth century Flemish weavers were invited to England, where the king was so eager to attract them that he joined a Flemish guild himself (Winder 2004: 34); over the next 200 years large numbers settled in London and in several provincial cities.[15] Many of the financiers of Europe were Jews. Although they faced discrimination, being excluded from most crafts and trades, they were often protected by the Crown as invaluable sources of loans, and for their national and international connections. When most of the Jews of Spain were expelled in 1492 they moved to Portugal, where they were initially viewed by the Portuguese monarch as an economic windfall.[16]

Two hundred years later when another religious minority, the Protestants of France, came under pressure they were also welcomed abroad. It was of these Huguenots that the word 'refugee' seems first to have been used. Among them were many wealthy families and craft workers whose skills were prized by other states. They were loosely viewed as incomers with special reasons for migration – those who had fled, having been forced to depart as the result of religious persecution. But at this period population movements had become so widespread across Europe that 'refugees' usually moved within the general stream of migrants. In England and the Low Countries, peasants had long been moving to towns and cities which were now growing rapidly. Emigration was also in full swing. In the sixteenth century, this had been canvassed as a means of removing social groups and political factions deemed undesirable or troublesome. In the case of England, a law was introduced to provide for transportation. This was 'An Acte for Punyshment of Rogues, Vagabonds and Sturdy Beggars': they were to be 'banished out of this Realm ... and conveyed to such parts beyond the seas as shall be ... assigned by the Privy Council.'[17] If 'a Rogue so banished' returned to England without permission he would be hanged.[18] In the late seventeenth century, the policy was extended to encourage emigration of Scottish crofters, Irish peasants and dissident soldiers, notably the Levellers of the English Revolution. In 1717 a new law provided that convicted criminals could be transported to the Americas instead of being flogged and branded. This was not merely a means to remove undesirables and to reduce the population of

England's crowded prisons but to line the pockets of shipping companies and plantation owners. Over the next 60 years some 40,000 men and women were transported to North America and the Caribbean to suffer what Hughes (1987: 41) calls a 'thinly disguised form of slavery'.

America – 'the asylum of freedom'

Among emigrants to the colonies were also those with capital – 'anticipatory' migrants who calculated that their investments would be more productive in the new economies. But as emigration stepped up in the late eighteenth century, most who made the journey were *compelled* to move: in the case of Britain they were 'forced to leave by grinding poverty, rapacious landlords or unsympathetic officials or politicians' (Cohen 1997a: 67–8). America was the main destination. It was often portrayed as a place of succour: one account from the 1780s set out an idealised picture of life in what its author called 'this great American asylum' (Rietbergen 1998: 379). According to Hector St John, in the American colonies,

> the poor of Europe have by some means met together ... Everything has tended to regenerate them; new laws, a new mode of living, a new social system; here they are become men: in Europe they were as many useless plants ... and were mowed down by want, hunger and war. (ibid)

St John portrayed America as 'the asylum of freedom' and 'the refuge of distressed Europeans' (Rietbergen 1998: 378).

Most migrants of this period were not identified formally as people seeking refuge. Their journeys were nonetheless undertaken as means of survival. From the late eighteenth century large numbers of people moved from Ireland to mainland Britain, fleeing an aggressive colonial regime, increased landlessness and hunger. By 1851 some 700,000 Irish emigrants made up 3 per cent of the population of England and Wales and 7 per cent of the population of Scotland (Castles and Miller 1993: 55). International migration had now taken on a complex character, for as such migrants crossed the Irish Sea, millions were leaving Britain, Ireland and other European countries to cross the Atlantic. Rietbergen (1998: 378) describes a mass movement of migrants 'who, in wave after wave, flooded across America, often in conjunction with economic calamities, political unrest or religious disputes'. Among them were increasing numbers of people who were refugees in the sense most often used during the twentieth century – those fleeing persecution or political upheavals.[19] Some also faced new or increased pressure because of their cultural status – their place of origin, language or religion – for economic change in Europe was often accompanied by campaigns of ethnic differentiation associated with the rise of nationalism and the formation of states (see Chapter 5).

Emigration, argues King (1995: 16), was an 'escape hatch' through which those expelled by Europe gained access to the labour-hungry economies of the New World. During the century from 1814, 17 million people migrated from the British Isles, over 80 per cent of them moving to North America, and most of the others to British colonies – Australia, New Zealand, South Africa and Rhodesia (Cohen 1997a: 68). The scale of these movements was an expression both of the upheavals caused by industrialisation and urbanisation in Britain, and by the opportunities – real and imagined – offered elsewhere. As capitalism reshaped economic and social relationships across Europe, more countries experienced mass emigration. The population of the United States grew rapidly: in 1800 it was 5.3 million, by 1820 it had reached 9.2 million, and over the next 20 years it doubled several times (Potts 1990: 131). Most immigrants arrived with expectations of rapid advancement as settlers on the land. The idea of a new rural idyll was encouraged by emigration agencies and shipping companies, complementing nostalgia for an earlier existence in Europe – one which most migrants' families had long since abandoned. Most underwent a different experience as poorly paid labourers in manufacturing industry, construction or the service sectors of the growing cities. Many suffered severe hardship: slavery was still in operation and many American employers were habituated to very high levels of exploitation of labour. Rietbergen (1998: 380) comments that 'for countless immigrants, the dream ... quickly became a nightmare after their arrival in the promised land'. Despite these experiences immigration continued at a hectic pace. Millions of Europeans were under intense pressure to leave: emigration of Jews from Russia, for example, 'was related far more to pogroms than to the trade cycle' so that as persecution increased the number of emigrants grew relentlessly (Taylor 1971: 106). By the early twentieth century, emigration was being maintained at higher and higher levels through the troughs and peaks of economic performance. Despite a serious slump in 1907, more migrants entered the United States than in all but one year of the preceding century (ibid). Europe was in effect ejecting millions of its poorest and most oppressed people.

During the early years of the twentieth century the flow of migrants reached gigantic proportions. By 1905 the population of the United States had risen to over 105 million, dwarfing that of all the major European countries (Potts 1990: 131). All manner of people continued to arrive, including large groups of those later defined as refugees, such as victims of persecutions which followed the 1905 revolution in Russia. Across Eastern Europe conflicts prompted by the intensification of ethnocentric nationalism also produced continuous mass emigration.

Prominent among the participants were Jews fleeing anti-Semitism: between 1881 and 1915 over 2.2 million moved to the United States (Kulischer 1943: 8). Zolberg (1989: 11) comments that throughout this period forced migrants moved uncontroversially, 'flow[ing] with the ongoing immigration tide'.

Patterns of migration

The element of compulsion in migratory movements of the nineteenth century has been understated. In the case of transatlantic migrations it has been obscured by accounts of a great adventure in which free individuals were involved in the making of America's new nations. Most migrants were not transported as slaves or indentured labourers – notionally they moved freely and there was often elaborate planning and mobilisation of family and community networks to facilitate the passage. The great majority of migrants, however, had no secure means of support: they had lost land or employment in the countryside and/or were living at the margins of urban society.

Typical were those who left Holland for the United States in the 1840s and 1850s:

> Socioeconomic problems [and] wars left the country in a weakened state, suffering from high taxes, unemployment, chronic pauperism, and a general feeling of disillusionment and bitterness. This was the situation when potatoes and rye, the basic food crops, failed three years in a row and brought the Netherlands to the brink of famine...The number of persons on government poor relief tripled [and] protests erupted in market towns (Swierenga 1986: 99).

The emigrants' journeys were not freely chosen but undertaken primarily as a means of escape. The selection of migrants was not arbitrary, nor was it usually related to a special sense of adventure or a particular ability to innovate. Rather, migration was linked directly to socio-economic status: it was intimately associated with structures of social class.

For some European states emigration served the purpose of removing undesirable and 'surplus' elements in the population – what Weiner (1995: 39) labels 'population dumping'. During the early decades of the nineteenth century upheavals across Europe produced widespread fear within privileged sections of society of movements from below, prompting Malthusian strategies including the export of undesired elements. Between 1815 and 1826 the British government carried out a number of experiments in state-supported emigration to North America designed to induce the indigent to emigrate. The Poor Law authorities alone 'helped' more than 60,000 people to leave (Taylor

1971: 98) – a strategy described as 'shovelling out the poor'. In 1843 Sir Thomas Carlyle called for the British state to organise emigration more formally as a means of removing political radicals, proposing a state emigration service which could be a 'free bridge' to carry away 'superfluous' workers who might otherwise turn to radical alternatives such as that offered by the Chartists.[20] There were long-standing precedents. In the fifteenth century the Portuguese began the practice of using colonial territories as prisons; from the seventeenth century, when Angola was settled 'it was almost exclusively populated with delinquents' – the *degredados* (Ferro 1997: 140). Spain too expelled convicts to 'the Indies' and Britain removed oppositional groups to the Americas. In the 1770s the American colonies rebelled, closing this outlet. Accordingly the British state turned to its most remote colonial possession, the vast and 'empty' territory of Australia. Over 80 years from the 1788 it transported 160,000 convicts and political prisoners, mainly Irish republicans. On arrival in Australia most underwent 'assignment' to landowners and entrepreneurs for whom they worked under intolerable conditions. Hughes (1987: 1) comments that a whole unexplored continent had become a jail.

Imperial diaspora

By the early nineteenth century vast areas of Africa, Asia and the Middle East were under the control of European powers. They urgently needed to establish bridgeheads for the colonial state or to strengthen communities already integral to it. There was therefore constant movement between the metropolitan countries and the colonies of administrators, professionals such as lawyers and engineers, and military men, charged with carrying out abroad roles with which they were familiar at home – most important that of supervising the colonial economies and securing territories in the face of competition from rival powers. They made up the core of what Cohen (1997a: 67) calls 'imperial diasporas'. Agencies which recruited for the colonial service and for commercial interests abroad developed sophisticated propaganda, using newspapers, illustrated magazines, postcards and exhibitions. These presented accounts and images of life abroad which endorsed notions of privilege, duty and of service to empire as part of a civilising crusade. A network of philanthropic organisations was established, including in Britain the Society for the Promotion of Colonisation, and the Fund for Promoting Female Emigration. Their competition for recruits was one index of the extent to which those who travelled under their auspices were true anticipatory migrants, able to exercise choice about their destination and the timing and manner of their journeys. The churches were also of great importance: Porter (1975: 25) comments that in the case of Britain their activity overseas expanded enormously at the moment that British industry exploded onto the world market – 'on the crest of the same wave of national dynamism and self-confident expansionism which came with the industrial revolution and the triumph of "progress" '. They carried the message of the twin blessings of Christianity and of commerce – 'the path to salvation for the savage', exporting networks of priests and church administrators, members of religious orders and missionaries (ibid).

The colonial authorities preferred in general to implant respectable middle-class citizens; in addition, rather than the unwashed masses of the Atlantic migrations they needed skilled labour. Cecil Rhodes, who directed British activities in Southern Africa, declared that the colonial project was for 'the rights of every civilised man ... white or black [*sic*], so long as he had a decent education, that he owned property or had a trade, in a word, that he was no loafer' (Ferro 1997: 83). In 1867 the colony of Natal in South Africa established a dictation test in which prospective migrants were made to write out and to sign a passage dictated by an official. The main aim was to exclude Indian immigrants but it also had the effect of discriminating against illiterates. Similar legislation was later passed in most of the Australian colonies, where the main aim was to exclude Chinese immigrants – part of a wave of Sinophobia which swept North America and Australia in the 1880s and 1890s (see Chapter 6). Immigration policy in the settled colonies became more and more discriminatory. British migrants to 'dominions' such as South Africa received substantial state help, including assisted passages, grants of land and subsidies. In addition, those who invested in agriculture or mining or traded local products benefited from preferences within the imperial commercial system. Many prospered, becoming part of the white supremacy. Meanwhile Australia attempted to close its borders to most migrants deemed non-European. In 1901 the first Australian federal government introduced the Immigration Restriction Bill, the aim of which was 'to preserve this island continent for all eternity for the white race'.

Algeria – making colons

In some cases European powers sought large numbers of migrants among the masses of metropolitan society. This was the case during the French colonisation of Algeria, where the state accepted all human materials as *colons* in a country which energetically resisted occupation. France invaded Algeria in 1832, in an attempt by a weak monarchical regime to win support from commercial interests and from the army, both of which were resentful of British expansion in Africa and Asia.

It was a calculatedly violent occupation and soon presented French generals with the problem of consolidating their hold over a vast area populated by an angry population among which many were prepared to organise against the intruders.[21] The solution chosen was that of mass settlement, as expounded by Marshal Soult: 'we cannot wait: it is absolutely imperative that we make colons and construct villages, summon all energies to sanction, consolidate and simplify the occupation we achieve by arms'.[22] The army set about the destruction of the indigenous economy, razing of villages, and the expulsion of local people from the urban centres. There was a crash programme of settlement from abroad: by 1845 there were 46,000 settlers, by 1853 there were 140,000 (Behr 1961: 26). All and any potential migrants, both voluntary and involuntary, were mobilised:

> Like immigrants the world over, the Europeans who settled in Algeria in the nineteenth century came from the least privileged strata of society. Some were sent to Algeria straight from state orphanages; in the early years of his rule, Napoleon III used Algeria as a convenient place to send political opponents, and Left-wing revolutionaries joined a motley collection of juvenile delinquents, prison offenders, and refugees from France's eastern provinces. (ibid)

Following failure of the 1848 revolution in France large numbers of republican workers were transported to the colony, followed three years later by more political deportees and by many of the unemployed of Paris. In 1871, after German military occupation of Alsace-Lorraine, large numbers of displaced people – described officially as 'refugees' (ibid) – were shipped to Algeria. They were soon joined by impoverished peasants who had been affected by ruination of many vineyards in Southern France by the disease phylloxera: immigration was strongest when the disease was destroying communities on the Mediterranean plain. By 1880 there were 276,000 settlers (Behr 1961: 27) but the regime required more manpower. France was a country of immigration, mainly from neighbouring states, and the colonial authorities struggled to find *colons*, looking further and further afield – to Italy, Spain, Greece, Cyprus and Malta. At one point they considered opening up Algeria to the Irish, to Indians, Chinese and to the Maronite and Coptic Christians of the Arab world.

By 1912 there were 781,000 Europeans in Algeria – a vast settlement but one in which only 20 per cent of the incomers originated in France (ibid). This diversity, superficially a multi-ethnicity, was subsumed beneath collective hostility to the indigenous population and an obsessive concern with French identity. The commander of the occupation force of 1832 had told his troops 'You are continuing the Crusades' (Clegg 1971: 26) and there was subsequently an intensive effort by the authorities to inculcate ideas of cultural superiority, especially in relation to religion. This was extremely important for a colonial regime which aimed to subordinate not only the indigenous masses but a settler community that had arrived impoverished and often highly politicised. The colonial elite – agrarian and industrial entrepreneurs and the merchants – had much to fear from both indigenous and imported sections of the population.[23] Its main concern was to mobilise the latter against the former. Some settlers received land; all received privileges vis-à-vis the Algerians in terms of employment, education and legal rights, underwritten by the French state. The culture of privilege vis-à-vis the indigenous masses succeeded in securing the interests of the minority and of the metropolitan state.

War and recession

All mass migrations bear the marks of socio-economic difference. Most involve a majority of propertyless people who begin their journey under duress. Most arrive at their destination poor and remain among the propertyless, unless – as in Algeria – they are part of a specific project organised by the state. A minority of migrants may command capital and/or may move as part of the attempt to establish or sustain local systems in which they are relatively privileged. For most of the nineteenth century the general character of emigration from Europe concealed these realities. All manner of people were on the move, including many who at a later date would be identified as 'refugees'. In the closing decades of the century and the years before the First World War the pace accelerated until, suggests Zolberg (1997: 279), 'the uprooted originated from every corner of the globe and migrated wherever land or work might be available'.

Analyses of movements during this period emphasise the unprecedented scale of events: 'a vast expansion of international migrations to unprecedented and hitherto truly inconceivable levels' (Zolberg 1997: 285). During the decade of the 1870s combined international flows within and across Europe and North America totalled 2.7 million; during the first decade of the twentieth century in these regions alone the number reached 11 million (ibid). But the First World War brought a sudden and dramatic change. Following the conflict international migration rapidly diminished and by the 1920s it involved a fraction of the earlier numbers. In the United States the annual average of entrants during the 1930s was less than 50,000 – about 6 per cent of the total admitted immediately after the war (Jacobson 1996: 48). The change was associated with erection of barriers to migration among all states earlier involved in both emigration and immigration, and with general hostility in North America and Europe towards non-citizens – 'aliens'.[24] For the first time there was widespread formal differentiation among migrants, including identification of 'refugees' as a special category.

During the closing decades of the nineteenth century there had been moves in the United States and in Britain to restrict entry of certain groups of immigrants but migration in general had continued apace. World war at first brought contradictory developments. The combatant states restricted emigration, demanding that 'their' citizens should be available to labour and/or to fight for the home country, and for the first time passports were widely introduced, largely to control exit. At the same time these states increased recruitment of labour abroad to support the war economy. In France a special agency was created, Service des Travailleurs Coloniaux, answerable to the Ministry of War, which brought in hundreds of thousands of West Africans and Maghrebis; Germany recruited mainly from Eastern Europe and from its colonies in Africa; and in the United States special arrangements were made to recruit Mexican farmworkers. At the end of the conflict, however, states declared most immigrants surplus to requirements. Germany removed those who had survived the experiences of shipment and of intense exploitation in militarised industries and on the land; in France repatriation proceeded so fast that by 1919 only 10,000 Maghrebis remained (Potts 1990: 134). In the United States, many Mexicans were forced to return under contracts which bound them to remain in the employment of the farmer who had recruited them or to face deportation. These policies were soon formalised in laws which brought a dramatic decline in immigration. By the early 1920s the era of mass movements had come to an end.

War was not a sufficient cause for the suppression of mass migration: more significant was the changed state of affairs within the world economy. In the century before 1913 international capitalism had expanded at a dizzying pace. World trade grew by a factor of 25 (Harris 1995: 3), with a tremendous spurt in the late nineteenth century. Notwithstanding the Great Depression of the 1870s, over four decades preceding the First World War, average annual growth of the world system reached 3.4 per cent (Harman 1996: 6). There was then a sharp change: if international trade in 1913 equalled 100; in 1920–25 it fell to 92; and by 1931–35 it had risen to just 93. Only in 1948 did it rise to 103, topping the 1913 figure (ibid). For 30 years after the First World War the world system contracted and although the severity of recession varied according to time and place its net impact was to severely depress demand for labour. At first the unevenness of economic change disguised this trend. On one estimate the combined industrial production of combatant states was a third less in 1919 than it had been in 1914 (Harman 1984: 54). The damage was concentrated in Europe – in the United States the immediate post-war period was one of boom, to the extent that the centre of world economic activity moved across the Atlantic. Here demand for labour was at first maintained but this was satisfied increasingly by internal migration, largely that of Black workers from the South to the industrial cities of the East and the mid-West. At the same time, new techniques of mass production and of labour management were introduced – Fordism and Taylorism (the 'scientific' regulation of labour) – which increased levels of productivity and depressed demand for imported labour. It was in this climate that draconian anti-immigration measures were introduced by the US government (see Chapter 4). The intense nationalism associated with war and the state-centred economic policies continued after the conflict were important related factors: the key issue, however, was the continued spiral of decline of the world economy as a whole.

In the late 1920s contraction of the world economy trigged global collapse – a second Great Depression. World industrial production fell by a third: in the relatively prosperous United States it fell by 46 per cent (Harman 1984: 55). Recession focused attention of states on local solutions to economic and political crisis. Control of capital movements took on new significance, especially as attempts to implement Keynesian measures became general. National frontiers became borderlines of great importance, enclosing territories within which currencies, interest rates, investment, and the labour force were closely regulated. All over the industrialised world immigration was halted. In the United States a mere trickle of immigrants was permitted; in Germany by 1932 the number of foreign workers had fallen to about 10 per cent of the annual total 30 years earlier (Potts 1990: 137). For the first time in 200 years mass migration ceased. States focused upon matters of national identity and national rights, including who should be denied such rights. After generations of relatively free movement, applications from potential immigrants were now scrutinised with obsessive care. Those compelled to migrate by economic, political and social pressures – the vast majority of all migrants – were categorised in novel ways. 'Refugees' emerged as a more distinct group but they too were subject to the regime of exclusion. Emigration had been an 'escape-hatch' through which for generations the poor, the desperate and oppressed had attempted to find different lives. When further traumatic developments in Europe required millions of people to flee they found that the escape-hatch had been shut.

Notes

1. The seventeenth century is usually seen as the 'early modern' era – the earliest period of radical change in economic and social life in North-Western Europe and of the consolidation of the colonial venture.

2. By the mid-nineteenth century 60 per cent of the land in Britain was in the hands of only 4000 proprietors and was cultivated by some 250,000 tenant farmers. Most rural people were agricultural labourers under relentless pressure to move to the towns (Hobsbawm 1962: 182).
3. Quoted in Potts 1990: 20.
4. In the case of movements from Hispaniola to the Bahamas 60,000 tied labourers were transported in mass shipments between 1509 and 1519: by 1520 only 800 remained alive (Potts 1990: 13).
5. Slavery was not an invention of European merchants. It had existed for millennia in various forms in many regions. Europeans had often been enslaved by other Europeans and by slave-traders from adjacent regions: as late as the 1630s Turkish slavers raided the English and Irish coasts (Hill 1969: 75). What distinguished the Atlantic slave trade was its integration of forced labour with commercial agriculture and with industry as part of a growing world market.
6. Quoted in Hill 1967: 227.
7. See Pirrenne (1933: ch VII) for account of protectionist measures introduced by European monarchs.
8. Quoted in Ferro 1997: 47.
9. During the eighteenth century over 40 per cent of the slave trade was in the hands of British merchants (Potts 1990: 40). Portugal and France were also prominent; by this stage Spain had ceased to be a slaving nation.
10. In the late eighteenth century ideas of 'free-market' competition began to supplant mercantilist doctrines. The classical economists, notably Adam Smith, argued against monopolies of trade organised within the imperial systems. The philosophy of an unfettered market did not however challenge the idea of the state which remained at the centre of their concerns. Sutherland comments that Smith's own vision of the world economy, 'represents the hegemonic ambitions of Britain at this time, as the centre of an international network of trade and consumption' (Smith 1993: xvii).
11. Among others Harris (1995) is mistaken in suggesting that the state regulation of migration was a development of the late nineteenth century. By then the state, in various forms, had been initiating, regulating and benefiting from migration for over 300 years.
12. Despite prohibition in 1830 at least 60,000 people were later transported from Africa. The trade continued until, Ferro argues, it became more profitable to retain Africans in their regions of origin, where they were employed in industries such processing of palm oil (Ferro 1997: 175).
13. Quoted in Ghai 1997: 161.
14. Fryer (1984: 134) comments that in the case of Britain: 'Once the English slave trade, English sugar-producing plantation slavery and English manufacturing industry had begun to operate as a trebly profitable interlocking system, the economic base had been laid for all those ancient scraps of myth and prejudice to be woven into a more or less coherent ideology: a mythology of race.'
15. There were almost 4000 in Norwich alone (Foot 1965: 80).

16. When they were expelled from Portugal, most joined Jewish communities in North Africa and the Middle East, largely in areas within the Ottoman Empire. Here, like other religious minorities, they enjoyed certain communal rights: in effect they exchanged their skills in trade and finance for a protected status.

17. Quoted in Hughes 1987: 40.

18. Quoted ibid.

19. A detailed analysis of migration to the United States from Europe between 1820 and 1924 confirms that the typical emigrant was 'the proletarian – an industrial or agricultural worker without means, though in many cases formerly a small holder of land' (Ferenczi and Willcox, quoted in Nugent 1992: 33).

20. Quoted in Cohen 1997a: 69.

21. Under the leadership of Abdel-Kader there was a 15-year resistance to the armies of occupation.

22. Quoted in Clegg 1971: 24.

23. Even in the 1950s there were only 20,000–30,000 landowners among the colonists. The vast majority of *pieds noirs* lived in two cities in which they were employed as state functionaries and industrial or craft workers, or were small traders (Clegg 1971: 29).

24. France was an exception to the trend. Massive losses of men during the First World War and continued high demand for labour in agriculture and mining resulted in high levels of immigration from neighbouring countries. Here too, however, deepening recession resulted in mass deportation of non-citizens.

4
Chain Migration to Forced Migration

New migrants

Global recession brought to an end the first era of long-distance migration. When mass migration resumed in the mid-1940s it was sustained by the longest continuous period of growth of the world economic system. New patterns of movement affected tens of millions of people in regions hitherto uninvolved in long-distance migration. When in the 1970s economic growth came to an end, migration could no longer be inhibited, because unprecedented pressures were forcing more and more people to leave countries of origin and to enter migratory networks which were part of a new global environment.

Following the Second World War the world economy expanded at an unprecedented rate, exceeding even levels attained in the nineteenth century: it grew twice as fast between 1950 and 1965 as between 1913 and 1950 and nearly half as fast again as during the period before the First World War (Harman 1984: 82). States which in the 1930s forbade entry of non-citizens now campaigned worldwide to recruit on behalf of labour-hungry employers. Western Europe accepted enormous numbers of migrants, millions of whom had been displaced during the war, especially from Eastern and Central Europe. In addition, there was mass movement westwards from territories occupied or likely to be occupied by armies of the Soviet Union. These forced migrants were absorbed so rapidly that governments of Western Europe began to compete aggressively to draw in more workers. Soon the ability of states to facilitate immigration became an index of national economic vitality. De Gaulle, president of France, called upon the French people to produce 12 million 'beautiful babies' in order to make good a century of demographic decline (Fysh and Wolfreys 1998: 31); at the same time the French government organised for mass immigration to satisfy immediate demands. Almost 500,000 Europeans travelled to France, most from Portugal, together with 500,000 Maghrebis, the majority from Algeria (Fysh and Wolfreys 1998: 32) Over the next 20 years some 300,000 immigrants also came from French colonial possessions in Africa, the Caribbean and the Indian Ocean (Castles and Miller 1993: 72). Like France, Britain and the Netherlands recruited in colonies and former colonies in Asia and the Caribbean, while Germany drew in a mass of contract workers – *Gastarbeit*er – from Southern Europe and later from North Africa, Turkey, the Balkans and even from East Asia. By the early 1970s immigrant workers made up over 10 per cent of the workforce in both France and Germany, and 30 per cent in Switzerland; of 11.5 million immigrants in Western Europe, 9 million were from countries of the Third World (Harris 1996: 9). Specific communities grew with great speed. In 1961 the number of Moroccans and Turks in Belgium was negligible: a generation later the two communities numbered 250,000, or 2.3 per cent of the total population (Lievens 1999: 718). Ease of movement did not mean that the migrants were privileged, however. Almost invariably they were employed on short-term contracts and were intensively exploited. Harris (1996: 10) notes that in Germany over 1 million native-born workers left manual occupations for white-collar jobs between 1961 and 1968, replaced by about half the number of immigrant workers.

The pattern of movement into North America also showed a dramatic rise in numbers. During the 1960s, 300,000 immigrants were registered annually – about six times the numbers admitted a generation earlier (Castles and Miller 1993: 73). Most came from Mexico. In 1942 the United States and Mexico had agreed the Bracero Program, which was to provide workers (*bracero* = labourer) for the war economy. After the war it became what Martin (2001: 91) calls 'a kind of rolling quasi-amnesty program' for seasonal workers, many of whom arrived illegally. It remained in operation until the mid-1960s, offering limited rights to approved Mexican workers. The irregulars – 'wetbacks' who crossed the rivers of the US–Mexico border – were, however, viewed periodically as violators who threatened the regime of migration control and during the mid-1950s almost three million were expelled under Operation Wetback (see Chapter 8). Large numbers were subsequently admitted legally but on temporary contracts, with the result that many lived in conditions of extreme insecurity. Mechanisation of much of the US horticultural industry in the mid-1960s brought the Bracero Program to an end and admission of migrant workers was subsequently regulated by 'labour certification' – laws which stipulated that employers must demonstrate a specific need to import workers. Large numbers came from Korea, China and the Philippines but Mexico continued to be the key source of supply. By 1996 there were 7.3 million people of Mexican origin in the United States (Binational Study 2000: 7).

The search for labour

Throughout the long boom employers in Europe and North America recruited aggressively in the main regions of labour supply. European states were increasingly competitive in their efforts to feed domestic industry – some offered paid passage, secure housing and even (for a minority of immigrants) – the right to settlement. Neighbouring states sometimes competed for the same groups of workers: during the 1960s Turkish miners in Belgium were induced to move to Germany, and on the promise of tied housing thousands of Moroccans in France were persuaded to leave for Belgium, Germany and the Netherlands (Harris 1996: 9). By the late 1960s Germany had abandoned its policy of recruiting single men to allow entry of women and of whole families – in effect, the German state encouraged existing immigrants to recruit all those in their countries of origin who could be induced to travel to Europe.

Initially migrants were solicited by state-run organisations such as Germany's Federal Labour Office (BfA). German employers were no longer able to recruit in Eastern Europe, the reservoir upon which they had depended for almost 100 years but from which West Germany was now separated by frontiers sealed as part of the Cold War. The BfA drew up contracts with governments of supplier states, first in southern Europe, then in North Africa, Yugoslavia and Turkey. Offices were established initially in Athens, Verona, Madrid, Istanbul, Belgrade, Lisbon, Casablanca and Tunis. They advertised for local applicants, vetted them, provided them with work and residence permits and organised collective transport in specially chartered trains directly to employers in Germany. Joppke (1999: 65) quotes one critic of the process who described such bureaucratic precision as 'chillingly reminiscent of the 1930s and 1940s'. In labour-supplying countries agencies of the local state encouraged emigration, their own aim being to benefit from repatriation of hard currency in the form of remittances. Kocturk (1992: 87) describes procedures used in Turkey. Here opportunities for work in Germany were widely advertised in Istanbul and the cities of Western Anatolia. Applicants were called for interview and underwent medical checks after which those approved waited for a vacancy; prospective employers normally paid passport and travel costs. The Turkish government did all it could to facilitate the process: its Employment Service (the TES) worked closely with the German state agency and registered all potential migrants. By 1975 Turkey had been rewarded by remittance income equal to 65 per cent of the country's entire export earnings (Kocturk 1992: 86).

Immediately after the Second World War the British Ministry of Labour recruited 80,000 refugees, known initially as Displaced

Persons, from refugee camps in Central Europe. The term Displaced Persons was viewed by the Ministry of Labour as inappropriate, so the recruits were renamed European Voluntary Workers (EVWs). They were tied to specific jobs and worked under insecure conditions but the government took some responsibilities for their welfare. It made no such commitment to the Irish workers recruited by the Ministry of Labour on behalf of the National Health Service and the construction and transport industries, who began to enter in large numbers in · 1946.[1] More labour was needed but the government faced two problems. First, laws passed after the First World War still excluded most potential immigrants (it did not apply to people from Ireland). Second, there was unwillingness to recruit certain Europeans (notably Jewish victims of Nazism) and non-Europeans, among whom citizens of the British Commonwealth (the former British Empire) were the most obvious candidates (see Chapter 8). Eventually intense demand for labour in post-war reconstruction led to new legislation which granted Commonwealth citizens right of entry. Public employers such as the London Transport Executive (LTE) recruited in the Caribbean, notably in Barbados, where the Barbadian Immigrants' Liaison Service organised loans to cover fares to Britain of several thousand workers. For the next 20 years LTE and other state agencies, together with the British Hotels and Restaurants Association, recruited widely in the region. Emigrants left in enormous numbers – between 1953 and 1962 almost 180,000 travelled to Britain from Jamaica alone (Pastor 1985: 70). From the mid-1950s British textile and engineering companies advertised in India and Pakistan, where local facilitators were labour agents who worked as middlemen for British employers. British businesses received work permits from the government and passed them to agencies which often sold them to workers already in Britain in order that the latter should recruit family members and friends from South Asia. Foot (1965: 126) describes the new migrants as 'a heaven-sent gift' for the Government and for labour-hungry employers, especially as they were under no obligation to supervise them, as with the EVWs. Numbers of immigrants increased rapidly, so that in 1961 almost 50,000 entered from India and Pakistan (ibid).

There was a similar pattern in France. In 1945 the Office Nationale d'Immigration (ONI) was established initially for recruitment of workers from Southern Europe. In theory employers were to apply for permits to the ONI and to pay a fee for each migrant accepted. In fact by the early 1950s immigrants were coming through formal and informal channels from Spain and Portugal, from the Maghreb, from West Africa and from overseas departments of France – colonies – in the Indian Ocean and the Caribbean. At this point there were 2 million immigrant workers but such was the demand for labour that the government signed agreements with North African countries for movement of hundreds of thousands more.

Impacts of the 'long boom'

What brought these migrants? Initially most were not under compulsion to travel long distances for work but were *induced* to do so. For the first time in the history of industrial capitalism very large numbers of people moved across continents on the basis of a relatively free choice. They were not slaves or indentured labourers nor, at this period, were they forced to escape unbearable conditions in countries of origin, like most of those who had crossed the Atlantic during the nineteenth century. Initially labour-importing countries struggled to attract workers, being forced to re-establish on a new basis the practice of long-distance migration which had come to an end during the 1920s. Their task was to generate chain-migration: to establish relationships with existing immigrants that would encourage continuing movements.

In general people of the labour-exporting regions were not under intense pressure to emigrate, for although conditions were difficult they were more stable and initially much more favourable than in the earlier period of colonial rule. For almost 30 years from the Second World War there was economic growth worldwide. Although this favoured dominant states it also had its impact upon most of Africa, Asia and Latin America. Bairoch (1975: 184) shows that during the 1950s the annual rate of GDP growth in the Third World as a whole, at 4.8 per cent, was more than double that for the preceding 20-year period and that during the 1960s it accelerated further to 5.1 per cent. Some states which recorded very high rates were oil-producers or were among the group of Newly Industrialising Countries (NICs) which underwent a specific experience of growth. Others were less well placed but nonetheless showed substantial advance. Turkey, Jamaica, Puerto Rico, Brazil, Nigeria, Mexico, Tunisia, Pakistan, Kenya, Lebanon and Tanzania were among a host of states from three continents which recorded annual rates of increase in GDP per capita of over 3 per cent during the period 1960 to 1973 (Warren 1980: 196–7). By the early 1970s the momentum was increasing rapidly: UN figures show that rates across the Third Word exceeded those of Western economies.[2] There were important regional variations, especially for growth per capita.[3] The general picture is clear, however: notwithstanding that most Third World countries were experiencing change from a very low base, in most regions the 'long boom' brought economic advance. For the mass of people this was experienced in various ways. Some regions were still under colonial rule and some independent states remained colonies in all but name. Here little changed; elsewhere, however, there were specific benefits, especially in improved access to land, greater food security and improved general welfare. In Africa, Asia and the Middle East there had been prolonged struggles for freedom from colonial rule and highly mobilised populations put great pressure on the new governments, which both drew upon and fed expectations of radical change, with the result that reforms introduced by the 'developmental state' brought tangible benefits for many of their citizens. In most parts of the world survival systems became more resilient as access to food, shelter and basic physical security improved. This was the outcome of a particular conjunction: the world economy was expanding rapidly, the mass of people demanded more, and the state was prepared to deliver certain changes.

Dreze and Sen (1989: 181) observe that when increased income per capita is allied to state intervention the mass of people can enjoy improved security:

> a high level of GNP per head provides an *opportunity* for improving nutrition and other basic capabilities, but that opportunity may or may not be seized. In the process of transforming this opportunity into a tangible achievement, public support in various forms (and influencing both the distribution of income and the relationship between income and basic capabilities) often play a crucial role. [emphasis in original]

For 30 years after the Second World War many states were active in consolidating food security. There was a range of strategies: direct aid; subsidy of dietary staples and of fuel for cooking; rationing; vouchers to ensure entitlements for the poor and development of food stocks to ameliorate crises. More general security was also achieved through provision of employment, health care, education and social assistance. The state as such was not benign. As Barraclough (1991: 169) observes in the context of food availability, 'political will' is required to satisfy basic needs of the mass of people and such will is usually the outcome of mobilisation from below. During the 1950s and 1960s rulers of many newly independent states struggled to suppress popular move- ments but at the same time were forced to make accommodation with them – one means being the guarantee of food and shelter and the pro- vision of at least rudimentary systems of education and health. The legitimacy of many governments was indeed linked to their perceived ability to provide increased general security. Reviewing circumstances across Africa, Asia and Latin America, Harrison (1993: 178) comments that for the mass of people these were 'relatively good times'.

There were nonetheless important changes under way. Rural economies were affected by the accelerating pace of commercialisation of agriculture, while attempts at industrialisation stimulated urban growth. In some regions the effects of decolonisation and/or continuing relations with former colonial powers produced abrupt changes in the structure of employment. The result was a very rapid increase in rural–urban migration. In some cases this was the outcome of specific state-directed policy: in several of the NICs of East Asia, for example, an energetic programme of industrialisation relied upon mobilisation of the rural population (Edwards 1992). Here most available labour was absorbed but in many other countries unemployment rose so that by the 1960s one survey showed that among 34 Third World countries, in 20 urban unemployment was above 10 per cent, in eight it was above 15 per cent, and in 4 above 20 per cent (Harrison 1993: 177). Although these figures need to be treated with care – people in the 'informal' sector were often treated as unemployed – it is clear that unemployment/underemployment grew rapidly, depressing wages in the cities. Initially this was the source to which recruitment agents turned in their efforts to secure labour for Western Europe and North America.

Chain migration

Most of the early post-war migrants were not unemployed before their departure for Europe. Growing pressure on jobs nevertheless affected their wages and made the promises of European governments and of labour agents particularly attractive. On board the *Empire Windrush*, the ship which in 1948 first took migrants from the Caribbean to Britain, the majority of passengers were of urban origin, were skilled and had had some vocational training (Hayter 2000: 17). Kocturk (1992: 88) shows that during the 1960s migrants from Turkey to Western Europe also came overwhelmingly from among employed urban workers: only 4 per cent were unemployed. She comments

> Emigration costs money and requires contacts, even when arranged through official channels. Although financial motivation was the primary reason for migration, those who came to Europe were not the poorest ... A typical emigrating worker at the beginning of the migration wave was a semi-qualified, literate, married man in his early twenties from the urban areas of the prosperous Marmara/Thrace and north-central Anatolia regions. (ibid)

Later, when migration paths were well established, many of those who travelled to Europe were of rural origin. In the case of Turkey, by the late 1960s the typical emigrant was no longer a male urban worker: he or she was much more likely to come from the Anatolian countryside. This reflected both the close relationship between rural and urban sectors in the Third World and the accelerating pace of internal migration. Migrants to Europe encouraged not only family and friends from the city to follow them but also others within their social networks who were from the countryside and who were more likely to emigrate as commercialisation of agriculture denied land to hundreds of thousands of share-croppers. In addition by the late 1960s the TES was targeting unskilled applicants from rural areas – an attempt to retain skilled labour and workers in strategically important urban sectors. A similar pattern was evident in the case of movements to Britain from India and Pakistan. Early migrants came mainly from East and West Punjab and from Kashmir, some having been displaced during the forced migrations associated with partition of India in 1947. Most lived or at least worked in urban centres, although they had strong rural connections which, as chain migration took hold, facilitated the movement of relatives from the villages. By 1970 most Pakistanis in Britain were of rural Kashmiri origin. Twenty years after receiving states had initiated these movements a ready supply of labour could be guaranteed. Recruitment agencies had had been forced to go further and further afield but had succeeded in establishing a self-replenishing system. This had become integral to European economies and had also had its effect upon countries of origin: most important, as European governments were soon to discover, the migratory experience had shaped new relationships between the two.

Migration networks

Sassen (1999: 1) comments of contemporary patterns of migration that, 'Immigration-receiving countries behave as though they were not parties to the process of immigration. But in fact they are partners.' The close relationship between sending and receiving countries became clear in the 1970s when the latter set out to restrict immigration. With the onset of global recession in 1973 states that had facilitated immigration erected new barriers to entry. They faced an immediate problem: they could neither halt existing movements nor contain those being generated by growing instability worldwide.

In Germany 20 years of aggressive recruitment abroad had enlisted over 2.5 million guestworkers. In 1973 the BfA ordered an immediate halt. The zeal which had been demonstrated in persuading people to leave their countries of origin was now evident, at least at an official level, in efforts to hinder entry and to persuade immigrants to leave, with the result that within three years their numbers had fallen by

25 per cent (Potts 1990: 141–2). Some were offered direct payments to go; others were confronted by new procedures which delayed approval of work and residence permits. Similar measures were taken in several European states, and mass deportation was discussed as a solution to what had suddenly become the immigrant 'problem'. But most migrants declined to leave. European governments were faced by the reality that, although it had been difficult to stimulate migration, it was now much more difficult to reverse it. Because they had seen immigrants merely as a resource – as objects of economic policy – there had been little concern for the latters' circumstances or for their views and preferences. As Weiner (1995: 99) notes, governments discovered that 'migrants were people with a will of their own'. Most wished to continue lives in which they had been encouraged to make a new investment of resources in relationships at work and in communities struggling to find security through establishment of self-help groups and of religious and cultural organisations usually built from scratch. Although authorities in some countries, notably Germany, had isolated workers in hostels, many migrants had developed relationships within the wider community, so that they also had a stake in the host society which greatly exceeded official expectations of what was appropriate for guestworkers.

Crucially, immigrants also maintained relations with communities of origin which were themselves being changed profoundly by long-distance migration. Kin groups and communities initially provided migrants with financial support and sometimes with education and employment skills. These were an investment made through complex networks of exchange based upon reciprocal relations.[4] Remittances fed directly into these networks and had become a key source of income in the sending regions. Ballard (1987: 22) comments on the implications for Pakistanis who had moved to Britain in the 1960s and 1970s:

> Richer, by definition, than those they left behind, emigrants are still expected to fulfil their kinship obligations, especially to the very old, the very young, and the destitute ... Not only do most migrants continue to rely on their home contacts but those back home also come to rely on them, especially when migration takes place on a large scale. Recipient households come to be increasingly dependent on the regular arrival of remittances for their continued financial health, as may the local and even the national economy.

A survey of Turkish workers in Germany in 1971 showed that each had an average of 4.6 direct dependents in Turkey (Kocturk 1992: 90). Many had intended to stay in Germany for a short period but found that jobs were less remunerative than they had expected and that they spent much more money on subsistence than anticipated. An average worker was not able to begin saving until two years after emigration, when about 36 per cent of income could be saved and an additional 11 per cent remitted (ibid). Strongly encouraged by employers many migrants extended their periods of work. They also facilitated continuing emigration, financing the journeys of others, for whom they usually organised accommodation and a reception point in Europe. These relationships were the outcome of years of sustained effort by labour-importing states. Chain migration was not a chance development but the product of strategies adopted by government and by private capital to create conditions in which labour flowed freely from regions in which emigration was certain to become integral to the local economy. Labour-importing states had intervened directly in the affairs of countries which remained physically distant from Europe but were now bound to the latter by new ties. They were indeed partners in the global networks of migration.

Whole regions in Southern Europe, Turkey, North and West Africa, the Balkans, the Caribbean and South Asia had become part of economic and social networks intimately connected to the major cities of Western Europe. By 1970 some 6 per cent of the workforce of Morocco was living abroad; in Tunisia and Algeria the figure was over 11 per cent (Harris 1983: 50). The density of economic, social and cultural connections between sending and receiving regions had reached the point at which migration was self-perpetuating – an example of processes in which, when network connections in an origin area reach a critical level, 'migration itself creates the social structure to sustain it' (Massey 1990: 8). There was a similar pattern in North America. Mexicans had been travelling north to work since the 1880s; in the 1930s the United States closed the border and some 400,000 Mexicans were expelled in order to 'free up' jobs for Americans (Martin 2001: 90) (see Chapter 6). With the onset of the World War, however, there was a huge increase in demand for labour. The initial aim of the Bracero Program, set up in 1942, was to use traditional areas of labour supply to support a militarised economy but the immigrants became integral to the activities of many employers and crucial to post-war economic growth: in 1965 when the Program was closed there were 4.5 million Mexicans working in the United States (Vernez 1993: 149). Until the 1940s most immigrants from Central America had been defined as sojourners. The Bracero Program changed this pattern, creating what Vernez (1993: 134) calls 'self-reinforcing migrant networks'. For 25 years Mexicans were encouraged to mobilise their communities of origin to provide a continuous supply of cheap labour, especially to California, where by the 1960s they made up 40 per cent of the agricultural workforce and where most had become long-term stayers – 'settlers' in the United States (Vernez 1993: 150). By the 1970s thousands of United States farmers were systematically using Mexican foremen to travel south to recruit seasonal labour. They visited Mexico during the winter months and enlisted workers who travelled illegally across the border in time for the harvest, so that well-established 'network recruitment' linked particular Mexican villages with regional labour markets in the United States. The Binational Study on Migration between Mexico and the United States concluded that the Program had established a 'tradition of migration' which produced new settler communities (Binational Study 2000: 51). It suggested that although the Program was meant to provide a temporary supply of workers 'one unintended consequence was to create a resident population' (ibid).

Community and reciprocity

The numbers involved in migration to Europe and North America were very large but give only a hint of the long-term impact upon communities of origin. Ballard has observed that, in the case of Pakistan, emigration should not be seen as 'a single, time-limited event' but as 'a process whereby a body of people have established a permanent overseas bridgehead, and where, having done so, there is a constant interchange of people and resources between the two ends of the migratory chain' (Ballard 1987: 29). This *transnational* exchange modifies economic, social and cultural relationships at both ends of the chain. Mutual assistance forges new links between communities bound by increasingly dense networks of solidarity and dependence and brings into being relationships which have meaning beyond the level of national societies (see Chapter 10).

In labour-exporting regions the migratory movements of the 1950s and 1960s left an indelible mark. In rural communities emigration greatly reduced the capacity to maintain irrigation systems, animal stocks, land fertility and local market networks. By removing a large part of the workforce it also radically reduced local communities' skill base, removing much of the social/technical capital upon which they customarily depended. This is clear in the case of the *barani* regions of Pakistan,[5] which supplied most of the country's emigrants to Britain and later to states of the Arab Gulf. By the 1980s many villages had lost much of their population while among those who had returned from the cities of Europe there was a preference to settle in the towns: Werbner (1990: 97) calls this 'a form of double urbanisation'. Most villages were also affected by the impact of remittances upon work practices, for with many families receiving income from abroad there was less incentive to maintain cultivation. Throughout the *barani* areas land was fitfully or poorly farmed and large areas were withdrawn from cultivation altogether. A region which once exported grain became an area 'in chronic food deficit ... slipping inexorably into a condition of dependency' (Ballard 1987: 33). These changes made remittances even more important to the sending communities, within which the option to return to the land became less and less feasible. Rather than attempt to revitalise agriculture most communities sought to despatch more and more migrants. Such developments are examples of what Massey (1993: 451) calls 'cumulative causation', a process in which each act of migration alters the context in which subsequent decisions about migration are taken, usually in ways which make further emigration more likely and which cement transnational linkages. As Weiner (1995: 28) observes: 'If there is a single "law" in migration, it is that a migration flow, once begun, induces its own flow.'

The case of Pakistan also provides a graphic illustration of the socio-cultural implications of chain migration and of processes associated with development of transnational communities. Clan groups of Northern Pakistan practise what is in effect an endogamous system of marriage. Traditionally, marriage of parallel- and cross-cousins has been preferred and siblings have first right of refusal with respect to the marriage of each other's children.[6] This has had its impact upon communities at each end of the migratory chain. Werbner (1990: 97) shows that among Pakistanis in Britain there has been a very high rate of first and second parallel- and cross-cousin marriage, and of exchange marriage and other arrangements between kin groups.[7] This implies not only the movement of potential spouses between Pakistan and Britain but also systematic attempts to equalise status of participating families, notwithstanding that they may be separated by thousands of miles. The fortunes of large kin groups are thus intimately connected at many levels, reinforcing reciprocal obligations of a material and symbolic kind. Migratory practices have been embedded in local culture, reshaping the expectations of whole communities, especially of young people in sending countries among whom there has developed a prospect of life abroad likely to affect their whole lives.

Relationships rooted in traditions of the sending regions are not necessarily weakened by distance or by time. Lievens (1999) shows how relations between communities of Moroccans and Turks in Belgium, and their communities of origin, have become closer as family networks arrange more and more cross-border marriages. Examining evidence from labour-supplying areas across South Asia with varying kinship patterns Ballard (2001: 9) suggests that claims on corporate resources of the kin group are invariably reinforced: 'the network of reciprocities between emigrants and those who stay behind guarantees their mutual investments in each other'. The density of connections reaches a critical mass, establishing a stock of social and cultural capital which physically distant communities draw upon in many areas of everyday life – an important example of transnationalism which is not part of the rhetoric of formal global theory. Escobar, Gonzalez and Roberts (1987) observe similar developments in Central America. By the 1980s, they suggest, migration from Mexico to the United States had become part of the culture of young adults. It had become an important experience in the transition to a full adult life, necessary for the establishment of a household and in effect for achievement of full adult status, allowing young people to meet obligations to their families and to establish themselves independently. Key influences upon women and men were the outcome of experiences in both countries: neither was necessarily a definitive 'home', rather each was an element within a dynamic cultural interaction between the village and the city. More and more Mexicans settled in the United States; meanwhile many others moved between the two locations, each of which was integral to their lives.

Recession and migration

By the mid-1970s almost 30 years of uninterrupted migration had reshaped the lives of tens of millions of people in sending communities. They soon faced further changes, for the recession which brought a halt to labour recruitment in the West had an even more serious impact in the Third World. Most economies were hit by falls in export prices and by multiple increases in the cost of oil and refined products. Between 1970 and 1975 the terms of trade of non-oil-producing countries fell precipitately: India's by 27 per cent, Peru's by 32 per cent, Sri Lanka's by 35 per cent (Harrison 1993: 353). As we have seen (Chapter 2) general crisis penalises Third World economies disproportionately severely in relation to those of the West. From the mid-1970s all the fragilities of the post-colonial order, earlier masked by general economic growth, became apparent. In the most vulnerable areas there were warning signs as survival systems came under great pressure. 'Famine' – the collapse of food availability – struck in the Sahel and in the Horn of Africa. Whole regions became vulnerable: by the early 1980s famine had again appeared in the Sahel and the Horn, this time affecting millions of people for whom it was the trigger prompting displacement over vast areas. The extreme weakness of the post-colonial state, evident in Central Africa in the 1960s, was manifested across the continent. Timberlake (1985: 162) comments

> In 1985 Africa was a continent in turmoil. Ten million people had fled their homes, some into famine centres, some into cities, many across national boundaries.
>
> Most of these were 'environmental refugees', people fleeing land that could no longer support them. Others had fled wars, civil wars and government

repression. But the connection between the wars of Africa and the 'droughts' of Africa were so tangled that it was impossible to tell who was fleeing for what reason.

Elsewhere regions which had become important areas of labour supply to Europe and North America faced repeated upheaval. In the case of Turkey, millions had left for the cities of Western Europe. Those considering return faced both deteriorating economic conditions and intense civil conflict in which organised labour and parties of the Left were targets for an authoritarian military regime. In response many prolonged their stay in Europe. When in 1983 the German government offered payment to those prepared to repatriate few took up the offer. Asian workers in Britain who sought to escape the effects of recession, especially mass closures in the textile industry, faced a worse scenario in their countries of origin: in case of Pakistanis, comments Ballard (2001: 27) 'the very phenomenon from which they were trying to escape was wreaking even more serious havoc back home'. Meanwhile North Africa experienced repeated mass protests against IMF-inspired programmes of economic reform: in Egypt in 1977, Morocco in 1982 and 1984, Tunisia in 1984 and Algeria in 1989. Regimes in each of these states were confronted by strong opposition movements, notably by Islamist currents which from the late 1970s grew rapidly to dominate politics across the region. Conflict between the state and the Islamists produced traumatic confrontations, including prolonged and violent clashes in Egypt, and in Algeria a military coup followed by a decade of bloodletting and terror. Large numbers of people fled the conflict zones of northern Algeria, which rapidly became the chief refugee-producing country of the region. As natal towns and villages became inhospitable the priority for many migrants was that of reunion with relatives within the country of *emigration*. Regions which had long been the target of labour recruitment by European states now exported *forced* migrants who moved along routes developed for a different purpose. As Castles (1993: 19) has pointed out: 'Migratory chains, once established, continue, even when the original policies on which they were based are changed or reversed.' By the 1970s 'chains' created for the specific purpose of obtaining cheap labour were delivering large numbers of involuntary migrants.

Increasingly Europe was viewed not only as a place of work and/or settlement but also as a sanctuary. In 1983 the number of applications for asylum in countries of the European Community was 70,500; within five years the figure had reached 290,650 (Collinson 1994: 13). Although the great majority of refugees from Africa, Asia and Latin America did not attempt entry to Western Europe – 95 per cent remaining within their regions of displacement – the increase in numbers applying for asylum corresponded almost exactly with the increase in the global total of refugees. Between 1985 and 1991 the total of officially recognised refugees rose by 70 percent, from 10 million to over 17 million. Over approximately the same period the number of applications to states of the EC increased by 120,000, also an increase of some 70 per cent (ibid). Many moved through migration networks modified to serve new needs. In the case of Sri Lanka, agents in Colombo had long been active in recruiting labour for the Gulf states. As ethnic conflict intensified and in 1983 became civil war the networks shifted their attention to movement of refugees, mainly Tamils. In a very important observation about the changing character of migratory networks McDowell (1996: 92) explains that the labour agents 'switched easily to the asylum routes and opened up the possibility of migration to those Tamils who did not have [existing] overseas contacts'. During the 1990s some 150,000 Sri Lankan Tamils sought asylum in Europe and North America (Crisp 1999: 7).

End of the 'miracle'

Mexico had initially been protected from the full impact of recession by oil income and by the cushioning effect of remittances. By the 1970s the country had also undergone 40 years of rapid economic growth – the 'Mexican miracle' – making it a paradigmatic case for theorists of modernisation. There had been spectacular growth in manufacturing and service industries, with the result that the share of agriculture in employment fell very sharply, from 65 per cent in 1940 to 28.9 per cent in 1980 (Lapati 1993: 67). In the countryside commercialisation had developed apace, with cash crops replacing maize and beans, and millions of subsistence peasants becoming rural proletarians. Meanwhile the state had expanded, becoming a major employer. Other aspects of the 'miracle' were largely ignored in official accounts, especially increasing inequality and increased impoverishment of the most disadvantaged sections of society – poor peasants and rural migrants who had entered the urban informal sector. Concealed within the narrative of prosperity was the fate of the poorest 10 per cent of the population, whose share of GNP declined from 2.4 per cent in 1957 to 1.1 per cent in 1977 (Lapati 1993: 68). In 1981 falling oil prices exposed Mexico's dependence upon massive foreign loans: the economy collapsed and Mexicans faced the worst economic crisis for 60 years. Between 1982 and 1986 real average industrial wages fell by over a third (Lapati 1993: 70); between 1980 and 1990 incomes of government employees halved (ibid). The number of poor people increased dramatically: from 32 million in 1980 to 41 million in 1987 (Lapati 1993: 72). One outcome was a sharp increase in urbanisation as the rural poor moved in their millions to the cities. In 1965, 55 per cent of Mexicans had been urbanites; by 1991 the figure was 73 per cent, by far the highest proportion in Central America (Thomas 1995: 2). Many urban poor entered the informal sector, where they were joined by cross-border migrants from neighbouring states in which economic crisis was accompanied by civil conflict and/or war. According to the Economic Commission on Latin America and the Caribbean (ECLAC), numbers employed in the informal sector rose by 80 per cent between 1980 and 1987.[8] Under intolerable pressure many attempted to move on to *El Norte* – to cross the border into the United States.

The Bracero Program had long been closed but migration continued by all means, so that the US Immigration and Naturalisation Service (INS) estimated that by the mid-1970s there were up to 6 million illegal immigrants, of whom most were Mexicans (Harris 1996: 49). The pattern of migration had changed, however, with many more migrants coming from towns and cities across Mexico and finding employment in manufacturing, construction and service industries. Their earnings were now a lifeline for millions of families: according to Gonzalez de la Rocha, during the 1980s over a quarter of families in one western Mexican city received dollar transfers regularly.[9]

Meanwhile remittances had became increasingly important to governments in all the labour-exporting countries. In 1965 remittances to Algeria had been $200 million – equal to over 30 per cent of merchandise exports. Algeria was an oil-exporting country and bene-fited from the rise in oil prices but even by 1973 the total of transfers from abroad, at $300 million, represented 20 per cent of foreign exchange earnings. In the case of Tunisia, transfers were 12 percent of foreign exchange earnings and for Morocco the figure was 25 per cent. In Turkey remittance income of US$1.4 billion almost equalled the value of commodity exports and had become crucial in covering rising trade deficits (all figures from Issawi 1982: 87–8). In Egypt migration to the Gulf had increased at a staggering rate: in 1974 remittance income was US$268 million; four years later it was officially more than US$1.7 billion. By 1980 remittances of US$2 billion were equal to the combined returns of cotton exports, Suez Canal revenues, tourism, and value added by the Aswan Dam, which over the preceding 20 years had brought vast new areas of land under irrigation (all figures from Ibrahim 1982: 71). Unofficial estimates put the real total of remit-tances at no less than US$22 billion (Lesch 1990: 100). The Egyptian government regarded emigration as having a specific political value. Ibrahim suggests that it performed a 'venting function', allowing many

young men whose expectations were frustrated by domestic unemployment to direct their energies into work abroad. At a time of general
social crisis the Egyptian state welcomed the activities of emigrants who
concentrated 'on "making money" instead of "making revolution" '
(Ibrahim 1982: 94).[10] Many other states pursued similar policies, so
that emigration became part of local development strategy. Labour-
importing countries had solicited migrants; at the same time, labour-
exporting countries had strongly encouraged them to migrate. Most
had established migration services to attract potential migrants and to
monitor remittances. Turkey had established the TES, Morocco set up
a Central Emigration Service, Tunisia an Office of Professional Training
and Employment, and Algeria the National Algerian Manpower Office.
Such states viewed emigrants as a high-value export: in the case of
Turkey workers were despatched on contract to Germany, Austria,
Belgium, the Netherlands, France and Sweden. Berberoglu (1982: 95)
suggests that the strategy was double-edged: it brought remittances but
increased the vulnerability of the economy in ways that could prove
damaging, even 'disastrous'. In the mid-1970s, following the halt to
recruitment in Germany, remittances to Turkey declined by 30 per
cent, requiring the Turkish state to borrow heavily on the international
market and adding to debt-service obligations which seriously affected
a growing balance-of-payments crisis (Berberoglu 1982: 110).

During the 1980s repeated crises of the world economy made remittances even more important. By the end of the decade migrants from
Pakistan provided over 50 per cent of the country's foreign exchange,
while return migrants and visitors brought large quantities of consumer
goods on which they were taxed, so that import duties became the
largest source of revenue to the Pakistani state. Ballard (1987: 37)
comments, 'No wonder the promotion of "manpower export" has
become one of the Government's central economic priorities.' So too
in Sri Lanka where remittances eclipsed the total of development assistance and humanitarian aid (Van Hear 2004: 14). Migration had been
factored into state planning and, as in many other labour-exporting
regions, migration networks had become functional to the health of the
economy and of the state apparatus itself.

'Nowhere to go'

Following the onset of recession in 1973, European states invited immigrants to leave. Return was a forbidding prospect. When in 1977 the
French government targeted 100,000 immigrants for repatriation, offering money to those who would go, it was mainly southern Europeans –
some 45,000 – who accepted (Harris 1996: 108). For those from

countries outside Europe, such as the states of North and West Africa, it was not a practical possibility: conditions 'at home' were deteriorating rapidly, making the migrants' presence in Europe more important to sending communities. Like the United States, Western European states had forged new ties with the Third World which they could not undo. They had originally wanted guestworkers but the demands of an expanding capitalism for continuous supplies of labour had instead brought long-term migrants, people whose place in the host society, and responsibilities to communities of origin and to new transnational networks, made them less short-term migrants than settlers. The first migrants of the post-war period had been solicited by labour-importing states and were largely, in Ghosh's words, 'opportunity seeking migrants' (Ghosh 1998: 35). Their journeys were made as the outcome of a choice, albeit from a narrow range of options. With the end of the boom the element of choice largely disappeared. Now most migrants from the Third World were under compulsion to move, as economic, socio-political and environmental collapse threatened basic security in many regions: they were 'survival migrants' (ibid). The equation which had governed long-distance migration for 30 years had been rewritten.

As Western states closed their borders and campaigned for repatriation, *forced* migration from the Third World increased relentlessly. The UN remarked on this coincidence, noting that: '[A] potent cocktail of increased pressure to migrate, set against hardening barriers to immigration, is developing. More and more potential migrants are emerging but there is nowhere for them to go.'[11] The observation was revealing. It reflected the official position of Western governments – that there was 'nowhere to go' – denying that societies of North America and Western Europe offered the possibility of relative security in a disordered world. It also suggested that continued efforts to move northwards could not be fruitful. But such efforts continued, by every means.

Notes

1. According to Castles and Miller (1993: 71) 350,000 Irish migrants arrived in Britain between 1946 and 1959.
2. Figures from UNCTAD quoted in Warren (1980: 195).
3. Between 1950 and 1970 GDP per capita grew annually in Latin America at 2.5 per cent and in Asia at 2 per cent (Bairoch 1975: 184). The pace was much slower in Africa, where on some calculations there may have been only marginal overall growth (Nafziger 1988: 23).
4. White (1999: 192), describing Turkish migration to Germany, places such reciprocity in the context of Bourdieu's reference to 'the gentle invisible form of violence'. This 'is never recognised as such, and is not so much undergone

as chosen, the violence of credit, confidence, obligation, personal loyalty, hospitality, gifts, gratitude [and] piety' (quoted ibid).

5. *Barani* regions – the fertile wheat-growing areas of the north of Pakistan.
6. Marriage customs vary enormously, even among groups from the same region. In the case of South Asia, clan exogamy is practised among most Hindus and Sikhs but Muslim communities across the subcontinent tend towards a preference for in-marriage.
7. Ballard (2001: 20) confirms that 60 per cent of all marriages among Pakistanis from the Mirpur region are between first cousins and most of the remainder between kin only slightly more distantly related.
8. Quoted in Lapati 1993: 71.
9. Quoted in Lapati 1993: 75.
10. Migration to the Gulf in fact had contradictory outcomes, as some emigrants used their time abroad to organise within Islamist currents which shortly became active in Egypt. See Hinnebusch 1985.
11. UNRISD quoted in UNHCR 1995: 194.

Part II

Rights

Part II looks at the notion of universal rights, focusing on the idea of the right to asylum. It considers the origins of the concept of sanctuary, and its later expression in the notion of refuge. It examines the idea of the refugee in early modern Europe and the ways in which this was shaped and reshaped over the course of 300 years. It considers how the changing practices of states have presented refugees at different times as heroes and as villains, as welcome guests and as enemies. It considers the refugee tragedies of the mid-twentieth century, asking what these experiences can tell us about the status of aliens in modern society. It looks at patterns of migration – legal and 'illegal' – and ways in which the changing policies of states in North America and Europe have affected the status of refugees today.

5

Refugees and Rights

Origins

In the twenty-first century forced migrants make claims for asylum on the basis of a *right* to refuge, what is usually seen as a 'universal' right to sanctuary. Where did such an idea originate and how has it been developed? There have been traditions of asylum for millennia: the literatures of Ancient India and of the Ancient Jewish tradition indicate that the institution was widely understood and respected. The texts of Judaism, for example, record the allocation by God of specific cities as places of refuge.[1] So too the traditions of Islam, in which refuge can be regarded as a foundational idea. The journey of the Prophet Muhammed from Mecca to Medina, the *hijra* or emigration, is associated with the idea of protection from persecution, and during the Prophetic period anyone who sought protection in a mosque or among the Companions of the Prophet was assured of security. The *Quran* and the *shari'a* affirmed the practice, identifying certain places, notably the Ka'aba in Mecca, as inviolable. Later the medieval theologian Ibn al-Arabi speci-fied the offer of protection as obligatory upon Muslims in the face of injustice and intolerance (Arnaout 1987, Eickelman and Piscatori 1990). The most profound influences on modern practice, however, seem to have been those of Ancient Greece and Rome. The word asylum comes from the Greek *sulon*, meaning pillage, with the negating prefix 'a' – hence a place in which pillage or plunder is forbidden. In Greece the institution seems to have had several functions, of which the most important may have been its role in protecting survivors of repeated conflicts between neighbouring city states. By assuring the safety of those taken in battle, states contributed to a reciprocal arrangement whereby their own citizens might survive continuing wars. Asylum was also afforded to those expelled by rival states. It was considered useful to accommodate them as exiles – people who were compelled to live under the protection of the gods of the host city. Places of sanctuary were typically those associated with local deities, temples and other sites of religious significance, at which an exile presence confirmed the power of the local gods and embellished the image of the host state at home and abroad (Gorman 1994).

These practices influenced attitudes in Rome, where the idea of exile was also recorded in a range of literatures. The word sanctuary comes from the Latin *sanctuarium* – a sacred or consecrated place. As in Greece, temples were key places of refuge: the *celia*, in which stood statues of the gods, was especially sacred and offered a special form of protection. Those who gained access to such places were regarded as touched by their qualities, and it was sacrilege to remove or injure them. Exiles were viewed as tragic figures: isolated from their homes and far from their gods they were powerless and deserving of protection. Their circumstances were celebrated in the works of numerous writers, notably Cicero, Ovid and Seneca (Claassen 1999). Expansion of the Roman Empire was the mechanism by which the idea of asylum became general across Southern and Western Europe, and when in the fourth century AD/CE the empire underwent Christianisation the institution gained new religious authority. When Rome retreated the institution remained, endorsed by canon law. By the early Middle Ages churches and other sites of religious significance were widely seen as places within which fugitives, debtors and others were immune from arrest or violence. Under the conditions of systemic conflict which obtained between European feudal states and fiefdoms, sanctuary had great importance, and for centuries religious sites were regarded as inviolable. When secular authorities transgressed these principles they challenged the powers of the Church and were liable to heavy penalties: hence the traumatic confrontation between religious authorities and the state which took place in thirteenth century England and is celebrated in T. S. Eliot's *Murder in the Cathedral*. The right to sanctuary for fugitives was finally abolished in England in 1623, not long before new ideas about refuge and the refugee were formalised.

Rights

The idea of sanctuary/asylum has an ancient lineage: the idea of the refugee is, however, a modern notion. It is intimately linked to ideas about rights and to the concept of the nation-state. In pre-modern Europe there had long been ideas about rights in property and about collective rights of certain groups. For centuries, corporate entities such as commercial and trade guilds, the clergy and the municipalities had invoked ideas of liberty and freedom in efforts to maintain their specific privileges and immunities. These claims did not refer to rights of larger groups or of people in general but to those of a particular status, who fought to maintain privileges granted, modified or revoked by local rulers. The clergy and monastic orders could, for example, apply for special freedoms and for lifetime rights to 'chartered sanctuary' in certain consecrated places.[2] Ideas about more general rights first appeared in the seventeenth century during the political upheavals which affected much of Western Europe. The first manifesto of rights was probably that set out by the Dutch writer Hugo Grotius, who was influenced by struggles in the Netherlands for independence from Spain. Grotius identified natural laws and declared for 'natural rights', an idea much more fully developed a generation later, when during the English Revolution of the 1640s a new discourse of rights became a key means of expressing demands for political change. The more radical were the forces engaged in struggles against the English Crown, the more embracing were notions of rights. Supporters of the mainstream parliamentary forces argued for specific rights of political representation, focusing on legal and civil matters, and said to be based in 'ancient rights and liberties'. In contrast, the radical Levellers asserted not only that all should have such rights but also that all should enjoy equal rights in property, guaranteed by 'the People'. When the radicals were suppressed it was the narrower definitions that emerged as state policy and were finally enshrined in a Bill of Rights (1689) as rights of 'people of this Kingdom' – English rights.

By the mid-eighteenth century ideas about rights had become a key element in exchanges between political activists and intellectuals in Western Europe and its American colonies. The aspirations of those who made the American Revolution of 1776 were assertively expressed in terms of rights. Initially the Americans argued against Britain's exactions by reference to their status as Englishmen, quoting the Bill of Rights and colonial charters issued by the British parliament. The latter responded that the colonists did have such rights but argued that as Englishmen they should be prepared to accept the authority of the Crown. This intransigence radicalised the Americans: the movement for independence became wider and deeper and the language of rights changed accordingly. Now American claims were expressed in the context of natural rights. The Declaration of Independence, issued by the Continental Congress, maintained that there were 'truths' which were 'self-evident', including 'certain inalienable rights … among these are life, liberty and the pursuit of happiness'. It was in this context that Americans claimed the right to national self-determination.[3]

The American example was an inspiration to the revolutionary movement in France – one deputy in the French National Assembly of 1789 declared: '[The Americans] have set a great example in the new hemisphere; let us give one to the universe'.[4] The French Revolution was the first to identify comprehensive rights associated with every person. The Declaration of the Rights of Man and Citizen set out 'the natural and inalienable rights of man' – rights to liberty, property and security, and the right of resistance to oppression. It outlined rights to equality before the law, admissibility to all public offices, protection from arbitrary orders or imprisonment, freedom of religion and freedom of the press. This initiated a long debate about rights of groups such as religious minorities and slaves: within a few years all civil and political rights were extended to Protestants, Jews, 'free blacks' and to slaves, although significantly not to women. The American movement had taken a more conservative approach. This is especially clear in the case of slavery: in the new United States, where one in every five people was enslaved, 'inalienable rights' did not encompass people of African origin. Many of the wealthiest people were slavers or were closely associated with the trade, among them leading activists of the independence movement. The glaring contradiction between their appeal to universal rights and their unwillingness to apply such rights led Samuel Johnson, a strong opponent of slavery, to observe: 'How is it that we hear the loudest yelps for liberty among the drivers of negroes?'[5] Slavery was not formally abolished for over 70 years, by which time there were over 2.5 million slaves in the United States (Thomas 1998: 659). The 'universal' rights identified in the Declaration of Independence had not been applied to all but according to the interests of those particular Americans who had means to implement them.

In France the commitment to universalism was declared a principle of the revolution but here too contradictions were soon evident. Organisations of journeymen and labourers, the *sans-culottes*, demanded economic, social and political rights which greatly exceeded those envisaged by leaders of the movement. As the radical leader Jacques Roux maintained of those who called for the most extensive change, 'it was not for the rich that they fight [*sic*], it was for liberty ... We adore liberty but we do not want to die of hunger'.[6] Much narrower ideas about liberty required that the *sans-culottes* should be suppressed and the republic which finally emerged from the years of revolution was led by men whose definition of rights was part of a more conservative approach to political order. Their approach was soon constituted the dominant discourse of rights in both Europe and North America. It spoke of universalism and at the same time insisted on much more limited, *particular* applications of rights.

Nation-states

Rights were also applied on the basis of differentiation by nation. For three centuries there had been increasing centralisation of states in Western Europe and manifestos such as those elaborated during the English and French revolutions assumed the local state as the context within which rights were to be defined. Such states were *nation*-states, entities within which the population was said to share certain characteristics – language, religious affiliation and association with certain traditions. Increasingly people of a nation-state were also encouraged to share a national*ism* – an identification with traditions said to define the qualities of 'their' nation-state as against Others. Such Others were of immense importance to those who encouraged nation-centred thinking. After centuries of conflict between neighbouring European states they had become central to the notion of national belonging, and around the notions of 'England', 'France', 'Spain' and other national entities there developed the idea of national *Self* against national Others. At the same time internal Others were identified as markers against which authentic national traditions could be recorded. Religious and linguistic minorities were particularly important: as early as the fifteenth century certain ethno-religious communities were declared to be outside the nation-in-formation and large communities were displaced. This was the fate of the Jews of Spain and Portugal, and later of the Protestant minorities of the Low Countries and of France. Where language was viewed as a key issue, speakers of 'non-national' tongues or even of unapproved dialects came under intense pressure. In France leaders of the revolution of 1789 declared that speakers of German who lived within the territorial boundaries of the republic consorted with 'enemies' (Hobsbawm 1990: 21). The revolution was followed by decades of pressure upon linguistic minorities with the aim of making a particular dialect of central France the official means of communication – an exercise in asserting the 'ethno-linguistic criterion of nationality' (ibid). Those in authority defined membership of the new nation-states – who was to be included and who excluded – and in effect they allocated rights. Because the state was widely perceived as the most advanced form of human organisation it was assumed that in time all people would come within the physical and socio-legal boundaries of a state – that all human beings were to be of the state. This was the context within which Lebrun, minister for foreign affairs in the revolutionary government of France, declared: 'our principles [of the Republican state] will spread everywhere by themselves … precisely because they are principles of pure reason'.[7]

Rights said to reside in individuals were meaningful to the extent that they were attributes of citizens or of subjects within a specific state. Citizens of other states did not in general enjoy rights on 'home' territory and conflict between rival states formalised policies of exclusion.[8] For 200 years before the French revolution the British state had been little concerned with the presence of non-nationals. During the revolution and the Napoleonic Wars, however, a series of Aliens Acts were passed with the aim of excluding non-citizens – 'aliens' – in wartime. In the 1820s, with the two states at peace, the acts were revoked; an important precedent had been set, however, for the more assertive the activities of the nation-state the more exclusionary its policies were to be. Transnational rights, such as the 'human rights' later formulated in international law, did not appear in legal statutes, in declarations or treaties, for throughout the seventeenth, eighteenth and nineteenth centuries such documents were written by national states exclusively about the status of those *within* such states. These developments had great significance for migrants. The more that states developed ideas about territorial control, and the more they encouraged notions of national belonging, the more they heightened a general awareness of those who crossed borders. The higher the profile of the nation-state, the higher was the profile of the migrant. The more that there was of rights, the more there was also a focus upon those who derived their rights elsewhere – upon 'aliens'. Among them were increasingly large numbers of displaced people.

Huguenots – the 'classic' refugees

The first people to be described as refugees were religious minorities who in the sixteenth century fled from the Low Countries to France to escape repression. These Calvinists were under pressure in several predominantly Catholic countries, from which many had been exiled: they described the communities of their diaspora as residing within *le refuge* and its individual members as being *refugies* (Cottret 1991: 7).[9] Much larger movements took place in the late seventeenth century when similar groups, the Huguenots, fled from France. Their circumstances are important, as they have often been seen to represent a definitive refugee experience. Zolberg (1989: 5), for example, suggests that the case of the Huguenots 'illustrates particularly well the refugee phenomenon'. Not only did they flee persecution, he argues, but their reception in host states showed that they had been identified in a particular way, as 'people to whom asylum and assistance were due' (Zolberg 1989: 6). They therefore represent 'the classic refugee' (Zolberg 1989: 9). For Adelman (1999: 89) the Huguenots bear all the defining characteristics of the forced migrant in the modern era. As Protestant dissenters who were victims of absolutism they were 'archetypically refugees of modernity' (ibid):

> The modern concept of a refugee is inseparable from the conceptions of Protestantism and its revolt against what it believed to be medieval superstition.

Protestantism stood for individual conscience ... Within the earthly realm, individual choice and human reason ruled ... Protestantism is identified with the celebration of the individual and the freedom of that individual, with instrumental rationality being the way to deal with the affairs of this world. Modernity is but the universalization of this Protestant ideology. (ibid)

This interpretation sees the Huguenots as an embodiment of philosophical principles which were themselves productive of global economic, social and political change. They were persecuted because they represented Progress: 'individualism, tolerance for different beliefs, and the rule of reason, at least in this world' (Adelman 1999: 90). They secured asylum, it seemed, on the basis of principles which were to guide succeeding generations of both refugees and host societies. This approach needs careful examination – not least because the Huguenot experience has indeed become a reference point for ideas about forced migrants and asylum rights.

The French Calvinists were an oppressed community whose circumstances had much in common with later migrant groups. They also had much in common, however, with other seventeenth century groups which did not secure asylum. Their designation as refugees reveals more about modern states and their approach to rights than about universal values and their application to those who seek sanctuary. The Huguenots were a minority deemed out of place in France, a predominantly Catholic society in which centralisation of the state was progressing rapidly. When religious conformity was imposed from the 1660s they began to lose the legal and political autonomy enjoyed for almost a century. Over the next 20 years repression was intensified until in 1681 state-inspired attacks – the *dragonnades* – became widespread, claiming many victims.[10] A process of emigration began that lasted some 40 years, reducing the population of 800,000 Calvinists by about a quarter.[11] The doctrine of mercantilism, which dominated thinking about economic matters in Europe, led the French state to limit these movements on the basis that economic and human assets should be retained at all costs in order to maximise resources available to the Crown. Calvinists were well represented among the aristocracy, the commercial bourgeoisie, and urban artisans and craft workers. Thus when the Calvinists' religious leaders were exiled the rest of the community was discouraged strongly from moving. The *dragonnades* nevertheless led many to attempt escape. Evading French troops and naval patrols, these early 'boat people' sought asylum mainly in the Netherlands and Britain but also in Switzerland, Prussia, North America and South Africa.

Up to 100,000 refugees moved to England and Ireland where they were received on the basis that they should enjoy liberty, including the right to religious freedom.[12] Zolberg (1989: 7) comments that the response of the British state to their plight was motivated by 'a sense of obligation towards fellow Protestants in distress', one which might be labelled 'humanitarianism'. He adds, however, that 'it should be understood that this humanitarianism was decidedly partisan … an astute move in the game of statecraft' (ibid). The view of the authorities might be better described as calculating, for the British state was also guided by mercantilist principles and saw the Huguenots as a valuable asset. A generation earlier Cromwell, the dominant figure in English politics, had made clear that the Calvinists were an important factor in his plans for gaining influence and even territory within France, Britain's main rival in Europe and in the colonial world. He declared that he wished to become 'the head and protector' of all Protestants; at the same time he wished to draw the French Huguenots 'to a dependence upon him, and thereby keep an interest in France'.[13] Hill (1969: 194) notes that at this period British writers on economic affairs advocated liberty of conscience 'precisely because it would attract foreign immigrants and discourage emigration', the particular target being dissenting communities of special economic importance. Ideas about rights which had been a key element within ideological struggles during the English revolution were being mobilised by the state as part of its foreign policy agenda.

In 1681 The English King, Charles II, made an appeal to Louis XIV of France:

> I conjure you in the name of the great [King] Henry, whose precious blood circulates in both our veins, to respect the Protestants who he looked upon as his children. If, as is reported, you wish to compel them to renounce their religion under pain of banishment from your Kingdom I offer them an Asylum in that of England.[14]

Charles issued a proclamation which combined a formal welcome to the Huguenots with a specific guarantee of their rights, set out as privileges which would allow them to pursue commercial and entrepreneurial activities. His offer included, 'letters of denization under the great seal without any charge whatsoever, and likewise such further privileges and immunities as are consistent with the laws for the free exercise of … trades and handicrafts'.[15] For centuries foreigners had been able to buy rights to become a denizen – a status intermediate between subject and alien; now the king offered free denizenship. Collections on behalf of the refugees were authorised in the churches and Parliament made generous grants for their support. Large sums of money were raised – £85,000 through public collections alone (Schwartz 1980: 60) – and a group of Huguenot aristocrats, known as the French Committee, was established to administer the money. The official reception of the refugees was unprecedentedly welcoming and supportive.

This approach contrasts starkly with attitudes at this period towards other people denied their rights, including religious rights. During the period of Huguenot immigration British forces were engaged in activities in Ireland similar to those of the French state vis-à-vis the Calvinist refugees. Following the conquest of Ireland by Cromwell's armies Catholic landowners had been expropriated and a policy of 'plantation' adopted under which Protestant immigrants, mainly from Scotland, were encouraged to settle. By the 1690s, 75 per cent of the land belonged to Anglo-Irish landowners or absentee Englishmen (Hill 1969: 164) and the Catholic majority of the population had been deprived of all political rights. These campaigns created large numbers of forced migrants: many Irish people fled to Spain and France, with which Ireland had strong commercial links. Large numbers were also deported by the British state, notably to its Caribbean colonies, to which they were sent as indentured servants.[16] Among deportees from mainland Britain were many members of dissenting Protestant groups. Levellers of the English Revolution, judged too radical for mainstream bourgeois taste, had already been expelled to the American colonies; in the late seventeenth century they were joined by Quakers who refused to take an oath of allegiance to the British Crown. The reception accorded the Huguenots also contrasted with the indifference shown to the Palatines, a largely destitute community in Germany which sought refuge in England in 1709. Their claims for sanctuary were rejected out of hand: the authenticity of their Protestantism and their poverty were questioned and they were accused of everything from introducing smallpox to stealing bread from the mouths of the English poor (Gwynn 1985: 124). Some 13,000 Palatines arrived; most were placed in emergency accommodation in wharves and warehouses along the Thames in London and several thousand were sent to 'the world's first official refugee camp' at Blackheath, south of the city, where they were accommodated in 1000 army tents (Winder 2004: 79). The government at first tried to disperse them across the country but then settled on a policy of deportation: 5000 were sent to Ireland and the rest to the American colonies. Winder comments that without money or skills they were doomed to rejection – 'they could not inspire the kind of ruling class support which helped the Huguenots to survive and flourish' (ibid).

'Profitable strangers'

The Huguenot refugees had not been received in Britain primarily because they were 'fellow Protestants in distress' or for 'humanitarian' reasons but because their presence was congenial to the British state. Their religious affiliation was important and their sufferings provoked sympathy and solidarity among those in power in Britain and among some of the wider population. The welcome they received was, however, a function of their particular value to the British state. Mercantilist principles asserted that the key task of the state was to maximise its resources, especially to increase the volume of trade under its control, and the quantity of bullion and numbers and skills of the people at its disposition. By the same token the state benefited if it could deprive rival states of their resources. A pamphlet published in Ireland set out the tasks of the British government in relation to the Huguenots:

> The present desolation of France may be a means of raising the power and the wealth of those neighbouring countries which have the wisdom and goodness enough to take hold of the opportunity … if we could draw in great numbers of French Protestants, this would be an Act of great charity to them; a great blow to the French king, and the greatest kindness that we can do to ourselves.[17]

In the late seventeenth century the population of France was some 20 million; that of Britain a mere 5 million. The British state aimed to benefit from the persecution of the Huguenots by encouraging 'a demographic haemorrhage' in the neighbouring country (Cottret 1991: 188). Although many Huguenot refugees were impoverished a large number had craft skills or connections in finance and commerce, and some had access to capital. An enormous quantity of money left France with the refugees, to the extent that 'French commerce was prostrated' while the exodus of artisans dealt a fatal blow to key areas of French industry (Reaman 1964: 62). Between 8000 and 9000 sailors, 12,000 soldiers and over 500 officers left the army of Louis XIV, many taking service with the Dutch and British forces (ibid), so that when William of Orange fought in the North of Ireland during the 1690s, winning decisive battles on behalf of the British colonial state, several of his regiments were composed of Huguenots. There were also implications for British activity in Africa and the Americas. The Huguenots were closely associated with the Atlantic slave trade, already a key part of the commercial activities of Britain and France, which had replaced the Iberian states as the most aggressive colonisers in the New World. Leading Huguenot merchant families in the Atlantic and Channel ports had a long tradition in slaving and after 1685 their networks were integrated into the British colonial venture.

Popular sympathy for co-religionists suffering intense persecution does not explain the unprecedented welcome arranged by the British authorities. The British state did indeed invoke ideals of freedom and for the first time offered asylum as a distinct policy consistent with its formal commitment to the new philosophy of rights. Its attitude to the Huguenots was, however, essentially an instrumental one.

The government faced widespread opposition to the refugees – from the Crown, from some sections of Parliament and the religious establishment, from some local authorities, from many commercial institutions and guilds, and from many ordinary people. A major problem was that although a minority of the immigrants – those of most interest to the state – were very wealthy, the mass was poor. Most, comments Foot (1965: 81), 'arrived destitute':

> They were not, as later panegyrics attempted to describe them, hardy well-dressed artisans who commended themselves immediately to their new hosts. On the contrary. Among the people with who[m] they had to deal on entry, they encountered resentment and bitterness. (ibid)[18]

There is evidence of hostility in particular from English craft workers who believed that they were being displaced by the incomers. In the 1670s there had been an economic downturn during which there was 'near hysterical opposition' to the admission of French artisans, including riots of journeymen, apprentices and master weavers protesting at their presence.[19] A decade later there were repeated petitions against them from guilds including the dyers, feltmakers, tailors and carpenters. There was also anger that the refugees were receiving financial help. Between June 1687 and August 1688 more than 10,000 Huguenots were given assistance by the French Committee, including help to establish themselves in trade or in craft activity (Cottret 1991: 223). This was resented by guilds and craft associations which believed their own privileges, strongly asserted in the revolutionary upheavals a generation earlier, were being undermined.

For generations the British state-in-formation had been inculcating an ideology within which France was the key rival power against which national identity was to be measured. For some people the Huguenots were therefore a manifestation of the enemy. They were attacked for wearing strange clothes, for their exotic food and for speaking an unfamiliar language, and characterised variously as indolent, as parasitical, as bearers of disease and as mad: Gwynn (1985: 121) comments that 'insanity ever haunted the refugees'. As early as 1682, before mass immigration, the Church of the Savoy, an important Huguenot centre in London, complained that in the country they had believed to be 'a sanctuary and a refuge of Protestants' they were envied and resented and treated like 'a kind of slaves'.[20] In Parliament there were outspoken statements against them, phrased in xenophobic terms. Sir John Knight, MP for Bristol, opposed a bill introduced in 1693 for naturalisation of the Huguenots. He declared

> should this Bill pass, it will bring as great afflictions on this nation, as ever fell upon the Egyptians, and one of their plagues we have at this time very severe upon us; I mean, that of the land bringing forth Frogs in abundance, even in

the chambers of their kings; for there is no entering ... the places of their hereditary kings for the great noise and croaking of the Froglanders ... Let us first kick this Bill out of the house, and then the foreigners out of the Kingdom.[21]

Meanwhile a clergyman in the East End of London, where many of the refugees had settled, declared:

This set of rabble are the very offal of the earth, who cannot be content to be safe here from that justice and beggary from which they fled, and to be fattened on what belongs to the poor of our own land and to grow rich at our expense, but must needs rob us of our religion too.[22]

In the face of these reactions the government mounted what Cottret (1991: 23) calls 'a wide ranging ideological campaign' in defence of the refugees. The media of the day produced a barrage of newsletters, papers, books and pamphlets, while senior figures of the Anglican Church instructed local clergy to collect donations in their parishes on behalf of the Huguenots. The Bishop of London directed ministers in his diocese to make congregations aware of both the moral responsibility to 'comfort and relieve' their co-religionists and the material benefits to be derived from their presence – 'the peopling of our country, increasing manufactures, industry, trading and the like'.[23] It was intervention of the state that turned the tide by mitigating the very ideas of national Self and alien Other to which it was deeply committed. The episode had spelt out the extent to which notions of general rights were contingent: the Huguenots had been beneficiaries of a particular interest in asserting ideas about liberty and the right to freedom of expression. Many of their contemporaries and many later generations of refugees were not so fortunate.

Exiles

A key feature of the Huguenot experience unnoticed in the literature on forced migration is that those who fled to Britain were treated as a *collective* refugee. This reflected the approach of the British state, which wished to acquire what it saw as group resources. Over the next two centuries, however, there was a steady move towards narrower definitions. Mass migration had become a much more general feature of world society. The international economy had expanded and there was an enormous increase in demand for labour, both 'free' and unfree. In Europe a large part of the rural population was in movement to the cities, while long-distance migration led many to the New World. Transportation grew apace: the Atlantic slave trade claimed more victims in Africa while European powers transferred large numbers of unwanted citizens to the colonies. Most of those on the move were forced migrants among whom it was increasingly difficult to identify the circumstances which had led to displacement. What characterised those dubbed 'refugees' was less the element of compulsion in their flight than the approach of specific states which chose to accommodate them. The refugee became a category into which states placed certain groups whose presence was deemed beneficial to the host society.

This development was associated with the emergence of more precise notions about rights and about the national character of citizenship. By the late eighteenth century the process of formation of nation-states was well advanced, so that those who wrote the manifestos of the American and French revolutions expressed the aspirations of these movements within the discourse of nation. The Declaration of the Rights of Man and Citizen adopted by the National Assembly in Paris in 1789 asserted in Article 2 that the aim of the revolution was preservation of the natural and inalienable rights of man; in Article 3 it added that, 'The source of all sovereignty resides essentially in the nation; no group, no individual may exercise authority not emanating expressly therefrom'.[24] Here, universal rights were rights of individuals who were *of* the nation. 'Liberty' was to be enjoyed by citizens of a specific nation-state; by the same token those not of the state would not enjoy liberty.

The French revolution had an enormous impact, drawing support from liberal intellectuals across Europe and from various movements of the oppressed and exploited. Apart from fitful support from the newly independent United States, however, France did not gain backing from other states, whose hostility increased when it became clear that the principles of the republic were to be spread forcibly by its new rulers – 'a French bourgeoisie whose appetites were, in their way, as limitless as those of the British' (Hobsbawm 1962: 109). Here the contradiction evident in the project of the nation-state was again evident, for the rationalism and universalism advanced by ideologues of the revolution was used to endorse military activity in Europe and overseas. The message of liberty, fraternity and equality was spread by armies acting for France as a self-consciously rational, enlightened and advanced *national* civilisation. It was in this climate of increasingly tense confrontation between European states preoccupied with ideologies of nation that refugees gained increased importance.

The British state had already declared as refugees those royalists in North America who were opposed to the movement for independence. Many left the United States for Quebec, Ontario and Nova Scotia where they received grants of land from the Crown. It was now that the term refugee, hitherto applied only to the Huguenots, was given wider usage. *Encyclopaedia Britannica* explained that the term applied not only to the French Protestants but to 'such as leave their country in time of distress, and, hence, since the revolt of the British Colonies in America we have frequently heard of American Refugees'.[25] During the revolution in France royalists and members of the clergy were deported; eager to assert a commitment to liberty under their own flags various European countries, notably Britain and Poland, offered asylum. Although there was still no formal definition of the refugee a concept was emerging which focused more precisely upon the idea of accommodating those unjustly treated by rival powers. The key issue was that of rights – their denial by unjust governments and their assertion and confirmation by the host. These were necessarily individual rights, now championed by all states, whether in the form of the French Republicans' Rights of Man, or the British version which emphasised historic rights associated with national tradition.

Exiles in Britain

European refugees of the nineteenth century came overwhelmingly from radical political movements in Germany, Austria, France, Italy and Poland. Most sought sanctuary in other European states after failed attempts at revolution, notably during the upheavals of 1830 and 1848. Most participants in such movements were artisans or urban industrial workers but few of these secured asylum – indeed, many were slaughtered, incarcerated or, in the case of France, deported to the colonies, notably Algeria (see Chapter 3). Those with the means to escape were mainly among the privileged: Marrus (1985: 20) notes that, 'the world of political exiles was that of the relatively well-to-do or, at least of the once well-to-do'. Exile was often short-lived: most states accepted large numbers of refugees but soon expelled them. Britain had a different approach. In 1826, with the Napoleonic wars long over, the British government abrogated its power to exclude aliens. Porter (1979: 1) notes that during the rest of the century the British authorities allowed all refugees to enter mainland Britain and did not expel a single one.[26] During the 1820s and 1830s most were nationalists from Italy and Poland; in the 1840s they were joined by Germans and by French socialists, and after the 1848 revolutions by Austrians, Czechs, Hungarians and by more Italians, French and Germans. Among them were many celebrated figures of European radicalism, including Giuseppe Mazzini, Louis Kossuth, Alexander Herzen, Felice Orsini, Karl Marx, Louis Blanc, Alexandre Ledru-Rollin and Victor Hugo.

Successive governments were content for Britain to be known as the centre of exile in Europe. British entrepreneurs, merchants and bankers were at the height of their confidence: the domestic economy was growing rapidly, British exports were flooding across the world and colonial ventures proceeded apace. The bourgeoisie declared for free trade and free movement, formally encouraging immigration and celebrating the presence of the exiles. The policy had a further purpose: the main audience for the rhetoric of free movement and of sanctuary was at home, where governments and the propertied class they represented also faced serious political difficulties. Growth of industry and the consolidation of empire was disturbed by a constant struggle with labour and with radical political movements, notably with Chartism. In this heightened atmosphere the political establishment struggled to maintain its discourse of nation and national identity. An added problem was the development among British workers of a new form of internationalism. Consciousness of events abroad was much more widespread than hitherto and the fortunes of movements in Europe were followed closely, so that in 1830 the upheavals in France had an 'electrifying' impact upon political activists across the country (Thompson 1968: 911). Committed to the idea of Britain as the home of inherited rights and freedoms, the major parties waxed eloquent about the welcome offered to exiles from regimes which had persecuted them. Porter (1984: 27) suggests that in this context the refugees had an instrumental value:

> If the people were persuaded that they were free, then there was less likelihood that dissent would grow to proportions that would require the trouble and expense of overt repression. Toleration of foreign refugees bolstered this mechanism, by highlighting the openness, freedom and stability of Britain's society by direct and stark contrast with her European neighbours.

It was in this context that refugees from Italy and Poland were lauded in Britain as 'brave aristocratic freedom-fighters shining in the glory of their recent exploits ... against foes who were the English Liberals' foes also' (Porter 1979: 4).

'Image of Britannia'

After the 1848 revolutions the presence of refugees became more contentious. All of Europe had been shaken by the upheavals and many politicians insisted that the open policy on asylum had gone far enough. When refugees such as Karl Marx arrived in London to establish a new revolutionary current hostility intensified. Letters to *The Times* in 1849 described refugees as 'scum and refuse' and as 'filth' (Porter 1979: 75) and in the House of Lords exiles from Poland were described as 'mostly syphilitic' (ibid). There was a tacit change in policy: some refugees were put under surveillance by undercover police, and from 1852 many were sent to the United States, their fares paid by the Secret Service Fund of the Foreign Office (Porter 1979: 160). In the same year a steamer patrol was despatched to prevent refugees landing on the Channel Island of Jersey, a favourite place of sanctuary for political activists from France. It was difficult for governments to retreat on their general refugee policy however. They had invested much in the idea of Britain as a sanctuary and, with the cause of the exiles pursued energetically by the Chartists and domestic radicals, the easier option was to tolerate their presence.

The question of the exiles became more and more highly charged. *The Times* set out the case for sanctuary: 'Every civilised people on the face of the earth must be aware that this country is the asylum of nations, and that it will defend the asylum to the last ounce of its treasure and the last drop of its blood.'[27] In parliament there were prolonged debates in which refugees of the past were summoned as testimony to the importance of offering protection to deserving communities. The story of the Huguenots was rediscovered.[28] In an unusually blunt assessment of their utility to Britain, Henry Brougham declared that they had proved an important asset, bringing 'their wealth, where they had any, and ... what perhaps, was more valuable, their industry and skills, which they poured into our lap' (Porter 1979: 5). Popular histories complemented narratives of nation which had become such an important part of domestic politics. In *The Huguenots* Samuel Smiles celebrated the reception of the Huguenots as a statement of national moral worth:

> The [British] people crowded round the remarkable sufferers with indignant and pitying hearts; they received them into their dwellings, and hospitably relieved their wants ... they deeply stirred the heart of the nation, and every effort was made to succour and help the poor exiles for conscience's sake. (Smiles 1868: 222)

Smiles's account, suggests Cottret (1991: 194), was part of an effort to ensure that the Huguenots were incorporated into 'the positive image of Britannia'.

The atmosphere was changing, however. Britain's liberal regime in relation to exiles did not mean that the state pursued a non-interventionist approach to migration in general. For decades transportation to the colonies had been a favoured means of dealing with criminals and political dissidents. Many went to Canada, where they were an important element in the colonial venture, and later to South Africa, where they constituted the first large body of British settlers in the Cape region; meanwhile tens of thousands were shipped to the penal colony in Australia. Many had been convicted of the most petty offences; others were trade unionists or radical activists such as the Dorset farmworkers who became known as the Tolpuddle Martyrs.

Meanwhile large numbers of Irish men and women were seized and deported for resisting the extreme measures used by British landlords and the colonial state. There could be no sharper contrast than that between the rights afforded European exiles – whose numbers in Britain during the nineteenth century never exceeded 7000 (Porter 1979: 16) – and the freedom denied to scores of thousands who experienced transportation.

'Race' and nation

By the 1870s states in general were becoming more concerned with control of migration and with rights of citizenship and definitions of the alien. Exclusionary laws began to appear – initially where they might least have been expected. The first measures were enacted in the United States against people of Chinese origin. Migration from Asia had begun in the 1850s. Following the Opium Wars with China, European powers had insisted on removing barriers to emigration, allowing foreign entre- preneurs to operate freely in 'treaty ports'. Initially this allowed move- ment of indentured labour from China to European colonies in South-East Asia which produced tropical commodities for the world market. Soon 'coolie' labour was being exported to the United States and when during the American Civil War of the 1860s the supply of domestic labour fell sharply there was a surge in demand. A semi-official recruiting agency, the American Emigration Company, was established and by the early 1870s over 20,000 Chinese were arriving each year (Zolberg 1997: 290). They were mobilised quickly in very low wage jobs, including work formerly carried out by slaves.

Although most employers welcomed the Chinese, the latter also encountered deep hostility, being viewed by some as a 'malevolent "invasion" ' which brought undesired influences (ibid). This reflected increased hostility in general towards groups declared alien to American society. As in Europe, a 'scientific' racism had been in the process of development – an ideology which sought to justify white domination in general and the superiority of certain groups of Western European origin in particular. Horsman comments on the views of the influential Harvard group of the 1840s:

> They believed that the national character was largely a matter of race, that liberty was a special attribute of the Germanic/Anglo-Saxon peoples, and that Providence had directed human progress westward to America where the United States was engaged in the fulfilment of that plan.[29]

Notions of race were inseparable from ideas about the nation-state and its mission to advance 'human progress'. While US capitalism demanded more and more people, some of its leading ideologues focused upon differentiation among and between them, and upon subordination of internal Others. Migration of millions of Irish people was encouraged; at the same time they were identified as inferior, especially on the grounds of their adherence to Catholicism. Meanwhile, expansion of the United States into the western and southern territories of North America brought the state into conflict with indigenous Americans and with Mexicans. The violence used against them was justified on the basis that expansion of the United States was an expression of progress vis-à-vis backward peoples. Just as in Europe, ideas about liberty and associated rights were part of the project of constructing a more stable state: ideologically this was to be built around certain 'racial' groups, while by the same token others were to be excluded. And as in Europe the contradiction of inclusion and simultaneous exclusion was accommodated by the idea of nation, the category required to bind a vast number of people of different classes and origins but one also rooted in the notion of difference. An independent United States had reconciled liberty with slavery; as traditional slave-owning came to an end new racisms were endorsed by leading academics and politicians.

After the Civil War the federal government announced a project of Reconstruction through which states of the Confederacy were to be integrated into a Union in which all would subscribe to an invigorated idea of nation. More and more attention was directed towards the socio-cultural and 'racial' character of the nation – and inevitably to those *not* of the nation. Thus although the war had brought liberties for some Americans, for others it marked the moment at which their rights in the United States were expressly limited. Until the 1860s migration had been largely unregulated; as the 'new' racism grew in influence the federal government devoted greater efforts to exclusion. Jacobs (1996: 46–7) notes this conjuncture – that as central government became 'the object of primary allegiance' it also took on the role of regulator of migration. Chinese people were the first to face official discrimination. The United States had at first responded to demands of employers by putting enormous pressure on China to allow emigration. In 1868 this resulted in the Burlingame Treaty, under which the Chinese authorities agreed to end controls by recognising the 'inherent and inalienable right of man to change his home and allegiance, and also the mutual advantage of the free migration and emigration of their citizens'.[30] The Treaty, records Hing (1993: 22), was greeted with 'fanfare and delight' in the United States: there were laudatory comments about Chinese people in general and the observation that China, the oldest nation, and the United States, the youngest, were linked by 'special destiny' (ibid). Meanwhile Sinophobia was becoming widespread. In 1863 the state legislature in California had introduced a law forbidding any Indian, any person with more than 50 per cent Indian blood, any Chinese and any Mongol [*sic*] from testifying for or against a white person. In 1870 the Congress, which had just ratified the Burlingame Treaty, forbade any Chinese the right to naturalise as an American cit-izen. In some areas Chinese workers had become an important part of the labour force: in California, for example, they made up 25 per cent of all wage-earners (Zolberg 1997: 295). Here there were repeated campaigns against them. In 1868, 40,000 Chinese workers were driven out of California; the following year thousands of rail workers were forced to flee Virginia (Parmet 1981: 28). Chinese people were attacked as 'pagan rat-eaters' who were said to be coming in such numbers that they would 'fill the land in every direction' (ibid). They were described as 'grovelling worms' and of being a 'regressive and inferior race'.[31] They met especially intense opposition from labour unions. In the early 1870s there were several attempts to use Chinese workers to break strikes and their presence in the United States became a key issue for labour: the Workingmen's Party of California adopted the slogan 'The Chinese Must Go' (Parmet 1981: 31). Racist sentiment was greatly increased by the economic crash of 1873 which initiated the Great Depression. During this period Chinese workers specifically were depicted as excess labour and Congress enacted a law directed ostensibly against 'headmen' – recruitment agents who were held to be guilty of moving Chinese labourers to the United States against their will. This measure was the first to control admission of immigrants directly; it was followed in 1882 by the draconian Chinese Exclusion Act. This established that all Chinese people attempting to enter the United States were 'coolies'; in addition, it asserted that all those resident in the United States were there illegally and were liable to deportation. When the Act was tested in the Supreme Court in 1889 – the Chinese Exclusion Case – the Court concluded: '[if Congress] considers the presence of foreigners of a different race in this country, who will not assimilate with us, to be dangerous to its peace and security ... its determination is conclusive upon the judiciary' (Joppke 1999: 44–5).

National identity

The 'liberal moment' of migration was at an end. States had long intervened to encourage or discourage migration but the pattern had been inconsistent – now it was becoming clearer. Two factors were critical in determining openness to immigration: one was the state of the labour market; the second was the relative weight of national

sentiment, which was associated with specific socio-political developments. Although migration policy usually accommodated the demands
of employers there was no necessary 'fit', so that those who wished to
recruit labour abroad might be frustrated by policies of exclusion they
viewed as irrational. In the years following the Chinese Exclusion Act
economic growth resumed and many employers who had relied on
Chinese labour faced difficulties. They looked elsewhere in Asia and at
first Japanese and Filipinos were recruited. Soon these too were
excluded, on the basis of the precedents set in the 1882 Act and of
general hostility towards people of Asian origin. Employers' problems
were only resolved when Mexicans began to move northwards,
establishing a migratory route which soon became indispensable to
American capitalism. Zolberg comments on the arguments raised about
immigration in receiving states such as the United States during the late
nineteenth century, identifying two axes of concern: one economic,
representing large manufacturers and others who wished for unhindered
immigration; the other 'moral', associated with traditional craftsmen
and skilled workers represented by the nascent labour unions:

> The 'moral', or political, dimension pertained to an assessment of the
> putative impact of immigration on the 'integrity' of the nation, anchored
> in 'scientific' and popular understanding of culture and psychology. As
> shaped by nationalist and imperialist rivalries, these involved prejudicial
> stereotypes regarding the 'character' of particular groups and their suit-
> ability for membership in the receiving nation. Paradoxically, the very qual-
> ities that made immigrants especially fit for their assigned role in the
> receiving country's economy – their 'brute strength', 'simplicity', and
> 'docility' – rendered them unsuitable for inclusion. Moreover, their appar-
> ent willingness to accept living conditions below the publicly approved
> standard of the receiving countries functioned as a self-fulfilling prophecy:
> in effect, they became the inferior beings they were imagined to be.
> (Zolberg 1997: 294)

This observation homogenises Americans, among whom many were
opposed to racist campaigns and demonstrated solidarity with people of
African origin and with incoming groups. It does however illustrate the
way in which ideas about nation, supported by racist definitions of
national character, identified aliens as a competitive and threatening
presence. Such a presence was *functional* to the ideology of the nation-
state, notwithstanding that campaigns against aliens were not always in
the interests of those who were most influential within it. The capitalist
state required 'inferior beings', both as labour and as imagined enemies.
Its difficulty lay in reconciling labour supply with the ideology of exclusion: its means to resolve the contradiction was in the attempt to exert
control over both.

By the end of the nineteenth century, comments Patterson (1997: 113), theories of race developed by American academics 'provided a rich medium for the ideas of scientific racism, hereditary racial differences in intelligence, inherited criminality and eugenics'. State officials did not hesitate to draw on their theories. In 1890 Francis Walker, director of the Census, declared that the United States was being overrun by 'less desirable immigrants' from Southern and Eastern Europe – 'beaten men from beaten races' who compared poorly to the sound stock which had earlier been imported from Northern Europe (Edmonston 1990: 11). It was in this context that movements such as the Immigration Restriction League became an influential lobby in campaigns for exclusion of Italians, Jews and other 'undesirables'. Similar developments were under way in Europe, especially in Britain, France and Austria. In all these cases the initiative came from within relatively privileged social strata, albeit that it often engaged those below. Zolberg (1997: 297) comments of the US movement that it was initiated 'by traditional social elites and quickly gained widespread support among what could be termed the *silent majority*' (emphasis in original). These anti-alien movements now became active participants in shaping migration policies which forbade rights of entry to those who most urgently needed to assert them.

Notes

1. See for example Psalms 16, 27, 36, 51, 52; and Isaiah 8.
2. Sanctuary in a church or other site was normally limited to 40 days.
3. For an account of the American colonies' various declarations and the genesis of the Continental declaration of 1776 see Zuckert 2000.
4. Quoted in Hunt 2000: 8.
5. Quoted in Thomas 1998: 476. Even the most celebrated figures of American liberalism were uncertain about emancipation. Benjamin Franklin, some of whose business associates were deeply involved in the slave trade, declared: 'Slavery is such an atrocious debasement of human nature that its very extirpation, if not performed with solicitous care, may sometimes open a source of serious evils.' Quoted in Thomas 1998: 479. On Franklin's business associates see Thomas 1998: 282.
6. Quoted in Rees 1999: 15.
7. Quoted in Jacobson 1996: 22.
8. The radicalism of the French Revolution produced a different arrangement – citizens of other states being granted voting rights.
9. Cottret (1991: 2) suggests that the term refugee was not used systematically until after the mass flight of Huguenots in 1685.

10. *Dragonnade*: billetting of troops – dragoons – upon civilians. Persecution was so intense that Calvinist texts including the Bible were seized and burned, clergymen were expelled, Huguenot lawyers and doctors were prohibited from practising their profession, and even 'poor washerwomen were excluded from their washing places on the river'. Quoted in Reaman 1964: 60.

11. This is the estimate give by Zolberg (1989: 4). Histories of the Huguenots give a variety of figures: Weiss suggests that there were 600,000 refugees, Lane-Poole suggests 300,000. For a review of the contending accounts see Lee, 1936: 11.

12. For a review of contending estimates of the numbers fleeing to Britain see Lee, ibid.

13. Quoted in Hill 1972: 156.

14. Quoted in Lee 1936: 11–12.

15. Quoted in Cottret (1991: 185). This formulation demonstrated that, notwithstanding the revolution of the 1640s, the Crown still had the authority to allow 'rights' – corporate immunities – outside general restrictions and regulations.

16. Williams (1964: 13) notes that the island of Monserrat 'became largely an Irish colony', adding of the practice of transportation to nearby Barbados that, 'So thoroughly was this policy pursued that an active verb was added to the English language – to "barbadoes" a person' (ibid).

17. 'The True Way to Render Ireland Happy and Secure', pamphlet issued in Dublin 1697, quoted in Lee 1936: 22.

18. Kershen (1997: 69) also notes the later development of a 'Huguenot myth' of the immigration of 'profitable strangers' whose industriousness, thrift and wealth-creation was for the public good (ibid).

19. Popular songs and poems attacked the French. According to one: 'The nation is it allmost quite undone, By French men that doe it dayly overrun.' Following the mass immigration which began in 1685 there was renewed hostility and new ballards against the French: 'Weavers all may curse their fates, because the French work under-rate.' Quoted in Gwynn 1964: 114 and 117.

20. Quoted in Gwynn 1985: 122.

21. Quoted in Gwynn 1985: 118.

22. Quoted in Kershen 1997: 72.

23. Quoted in Gwynn 1985: 128.

24. Quoted in Rietbergen 1998: 338.

25. Quoted in Rudge 1992: 99.

26. Porter's detailed account of the circumstances of refugees in Victorian Britain suggests that they were not inhibited from admission to mainland Britain: there were, however, exclusions from the Channel Islands. See Porter 1985: 160–3.

27. *The Times* of 28 February 1853, quoted in Porter 1979: 7.

28. Individual Huguenot families and groups retained their identities and some histories already recalled the events of the 1680s. See for example

Memoirs of a Huguenot Family, a remarkable account by Fontaine (1852 [1712]) of his escape from France, passage to England and settlement in Devon and later in London.
29. Quoted in Patterson 1997: 112.
30. Quoted in Hing 1993: 22.
31. Quoted in Dinnerstein *et al.* 1979: 194.

6
Towards Disaster[1]

Menace from the East

During the first half of the nineteenth century the nationalism of Western Europe and North America had a liberal tone. This was the 'age of emancipation', which saw abolition of slavery, the civil and political emancipation of the Jews, widespread support for movements of self-determination in Southern and Eastern Europe and a relatively accommodating approach towards refugees. From mid-century a narrower nationalism began to take hold – one based upon much more precise ideas about difference. It drew upon the 'race science' of biologists and anthropologists such as Knox, Blumenbach, Nordmann and Gobineau, appealing strongly to bourgeois classes which felt under pressure from without and within. Rulers of the rival European powers were engaged in increasingly frenetic struggles for domination of Africa and the Arab East; at the same time they faced growing domestic threats from organised labour and from the first mass parties of the left. More precise ideas about race seemed to provide rationales which could cohere volatile populations and drive forward the imperial venture. MacMaster (2001: 14) comments that in Europe race science spread rapidly as 'the dominant epistemology, a tool for the unlocking of every conceivable social, cultural and political phenomenon ... the discourse of race infiltrated gender, class and nation'. For the first time ideas about national belonging were correlated closely with those of race – a development which was to have a profound impact upon generations of migrants.

Domestic politics was infused with ideas about national belonging and with fear of the alien. The latter might be any external or internal enemy but was most often represented as an 'Oriental'. In the United States the focus was upon the Chinese, now characterised as racially inferior, criminal, disease-ridden and sexually perverse. New techniques in microbiology were used to support ideas about the racialised human body, apparently confirming the idea that Orientals were vectors of disease *par excellence*, and with the result that entry of immigrants from Asia was regulated closely by police and public health authorities. Many Chinese communities were ghettoised: in the case of San Francisco's Chinatown borders were carefully demarcated and intensive efforts made to control the movement of its residents, with the aim of preventing contamination of the city's other inhabitants. The quarter was identified as a menace to the population as a whole – it was 'the pre-eminent site of urban sickness, vice, crime, poverty and depravity' (Shah 2001: 1) A dual menace had been identified – that of an alien group without and within, and it was under these circumstances that the Chinese Exclusion Act and other exclusionary measures brought an end to immigration from Asia. There were similar developments in Australia, where in the 1880s an 'anti-Chinese paranoia' took hold (Kingston 1988: 137).

In Western Europe, the focus was upon a different 'Oriental' threat – that of the Jews. The new racial determinism had already set Europeans in general against all Others, renewing in a more precise form the racisms of slavery and the early colonial period, and justifying more oppressive and exploitative regimes in the colonies. At the same time it racialised the competitive nationalism of the major colonising powers, so that the scramble for Africa and for the Arab East became a test of vigour of contending nations/races. The focus on Black Africans, Orientals and the 'races' of Europe barely concealed concern about other internal enemies, principally the threat from below – that of workers' movements for collective rights and for the franchise. In addition many European states faced the challenge of national movements at home: Britain was confronted by an energetic movement for Irish independence, and the empires of Central and Eastern Europe were challenged by a host of campaigns for self-determination. In the case of Britain, by the 1860s the 'dangerous classes' were routinely identified in conservative circles as 'savages' and 'negroes', as an increasingly insecure bourgeoisie constantly played upon and interwove the rhetoric of race and class, making the domestic proletariat 'Blacks without Blackness'.[2] The working class and urban poor (including many Irish people) were in effect members of a degenerate race, identified by means of the same markers said to characterise Africans and others of the colonial world: they were physically inferior to the good racial stock of the middle classes; they were dirty and carried disease (especially sexually transmitted disease); they were lazy and open to moral subversion; and they posed a danger to the national/racial project. There was in addition an internal enemy – the Jew, defined for the first time as racially distinct from and antipathetic to the whole of European society.

Jews were becoming increasingly mobile. From the 1840s they had been migrating from Russia and Eastern Europe to North America, smaller numbers settling in Western Europe. They were among the millions displaced by industrialisation and urbanisation: Litvinoff

(1989: 198) comments that those flocking westwards were 'the depressed classes, Irish, Italians, Jews and Serbs, from the stagnating fringes of the old continent'. From the 1880s the pace of economic change accelerated, bringing immiseration to sections of the population associated with traditional occupations, especially the many Jews who were artisans and small traders. Meanwhile general political instability in the region produced increased repression, including state campaigns of anti-Semitism. For the first time anti-Semitism became a coherent ideology shared by writers and by political activists in several countries, as shown by representation at the First and Second Anti-Jewish Congresses held in 1882 and 1883, with participants from Germany, Austria, Hungary, Russia, Romania, Serbia and France. Following the assassination of the Tsar in 1881 there were pogroms across Russia, many organised by the state and some involving mass killings. In 1882 the Tsarist interior minister, Count Nikolai Ignatiev, set out the imperial policy, declaring: 'The western frontier is open to the Jews.'[3] A large part of the Jewish population began to move. Not all were escaping specific persecutions – the Jewish experience varied widely from place to place and over time, with some communities facing repeated systematic violence and others enjoying relative calm. But everywhere there was the threat of hostility. The culture of terror had a demonstration effect, forcing more and more people into flight: Kushner and Knox (1999: 20) comment, 'the *fear* as well as the *reality* of violence was of great importance' (emphasis in original). Jewish emigration accelerated: between 1881 and the outbreak of the world war in 1914 over 2.5 million Jews moved westwards (Marrus 1985: 28). They entered states in which anti-alienism in general and anti-Semitism in particular had taken a strong hold within the discourse of nation. In Germany Wilhelm Marr had founded the Anti-Semitic League in 1879.[4] In France the first openly Judaeophobic newspaper, *L'Anti-Juif*, had been published in 1881, soon followed by *L'Antisemitique*, by a host of Judeophobic books and pamphlets, and by political organisations including the Ligue Antisemitique, founded in 1889. It was in this climate that in 1894 the Dreyus Affair unfolded: a long-running campaign against a Jewish army officer which imagined a Judaeo-German conspiracy against the French state. Similar developments in Britain had even more serious outcomes, producing the first European legislation to specify race as a criterion for exclusion.

In Britain the recession of the 1870s stimulated a policy of economic protectionism, accompanied by heightened nationalism. Hostility towards immigrants increased steadily. As in the United States, establishment politicians led the offensive and were joined at various points by leaders of organised labour. During the 1890s conservative nationalist organisations appeared, such as the British Brothers' League, which had an explicitly anti-Semitic agenda, and in 1898 a first bill to restrict immigration was introduced on the basis that 'alien elements' threatened 'English' society (Foot 1965: 87). Race science, which had proved so important in shaping the discourse of Sinophobia in the United States, was focused upon a different 'Oriental' but with similar outcomes. Jews were racialised – depicted as criminal, diseased and likely to import moral decay. In a typical characterisation Jewish immigrants were likened to diseased cattle and the areas in which they lived were identified as zones of infection and of corruption – by this means traditional fear (and fascination) among the English middle class of the East End of London was given a new racist inflection (Foot 1965: 89–90). A Royal Commission on the Aliens Question was established which found against all the allegations raised by anti-alien campaigners but which concluded, paradoxically, that 'undesirable' immigrants should be excluded. In 1905 Parliament passed the Aliens Act – the first legislation in Britain for over 300 years to impose mechanisms for control of immigration during peacetime. The new law restricted entry of steerage passengers arriving on 'immigrant ships' who were judged not to be self-supporting, who might become a cost to the state, who were mentally ill or who were perceived as travelling en masse – defined as a group of more than 20. In effect, it targeted the poor and the vulnerable and was a thinly disguised means of excluding Jews. The Act also distinguished for the first time between migrants in general and those much later to be defined as refugees. Although refugees were not named as a category, the law specified that certain migrants should not be refused: those seeking 'solely to avoid persecution or punishment on religious or political grounds or for an offence of a political character or persecution involving a danger of imprisonment or danger to life or limb, on account of religious belief'.[5] An incoming government soon added the provision that asylum could be granted on a discretionary basis: the right to sanctuary for certain persons which was implicit in the Act was to be a right recognised at will by those in power. It allowed for the granting of asylum as an *ex gratia* act in which the government did not surrender control over entry. Schuster and Solomos (1999: 54) observe that this established an important precedent in British law: asylum was to be an act of charity in which the status of the applicant was to be determined on a subjective basis by officials of the Home Office. This had important long-term implications for British immigration policy, granting the government of the day flexibility 'to admit those whom it chooses and to reject those it does not want or need' (ibid).

Age of exclusion

Following the recession of the 1870s the world economy continued to grow at an unprecedented rate. Sustained increases in world trade and finance had produced more complex links across continents – a development later to be identified as an early expression of globalisation.[6] Competition between the European powers had meanwhile intensified; the colonial world functioning as an arena within which to express rivalries which in 1914 erupted into war. The conflict was also a clash of nationalisms. Combatant states poured their energies into rival propaganda efforts and unprecedented levels of hostility were generated vis-à-vis citizens of other states assumed to be antagonistic to the domestic population. Surveillance and regulation of the population reached new levels of intensity. Passports were introduced across Europe: hitherto their use had been uneven and sporadic, now they served to regulate emigration (minimising loss of labour, skills and military personnel) and to identify citizens and Others. Supported by a mass of documentation which variously confirmed antecedents, place of birth and residence, and sometimes ethnic markers (language, religion, 'race') the passport marked out a new national status. Introduced as a means of *control* it was a bureaucratic assertion of the power of the state vis-à-vis 'its' citizens. In the case of Britain a new law rushed through parliament at the start of the war also targeted all foreigners. Foot comments (1965: 101):

> all the liberal arguments, all the 'traditions of asylum', all the high-blown talk about the free haven of Britain, all the long, tumultuous opposition of liberals and socialists to strict immigration control were washed away by a single Act passed through all its parliamentary stages on a single day.

This legislation, the Aliens Restrictions Act of 1914, brought special supervision of aliens, who could be prevented from entering under any circumstances, while those resident in Britain were to register with the police and could be deported at will. The Act abolished provisions of the 1905 law which had permitted entry of those fleeing persecution and allowed for any other measures 'which appear necessary or expedient with a view to the safety of the realm'.[7] Between 70,000 and 75,000 people were classified as enemy aliens; some 32,000 were interned and a further 20,000 deported (Kushner and Knox 1999: 45).

While existing states became hyper-nationalist, the old empires of Europe fragmented into new national units. Following the war a series of peace treaties written by the victorious powers dismantled the Russian, Austro-Hungarian and Ottoman empires and in their place appeared a host of nation-states. In 1871 there had been 14 states in Europe; by 1919 there were 26. The new entities brought a mass of problems for those included within them or excluded from them.

Dominant models of the state assumed that citizens were people of 'national origin' and that states should be ethnically homogenous or at least be based upon overwhelming dominance of those considered to possess national characteristics. But among the new states of Eastern Europe and the Balkans there was great ethnic heterogeneity. According to Arendt (1986: 270), the situation was 'preposterous':

> The Treaties lumped together many peoples in single states, called some of them 'state people' and entrusted them with the government, silently assumed that others (such as the Slovaks in Czechoslovakia, or the Croats and Slovenes in Yugoslavia) were equal partners in the government, which of course they were not, and with equal arbitrariness created out of the remnant a third group of nationalities called 'minorities', thereby adding to the many burdens of the new states the trouble of observing special regulations for part of the population. (ibid)

'National' groups which did not acquire states viewed the Peace Treaties as unjust – they had handed out 'rule to some and servitude to others' (ibid). Meanwhile the associated Minority Treaties, which guaranteed rights for 'non-national' groups within the new states, infuriated the latters' nationalist leaderships.

One outcome was mass population movement across Eastern and Central Europe. Movements to nation-states in which migrants had the correct ethnic 'fit' had been under way for decades: in the mid-nineteenth century, for example, large numbers of Greeks moved from their regions of origin within the Ottoman Empire to the independent state of Greece. The Peace Treaties now brought movements across scores of countries, as those identified as aliens in one state were welcomed as the citizens of others – or were simply excluded as stateless people. A strategy later identified as ethnic cleansing affected scores of millions of people: it was energetically pursued in the Baltic states of Estonia, Latvia and Lithuania, and in Austria, Czechoslovakia, Hungary, Poland and the new state of Yugoslavia. In the former Ottoman regions there was a sustained, violent assault by Turkish nationalists upon the Armenian population, whose presence in Anatolia was seen as inconsistent with plans for independent Turkey. A million Armenians were driven out of eastern Anatolia, most into the Syrian desert, where vast numbers perished. This forced mass movement of aliens was a harbinger of events to take place in Europe a generation later.[8]

The Minority Treaties identified ethnic groups as people with their own interests. This was a first move towards notions of collective rights and potentially a means of giving protection to those disowned by the state system. It also reflected, however, the wish of dominant states to pre-empt problems among groups which might cause political instability and might violate the many new national political borders. There was a further difficulty: the Treaties were premised upon the idea that only nations could guarantee rights. The national character of the latter, implicit in all approaches to rights since the seventeenth century, was now formalised. Arendt (1986: 275) comments:

> The Minority Treaties said in plain language what until then had been only implied in the working-system of the nation-states, namely, that only nationals could be citizens, only people of the same national origin could enjoy the full protection of legal institutions, that persons of different nationality needed some law of exception until or unless they were completely assimilated and divorced from their origin.

Although the Minority Treaties focused upon rights, these were vested in states, which had sole authority in allocating citizenship and in matters of immigration. 'Minorities' were those with an affiliation other than that of the states or states in which they found themselves: they were 'exceptions' – 'misfits' whose presence posed new problems for all nation-states. Discussions on their status marked a recognition of the complexities of post-war Europe. This was short-lived however. The peace of 1918 initially brought world economic recovery but as conditions deteriorated and many European governments faced strong radical opposition, minorities quickly became scapegoats. Governments preoccupied with internal matters relegated non-national peoples 'to the ranks of outsiders and aliens who threatened national and cultural cohesion' (Loescher 1993: 34). Refugees' problems became more acute. New migrations from the Balkans brought large numbers of people into Eastern and Central Europe, while the fallout from the Russian Revolution of 1917 and from subsequent military conflicts with Communist Russia initiated by Western states caused large movements to Western Europe, Eastern Europe and North America. By the early 1920s millions of people were moving back and forth, confronted by a new mosaic of state authorities, each with its own national agenda – its own approach to inclusion and exclusion.

Immigration had been integral to the growth of industrial capitalism in Europe and North America. After the First World War it slowed dramatically as states focused upon the problem of deepening economic crisis, declaring policies of 'no entry' to most migrants. In the United States the Immigration Act of 1917 imposed a numerical limit on entries and included a literacy requirement which discriminated against immigrants from Southern and Eastern Europe. In 1921 a further Immigration Act established a quota system, limiting entrants of a specific national origin to 3 per cent of the numbers of 'their' foreign-born European ethnic group resident in the United States in 1910. This was developed with the help of the US Bureau of Census, which provided analyses showing how limits could be set for immigrants of specific national origins by choosing a benchmark year which would guarantee admissions weighted to Anglo-Saxon applicants. Yet another Immigration Act was passed in 1924. This revised the benchmark year to 1890 – the moment before intensification of migration to the United States from Eastern Europe, mainly of Jews, and from Southern Europe, mainly of Italians.[9] Jacobson (1996: 47) notes that proponents of the legislation cited the importance of racial homogeneity and claims of Anglo-Saxon superiority, while attacking arguments for the United States as an ethnic melting pot as 'fallacious'. Echoing the Supreme Court decisions of the 1890s they warned of 'racial indigestion' (ibid). Country-of-origin quotas remained the basis for official immigration policy for the next 40 years.

During the 1920s new techniques of mass production and of labour management intensified exploitation of the American workforce. 'Scientific' regulation of labour – Taylorism and Fordism – increased the pace of production in manufacturing industry and at first reduced the need for immigrant labour.[10] At the same time world recession drew closer and in the late 1920s became economic collapse – a new and much more serious Great Depression. All over the industrialised world mass migration was halted. In the United States the annual average of entrants during the 1930s was less than 50,000 – about 6 per cent of the total admitted in 1921 before the first Immigration Act (Jacobson 1996: 48).[11] So too in Europe: in Germany by 1932 the number of foreign workers had fallen to about 10 per cent of the total 30 years earlier (Potts 1990: 137). Many states implemented policies of 'no exit'. In some cases, such as the Soviet Union, this was public policy; in others, intending migrants discovered only at the border that controls had been put in place. New displacements meanwhile continued to add to the total of forced migrants. By 1926 almost 10 million had been displaced people across Europe and for the first time they were routinely referred to as refugees. Many had come from Russia and from the Balkans; they were joined by Italians fleeing the Mussolini regime and later by those escaping authoritarian governments in Spain and Portugal. They were perceived by most European states as unwelcome, indeed as threatening: most were poor and vulnerable and were deemed highly undesirable as immigrants. Their presence was taken as a further token of general instability in Europe and as an index of the need to reinforce barriers to entry. This pattern was to recur, becoming the most important feature of the relationship between states and forced migrants in the twentieth century – for when access was needed most urgently states were most aggressive in developing regimes of exclusion. Such policies – narrow nationalisms which sought to deflect onto migrants the responsibility for systemic crises – led to repeated tragedies. The first of these followed hard on the events of the 1920s.

The Nazi project

Fascism was the apotheosis of the idea of nation. In common with other nationalisms it maintained that the state was an expression of specific local values. But it also viewed the state as the means of fulfilling an historic mission of self-assertion – to confirm the superiority of the race/nation vis-à-vis Others said to threaten it from without and from within. In the case of Nazism, the German people were charged with a mission of rescue of national society from alien forces bent upon its destruction. This involved the ultimate measures of population control – racial 'purification' of the nation by mass extermination of the alien.

The rise of Nazism posed a series of questions to the governments of Europe and North America, prominent among which was the policy to be pursued vis à vis the movement's many victims. Violence directed at political rivals and minority populations was integral to the Nazis' programme. Among their first priorities was a violent assault upon workers' movements and the Left; the main concern, however, was with Jews, and on taking power in 1933 they set out to expel as many as possible. Jews were judged not merely to be racially inferior to Europeans in general and to Aryan Germans in particular but to be irredeemably corrupt. Eugenics and race science were mobilised to show that Jews carried disease and decay, and that their presence corrupted and weakened the strong racial stock of Germany. They could not be reformed, for Jewish 'blood' bore base influences: the main task was to prevent contamination of the wider society by taking radical preventative measures. From 1933 large numbers of Jews left Germany and over the next five years increasingly violent anti-Semitism drove out some 300,000 people. The Nazi leadership was not satisfied, however: in 1938 Hitler ordered the emigration of Jews 'by every possible means'[12] and by 1939 the majority had left.[13] Union with Austria, the *Anschluss*, also produced attempts at mass exit. These movements were *planned* by the Nazi regime as part of its effort to rid German territories of alien influences; they were a phase in the programme of ethnic cleansing that eventually, when emigration of Jews was halted, produced the death camps of the *Endlosung der Judenfrage* – the 'Final Solution to the Jewish Problem'.[14] Those able to flee mostly survived; those who did not attempt to leave, or who were unable to do so, were murdered systematically as from 1941 the German high command launched the Holocaust proper. At this point the project was straightforward: the Nazis killed as many Jews as they could.

The circumstances associated with Jewish flight from Nazi-controlled areas have been the subject of prolonged debate. Did potential countries of asylum understand the realities of Nazi anti-Semitism? Did they systematically exclude its victims? Why did some Jews remain, to be consigned to the death camps? Did the Allied powers of the Second World War reject the option to rescue Hitler's victims? Were they effectively complicit in genocide? These questions are of immense importance in the history of forced migration: not only do they relate to the fate of millions of people but they have implications for all subsequent generations of forced migrants.[15]

The conduct of the Allied powers is of special importance, primarily in relation to the lives of victims or potential victims of fascism, but also because of the role played by these governments in shaping ideas about refugees and their rights. The balance of evidence suggests that although the majority of German Jews did escape, many faced serious obstacles in the search for sanctuary, including in the most obvious places of refuge – Britain, France and the United States. This was not primarily because of a focused anti-Semitism in these states but because of the policy of states in general that their borders should remain closed, and the fixation of national politicians with regulation of popu-lation. Preoccupied by continuing economic crisis, all governments focused upon their own stability. They saw little to be gained by accommodating displaced people, who were at best viewed as a cost to the state and hence as undesirable. Loescher (1993: 41) comments

> there was a broad consensus in almost every industrialized nation, particularly during the years of the Great Depression, that national interests were best served by imposing and maintaining rigid limits on immigration; that humanitarian initiatives on behalf of refugees had to be limited by tight fiscal constraints and the need to employ the nation's own citizens; and that no particular foreign policy benefits would accrue from putting political and moral pressure on refugee-generating countries or from accepting their unwanted dissidents and minority groups.

Refugees of many origins were left to face the consequences. During the early 1930s consolidation of Stalinism in the Soviet Union brought victimisation of all manner of real or imagined opponents of the regime. Most of the activists who survived from the revolutionary movement of 1917 were eliminated, while several non-Russian nation-alities were forcibly removed and resettled. Western governments in knowledge of their plight largely ignored it, abandoning the discourse of rights associated with the Minority Treaties. In the United States the 'quota acts' of 1921 and 1924 had marked the end of general immigration. The annual quota for immigrants from the Soviet Union was a mere 2712, so that even those who escaped the early persecutions of Stalinism had little chance of admission (Rubinstein 1997: 32). Similarly, tens of thousands fled the effects of Civil War in Spain but with the annual quota for Spanish immigrants set at 252 a mere handful found refuge in the United States. During the entire course of the war, from 1936 to 1939, fewer than 1000 people were admitted (Rubinstein 2000: 34). Following the First World War, France had become an important place of refuge. Shortage of labour associated with immense loss of life during the conflict had encouraged a liberal immigration regime but world recession soon brought a change in attitudes. By the mid-1930s employers who had earlier scoured the continent for labourers 'clamoured for foreigners to be sent home' (Marrus 1985: 146). New restrictions were introduced which soon affected German Jews fleeing Nazism, some of whom were turned back at the border. Marrus (1985: 147) notes the insistence of senior officials that France 'would not become a dumping ground for refugees', who were accused of stealing the rights of Frenchmen, undermining France's cultural purity or trying to embroil France with Hitler. After a brief liberalisation at the time of the Popular Front government in 1936, pressure again increased. France was said to be 'saturated' with refugees and for the first time there was talk of an illegal presence – '*les clandestins*'. Meanwhile military victory for the nationalists in Spain resulted in a mass exit of Republicans to France. Some 400,000 crossed the border but almost half were soon repatriated (Marrus 1985: 193). Britain maintained a more restrictive policy. When Jewish refugees began to arrive from Germany in 1933, attempts to loosen regulations were firmly rejected by the government, which insisted that no immigrant should be a cost on public funds. The Home Secretary asserted that, 'aliens are only allowed to come in for residence if their settlement here is consonant with the interests of this country ... the interests of this country must predominate over all other considerations'.[16]

'Invaders'

These attitudes were consistent with growing official racism in Western Europe. During the First World War Britain, France and Germany had transported large numbers of their colonial subjects to serve in the armed forces and within domestic industry. Following the Russian Revolution of 1917 and the end of the war there was political upheaval not only across Europe but in Asia and the Middle East, leading to fear of contact between immigrants and European radicals sympathetic to anti-colonial struggles. France demobilised and expelled all but a handful of those imported from the colonies. Britain had recruited thousands of seamen; most were also expelled and the government hounded those who remained, including those who were British citizens. In 1925 it enacted the Coloured Alien Seaman Order, which licensed general harassment by police and enforced deportation. In both Britain and France, suggests

Macmaster (2001: 124), governments endorsed racial subordination and were parties to strident propaganda campaigns:

> The authorities created a climate of opinion that would readily accept the necessity for special controls and policing through the dissemination of highly racialized images of black immigrants as primitive 'invaders' who threatened European society through the transmission of dangerous microbes, criminal activity (pimping, drugs, gambling), by the sexual danger presented to women and children (rape, molestation), and the proliferation of squalid ghettos (ibid).

Many leading European politicians accepted race science and ideas about the dangers of miscegenation and the pernicious influence of alien communities. These notions played an important role in shaping government efforts to assert authority during periods of social and political turmoil, and were part of the rationale for immigration control. They also both encouraged and were stimulated by parties of the extreme right. State-sanctioned discourses of racism gave legitimacy to fascist organisations such as the Parti Social Français, the Parti Populaire Français and the British Union of Fascists (BUF). The latter had absorbed much of the Nazi programme and was active in campaigning against all immigrants, reserving special venom for those it termed the 'refujews' (Kushner and Knox 1999: 149). In a typical campaign the BUF railed against all who sought asylum:

> Why support a fund to give relief to aliens when poverty and unemployment are rife in Britain? We have been asked in the past four years to support Abyssinians, Basques, Chinese, Austrians, Spaniards, and now Jews. [BUF leader] MOSLEY SAYS ... CHARITY BEGINS AT HOME.[17]

The BUF's stridency and anti-Semitism set it apart from other political organisations in Britain. Its hostility to aliens was not unique, however. The organisation had emerged in the context of years of officially sanctioned racism which was so intense that it amounted to the 'recolonization and racialization' of minority communities (McMaster 2001: 124).

In the United States by 1930 there were 12 million unemployed, with at least another 6 million on short-time working (Edsforth 2000: 46). Non-citizens were viewed by the state as an unbearable burden on the economy and presented as a threat to the indigenous workforce. In 1930 President Hoover effectively closed down immigration, directing US consulates to enforce restrictions to the letter, and ordering the INS to step up efforts to deport aliens. Mexicans were the main target. Aggressive lobbying by the horticultural industry had ensured that immigration from the south was not restricted by quotas, and Mexicans had become integral to the economies of Texas, Arizona, Colorado and

California. Large communities had developed in many cities – by 1930 Los Angeles had a Mexican population of almost 100,000 (Watkins 1999: 396). Immigrants had also moved to the mid-West, where they worked in the new industries, notably in motor manufacturing: there were some 20,000 Mexicans in Chicago alone (ibid). Hoover's Emergency Committee for Employment targeted such communities as a means to tackle unemployment. The policy was unambiguously racist: Labor Secretary William Doak, responsible for the INS, declared: 'My conviction is that by a strict limitation and wide selection of immigration we can make America stronger in every way, hastening the day when our population shall be more homogenous' (ibid). Local authorities played a key role in enacting state policy. In cities with Mexican populations they identified Spanish names on lists of those who had applied for relief and targeted them for deportation. The intention, according to officials in Los Angeles, was 'to scare many thousand alien deportables [*sic*] out of this district which is the result desired': they termed this 'scareheading' (Watkins 1999: 400). Hoover claimed publicly that hundreds of thousands of people had been removed and that the United States had ceased to be a country of immigration – now it was to be a country of emigration. Edsforth (2000: 65) comments, 'The Hoover administration's policy of using immigration law to reduce unemployment reflects the way that the Great Depression encouraged xenophobia even [sic] in the United States.' The incoming Roosevelt administration of 1932, pledged to a 'New Deal for the American people', did not revoke the policy.

Many local administrations in the United States introduced strict residency requirements for those receiving publicly funded relief. They also discriminated against African-Americans, Hispanics, Asian-Americans and Native Americans, who seldom received assistance equal to that provided for citizens of European origin. Extensive programmes for 'transients' were put in place so that by 1935 some 300,000 people were receiving aid: this was denied, however, to cross-border seasonal migrants (Rose 1994: 39). In an account of employment practices in Arizona, Bustamente (1998) shows that 'Anglo' workers were routinely given preference over Mexicans and that even when the latter got work they were paid a fraction of the 'Anglo' rate. The City of Los Angeles sacked scores of Japanese transit workers, while in New Orleans the local authority passed a law forbidding employment of African-Americans in the docks. Organisations of the right made a rapid advance. In many Southern states there were campaigns for 'Negro Removal' in which a revived Ku Klux Klan was prominent. There was also a dramatic increase in lynchings of Black men. Traditionally a bloody feature of white supremacy in the South, these killings began to take place elsewhere, including in the industrial East and the mid-West.

Meanwhile hundreds of small fascist and anti-Semitic groups emerged, although most collapsed as quickly as they had emerged.[18] Edsforth (2000: 90–1) concludes that in this heightened atmosphere, 'White supremacist politics and race war were not inconceivable outcomes of the collapse of American capitalism'.

Racism and exclusion

Without exception those who controlled the states of Europe and North America promoted ideologies of nation which complemented their attempts to assert economic independence or even autarky. The more that recession and the accompanying socio-political crisis deepened, the more they emphasised national unity, heightening consciousness of the national collective vis-à-vis Others. It was in this atmosphere that states formulated policies vis-à-vis the refugees from Nazism.

In the early 1930s the plight of Jewish victims of Nazism was well understood by Western governments. Although none could know of the fate awaiting those who did not escape they were well informed about the effects of increasing anti-Semitism in Germany. London (2000: 28) notes that in 1933 the British Cabinet was aware of Hitler's strategy to target all German Jews for expulsion, and that a special committee discussed the implications for immigration policy. Meanwhile the Press in Europe and North America commented extensively on Nazi ideology and practice. Lipstadt (1994) shows that throughout the 1930s newspapers and magazines in the United States reported on and editorialised against Nazi repression. The British Press, with some prominent exceptions, was hostile to fascism and also reported regularly on the atrocities. In addition all governments received information from a new source – the High Commissioner for Refugees from Germany. This position had been created in 1933 but owed its existence to events more than a decade earlier. In 1921 the League of Nations had established an office to regulate the movements of refugees from Russia – the High Commissioner on behalf of the League in connection with Russian Refugees in Europe. The Commissioner, Fridtjof Nansen, was mandated to carry out specific tasks: he was to work only with Russian refugees and to use his limited budget for administration, not for relief. He was also instructed that any assistance provided for the refugees was to be temporary – there was to be no permanent protection or right to settlement. As instability continued across Europe Nansen was required to intervene in Greece, Turkey and in the Balkans, organising exchanges of population which were part of the regulation of ethnic groups associated with establishment of new nation-states. These activities helped to delineate a status – 'the refugee' – which was recognised informally by most governments, although it referred only to those displaced from specific countries, initially from Russia and Armenia. States troubled by continuing instability in Europe were moving slowly towards definition of a category of displaced persons. This was not to be a universal status, however, or to hint at any limitation on states' sovereign right to include or to exclude.

When Hitler came to power in 1933 the League of Nations established the office of the High Commissioner for Refugees from Germany – tacit recognition of the seriousness of problems faced by victims of the new Nazi regime. In 1935, when he failed to secure admission to desired places of asylum for those wishing to leave Germany, the High Commissioner, James McDonald, resigned. In a widely publicised letter he described in detail Nazi persecution of Jewish and 'non-Aryan' populations and predicted that many of those threatened would try to flee. He called for concerted international action on behalf of the refugees, arguing that German Jews constituted a minority whose protection, like that of all racial, religious or linguistic minorities, 'was hardening into an obligation of the public law of Europe'.[19] The McDonald Letter was widely discussed in North America and Western Europe. Governments ignored it: in the case of Britain, its conclusions were explicitly rejected (Sherman 1994: 65).

It is implausible to suggest that European and North American states conspired against the refugees: as we shall see, some who fled Nazism were warmly received. But neither is it the case that they came to their aid. This is evident from detailed accounts of debates within the British government which confirm that the political establishment was reluctant to permit any increase in immigration. Its initial attitude is summed up by a message sent to the British embassy in Paris in 1933, noting that it was policy 'to do *nothing* to *encourage* further immigration' (emphasis in original) (London 2000: 55). Meanwhile queues at consulates in Germany and Eastern Europe grew longer and warnings from British diplomats became more alarmist. In 1935 a senior figure in Germany reported to the Foreign Office that 'the Jew is to be eliminated and the [German] State has no regard for the manner of the elimination'.[20] In the same year the ambassador in Berlin, commenting on the Macdonald Letter, agreed with its author that, 'the position of the Jews is becoming so desperate as to make it apparent every day that ... the present Nazi policy threatens the Jewish population in the Reich with extermination'.[21] In 1938 Anschluss created panic among Austrian Jews. Thousands besieged consulates in Vienna and others attempted to flee through Czechoslovakia. Such was their desperation that, according to a contemporary account, hundreds committed suicide every day (Sherman 1994: 86). Their plight was discussed by officials in London who concluded that mass movement of refugees was likely and that this might bring 'social and labour problems' in Britain.[22] The Home Office decided to introduce a visa system so that entry of German and Austrian nationals could be more tightly controlled. Its main aim was to avoid 'the creation of a Jewish problem in this country [Britain].'[23]

A stream of diplomatic messages gave detailed accounts of the plight of the Jews. In April 1938 the British Consul-General in Vienna described the Jews of Austria as 'terror-stricken, despoiled and fearful of what the morrow may bring forth'; what was needed to solve the problem, he suggested, was 'a long-term policy, a comprehensive scheme, the best brains, and ample finance'.[24] A month later he reported that the situation was worsening:

> the distress and despair amongst the Jews are appalling. This consulate-general is literally besieged every day by hundreds of Jews who have been told to leave the country and come vainly searching for a visa to go anywhere. Every consulate in Vienna is in a similar position.[25]

The British government resolved not to lift controls. So too in the United States, where in 1930 Hoover had instructed consulates to enforce rigorously a provision of the 1917 Act which forbade entry to those 'likely to become a public charge'. Visas were granted only to those who could show that they could support themselves indefinitely or to those with guarantees from relatives or friends. The incoming Roosevelt administration relaxed the rules but not the principles of exclusion and eventually, after growing public pressure, the president initiated an international meeting to address the issue of the refugees. This took place in July 1938 at Evian in France, bringing together delegates from 32 countries including all the major powers except Germany and the Soviet Union. The chances of an outcome favourable to refugees were slim – the invitation to the conference stated that 'no country would be expected to receive a greater number of emigrants than is permitted by its existing legislation'.[26] The proceedings were low-key, with nothing to suggest the massive crisis under way in Germany and Austria. Most states emphasised that they had already accepted large numbers of refugees – a fiction – and that they could take no more. Britain contributed a vague plan to settle refugees in Kenya or in Guiana, its colony in South America. The only substantial offer came from the Dominican Republic, a tiny Caribbean state which offered to accept 100,000 refugees as rural settlers to work on the land. Politicians in all the desired countries of asylum made clear that offers of sanctuary would act as a signal for mass emigration of Jews, bringing them unwanted inflows of aliens.

Within days of the conference the situation in Austria had again deteriorated. In August 1938 there was an upsurge in violent anti-Semitism, producing panic among the Jewish population. At the consulates 'hordes of would-be migrants competed frantically for places in queues from which the Gestapo and Nazi Party functionaries would occasionally make random and brutal arrests' (Sherman 1994: 133). Still there was no change in policy and it was not until November 1938 that Western governments reluctantly made concessions – an outcome of pressure from the public following the events of *Kristallnacht*, 9 November 1938, a pogrom across the entire area under Nazi control. Governments now edged towards relaxation of immigration policy but every move was marked by extreme reluctance: in Britain ministers continued to complain that a more liberal policy was impossible unless Germany paid host countries to accept refugees. It revealed that during the whole five years of Nazi rule it had accepted a total of 11,000 immigrants (Sherman 1994: 179). Eventually public pressure made the British government's position untenable. Already forced by persistent lobbying to accept Basque victims of the conflict in Spain, it was now obliged to respond to those campaigning for Jewish refugees – a minister conceding that, 'It is largely public opinion which must be the determining factor' (Kushner and Knox 1999: 140).[27] In February 1939 Britain agreed in principle to participate in a programme to help remaining Jews to emigrate – but insisted that they should be directed out of Europe. While the debates went on those Jews who could escape travelled far and wide to find sanctuary. There were sustained attempts to reach Palestine, often through networks established by the Zionist movement and periodically inhibited by the British colonial authorities. By mid-1939 there were some 14,000 refugees in Shanghai, a European enclave within China (Rubinstein 1997: 40). Refugees also reached the Latin America and the Caribbean, where looser controls on immigration meant that several communities were established. Eventually Britain relaxed domestic controls and by September 1939 official figures showed that a total of 50,000 Jewish refugees had entered the United Kingdom, albeit on temporary visas (Sherman 1994: 271). In the United States similar pressures on government brought an increase in the number of refugees accepted, from some 19,000 in 1937–38 to 43,000 in 1938–39 (Rubinstein 1997: 35).

'Money speaks'

Some victims of Nazism had for years been freely accommodated. In 1933 the British Cabinet discussed the unfolding crisis in Germany and resolved to maintain the policy of exclusion of any alien who might become a public charge; at the same time it agreed that the public interest would be served by accepting certain refugees. The government's aim should be to secure 'prominent Jews' expelled from Germany, those who had 'achieved distinction whether in pure science, applied science, such as medicine or technical industry, music or art'.[28] There was a specific purpose to the initiative: 'This would not only obtain for this country the advantage of their knowledge and experience, but would also create a very favourable impression in the world, particularly if our hospitality were to be offered with some warmth.'[29] The Cabinet agreed to recommend to its Committee on Alien Restrictions that offers of hospitality should be made to refugees from Germany who were 'eminent in science, technology, art and music'. Some Jews were to be approved for admission in order to bring technical expertise or special skills and to embellish Britain's international reputation. In 1938, with the refugee crisis at its height, the government still asserted that the test for admission for a refugee was whether an applicant 'is likely to be an asset the United Kingdom'.[30] Those deemed acceptable and who were to be granted visas without delay included leading academics and researchers; artists, architects and designers who could maintain themselves; and industrialists who intended to transfer well-established businesses to Britain. Schuster and Solomos (1999: 56) describe the policy as 'cynical manipulation of the Jewish exodus for practical and propaganda purposes'.

There was a similar approach in the United States. Rubinstein (1997: 37) comments that luminaries such as Einstein, Schoenberg and the non-Jewish Thomas Mann had little or no trouble gaining entry, as their presence operated 'to symbolise both the barbarism of Nazi Germany and the best aspects of American democracy'. Litvinoff (1989: 297) observes that such figures were so desirable to host countries that they became the object of competitive efforts: 'visas existed in abundance for the eminent. Competition waxed furious among the world's universities for celebrated [Jewish] writers and scientists. Everyone wanted the Nobel laureates'. He adds that, 'money too could speak all languages' (ibid), so that the few who were able to escape fascism accompanied by their capital were also accommodated. The vast majority of Jewish asylum-seekers – the workers, craftspeople, small traders, professionals, unemployed and orphaned children who were the anonymous applicants queuing outside the consulates – continued to face a web of restrictive regulations.

The governments of Britain, the United States and other states which were desired countries of asylum were not focused upon the 'redemptive' anti-Semitism which led Nazism to campaign for the annihilation of its imagined enemy. They did, however, draw upon ideologies of assertive nationalism. They were obsessed with surveillance and control of populations within which they too saw alien elements, usually ethnic minorities, and against which they organised formal discrimination. This helped to create the circumstances within which currents of the right could grow, intensifying demands for exclusion or focusing attention on domestic minorities. The state nourished the discourse of the alien, promoting a 'fundamental ambivalence to Jews and Jewish suffering' (Bloxham and Kushner 2005: 194). Throughout the 1930s the United States and European states discussed refugee issues as problems associated with instability and disorder. Displaced people were identified with conflict and social turmoil. Their presence as refugees, it was argued, would threaten domestic order: they were unwelcome and should be contained as far as possible within the area of their displacement. International collaborations confirmed the local pattern. In 1938 the Evian Conference notionally provided an opportunity for change. In fact it marked an accommodation to the regime in Germany, encouraging the latter to believe that it could continue persecution unchallenged. Evian demonstrated the extent to which, even if they did not endorse Nazi practices, governments of the liberal democracies recognised and comprehended them. The policies of Hitler could be seen as extreme and as potentially destabilising but could be 'understood'. Loescher (1993: 45) passes a damning verdict:

> Germany regarded Evian and the Western nations' policy of closing their doors against refugees as exonerating its policies and began to use more draconian measures to rid the Third Reich of its Jewish population. Thus, the subsequent mass murder of Jews by the Nazis was tacitly tolerated by most of the Western world until it was too late for effective counteraction.

The politics of exclusion had an inexorable logic. In conditions of general crisis borders were strengthened within and between states. A discourse of the alien became general among establishment politicians, whose rationales for exclusion became part of the practice of the state at the national and local levels. The victims of Nazism were aliens in Nazi-occupied territories; when they attempted to flee they remained aliens who, it was believed, would continue to threaten states in which they sought asylum. It is in this context that Feingold (1980: xiii) comments of policies in the United States that the root of the problem lay less in the State Department or in the attitudes of specific officials than in 'the nature of the nation-state itself'.

Notes

1. In this chapter I have examined a complex literature dealing with the refugee crises of Europe in the 1930s, including developments leading to the Holocaust. For a perceptive analysis of contending views see Bloxham and Kushner 2005.

2. These observations by Macmaster (2001: 64–5) are developed in an insightful analysis of the relationship between slavery, colonial rule and the metropolitan order.

3. Quoted in Marrus 1985: 28.

4. Macmaster 2001: 94. Use of the term, with its implications of 'racial' difference, marked a change from earlier anti-Jewish attitudes, with their emphases on religious identity.

5. The Aliens Act 1905, Section 1[2].

6. Between 1870 and 1923 world trade grew by an average of 3.4 percent a year. Harman 1996: 6.

7. Quoted in Kushner and Knox 1999: 44.

8. In a very striking exception to this pattern, the revolutionary government which took power in Russia in 1917 facilitated formation of independent states and their secession from the former Russian empire. Most soon declared for federation with the Soviet republic. Many were in ethnically complex regions in which, at first, minorities were accommodated; Stalinism later asserted Russian cultural hegemony and denied all but the most token forms of local self-expression.

9. Quotas for the main countries of emigration were fixed at 65,721 for Britain, Germany 25,957, Ireland 17,853, Poland 6524 and Italy 5802. Quoted in Rubinstein 1997: 33 n53.

10. It later brought greatly increased demand for labour, satisfied in part by increased internal migration, for example in the United States of Black rural populations from the South to the manufacturing centres of the mid-West.

11. France was an exception to the trend. Massive losses of men during the First World War and continued high demand for labour in agriculture and extractive industries resulted in high levels of immigration from neighbouring countries. But here too deepening recession resulted in mass deportation of non-citizens (Castles and Miller 1993: 60–1).

12. Quoted in Gluckstein 1999: 175.

13. According to Rubinstein (1997: 16) by 1939 the great majority of German Jews – no less than 72 per cent – had emigrated. This is one of many contentious statistics mobilised as part of the debate over abandonment/rescue of European Jewry. According to Fox (1988: 74) less than a third of German Jews had left by November 1938 suggesting that, if Rubinstein is correct, there was a mass exit in the 10 months before the outbreak of war. Although numbers of refugees greatly increased, the evidence does not suggest that they reached this level.

14. Nazi plans to exterminate all Jews in areas under their control were probably not formulated until 1941. See Gluckstein (1999: ch 8) for a review of contending arguments and evidence.

15. For 20 years after the war most accounts of the Holocaust focused on Nazi guilt and upon the positive actions of the Allies in ending mass extermination. From the late 1960s however a series of analyses argued that apathy or even anti-Semitism in the United States and Western Europe

contributed to the catastrophe by ensuring that governments retained or even raised obstacles to immigration. See Rubinstein 1997.

16. Quoted in Sherman 1994: 28.
17. Quoted in Kushner and Knox 1999: 149.
18. In 1930 a short-lived organisation calling itself the Black Shirts recruited 40,000 people around the slogan 'No Jobs for Niggers Until Every White Man Has a Job' (Edsforth 2000: 109).
19. Quoted in Sherman 1994: 65.
20. Quoted in Sherman 1994: 62
21. Quoted in Sherman 1994: 63.
22. Quoted in Sherman 1994: 86.
23. Quoted ibid.
24. Quoted in Sherman 1994: 98.
25. Quoted ibid.
26. Quoted in Kushner and Knox 1999: 253.
27. Admission of refugees from Spain demonstrated the effectiveness of vigorous campaigning by a network of solidarity groups in Britain. Kushner and Knox (1999: 106) show that the National Joint Committee for Spanish Relief, formed in 1937, co-ordinated at least 150 fundraising groups and that by 1939 it was associated with some 850 local and national bodies. Four thousand refugee children were eventually accepted.
28. Quoted in Sherman 1994: 32.
29. Quoted ibid.
30. Quoted in Sherman 1994: 91.

7

From Ambassadors to Aliens

Repatriation

The Second World War displaced some 40 million people across Europe.[1] Following the conflict many wished to return to their places of origin but many did not. In the light of the refugee disasters of the 1930s, their wishes might have been accommodated – in fact they were the object of a campaign of mass transportation. In 1943 the Allied powers had created the United Nations Relief and Rehabilitation Agency (UNRRA), initially charged with assisting in reconstruction and later with returning the refugees. From 1945 it set about repatriation with zeal, backed by a staff of almost 30,000 and a budget which reached the unprecedented figure of US$3.6 billion (Loescher 1993: 47). UNRRA worked closely with Allied forces to identify displaced persons (DPs), separate them into national categories, and put them in trucks and box-cars to be shipped to the countries from which they had come. The operation was conducted with only token reference to the wishes of the refugees: for those who had already been victims of the conflict, and were unwilling to be moved, it was a new forced migration.

Among those repatriated were large numbers of citizens of the Soviet Union and of Eastern European countries which soon came under Soviet control. Britain and the United States had undertaken to repatriate Soviet citizens and prisoners-of-war held by the Nazis – by force if necessary. Many were regarded with suspicion by the Stalinist regimes and ended up in labour camps; those reluctant to return were characterised by Moscow as war criminals and traitors, and in displaced persons' camps in Western Europe there were protests and even suicides among those scheduled for repatriation. Cesarani (2001: 39) notes that, 'It became necessary to move thousands of the "recalcitrants" by force, often under traumatic circumstances'. Some had been members of Nazi units recruited among Russians, Cossacks and various

141

Eastern European nationalities, and could expect summary treatment from the Soviet state. Others were simply swept up in the repatriation programme: American and British troops who 'bludgeoned' them into freight cars were deeply unhappy about their task (ibid). Opposition to the programme became so intense that special camps were established to hold those opposed to return, with the aim of preventing them from influencing other DPs.[2] Meanwhile Jewish survivors of the Holocaust, similarly categorised as aliens, were also held in camps until their fate could be decided. Kochavi (2001: 32) comments that the Allies' attitude was that Jews, like all other displaced persons, 'ought to return to their countries of origin and pick up their lives as soon as possible'. Some remained in former Nazi concentration camps for years while the authorities debated their fate: in January 1947 there were still over 10,000 Jews in Belsen–Bergen camp (Kochavi 2001: 56). UNRRA's activities only came to an end when the US government decided that continued repatriation to the Eastern bloc was assisting its Cold War rival and in 1947 it created the International Refugee Organisation (IRO), mandated to resettle those who had not been returned. The abrupt change of strategy was too late for the millions transported to the East. UNRRA had been so successful that within five months of the end of the war almost 75 per cent of all the displaced in Europe had been repatriated (Loescher 1993: 48). The organisation had not been charged with attending to the preferences of the refugees but with the priorities of states which had emerged victorious from the conflict. In the light of the events of the 1930s the strategy appears startling, and it soon become one of the most contentious matters of debate at the newly created United Nations. Why were the Allied powers intent upon re-organising, in effect eliminating, the refugee presence in Europe?

For 400 years nation-states had been premised upon ideas about difference. Among Europe's independent states the nation had been defined mainly in relation to other local powers, those in authority in each state maintaining relentless efforts vis-à-vis their rivals. Shafer (1972: 166–7) comments on developments during the nineteenth century:

> 'Other' nations were always believed to be stronger; 'other' nations' motivations were always suspect; and hence the 'other' nations were always dangerous. ... Each nation had to be strong, powerful, had to prepare for any eventuality, strengthen itself economically, acquire colonies, increase its armies, make alliances, while it did everything it could to ensure the loyalty of its own citizens. Each effort of each nation meant that other nations had not only to make similar exertions but exceed them.

The ideological accompaniment to such competition and conflict was a heightened sense of difference in relation to Others, so that as new states emerged across Europe ideas about the alien permeated the discourse of nation across a whole continent. Everywhere there were sustained attempts to marshal the population behind monarchs, governments and parties committed to the vision of nation. Histories became overwhelmingly narratives of nation, embellishing or inventing traditions in which the mass of citizens might find a focus for attachment (Hobsbawm and Ranger 1983). As a corollary, those unwilling to accept the dominant ideology were disciplined in the name of nation. Internal conflicts were often focused upon linguistic and ethnic minorities, political radicals and religious dissenters, as well as those deemed to be dysfunctional to the national project – criminals, the poor and the indigent. These groups were often declared 'alien' and were the object of campaigns of persecution which included deportation.

Everywhere the idea of national belonging was accompanied by the notion of alienage – the defining characteristic of the non-national, or the citizen deemed inadequately 'national' on account of their language, religion or antecedents. This was the basis for the first exclusionary laws in the United States and Britain. It was also the rationale for discrimination like that which penalised immigrant workers during the Depression, and in its most acute form produced the mass murders of the Nazi era. In wartime a focus upon aliens affected all combatant states: during the Second World War Britain arrested 30,000 'enemy aliens', most of German origin, among whom were many Jews recently accepted as refugees. Meanwhile the United States interned several thousand Germans and some 120,000 American citizens of Japanese origin, and launched an additional 'enemy aliens' programme to target people of Italian, German and Japanese origin living in Latin America. US forces violated the borders of 15 Latin American countries, kidnapping some 6000 people, also described as 'aliens', with the aim of using them in prisoner exchanges.[3] At the end of the war the United States forcibly 'returned' many people to Germany, including children born in the United States to immigrants of German origin. At the same time it showed extreme reluctance to accept refugees *from* Europe. Notwithstanding widespread public distress at revelations of the fate of victims of Nazism the US state maintained a policy of tight control over entry, so that even 12 months after the end of war in Europe only 5000 DPs had been accepted (Divine 1957: 113). Immigration policy had not changed since the Quota Acts of the early 1920s, and was not substantially modified until the mid-1960s: in the mid-1940s it was still marked by the commitment to maintain what Joppke (1999: 23) calls 'an ethnic core of protestant Anglo-Saxonism'. This permitted the entry of modest numbers of northern Europeans while continuing to restrict admission of others seen as definitive of the alien, notably Jews, so that American Jewish organisations were compelled to make strenuous efforts to ease controls even for survivors of the Holocaust.

This is the context in which the victorious Allies set about aligning the displaced people of Europe within the boundaries of their states of origin, seizing the opportunity of military victory to assert the national principle of political organisation by re-emplacing refugees. The project continued until the priorities of the Cold War dictated a change of strategy, although even the new policy did not imply a change in attitudes towards aliens, for the Cold War brought fears about new enemies. In the case of the United States the alien threat was said to have become ubiquitous – a Senate committee declared that the country was under immediate threat from Communism, an ideology said to have emerged in 'alien lands' (Loescher and Scanlan 1986: 28–9). In a forceful assertion of American national identity against menacing Others it declared Communism a general conspiracy antipathetic to the American character.[4] All who attempted to enter the United States – all aliens – were to be treated as potential subversives bent upon violating American traditions.

Human rights

It was in this atmosphere that the first international agreements about human rights and refugees were concluded. They were written against a background of regret for the tragedies of the 1930s also but of continuing fear and rejection of Others. They did not set out means of assuring the entitlements of those affected en masse by repression or war; rather, they were narrow formulae which focused upon the specific rights of certain individuals.

Those in authority in the modern state had long assumed that every person was allocated citizenship by the specific state with which they were associated, and they had great difficulty accommodating citizens of other states. The rights they defined were conceived as 'universal' but were shaped by a concern for specific groups of persons. Maher (2002: 21) comments of this approach that it is 'a cultural logic in which even human rights are framed as entitlements exclusive to citizens': in which 'universal personhood' is subordinated to specific citizenship. When the first statements of human rights in relation to refugees were being written, unplanned population movements – the intrusion into state territories of non-citizens – were particularly unwelcome and usually unacceptable. There was an assumption that they should be prevented, and when this was not possible, reversed as soon as possible. There was a compulsion to place aliens, non-citizens, in the correct physical space – the territory within which they had originated and in which they derived their rights.

The discourse of 'universal' rights had developed in the early 1940s, stimulated largely by discussions in the United States about involvement in the Second World War. These debates were dominated by exchanges between, on the one hand, American isolationists, and on the other hand those such as President Roosevelt who saw the pursuit of rights as a key rationale for involvement in war and as part of the effort to position the United States as the dominant state in a post-war world order. According to Roosevelt there were four key freedoms to which all should have access by right: freedom of speech, freedom of religion, freedom from fear and freedom from want. In pursuit of these freedoms for all, he argued, the United States must engage more fully in world affairs. He maintained that the four freedoms were consistent with Americans' own anti-colonial struggle and with the founding documents of the independent US state. Evans (2001: 21) suggests that they were highly selective – they were 'liberal' rights which complemented dominant ideas of the American political tradition. In effect they made general the particular entitlements enshrined in the US Constitution; at the same time – and paradoxically – they limited these entitlements, for in reality they were to be guaranteed only to specific groups of citizens.

The Charter of the United Nations, issued in 1945, made only a general statement about rights – that commitment to human rights was the basis upon which the organisation would work to prevent war, and to assert the dignity and worth of the human person. In 1948 the organisation adopted the more specific Universal Declaration of Human Rights (UDHR). This affirmed a series of rights including security of the person, freedom from slavery, freedom from arbitrary arrest or interference in private life, freedom of association, religion and opinion, right to choose a form of education, right to marry and to own property, and the right to seek and to enjoy asylum. Although these were expressed in general terms and were not binding upon states – the UDHR was not a treaty – the notion of universal rights as unconditional entitlements caused particular concern to the United States. In a world of rapid change and rising aspirations American politicians feared that such ideas could be seized upon to legitimise radical agendas which threatened US interests. Washington therefore determined to limit the discourse of rights and in particular to 'debase' debates on rights at the UN (Evans 2001: 25). These were already being shaped by the rivalries of the Cold War: while Washington argued for certain civil and political rights, Moscow minimised their importance. By the same token the United States rejected the economic and social rights advanced by the Eastern Bloc and by many newly independent states of the Third World. It opposed the right to safety in the face of war, generalised violence or natural disaster; the right to work; rights to education, health and housing; and collective representational rights such as those of organised labour. At the United Nations it withdrew from most formal debates on the subject, with the result, suggests Moskowitz, that for years an organisation founded upon the commitment to rights 'pirouetted around a missing centre'.[5]

The Convention Relating to the Status of Refugees, the Geneva Convention, was shaped by similar concerns. Since it was approved in 1951 the Convention has often been seen as a model statement of asylum rights: the UNHCR (1995: 58), for example, has viewed it as a statement of 'fundamental rights and freedoms'. In fact the agreement set out a narrow and partisan approach. During the 1940s discussions about the Convention were dominated by the United States and its European allies, not only because of their general influence in world affairs but because states of the Eastern Bloc, with the exception of Yugoslavia, boycotted the proceedings. There were disputes, nonetheless, among the Western allies: Britain wished for a broad definition of the refugee and a formulation which would accommodate those who might be displaced in the future. The United States and France wanted a much narrower definition and insisted on restricting the formula to people displaced within Europe. Given US dominance the outcome was not in doubt: when the agreement was finalised it was applied only to those who had become refugees in Europe and only as a result of events occurring before 1 January 1951. In addition, the Convention viewed the refugee as a person denied specific civil and political rights: there were no references to economic and social rights. The key issue was that of 'persecution'. Loescher (2001: 44) comments that this was made to fit 'a Western interpretation of asylum-seekers'. He observes bluntly 'The Convention was intended to be used by the Western states in dealing with arrivals from the East, and largely reflected the international politics of the early Cold War era' (ibid). It perceived refugees to be victims of oppressive, totalitarian regimes, with the implication that the guilty parties were to be found east of the Iron Curtain. It was not intended to embrace refugees in general, groups of displaced people, or those fleeing from international or internal conflicts. Most important it did not mention a 'right' to asylum. Contrary to many later interpretations it was not a statement of universal rights in the form of unconditional entitlements of displaced people.

Despite these very severe limitations the United States did not ratify the Convention or back the UNHCR, which had been established in 1950 as a dedicated body with responsibilities for refugees. The United States already had full control over the IRO and its activities, and expected the same authority over the UNHCR. When this was not forthcoming from the United Nations the United States boycotted the UNHCR, treating it as 'a sideshow and as a mostly irrelevant organization' (Loescher 2001: 54). Meanwhile it ignored the Convention, which had been largely written by its own officials, producing instead a new law based paradoxically upon a much more open definition of the refugee. The Refugee Relief Act (RRA) of 1953 appeared to offer asylum to most forced migrants. It declared that a refugee was:

> any person in a country or area which is neither Communist nor Communist-dominated, who because of persecution, fear of persecution, natural calamity or military operations is out of his usual place of abode and is unable to return thereto, who has not been firmly resettled, and who is in urgent need of assistance for the essentials of life or for transportation.[6]

Under the RRA refugees were not only to be admitted to the United States on the grounds of persecution but because of all manner of problems including the catch-all 'calamity'. Loescher and Scanlan (1986: 46) comment that the Act 'effectively eliminated the need to distinguish so-called "economic migrants" from "political refugees" '.[7] Among its most important provisions were means to accommodate certain groups of 'escapees' from the East, together with communities of Southern Europeans whom the administration wished to accept for reasons of electoral advantage.[8] Under the Act, over 200,000 people were admitted in the first major transAtlantic immigration since the Quota Acts of the 1920s. Both the Convention and the RRA demonstrated how, in the post-war era, refugees remained objects of instrumental political initiatives.

'Ambassadors'

For two decades after the Second World War refugees occupied a special status. They were viewed in the West as individuals whose specific experiences of persecution under repressive regimes made them deserving of sanctuary. Those accepted originated almost exclusively within countries of the Eastern Bloc – as 'escapees' from Stalinist rule they moved in small numbers from East to West. Large groups were rarely accepted – the early exceptions being the Southern Europeans received in the United States under the RRA. In the context of superpower rivalries refugees had great ideological significance. Their flight was depicted as a rejection of Communism and their presence in the West as testimony to the virtues of liberal democracy. They were identified as citizens of states which had disenfranchised their populations – they were victims of culpable action undertaken by totalitarian regimes and were entitled to sanctuary and to enjoy rights denied by their 'own' states.

The 1951 Convention prescribed that eligibility for asylum should be assessed on the basis of 'well-founded fear of being persecuted' for reasons of race, religion, nationality, membership of a particular social group or political opinion. The formula embraced 'persons' – anyone whose appeal to rights as an individual might be endorsed by the receiving state. But such rights were limited to those favoured by Western states and in effect they defined the social status of migrants such states were prepared to accept. The Stalinist regimes imposed forms of exploitation and of repression which abused whole populations but Western governments were interested in selected victims: those educated and preferably articulate individuals who could testify to their particular predicaments. In the United States the National Security Council was precise about its preferences, believing that damage to Eastern bloc states and advantage to the West would be maximised when 'emigration pertained to professionals'.[9] Tuitt comments of those granted asylum at this period that they were largely 'of an elite class able to perform a relatively sophisticated ambassadorial role on behalf of the host state, albeit unwittingly' (Tuitt 1996: 17). They functioned as 'ambassadors of the Cold War period … living witnesses of "corrupt", "evil" and "oppressive" governments and to the "heraldry" of the host state' (ibid). To assist in recruitment of such ambassadors, the United States in 1951 established the Inter-governmental Committee for European Migration (ICEM) and the following year initiated the United States Escapee Program (USEP).

In 1952 President Truman spelt out the official approach towards refugees, emphasising the importance for the US state of citizens of Eastern Bloc countries:

> we want to stretch out a helping hand, to save those who have managed to flee into Western Europe, to succor those who are brave enough to escape from barbarism, to welcome and restore them against the day when their countries will, as we hope, be free again.[10]

These offers were particularly striking in view of refugees' predicaments outside Europe. At the end of the Second World War the retreat of colonial powers and the emergence of new states had brought huge population movements, especially in Asia and the Middle East. In 1947 over 11 million people crossed border zones during the partition of India, and a year later almost a million Palestinians fled to neighbouring Arab states. These were dramatic collective movements which shaped the circumstances of large numbers of people and had enormous significance at the level of regional politics. But in the context of what Suhrke (1997: 219) calls the 'Eurocentric orientation of the early refugee regime' they were ignored or approached quite differently to those in Europe. In a comment which anticipated many later reactions in the West to refugees in the Third World, *The Times* of London laid blame for turmoil in India upon the refugees themselves. It identified them as 'carriers of an infectious hysteria or mental derangement' that was a principal cause of unrest.[11] The IRO, mandated to operate only in Europe, refused to intervene. In the case of Palestine, where the United States judged that the risk to Western interests was much greater, a special agency was established with the aim of managing the refugees and containing their potentially destabilising influence. The United Nations Relief for Palestinian Refugees, later renamed the United Nations Relief and Works Agency (UNRWA), was created to administer refugee camps and work programmes so as to minimise disturbance to the Arab states – displaced people from Palestine having been distributed across four neighbouring countries. The US Secretary of State told Congress that this was an essential measure to safeguard against Communist subversion in the region.[12]

The United Nations was also represented in Korea – but for different reasons. The Korean War of 1950 to 1953 directly engaged the superpowers and its crises of mass displacement produced an immediate response, with refugees from Communist North Korea received enthusiastically in Western-backed South Korea. Contrary to the provisions of the Convention and the mandate of the UNHCR, Koreans benefited from a huge UN relief effort. This was achieved by the establishment of another independent organisation – the United Nations Korean Reconstruction Agency (UNKRA), for which the United States agreed to pay up to 70 per cent of all costs. Meanwhile the United States still refused to contribute to the UNHCR. Despite a warning from the latter's secretary general that for want of money it would be condemned to simply 'administer misery', the Americans continued to view the agency with suspicion (UNHCR 2000: 22).[13] In Europe, Washington lavished support on USEP – the escapee program. In 1951 Congress agreed to spend a vast sum, up to US$100 million, on assistance to escapees from the East, defined in a new act as those likely to 'contribute to the defense of the North Atlantic area and to the security of the United States'.[14] Those who escaped from Eastern Bloc countries were screened in reception centres in Western Europe, usually by US Military Intelligence, and when judged useful for 'psychology warfare purposes' were used by American intelligence groups and by radio stations which broadcast to the East, notably Radio Free Europe and Voice of America.[15] Meanwhile the Stalinist regimes made their own contribution to this tug-of-war, organising in remaining refugee centres in Western Europe and encouraging re-defection to the East. Conditions in the camps were often very poor and these efforts met with considerable success – a key factor causing the United States eventually to turn to the UNHCR and its programmes for refugee support and settlement in Europe. When the United States finally backed the organisation in 1955 it was 'in our own self-interest'.[16]

Cold War preoccupations shaped international refugee policy for the next 15 years. In the case of the Hungarian uprising in 1956, which produced 200,000 refugees,[17] the main factor influencing governments in the West was a continuing desire to seek advantage vis-à-vis regimes of the Eastern Bloc. But Western states were also under pressure from their own populations to accept the refugees – there were demonstrations of support for the Hungarians which governments committed to Cold War rhetoric found it difficult to ignore. They could only offer asylum, however, by modifying or reinterpreting the Geneva Convention, which applied strictly to those displaced by events before 1951. The Hungarians were therefore designated refugees on the basis that their displacement was the outcome of events before that date: in effect the Convention was modified to allow for a new collective refugee. So too with the UNHCR mandate, which was reinterpreted in order that the organisation should play a leading role in managing the migrants.[18] The question of settlement in Western Europe was relatively straightforward. Most refugees were young, skilled and well educated: Loescher (2001: 87) describes their exit from Hungary as a 'brain drain' which greatly benefited labour-hungry economies. There were problems in the United States, however, where immigration law was still restrictive and suspicion of aliens, especially incomers from Eastern Europe, a strong influence. Eventually the administration agreed to 'parole' selected aliens into the country, receiving what one official called 'a valuable economic bonus' (ibid).

'New' refugees

It was another ten years before dominant world powers began to make real changes to the international refugee regime. By the late 1960s the long boom of the world economic system which followed the Second World War had started to falter; struggles for independence from colonial rule had intensified, and political instability was becoming more general. The mandate of the UNHCR was modified several times, so that the agency's 'good offices' could be extended to people displaced by war and other local disruptions. A new status emerged, that of the *de facto* refugee, a forced migrant in need of sanctuary and given tacit recognition through forms of 'temporary' asylum, often negotiated by the UNHCR. By 1969 two-thirds of the organisation's programme funds were being spent in Africa, illustrating the shift in its geographical focus over the course of a decade (UNHCR 2000: 37). Most refugees were now part of mass population movements and increasingly these affected whole regions, with the result that refugees were compelled to travel greater distances to find security. Suhrke (1997: 219) comments, 'The West recognised that if left unassisted, large refugee populations could cause instability and create situations ripe for exploitation by radical or Communist forces.' In 1967 a Protocol was signed in New York giving worldwide applicability to the Geneva Convention, and the UNHCR became a body with a world mandate. Even the United States acceded to the agreement: worried that refugee communities would become 'seedbeds of instability' it endorsed the organisation as a vehicle for intervention in crisis zones of the Third World.[19]

The 1970s was a decade of repeated economic crises and political upheavals. For Western states it had become a matter of urgency to see refugees *contained*, as far as possible within their areas of origin. The Convention had originally focused upon a migrant who was able to journey into exile in North America or Western Europe – typically this had been an individual adult male from an Eastern Bloc country. By the 1970s, however, the majority of refugees were women and children in vulnerable regions of the Third World who had fled hunger, famine, economic collapse, state repression or civil conflict – or combinations of these. The idea of overseas resettlement, which had underpinned the whole approach to the European refugee problem, was judged not to be an option for these new migrants. Some Western states continued to accept refugees from political conflicts on programmes which had continuity with the earlier Cold War reception projects: Chileans and Vietnamese, for example, were viewed as victims of specific persecutions by the state of origin and some found their way to the West on quota programmes. But they were already exceptions to a new rule: most refugees no longer provided a means of ideological self-assertion for Western governments; rather, they were problem-people, whose predicaments raised uncomfortable questions about the legacy of colonialism and the instability of the world system.

'Invisible' refugees

By the mid-1980s hosts of people were living in long-term exile, and a larger proportion than hitherto were becoming long-distance refugees. Some were officially recorded and received protection and various forms of support in emergency centres, holding stations and camps (see Chapter 10). An increasing number, however, encountered a fundamental problem – that of their visibility as refugees. The right to asylum defined in the 1951 Convention was limited to those experiencing forms of persecution associated with the formal politics typically

conducted by men. The Convention excluded most activities in which
women might be the key actors – economic and social life and the
'private' sphere in general. States and refugee agencies had assumed
passivity of the female in the political arena, viewing women's beliefs,
activities and statuses as meaningful only in relation to those of male kin
or male activists. Since 1951 refugee law had been refined largely
though the examination of cases in which men were applicants for asylum, women appearing only incidentally as dependent relatives of adult
males or as subordinates of political activists who were also invariably
men. For Tuitt (1996: 25) the authorities' concern with 'malehood,
adulthood and conventional sexual and social mores' had produced a
'mythical' refugee. Meanwhile the pattern of economic and political
development worldwide ensured that women faced increased pressure
in every area of their lives, making it more and more likely that they
would be centrally involved in crises of mass displacement.

The 'new wars' had already produced a new pattern of civilian involvement. They involved not only forces of the state but also paramilitaries,
militias and informal armed groups, among which conventional warfare
was often less important than strategies of terror in which non-
combatants were the key target (see Chapter 11). The outcome was an
unprecedented number of civilian casualties. In the First World War the
proportion of civilian casualties was 5 per cent; in the Second World War
50 per cent; in the Vietnam War 80 per cent; by the 1990s the figure had
reached over 90 per cent (Summerfield 1995: 17). Women and children,
who were in general non-combatants, accounted for most of the dead
and injured; they also featured prominently in associated mass displacements. Meanwhile women had also become a particular target. During
periods of social crisis, civil conflict and war, gender relations become
increasingly important. Women are invariably central to the definition of
cultural authenticity, being viewed as a repository of key communal
values and an expression of identity of the kin group, ethnic collectivity
or nation. Not only are they reproducers in the biological sense but
through parental and familial relations women transmit core cultural
values which maintain the integrity of the group. Subordinated in formal
economic and political life, they are exalted in the context of community
and of national culture, often appearing as maternal figures representing
collective identity and honour. Yuval-Davis (1997: 45) comments

> A figure of a woman, often a mother, symbolises in many cultures the spirit
> of the collectivity, whether it is Mother Russia, Mother Ireland, or Mother
> India. In the French revolution its symbol was 'La Patrie', a figure of a
> woman giving birth to a baby; and in Cyprus, a crying woman refugee on
> roadside posters was the embodiment of the pain and anger of the Greek
> Cypriot collectivity after the Turkish invasion.

Women are also central to the domestic agendas of national groups and nation-states. They may be invoked to produce more children or even compelled to do so; alternatively women's membership of certain ethnic groups or social classes may mean that they are targeted in efforts to reduce fertility. All states regulate marriage and may limit or forbid union between those of certain statuses, ethnic or religious groups: it is usually women who are targeted and who lose citizenship rights if they marry outside the community. Women usually define the limits of the group and, when boundaries become more fluid or are under threat, gender relations take on increased importance. Moghadam (1994: 2) observes,

> Women frequently become the sign or marker of political goals and of cultural identity during processes of revolution and state-building, and when power is being contested or reproduced. Representations of women assume political significance, and certain images of women define and demarcate political groups, cultural projects, or ethnic communities. Women's behaviour and appearance – and the acceptable range of their activities – come to be defined by, and frequently are subject to, the political or cultural objectives of political movements, states and leaderships.

When conflict intensifies women can become a key target. In the assault upon women, men of the community are also humiliated and weakened – hence sexual violence is an instrument of state repression and of war and is used systematically against communal enemies. When rival groups with ethnocentric/ national agendas collide the cost to women may be enormous, as during inter-ethnic conflicts in the former Yugoslavia in the 1990s when soldiers of all the contending groups engaged in rape (Korac 1998). Taylor (1999: 157) notes that in the case of Rwanda the incidence of rape in peacetime was relatively low. In the early 1990s, as communal tensions intensified, it increased dramatically. Violence was directed primarily against Tutsi women by Hutu militias: in the light of later events it can be seen as a prelude to genocide. During the mass killings of 1994 tens of thousands of women were abused, mutilated and murdered, suffering rape, oblation of breasts, evisceration (especially among those bearing children), impaling, forced incest and forced cannibalism of family members. Taylor (1999: 105) suggests that these were assaults on the Tutsi as a group, which aimed to attack the capacity to reproduce and to destroy core cultural symbols by negating the female as an expression of collective identity. The Rwandan events were particularly traumatic but there have been many other conflicts in which women have been targeted in similar ways even if the scale of the atrocity has been less appalling. Along with rape goes the exploitation of women and girls seized by armies or militias and compelled to work as cooks, maids, labourers and/or prostitutes – part of the utilisation of the most vulnerable which also produces the phenomenon of child soldiers. In all these respects women have featured as victims, but in some conflicts they have played an active public role, contesting their persecution as women directly, or participating on the same basis as men – joining armies and militias in which they have taken leadership positions, and in which they too have been responsible for abuses, including those directed against women and children.

By the late 1980s changing patterns of conflict showed overwhelming evidence of the fuller involvement of women, most as victims: so too with the pattern of forced migration. The contradiction between the actuality of refugee movements and the expectations of the international legal regime had become acute, for the legitimate refugee was still the adult male political activist identified by the Convention, an individual whose civil rights had been violated by an authoritarian state unfriendly to the West.

Hordes of aliens

Since the 1980s all refugees wishing for recognition in countries of the West have been confronted by an apparently contradictory asylum regime. On the one hand, they have been required to demonstrate *individually* their fear of persecution. On the other hand they have been treated increasingly as collectives – as groups of aliens who pose a general threat to their potential hosts. The standard reference to refugees in Europe, North America and Australia has suggested movements of dehumanised masses. They have been described as moving in 'hordes', 'waves', 'surges' and 'tides', threatening to 'inundate' host states (see Chapter 10). With rare exceptions the particular circumstances faced by those involved have not been examined publicly; refugees have seldom been invited to account in detail for their flight or to reflect upon its wider significance. This is a stark contrast to the refugee discourse of the Cold War period, when those who had escaped regimes of the East were encouraged to attest to the shortcomings of Communism. Their presence in exile was an assertion of values of the host society – a mirror within which the protagonists of ideological conflict could admire their works and which could be mobilised within popular constructions of liberal democracy. The presence of refugees of Third World origin, who were often poor, female, and lacking formal education, had different implications. It focused anxieties about an unstable world – a system which would not operate according to the economic and political principles to which Western governments were attached.

In the United States asylum had long been used blatantly as an ideological weapon. Between 1956 and 1968 a total of 233,436 refugees were accepted for asylum: all but 925 were from Communist countries (Loescher 2001: 55). Over the next 20 years the pattern hardly changed, even by 1986 over 90 per cent of all those granted refugee status originated in states with Communist or radical nationalist governments (Sjoberg 1991: 10). Refugees from states friendly to the United States were routinely denied admission, whatever their circumstances: the United States simply had no policy for accommodating them. During the 1970s tens of thousands of people fled Haiti, Guatemala and El Salvador, all ruled by strongly pro-American regimes. They were classified in the United States as 'no status' and denied asylum; many were imprisoned until they could be expelled. In the case of Haiti, ruled by a particularly ruthless and aggressive regime, 30,000 people fled to the United States between 1972 and 1980; less than 50 – a fraction of 1 per cent – were granted asylum (Sjoberg 1991: 9). From the early 1980s the numbers of those seeking entry to the United States grew rapidly. Economic crisis in Central America impoverished tens of millions of people who were forced from the countryside into the cities and among whom many attempted to move on to the United States (see Chapter 8). Meanwhile conflicts in states such as El Salvador, Guatemala and Nicaragua led over 500,000 people to flee to Mexico, from which many attempted to move further north. Washington treated them officially as illegals liable to arrest, detention and deportation. The United States now took great care to separate its traditional policy of mobilising refugees for ideological purposes from notions about playing host to them. When refugee groups were sponsored as part of Cold War campaigns to contest Soviet influence their activities were backed largely *within* the region of conflict, so that although the United States financed and equipped the anti-Soviet Afghan *mujahidin* for over a decade, Washington did not embrace Afghan refugees. A decade after the Soviet invasion, with several million Afghans displaced into neighbouring countries, only 22,000 had been offered asylum in the United States (Zolberg 1989: 154).

In Europe the negative response to refugees was even more marked, partly because of an unprecedented level of collaboration on asylum policy among EU governments. Refugees were recast as key figures within national and pan-European political discourse. They ceased to represent the struggle for freedom from totalitarianism of the East, becoming variously illegal, opportunistic and fraudulent, and presented once more as alien within Western culture. Here alienage was not merely a legal status but a condition of people deemed out of place because of their *fundamental* difference vis-à-vis the host society. Since the early 1980s intensification of racism in Europe has been closely

associated with crises of the regional economy. Joly (1996: 21) comments on the close link between economic circumstances and attitudes
towards migrants: 'In times of economic boom [immigration] policies
are generally more generous and relaxed', while in times of recession
migrants can be identified as 'competitors threatening the jobs of
autochtonous people'. Such 'competitors' are officially excluded on the
basis that as aliens they do not enjoy rights accorded to citizens.
Drawing upon a long history of official discrimination, this practice has
heightened popular awareness of the alien, legitimising and encouraging perceptions of difference and facilitating the spread of racist ideas.

In the mid-1980s Western European governments began to lay the
foundations of a region sealed against the majority of immigrants.
Harmonised legislation on immigration made for a 'Fortress Europe'
which measured the alien in legal terms; at the same time it was an
active element in the making of popular racism, with its perceptions
of essential biological/cultural difference. State-sanctioned policies of
exclusion have since stimulated and been stimulated by organised racist
currents, so that it is difficult to separate the action and interaction of
the two. The outcome is clear, however: refugees have become central
to the discourse of racism and have become targets of a rejuvenated
European fascist movement. During the 1980s the extreme Right
re-emerged from the margins of European politics to target enemies
familiar from an earlier era – Jews, gypsies, homosexuals, Communists –
and also migrants of Third World origin. Jean-Marie Le Pen, leader of
the Front National (FN) in France, conjured the vision of an immigrant
'invasion' which would submerge Europe under a 'wave of Third World
misery', bringing crime, delinquency, drug trafficking, moral permis-
siveness and general breakdown of law and order (Evans 1996: 49). In
Germany his co-thinkers targeted migrants in general and asylum-
seekers in particular: the German People's Union (DVU) called upon
German citizens to stem a 'flood' threatening to 'swamp' the indigenous population (Evans 1996: 48). As in racist propaganda of an earlier
era, biological metaphors were mobilised to emphasise the dangers
presented by these new enemies: the DVU, for example, described
refugees as bearers of 'plague' (ibid). They were viewed as a pathological influence, one which weakened the healthy body of the host society
and must be excised. In the mid-1980s official hostility to refugees
greatly encouraged the extreme Right. Bosswick (2000: 47) comments
on the 'obvious' link between heated public debate in Germany and
attacks on refugees and foreigners in general. In 1986–87, during the
course of a bitterly contested national election campaign, violent
attacks on foreigners increased by 134 per cent (ibid). The German
government identified the presence of refugees as a key problem and
argued that numbers must be reduced in order to combat the violence.

A new Aliens Act came into force in 1991, aimed to speed up process-ing of refugees and expulsion of most applicants. The following year violent offences against foreigners almost doubled: over three years to 1993 almost 50 migrants were murdered (Bosswick 2000: 48).

During the 1980s economic recession across Europe provided the Right with new opportunities, and in a series of countries fascist currents made spectacular electoral gains. Mainstream political parties in fear of losing votes responded by adopting increasingly racist poli-cies. In France the future Gaullist Prime Minister Alain Juppe joined with other conservatives to declaim, 'we must stop this invasion', while his campaign newspaper evoked the link between 'clandestine immigra-tion, delinquence and criminality' (Fysh and Wolfreys 1998: 44). A leading regional politician declared against asylum: according to the mayor of Toulon,

> [France] was never supposed to have a role as a refuge for the unemployed of Africa and Europe. Our country has become a dustbin for the collection of revolutionaries, delinquents and anarchists of all types. We should kick them out. (Fysh and Wolfreys 1998: 45)

By the 1990s refugees were viewed by much of the political establish-ment and by the media as menacing to European society. In a typical assessment the British Conservative Tom Spencer, leader of the European Parliament's Security and Defence Policy Committee, warned of immense pressure from people of the Third World. In an echo of Kaplan's warning to the West of Third World 'anarchy', Spencer argued that economic crisis, population growth and political collapse were likely to drive northward tens of millions of desperate people – 'the wretched of the earth' – and called for urgent exclusion-ary action before 'civilisation' was submerged by a 'tide of misery' (*Independent*, 11 June 1997). In France, asylum-seekers were suspected of being *clandestins*, in Italy they were *clandestini*, while in Britain they were 'bogus' applicants seeking to exploit a credulous host society and its welfare state. In Germany the government borrowed language routinely used by fascist groups to declare refugees unwel-come. In 1997 Foreign Minister Klaus Kinkel declared that no more refugees could be accommodated because 'our boat is practically full'.[20] This phrase had been first been used in Switzerland in the 1930s when Jews from Germany were refused asylum;[21] later it became a slogan of the neo-Nazi Republican Party (REP). Vachudova (2000: 156) comments that Europe's political leaders had taken on the preoccupations of the extreme right: 'In essence, they co-opted the extreme right's diagnosis of what was ailing society (foreigners) as well as its prescribed cure (the removal of foreigners).' As restrictive policies were harmonised across the European Union the extreme Right saw some of its earlier demands implemented. External borders of the Union were policed in the style of the former Stalinist regimes, but now to keep migrants out, while tens of thousands of asylum-seekers were arrested and incarcerated in holding centres and prisons (see Chapter 12). In Italy a government campaign to arrest and deport asylum-seekers was accompanied by demands from the parliamentary right that immigrants should be tat-tooed with identification codes (*Guardian,* 7 August 1998). This bla-tant reference to Nazi practices of the 1930s showed how official policy towards refugees encouraged a politics earlier dismissed as barbarism.

Scapegoats

The 'tide of misery' which bore new threats towards Europe was iden-tified primarily with the Third World. From the late 1980s, however, an older enemy was conjured by the extreme Right and soon by the state itself. Collapse of the Stalinist regimes had been accompanied by an efflorescence of local nationalisms in Eastern Europe and the re-emergence of open hostility towards ethnic minorities, especially the Roma. The revolutions of 1989 and 1990 led people of the region to anticipate further progressive change. Instead implementation of the market model brought increased inequality, and widespread immisera-tion and social dislocation. Over the next decade Roma communities which had long been marginalised came under increased pressure, sometimes facing physical assaults on a massive scale. Kenrick comments that this came at a time when European governments were officially commemorating the Holocaust:

> As we recall the events of the Nazi period, it is shocking to see the beginnings of a new genocide against Gypsies in eastern Europe. Romanies have replaced the Jews as scapegoats for real or imagined ills of the majority population. (Kenrick 1998: 13)

Roma were among the first from the East to claim asylum rights in the European Union – and among the first to experience attacks from organisations of the Right that were gaining in confidence. In Germany the DVU and the REP targeted them 'as non-conformist nomads, part of a general "gypsy plague" engaged in the systematic harassment of ordinary citizens' (Evans 1996: 48). When Roma moved further west, attempting entry into Britain, France and Spain, they met a similar response. In Britain the provincial press led a furious racist campaign, branding Roma 'bootleggers', 'scum of the earth' and 'human sewage'; one editorial proclaimed: 'We want to wash them down the drain'.[22] The attacks were so widespread that the Refugee Council (1999) identified a 'media pogrom'. Large numbers of Roma were imprisoned and deported – a fate they also met in France and in Spain.

In 1999 there was an outcry in many European countries when the Freedom Party in Austria campaigned on the basis of an end to *Uberfremdung* – 'swamping by foreigners' – an open attack on refugees. Within a few years the party's co-thinkers in Western Europe were in government. Aggressive campaigns against refugees were conducted by populist parties in France, Belgium, Switzerland, the Netherlands, Denmark and Norway. In the Netherlands a new leader of the right, Pim Fortuyn, declared that the country was 'full', that its borders should be closed and the number of immigrants radically reduced (Marfleet 2003). A centre-right coalition government promptly took on much of his immigration and asylum agenda, introducing measures to deport 26,000 applicants for asylum who failed new tests for residence permits. Despite criticism from human rights organisations worldwide, in 2004 the Dutch authorities initiated what Fekete (2005: 11) calls 'the biggest forced exodus from Europe since the Second World War'. In Denmark the People's Party made hostility to refugees the key principle of its electoral programme: in government it soon introduced the most restrictive immigration rules in Western Europe, authorising police to return forcibly those immigrants whose applications for asylum had been refused. Domestic critics noted that 50 years earlier Danish activists had been pioneers in developing liberal asylum policies.

These regimes have been extended across Europe. Reports published by the Jesuit Refugee Service (2004) and the Institute of Race Relations (IRR [Fekete 2005]) detail measures of detention and deportation not seen on the continent since the high age of anti-alienism in the 1930s and 1940s (see Chapter 12). The IRR traces development of a co-ordinated EU policy on forced removals, including establishment of an EU Agency for the Management of Operational Co-operation at External Borders, and an Expulsions Agency dedicated to joint efforts at deportation. The overall aim, suggests Fekete (2005: 5) is 'creation of a conveyor-belt system of removals designed to meet government targets'. As part of this programme large numbers of refugees are being returned to conflict zones declared 'safe', even though EU states warn their own nationals not to enter such territories. Britain has deported to the Democratic Republic of Congo (DRC), Zimbabwe, Iraq and Afghanistan, all states experiencing intense conflict. During 2004 it compelled over 100 Somalis to enter southern Somalia, a territory without a central political authority and in which even the unrecognised Transitional National Government had warned against forced returns. Meanwhile Germany has carried out mass expulsions to Turkey; Switzerland to Senegal, Ivory Coast and the Russian

Federation; Malta to Eritrea; and Italy to Libya. In addition there have been many individual cases of enforced return to a wide range of destinations.[23] Fekete (2005: 7) observes that there is no systematic effort to monitor outcomes, despite evidence that return can be fatal for the deportees. She comments:

> asylum seekers are lower in the order of things than animals. Every cow which goes in and out of Europe is tagged, documented and monitored so that EU officials know details of its movements and its whereabouts. It is fully traceable. But the fate of asylum seekers is nobody's concern. They have less value than livestock.

Balkan 'ambassadors'

There have been recent episodes during which EU states have viewed forced migrants differently. These have served to illustrate more precisely the constructed nature of ideas about refugees. During the Bosnian war of the early 1990s almost 3 million people were displaced by ethnic cleansing. They were *collective* victims, however, and were not eligible for asylum as Convention refugees who could demonstrate individual persecution. Consistent with recent patterns of mass displacement the majority were women and children, most driven from their homes by campaigns of terror in which sexual violence was a key weapon. As the crisis intensified, EU states attempted every means to avoid offering asylum, including 'internalisation' – the provision of 'safe havens' aimed to contain refugees within the region. During the height of the conflict many Western European states demanded visas from those who had been displaced: Britain required asylum-seekers to obtain them by application to consulates in the war zone, where in fact no British consular service was functioning. When such attempts failed to discourage requests for asylum EU governments quarrelled about allocation of refugees and the problem of 'burden-sharing'. Eventually they admitted over a million refugees, most under schemes for temporary protection. No sooner did the level of conflict diminish than programmes of repatriation were under way, even though most refugees could not hope to reclaim their former homes.

Such reluctance to recognise the needs of people in immediate danger can be contrasted with attitudes of EU governments a few years later. In 1999 European states collaborated through Nato in a military offensive against Serbia, their rationales for war focusing upon the plight of refugees in Kosovo. Initiating a campaign of bombing in March 1999, British Prime Minister Tony Blair explained that European states were under an obligation to assist oppressed people in a neighbouring region.

For a few weeks Kosovan refugees were heralded, like the refugees of an earlier era, as victims of oppression who by right should be granted sanctuary, notwithstanding that they could not show reason to be admitted as Convention refugees. Applicants for asylum from Kosovo and neighbouring Albania had for several years been among those systematically excluded by countries of the EU: for a short time some were admitted to the Union as a collective refugee. When Nato's immediate military aims were achieved, however, they came under pressure to return. Van Selm (2000: 206) observes that the memory of 'those poor Kosovar refugees' soon faded, replaced by images promoted by the media of illegal migrants being smuggled into Western Europe. This 'paradoxical labelling' had first presented those in the conflict zone sympathetically; when they sought sanctuary in Europe they were transformed into the 'illegal, scrounging immigrant' (ibid).

The belief that victims of mass violence threaten the integrity of potential host states is not novel. It lay behind the strategy adopted by Allied governments in Europe in the 1940s when UNRRA moved large populations of displaced people into alignment with national frontiers in order to restore 'order'. Such demographic adjustments to rules of national identification are responses of states to increased instability. The main difference between earlier approaches and the hostile stance taken towards refugees today is that the scale of crisis at a world level is unprecedented and the obstacles erected to refugee movements are proportionately much greater.

Notes

1. Estimate of the US State Department, cited in Loescher and Scanlan 1986: 1.
2. See Salomon (1990) for an account of the activities of UNRRA and the IRO in the camps. Cesarani (2001) makes clear that among those claiming to be Displaced Persons were many Eastern Europeans and citizens of Baltic states who had been active in the Nazi forces, or who had been collaborators. The approach of the Allies towards these groups was compromised by the wish to exploit their potential in various ways: the Americans by selecting scientists and technicians they wished to use for US military programmes, and the British by their desire to import labour from selected ethnic groups (see Chapter 8).
3. For testimonies of those seized by US forces see Higashide 2000.
4. According to the committee no American would voluntarily accept Communism: 'It is inconceivable that the people of the United States would, of their own violition [*sic*] organize or become part of a conspiracy to destroy the free institutions to which generations of Americans have devoted themselves' (Loescher and Scanlan 1986: 28–9).
5. Moskovitz, quoted in Evans 2001: 25.

6. Quoted in Loescher and Scanlan 1986: 46.
7. It had been preceded by complex arguments about immigration policy within the American political establishment. Conservative opinion emphasised the integrity of US borders, the need to exclude Southern and Eastern Europeans (with the aim of perpetuating a racist immigration policy), and a mistrust of incomers that was part of the security mania of the McCarthy era. More liberal elements associated with the Truman administration wanted greater flexibility. See Loescher and Scanlan 1986.
8. The need for labour, usually a key factor in immigration policy, seems to have been a minor consideration, probably because large numbers of Mexicans were still being employed through the Bracero Program. A key issue was the president's wish to favour Greek and Italian communities in the United States which were pressing for larger immigration quotas and whose votes he was keen to secure. For a detailed discussion of these issues see Loescher and Scanlan 1986: ch 2.
9. A National Security Council document issued in 1953 was entitled 'Psychological Value of Escapees from the Soviet Union'. It stated that it was US policy to 'encourage defection of all USSR nationals as well as "key" personnel from the satellite countries', as this would inflict 'a serious psychological blow on Communism' and 'material loss to the Soviet Union' insofar as the emigration related to professionals. Quoted in Sjoberg 1991: 10.
10. Quoted in Loescher and Scanlan 1986: 26.
11. Quoted in Schechtman 1963: 98.
12. George McGhee told Congressional hearings that 'The loss of the Middle East would be a major disaster' and that all measures must be taken to ensure that the Soviet Union did not advance its position in the region in relation to the Palestine issue. He maintained: 'As long as the refugee problem remains unsolved ... attainment of a political settlement in Palestine is delayed ... [and] the refugees ... will continue to serve as a natural focal point for disruption by communist disruptive elements which neither we nor the Near Eastern governments can afford to ignore.' Quoted in Loescher 2001: 56.
13. The UNHCR continued to function largely because of support from the Ford Foundation, which gave its first grant in 1951 (UNHCR 2000: 22).
14. Quoted in Loescher and Scanlan 1986: 39.
15. Report on refugees in Austria by the US embassy in Vienna, 1955, quoted in Loescher 2001: 73.
16. Report to US Congress, quoted ibid.
17. According to the UNHCR, during December 1956 and January 1957 some 200,000 people fled Hungary, most to Austria and to Yugoslavia (UNHCR 2000: 29).
18. This involved a creative reassessment of the process through which the Convention had originally been agreed. For a detailed account see UNHCR 2000: 30–1.

19. According to a US Senate Judiciary Committee refugees might also be 'probable prey to agitators and potential reservoirs of political and quasi-military opposition to existing regimes'. Quoted in Loescher 2001: 139.
20. German Foreign Minister Klaus Kinkel, quoted in *The Guardian*, 20 March 1997.
21. See Dale 1999: 137.
22. Editorials in newspapers in the south-east of England, quoted in *The Independent*, 17 November 1998.
23. For a full account of the deportations record see Fekete 2005, chapter 3.

8

Legality and Authenticity

Who is 'illegal'?

Western states make the assumption that most applicants for refugee status are inauthentic – that they do not move under compulsion, seeking security, but are opportunists whose aim is to exploit potential host societies. Increasingly they also view refugees as 'illegals' – people who evade migration controls and who, placing themselves outside the law, abandon their rights to asylum. In the case of the United States, suggests Maher (2002: 28), migrants who have 'chosen' to cross state borders without authorisation 'are imagined to have consented to the conditions of "rightlessness" '. In the contemporary discourse of the refugee, irregular movements are associated with criminality and in particular with the activities of human smugglers and traffickers. Those involved are implicated by the authorities in transnational crime networks, with their connections to drugs- and arms-dealing, and with other activities seen to threaten the integrity of the state. They are seen as doubly duplicitous – as invoking the idea of rights while violating the legal structures which guarantee them. A mass of evidence from Europe and North America shows, however, that states themselves have facilitated the establishment of irregular networks. They have often encouraged and stimulated clandestine activity, and *at the same time* targeted 'illegals' as a malign, undesired presence. This apparently contradictory strategy is explained by the readiness of politicians to develop populist, anti-immigrant policies, and their wish to satisfy the needs of employers for cheap labour, preferably for a vulnerable and compliant workforce. The outcome is a situation congenial to employers, governments and migration agents but seldom beneficial to those compelled to enter the irregular networks.

The status of the migrant is a contingent issue. A complex of factors determine official policies: who is on the move? from which state and to which state? who is facilitating their passage? who champions their case? what are the domestic implications of their presence? Laws on exit and entry may be interpreted narrowly or very widely, or they may be disregarded or suddenly amended, rendering today's licit migrant tomorrow's law-breaker or leaving many people in an uncertain zone between legality and illegality. The key issue is the attitude of states towards particular migrants. Many states may be involved: that in the country of origin, that or those en route, and that in the country of immigration. Increasingly the status of migrants during their journey is of concern to authorities in the country of immigration, as those who travel by clandestine means are often assumed to intend a final illegal entry. Legal status may not, however, be an issue for the authorities: many 'illegal' migrants are accepted informally at their destination and occupy a quasi-legal status, and many may be amnestied or otherwise regularised. In addition informal networks often operate in collusion with employers in destination countries, and state officials may openly or tacitly endorse their activities. This creates complex problems of terminology: in this book migrants who evade controls are described as 'irregular' or 'informal': the term 'illegal' is used only to refer to breaches of specific laws, or when it is has been used by states, media, researchers or other sources.

In praise of informal migrants

For centuries refugees have used irregular means to leave their countries of origin, to travel across borders, and to enter potential host states. In the seventeenth century Calvinists fleeing France were compelled to travel clandestinely, using hired guides to help them across borders into neighbouring countries or paying to be smuggled across the Channel to England. These measures have been identified as among the characteristics which mark the Huguenots as refugees in the formal sense: as the UNHCR has observed, their movement into exile 'had many features in common with the situation of refugees today: emergency assistance, protection, refoulement, pirate attacks on "boat people" at sea, integration problems, resettlement, repatriation'.[1] There have since been many mass irregular movements supervised by agents paid to guide migrants along routes which bypass the authorities. Following the American and French revolutions of the late eighteenth century, Royalists who fled to states which were enemies of the new republics were often compelled to use underground networks. Those who facilitated their escape were lauded and even romanticised, as with the 'Scarlet Pimpernel', in whose imagined adventures, authored by the

Hungarian-British writer Baroness Orczy, French monarchists were led to safety in England.

In the twentieth century victims of fascism paid migration agents to facilitate exit from countries under Nazi control or influence, and to enter countries of refuge through informal channels. Those who worked to protect victims of Nazi persecution or to facilitate their escape, such as Oskar Schindler, Raoul Wallenberg and Frank Foley, were later lauded for their efforts even though they had engaged in specific illegal activities. Following the Second World War the United States used irregular channels of migration as part of its Cold War strategy. Its purpose was to rescue the perpetrators of war crimes: American officials arranged for the movement of hundreds of selected Nazis from Germany, together with Nazi collaborators from Eastern Europe, the Baltic states and the Balkans. Many were scientists whose expertise the United States wished to exploit for military purposes. As part of Operation Paperclip, authorised by the Truman administration in 1946, they were taken through clandestine networks and entered the United States on fraudulent visas, so that for many years their identities were concealed from immigration officials and from the wider public. According to the head of US secret operations they were 'freedom fighters' who had been allocated key roles in anti-Communist operations.[2] Later, refugees from Eastern Europe were encouraged to evade controls by organisations such as USEP, the escapee programme established by the Truman administration. The United States went to great lengths to encourage defection, even drawing into its clandestine operations the International Rescue Committee (IRC), created in the early 1930s by political radicals to assist refugees from fascism (Levenstein 1983). By the late 1940s the IRC was engaged in psychological warfare projects, intelligence gathering and systematic efforts to move selected escapees out of the Soviet Union and neighbouring states. It was financed by budgets running into tens of millions of dollars (Chester 1995). Here irregular movements, including operations hidden from most departments of the state, were endorsed by the same government which pursued vigorous campaigns of exclusion against 'alien' intruders.

At the same period a very different sort of irregular migration took 70,000 Jews to Palestine. During the 1930s the leadership of the Zionist movement had created a special agency to facilitate movement through European states and to evade controls imposed by the British colonial authorities. By the late 1940s Mossad Le'Aliya Bet, the Organisation for B [unauthorised] Migration, organised complex networks which by-passed state controls and negotiated secret agreements to allow passage through immigration checks. During 1947 and 1948 it moved Jewish refugees from cities and refugee camps all over Europe to ports at which they could embark on ships which attempted to run the British blockage on Palestine. These activities, later celebrated in the novel *Exodus* and a film of the same name, have been seen as a heroic episode in the history of the Zionist movement and the establishment of the state of Israel. The Mossad agents involved have been given a special place in Israeli history: several accounts record that they performed a mission crucial to the whole national enterprise (Hadari and Tsahor 1985, Lertal 1998). In this case irregular migration was functional to the making of the state itself.

For most of the Cold War period refugees originating in Eastern Bloc countries were accepted enthusiastically by Western governments, which often organised their irregular movements, citing refugee rights under the 1951 Convention. This had recognised, in Article 31(1), that refugees might have to use illicit means of entry into a safe country and required that host countries 'shall not impose penalties' on this account. These were among the grounds for accepting refugees from Hungary in 1956. Following the Soviet invasion, President Eisenhower committed his administration to accepting Hungarians, transporting them to the United States and resettling them as soon as possible. Despite the fact that many had left Hungary irregularly and passed through neighbouring states along clandestine routes, they were welcomed as victims of repression who enjoyed a right to asylum in the West. During the 1960s the United States also strongly encouraged irregular exit and travel from Cuba, another Cold War enemy. An official report recommended that Cubans should be mobilised not only for symbolic purposes but in order to form the basis of an exile army, 'a striking force capable of sustained guerrilla action against Castro' (Masud-Piloto 1996: 51). The United States organised an economic blockade together with an ideological offensive designed to stimulate outward movement. This included the extraordinary Pedro Plan (later the Cuban Children's Program), which attempted to persuade parents to send their unaccompanied children out of Cuba 'to avoid Communist indoctrination' (Masud-Piloto 1996: 39). Emigrants were encouraged to evade the Cuban authorities and on arrival in the United States were welcomed and absorbed into a well-financed network of agencies responsible for settlement. When US policy towards Cuba was modified attitudes changed radically: the 'refugees' of an earlier period were declared unwelcome and characterised by the federal government as illegitimate – people bent solely upon economic advance whom the United States could not be expected to accommodate, and who must be rejected because of their irregular status. Large numbers were imprisoned as 'excludable aliens' who were 'unfit for American society' (Masud-Piloto 1996: 100).

There have been hosts of similar cases. Migrants who violate laws on cross-border movement may be received by governments for which the violation itself is of exemplary value as an opportunity to seek propaganda advantage over other states. Those who move in similar circumstances may later be rejected as irregular/illegitimate by the same receiving states, even by the same governments, whose policies and 'principles' have changed. In the late 1980s European states were aware that many activists of the Democracy Movement in China had reached safety in Hong Kong, then a British colony, with the help of 'snakeheads' – crime syndicates. This did not prevent EU governments offering asylum. When repression in China continued and larger numbers of victims sought to emulate the refugees of Tiananmen by leaving through underground migration networks they were rejected as illegals. In the case of the United States, supporters of the Democracy Movement were initially given celebrity status; others who followed them by sea were declared to be participants in smuggling operations and seized as illegal immigrants (see Chapter 11). President Clinton declared that they presented a risk to US state security and ordered the National Security Council to intervene. Some of those arrested were held for years in prison without entering the process of refugee determination (Copeland 1998: 436).[3]

Amnesties

The fate of those seeking asylum cannot be isolated from wider patterns of migration and from states' changing immigration policies. Governments have long behaved as if immigration can be turned on or off at will, with the result that today's welcome guest can become tomorrow's 'illegal' immigrant. In general during periods of high demand for labour, employers and government bodies solicit migrants. Restrictions on entry may be ignored, encouraging entry of vulnerable and compliant migrants who can be exploited more intensively than those with legal status. When conditions change, states may make efforts to reduce immigration – a response to economic changes and/or to a wish to emphasise 'national' rights within all or part of the labour market. Irregular migration comes into focus, with the emphasis upon criminality of labour agents, 'facilitators' (smugglers and traffickers) and those who use their services, including refugees. Over the past 30 years these offensives have, however, been primarily of an ideological nature: states have rarely attempted to shut down immigration and have often continued in practice to accept the presence of irregulars. As a result, conclude Kyle and Koslowski (2001: 10), almost every new measure of control has *encouraged* immigration: most have been accompanied by so many 'loopholes, back doors, and side doors' that they have brought more irregular migrants, often from a wider range of countries of origin. In addition, many governments have accepted irregular migrants through the 'front door' by means of amnesty, the formal aim being to regularise their status, to guarantee rights, and to resolve complex legal issues which clutter the courts. Data from Europe and the United States show the scale of the practice.

Country	Date of amnesty	Number of applications
France	1981–82	150,000
	1997–98	152,000
Belgium	2000	60,000
Greece	1997–98	397,000
	2000–01	350,000*
Italy	1987–88	119,000
	1990	235,000
	1996	259,000
	1998	308,000
Portugal	1992–93	39,000
	1996	22,000
	2001	100,000*
Spain	1985–86	44,000
	1991	135,000
	1996	21,000
	2000	127,000
	2001	314,000*
United States	1986	2,685,000

* process incomplete.

Source: Pinkerton *et al.* 2004: 40–1.

The effects of amnesties can be dramatic: in some cases they redraw the boundaries of legality for vast numbers of people: in the United States the amnesty of 1986 brought some 2.6 million applicants, almost a quarter of the total recorded foreign population; in the case of Greece the amnesty of 1997–98 brought almost 4000,000 applications – 2.5 times the number of the recorded foreign population (Pinkerton *et al.* 2004: 40–1). The long-term impact is also of great importance, for amnesties stimulate irregular migration networks and the activities of employers who rely on them. Pinkerton *et al.* (2004: 39) observe that regularisation programmes 'have a tendency to become recurrent'. When this happens, they suggest, more irregulars may be encouraged to enter, hoping to benefit from the next round of legalisation. 'For this reason, governments usually state that they do not intend to repeat the exercise. In reality, amnesties breed: most countries that have had one go on to have another' (ibid). The practice becomes habit-forming because it offers employers and states a steady supply of labour. Its effect is that immigration control erects only notional barriers to entry or operates on the basis of informal 'rules of the game', whereby officials, employers and migration agents share an understanding that clandestine activity is part of the routine of migratory movements.

Coyotes

Miller (2001: 328) warns against 'anti-statist bias' in the analysis of policies on unauthorised migration, maintaining that this has marred much public and scholarly discourse on the issue. He argues that immigration policies are not necessarily 'evil or oppressive', and that European and North American states should take further steps to curb illegal entry (ibid). At the same time he recognises 'a terrible paradox' – the more that states enforce laws against illegal networks, the more they create conditions conducive to such activity. Nowhere is this clearer than in the United States. From the 1940s very large numbers of Mexicans entered the United States as irregulars. On one estimate, for every legal worker employed on the Bracero Program four entered irregularly (Potts 1990: 150). The US government moved between policies of tolerance and hostility: Joppke (1999: 30) describes its attitude as 'lax, with intermittent shows of toughness'. For long periods irregulars were accepted as an indispensable part of the movement from the south. Under the Texas Proviso of the Immigration and Nationality Act of 1952, inserted to accommodate the demands of the horticulture industry, employment of irregulars did not constitute the criminal act of 'harboring' – it was legal to employ irregular immigrants, who could still be deported. When major campaigns of arrest and deportation were implemented, as after the Korean War when demand for immigrant labour lessened, 'wetbacks' were pursued en masse and ejected, only for some to be readmitted legally or 'paroled' back to their original employers as irregular workers. For 20 years from the mid-1950s state and federal authorities ignored the formal status of most Mexicans who worked in the United States. This became a matter of interest only in 1973 – the year of the global oil crisis and of sudden and severe recession. Nevins (2000: 101) points out that it was at this time that the US media began to highlight problems associated with irregular entry and that national and local politicians 'helped to construct the perception of the crisis and to stoke public fears'. Senior officials revived the spectre of invasion: in 1978 the director of the CIA, William Colby, described Mexican immigrants as the greatest security danger facing the United States – a threat greater, he said, than that posed by the Soviet Union (Rodrigez 1997: 227). The result of such pressures was a new border regime which penalised those who had earlier crossed many times without hindrance.

After years of dispute about immigration between employers on the one hand, and labour unions and organisations of the Right on the other, an official report of 1980 declared that the United States could not 'become a land of unlimited immigration'.[4] It argued for 'closing the back door to undocumented/irregular immigration [and] opening the front door a little more'.[5] Mass irregular migration continued, however, and those employers who wished for a freer flow of labour lobbied aggressively for regularisation – one US senator declared that, 'The greed of the growers ... is insatiable'.[6] In 1986 Congress passed an Immigration Reform and Control Act (IRCA) which included a 'once-for-all' amnesty and permanent settlement to those who had entered without authorisation. Officials received some 2.6 million applications of which 70 per cent came from Mexicans. This was a boost for labour agents and for facilitators – the 'coyotes' who smuggled migrants across the border.[7] It recognised that there were two channels of labour supply, formal and informal, which operated in parallel. In the early 1990s, in the context of a further world recession, the anti-immigration lobby gained strength and President Clinton responded with a campaign to 'regain control' of the border with Mexico. At the same time his administration pursued neo-liberal reform in Central America, establishing Nafta and greatly intensifying pressures in Mexico for movement to the north. In 1993 it launched a series of initiatives to control irregular movements – Operation Blockade (later renamed Operation Hold-the-line), Operation Safeguard and Operation Gatekeeper; a further campaign, Operation Rio Grande, was introduced in 1997. Irregular migration nevertheless increased so that in 1995 over 1.3 million people were apprehended for crossing from Mexico 'without inspection' (Binational Study 2000: 11). This figure was a mere fraction of the total of irregular entries, as for every irregular migrant who was apprehended two or three managed to cross the border (Ghosh 1998: 10). Despite the 'crackdown', which received enormous publicity in Mexico and in the United States, by the mid-1990s a third of the 7 million people in the United States of Mexican origin were thought to be irregulars (Binational Study 2000: 7).

Decades of migration had created networks in which the distinction between formal and informal channels had been blurred, especially at times of labour shortage. Today thousands of US employers engage irregular workers, confident that the latters' vulnerability will allow evasion of social security charges, taxes and overtime pay, reducing costs by a sum which could be up to two-thirds of the wage bill. They also know that ready availability of cheap labour keeps land prices high and, correspondingly, that shortages of labour and increased wages

depress prices. Employers and coyotes have therefore for decades cultivated a mutually beneficial relationship, often drawing in state officials:
Spener (2000) shows that immigration officers and border guards have
regularly been part of the clandestine networks.[8]

Capitalism's 'lubricant'

In 1993 the INS budget began to rise and by 1997 it had doubled to
US$3.1 billion, of which some two-thirds was spent on border policing
(Eschbach *et al.* 1999: 447). Under the Gatekeeper Program the
strength of the Border Patrol was increased to 5000, triple fences were
erected in vulnerable areas, and a steel barrier constructed which
extended 100 metres into the Pacific Ocean near the city of San Diego.[9]
In addition some border areas were militarised, using units of the US
National Guard and even the regular army.[10] In 1996 a new immigration law, the Illegal Immigrant Reform and Immigrant Responsibility
Act (IIRAIRA), was introduced to speed up removal of aliens and
'phoney asylum seekers' (*Trafficking in Migrants*, December 1996).
Although there was little impact on irregular movement overall there
were fatal consequences for some of those using coyote networks, who
were compelled to attempt crossings through desert and across fast-
flowing rivers, with the result that by 1999 deaths of irregulars as the
result of heatstroke, hypothermia, exposure or drowning had increased
six times to 360.[11] The coyotes ensured that the poorest migrants faced
the greatest dangers: those with US$150 to pay might be taken to the
border where they faced a potentially fatal desert crossing without a
guide; those with US$450 might be escorted across the desert to a city
in Texas or Arizona; those with US$700 might get close escort along
tried and tested routes and make it to Los Angeles (Stalker 2001: 52).
Those not threatened by the journey itself might have a different fate:
in 1997 there were claims that federal troops had shot irregular crossers
on sight (*In Motion*, September 14 1997). By 1999, estimated Eschbach
(1999: 430), there had been 1600 deaths over the previous five years:
the victims had become the *desaparicidos* – the disappeared – of the
border. The toll rose steadily: in 2000, 490 people died attempting
the crossing (*Guardian*, May 25 2001). The American Civil Liberties
Union commented that migrants in general 'face the death penalty for
seeking a job'.[12]

Some US officials have declared that their policy is to discourage
smugglers and all irregular immigrants. This is implausible. Harris
(1996: 98) comments that in the 1980s INS patrols were 'laughably
inadequate' for the 2000-mile border with Mexico and even measures
introduced to enforce Gatekeeper restrictions could not hope to close

the frontier. In 1998 only 3.2 per cent of those detained faced proceedings and over 90 per cent returned to Mexico without penalty (Spener 2000: 122). By 2001 the INS had ceased to search for irregulars within US territory. Meanwhile sanctions against employers who routinely hired irregulars were applied so patchily that millions of irregular entrants could expect to find work without difficulty. Weiner (1995: 186) comments that in the mid-1990s few INS officials, and none at all from the Labor Department, were assigned to the task of pursuing such employers. The Binational Study (2000: 29) found that the main beneficiaries of increased controls were the coyotes, whose operations had been diversified. They offered new 'packages of services' to migrants and options to pay for the cost of clandestine border crossing, including work in pre-arranged jobs (Binational Study 2000: 28). By 2001 coyotes were said to be making more than US$600 million annually (*Guardian*, 17 March 2001).

Miller (1999: 23) notes criticisms that the US state 'tacitly tolerates unauthorized alien entry as it benefits certain politically influential economic actors'.[13] This could be put more plainly: the US state accepts irregulars because powerful business groups demand cheap and vulnerable labour. According to the Cato Institute, a conservative American think-tank, in 2001 the benefit to the US economy of importing irregular migrants amounted to US$30 billion annually (*Observer*, 3 June 2001). It described the workers as 'the lubricant to our capitalistic economy', valued especially because of the competitive advantage acquired by US companies in relation to European rivals (ibid). In this context the high-profile campaigns directed against coyote networks have not aimed to stop irregulars but have been mainly of symbolic value to politicians with populist agendas. Far from rejecting and penalising facilitators the US state has routinely made accommodation with them; it has accepted that millions of their clients will be taken on by American employers whose hiring policies are of little concern to state or federal authorities. During the 1980s and 1990s an increasing number of the coyotes' clients were forced migrants. Many had been displaced by upheaval associated directly with neo-liberal reform in Mexico and neighbouring states, others were Central Americans who had moved to Mexico as a result of war and civil conflict in neighbouring states. By the late 1980s there were up to 400,000 such cross-border migrants in Mexico, for many of whom the country was seen as 'a corridor' to the United States (Zolberg *et al.* 1989: 215). Only a fraction of them had refugee status and few expended energies securing a formal legal standing, for the priority was to move to a more secure environment. Together with Mexicans they entered coyote networks in the knowledge that for many American employers what mattered was their irregularity and suitability for intensive exploitation.

Those with a case for recognition as refugees under asylum law moved with the mass of others declared to be 'economic' migrants. By 2001 new estimates placed the number of irregular migrants at some 8.5 million (Pinkerton *et al.* 2004: 22).

France: welcoming *clandestins*

Andreas (2001: 122) sums up relationships between the US state and the irregular networks as 'conflictive but in many ways symbiotic'. In Europe the situation has been more complex but reveals a similar pattern. For over 30 years after the Second World War several European governments operated as if their migration controls did not exist – Ghosh (1998: 5) concludes that most took a 'benign' attitude towards informal entrants. In the immediate post-war period it was the French government which expressed the greatest enthusiasm for immigration. De Gaulle's appeal to make 'beautiful babies' was followed by a policy statement from government planners that population issues were 'the number one problem in the whole of French economic policy'.[14] Officials estimated that up to 5 million immigrants would be needed to restore the country to economic independence and openly welcomed undocumented workers as a way of resolving the country's employment crisis. Employers' organisations praised immigrant labour for its flexibility, lauding those 'ready to move from one region or workplace to another and, if necessary accept a period of unemployment', as well as for saving the national economy the costs of education, health care and pensions, as the migrants were largely adult, young and healthy.[15] Following Algerian independence in 1962 almost a million former colonists moved to France, the economically active element being quickly absorbed into the national workforce. In 1966, with demand for labour still rising, the Minister for Social Affairs asserted that all immigrants, including those who arrived without authorisation, were to be accepted. He declared: 'clandestine immigration in itself is not without benefit, for if we stuck to a strict interpretation of the rules and international agreements, we would perhaps be short of labour'.[16] Irregulars were acceptable to the French authorities as long as they were deemed to serve an economic purpose: in effect the state declared publicly that the law should be disregarded in the interests of employers. By the late 1960s the vast majority of immigrants were irregulars: the ONI revealed that 82 per cent of those admitted had failed to pass through formal channels and were counted as *clandestines* (Castles and Miller 1993: 68). Regularisation now became the main means of formalising the immigrant population: between 1945 and 1970 this was the principal mode of admission to residency. Collinson

(1994: 49) comments that the role of the ONI had been reduced to one of '*a posteriori* regularization of immigrants who had already entered and established themselves'.

When the labour market collapsed in 1973–74, the impact upon migrant flows was immediately clear: according to official figures, in 1971 some 212,000 migrant workers entered; by 1974 numbers had fallen to 64,000 and by 1977 to 22,000 (Potts 1990: 145). At the same time immigrants came under attack as a drain on national resources and as destructive of harmonious social relations. The ministries of the interior and of employment called attention to irregular entry and for a halt to regularisation. In 1974 the government created a new position for a Secretary of State for Immigrant Workers, who was charged with bringing order to irregular movements; it also issued a formal 'stop' order suspending entry of workers on contract. As economic growth resumed, however, both formal and informal entry continued and there were new regularisations, so that some 450,000 people were legalised in amnesties in 1981–82, 1992 and 1997. Meanwhile violations of labour law by French employers were routinely ignored. In 1981 employers were forgiven past offences if they would confirm that named irregulars wishing for regularisation had worked for them. This encouraged production of false documentation and demands from employers for payment by applicants for formal status, and while some employers sold authentication many legitimate claimants who could not afford to pay remained outside the process. Labour agents and clandestine networks received an enormous boost and were able to cement relationships with employers through whom they could in effect sell residency in France.

In the early 1990s the combined impact of world economic recession and of growth of populist movements of the Right brought stricter controls – tighter laws on entry and new visa requirements. The neo-fascist FN argued that unemployment problems were associated directly with immigration. Its main targets were refugees from Algeria, where a military coup followed by civil war had displaced hundreds of thousands of people. Irregular entries nonetheless increased: the push factor was compelling and migration networks so well established that by 1996 there were some 350,000 irregular immigrants (Ghosh 1998: 12). Under pressure from the Right the government accepted that refugee status would only be granted 'under conditions compatible with the national interest' and by 2000 the rejection rate had risen to 90 per cent (Delouvin 2000: 71). Thousands of refugees were now irregulars; to complicate matters regularisation was still taking place at such a rate that the number accepted each year exceeded the number of new formal – 'legal' – immigrants, and in 2001 French officials estimated that over 76,000 people living 'illegally' were eligible for regularisation.[17]

Germany: from guestworkers to refugees

Developments in the United States and France make it difficult to understand the assertion of some writers that anxiety about popular opinion causes governments to avoid gestures that could encourage immigration. Hollifield (2000: 150) suggests that liberal governments fear moves to expand immigrants' rights: they remain anxious that these 'could open up the floodgates ... such change (like amnesties or whole naturalizations) would send the wrong message to those wanting to immigrate'. On the contrary, for years the American and French governments sent messages which brought many migrants, albeit by irregular means. In Germany, the main country of immigration in Europe, there has been a somewhat different approach. Here the state has maintained a formal policy of close control and there have been no declarations of open borders or mass legalisations. Nevertheless by the 1990s Germany was host to the continent's largest population of irregular immigrants.

The guestworker scheme of the post-war period had initially assumed return migration. *Gastarbeiter* were normally males under the age of 40, employed on 12-month contracts, and accommodated in dormitories or hostels. Joppke (1999: 65) describes the worker's status under this arrangement as that of 'a conjuncturally disposable commodity without social reproduction and labour costs' – immigrants were units of labour with no meaningful relationships apart from those which bound them temporarily to an employer. The system aimed at 'rotation' of immigrants – in effect it provided temporary workers for permanent jobs. This brought problems for employers who wanted to retain a trained workforce. They increased pressure on the government to extend work and residence permits but the state maintained an official position which defined immigrants as disposable. The Aliens Act of 1965 set out its policy in blunt terms: immigrant labour was to be 'a manoeuvrable resource ... for solving ... economic problems'.[18] This arrangement provided labour *and* allowed federal authorities to control formal, contract-based immigration through the BfA. Thus when the long boom of the world economy suffered from the first tremors of a new world recession the number of migrant workers in Germany was reduced rapidly – from 1.3 million in 1966 to 903,000 in 1968 (Potts 1990: 141–2). Continuing rapid growth then produced a huge increase in numbers, to 2.6 million by 1973 (ibid). Migrant labour was operating as a *Konjunkturpuffer*, a 'buffer' against effects of cyclical economic change.

In 1973 the *Anwerbestopp* – recruitment stop – brought a modified approach. There is strong evidence to suggest that freezing of recruitment was less a mechanical response to immediate or anticipated 'excess' of labour (demand for low-cost labour persisted) than to the government's anxiety to avoid 'social tensions'.[19] In effect it wished to maintain control over immigration and at the same time to pre-empt demands from political rivals who sought to mobilise around populist anti-immigrant agendas. Following the *Anwerbestopp* immigration at first fell sharply and Right-wing politicians demanded deportations and rigorous implementation of 'rotation' – a means of ensuring that immigrants would not be allowed to return. As anti-immigrant sentiment intensified, those who applied for refugee status attracted special hostility. The term *Asylant*, often with a pejorative connotation, emerged within the state apparatus and was used widely in election campaigns by parties of the Right, which called for more forceful immigration control. In 1980 attacks on refugees resulted in the murder of two Vietnamese in a hostel in Hamburg. There were to be more killings.

With the *Anwerbestopp* guestworker status came into question. Foreign workers were now depicted less as a resource than as a threat and demands for rotation became more insistent even though they were not translated into government policy. In fact rotation/deportation was never an option. Key areas of German industry had for years been wholly dependent upon these workers. Sixty per cent of all immigrants were employed in the key export industries of mechanical engineering and chemicals, while 45 per cent were employed in manufacturing, the driving force in national economic growth (Harris 1996: 10). Many major factories were entirely reliant upon foreign workers: at the Ford vehicle plant in Cologne 75 per cent of the workforce was of Turkish origin (ibid). No government could risk removal of immigrants, without whom the spectacular economic growth of the postwar decades would not have been possible.[20] The federal government found itself in a position like that of other states which wished for a ready supply of labour *and* for migration controls which complemented a nationalist agenda. It first reduced immigration and then initiated a long series of reforms to limit entry and to clarify the rights of aliens. The immigrant presence fell sharply: during the first two years of the recruitment ban an estimated 400,000 workers left the country (Kolinsky 1996: 82). New laws were introduced based upon the assertion that Germany was not 'a country of immigration' (*kein Einwanderungsland*) but after the initial decline the number of foreigners again grew quickly, apparently in defiance of this policy.[21] In fact although the government had introduced many restrictions on entry it continued to allow immigration in the form of family reunion, through new forms of temporary contract, and also by claims for asylum, which became an increasingly important means of securing cheap labour. Only two years after the *Anwerbestopp* the federal government relaxed a general work ban imposed upon asylum seekers. It also agreed to distribute the growing number of asylum seekers across the country, making the main industrial areas of the Ruhr and Rhine-Main accessible from peripheral *Lander* (states of the federal republic) through which most refugees entered Germany. As asylum seekers were automatically granted entry and a work permit these measures amounted to 'invitations to pursue the asylum strategy of immigration' (Joppke 1998: 125).

In the early 1980s there was an outcry over *Scheinasylaten* – 'seeming' or 'apparent' asylum seekers. Schonwalder (1999: 78) comments that at a time when many West Germans were beginning to lose confidence in the economy, new public debates focused upon refugees as 'an illegitimate and threatening "stream" of paupers'. Government policy now changed dramatically: restrictions on work for refugees were reimposed and entry requirements extended to cover countries from which many applicants had been arriving. Although labour agents had long been bringing migrants into Western Europe their activities in Germany during this period mark a key development, demonstrating the continuity between recruitment of guestworkers and, from the early 1980s, that of irregular migrants. Networks which had been initiated by employers and by the BfA continued to operate, notwithstanding official prohibition on entry. Castles's comment on the development of the 'migration industry' might be applied precisely to this conjucture:

> Once a migration gets under way, needs arise for a variety of services. The migration industry includes travel agents, lawyers, bankers, labour recruiters, brokers, interpreters, and housing agents. If a government decides to curtail migration, it may have difficulties, because such agents may go on organizing migration, though the form may change (e.g. from legal worker recruitment to asylum migration or undocumented entry). (Castles 2004: 209)

German employers now sought out irregulars, who could be hired for a fraction of the sum paid to legally employable workers, in some cases a tenth of the wages paid to the latter and, when hired as self-employed, without the employer's obligation to pay social security contributions. The relationship between employers, the state and the labour agents was not conspiratorial; rather, as in the United States, it expressed an accommodation between them. Employers got access to cheap labour while the state was able to insist that it had an effective migration policy. Meanwhile labour agents extracted vast sums of money from increasingly desperate clients.

Between 1983 and 1992 regulations on asylum were changed no less than 18 times. Initially there was a fall in the number of applications but by end of the decade they were again rising sharply: by 1990 there were over 250,000 applications and by 1992 the figure was almost 440,000, most from the former Yugoslavia (Joppke 1998: 126). By the mid-1990s, with the Balkan wars in a different phase, numbers had halved but recognition rates had fallen far more steeply. This change was correlated with a new wave of hostility towards refugees. During the turmoil associated with German reunification, movements of the new Right attacked foreigners in general and refugees in particular: in an atmosphere of 'overall confusion and at times near hysteria' the latter were repeatedly targeted, becoming *Sundenbocke* – 'scapegoats' – for all manner of ills (Marshall 2000: 87). By the mid-1990s, after further changes in the law, the recognition rate had fallen to 4 per cent, less than a fifth of the figure 10 years earlier (Marshall 2000: 101). Hundreds of thousands of applicants were being rejected and very soon 'disappeared', becoming part of the irregular population. They now made up a crucial part of the workforce – on one estimate there were 500,000 irregulars in the construction sector alone, more than double the number of all workers admitted on seasonal contracts (Marshall 2000: 28 and 33). By 2004 the state ombudsman for foreigners suggested that there were up to 1.5 million irregulars (Pinkerton 2004: 36). Their presence was the outcome of a long process in which networks established by the state a generation earlier had continued to operate, encouraged by the desperation of immigrants, among whom more and more came from the forcibly displaced. They made up 'an emerging underclass of socially and economically exploitable, but also highly flexible and motivated individuals' (Marshall 2000: 29).

Britain: legacy of empire

Alone among the major states of Western Europe Britain has undertaken no official assessment of the size of the irregular migrant population. Despite the highly charged nature of debates about immigration, there has been no count of irregular residents or the irregular workforce. In effect successive British governments have been in denial of the irregular presence.

In the post-war period British employers struggled to compete for labour with counterparts in mainland Europe. In 1944 the government established a Royal Commission on Population, which examined a range of options for immigration and emigration. It concluded that immigration 'could only be welcomed without reserve if the immigrants were of good human stock and were not prevented by their religion or race from intermarrying with the local population and becoming merged with it'.[22] Cesarani (2001: 73) observes that this approach found its way into a series of policies on labour recruitment 'shot through with racist assumptions'. The European Voluntary Worker programme, which began in 1947, selected on the basis of a racial hierarchy. It favoured northern Europeans as against those from the east – and rejected Jews, who 'remained beyond the pale' (Cesarani 2001: 77–8). Despite the presence of thousands of Holocaust survivors in the British military zone in Germany, many calling urgently for asylum, Jews were excluded from all recruitment projects and only a handful were accepted in Britain on any grounds; meanwhile irregular migrants from the Baltic states – 'illegal landers' – were accommodated.[23] Other potential recruits – people of the British colonies and former colonies – were also viewed with outright hostility. Eventually demand for labour became so intense that immigration controls were lifted and soon immigrants from the Caribbean and South Asia began to arrive in large numbers, the Jewish refugees being ignored and effectively forgotten. For 15 years Commonwealth states supplied the needs of a growing economy.

Successive governments now faced a growing difficulty: they were under pressure to satisfy employers' demands and, at the same time, to bend to hostility towards immigrants closely associated with the state's own long engagement with colonial rule and its ideologies of racism. Politicians of the mainstream parties were highly sensitive to the anti-immigrant Right and, when economic growth flagged, soon accommodated the latter's demands, moving from an official commitment to open migration to one of racist exclusion. In 1962 a Commonwealth Immigration Act specified that entry would be conditional on possession of a voucher issued by employers through the Ministry of Labour. According to a senior member of the government, 'its aim is primarily social and its restrictive effect is intended to, and would in fact, operate on coloured people almost exclusively'.[24] The Act did not halt immigration, however. Economic growth resumed and employers again demanded a consistent flow of cheap labour, employers recruiting mainly in India and Pakistan by using agents or through family networks of existing employees. Possession of a voucher virtually guaranteed entry, so that rather than restricting immigration, the new system speeded it up. Ballard (1987: 25) comments of Pakistan that in the main region of emigration virtually every able-bodied man not otherwise engaged now set off for Britain. Wittingly or unwittingly the government also encouraged labour agents to organise clandestine entry. The Act allowed that any person who bypassed border controls and remained in Britain for 24 hours could stay in the United Kingdom: those able to evade the authorities at the time of entry were therefore assured of regularisation. Further legislation followed in 1965 and 1968, tightening restrictions but not excluding those who went undetected: in the 1968 Act irregulars were free from prosecution if they were not apprehended within six months of arrival.

Despite the official rhetoric with which the laws were introduced they did less to halt immigration than to legitimise racist attitudes. One immediate outcome of the 1968 act was that leading politicians began to campaign specifically against irregulars, generalising the idea that people of African and Asian origin should be treated with suspicion.[25] Many were apprehended and demands made for production of papers and passports, so that in an early review of the law Moore and Wallace (1975: 117) describe a regime of 'documentation and surveillance ... [which] heightens the sense of insecurity and makes people feel they are being continuously checked'. In fact there were relatively few deportations and many of those who evaded immigration controls were amnestied[26]: in 1972 irregulars who had arrived between 1962 and 1968 were declared to have entered through a 'gap' in the law and were regularised.[27] In 1971 a new Immigration Act formalised exclusion on the basis of race by allowing immigration of 'patrials' – those with a British parent or grandparent – and denying entry to most others. This ensured that White Commonwealth citizens had access to Britain while Black Commonwealth citizens lost remaining rights of entry. Joppke (1998: 134) describes the patriality clause as 'the revenge of empire, planting the virus of racial discrimination deep into the heart of British immigration law'.

These developments took place as a new era of forced migration was about to begin, with the result that when the number of refugees increased the state was well prepared to criminalise them. In the late 1980s numbers rose abruptly, with applications for asylum increasing almost three times in 1989 and almost doubling in 1990 and 1991. Like its European neighbours Britain was now suffering the effects of deep and prolonged recession. The government sought to reduce public spending by all means and targeted refugees as 'cheats' – fraudulent claimants who wished to enter Britain with the intention of exploiting the welfare system. The majority of asylum seekers were said to be both dishonest and illegal, as the government associated questions of authenticity with those of entry status. In 1993 it introduced an Asylum and Immigration Appeals Act which aimed to exclude 'bogus' applicants for asylum and to allow selection from among 'genuine' refugees those whom the government deemed to be of benefit to the host society. What had earlier been the rhetoric of the populist Right was now government policy. Leading members of the ruling Conservative Party told Parliament that Europe was threatened by 'a vast horde of aspirant economic migrants' masquerading as refugees.[28] Prominent figures in the opposition Labour Party concurred: a senior figure declared that 'bogus asylum seekers must be prevented from entering the country'.[29] The rate of refusal of asylum applications rose dramatically: from 16 per cent in 1993 to 75 per cent in 1994 (Joppke 1999: 138).[30] Thousands of those earlier treated as legitimate applicants were rejected. During the 1980s most refugees from war in Sri Lanka had been accepted without hesitation; by the mid-1990s, despite escalation of the conflict to levels of extreme violence, most were refused and by 1997 British officials were rejecting all but a fraction of claims. Some Sri Lankans were granted 'exceptional' leave to remain; others in effect became irregular migrants.[31] Like many other rejected applicants they were unable to return to their country of origin and maintained a semi-legal existence in Britain. Those who employed irregular entrants and 'overstayers' were meanwhile ignored: in a detailed study of British policy in 2002 Immigration Minister Lord Rooker admitted that prosecutions of employers of irregular labour were 'non-existent' (*Independent*, 21 January 2002). Eventually the British government quietly introduced what was, in effect, a first formal amnesty. When in 2004 eight Eastern European states joined the European Union, gaining rights for their citizens to work in member states, some 90,000 registered to work in Britain (*Independent*, 11 November 2004). According to the British Home Office, almost half had already been working in the country illegally: their registrations were accepted without comment (ibid).

In 2005 British researchers produced the first detailed study on forced labour and migration to the United Kingdom. It demonstrated that irregular labour had for years been used routinely in key areas of economic activity, notably construction, catering, contract cleaning, agriculture and care services (Anderson and Rogaly 2005). Workers were paid at levels far below the minimum wage, with employers benefiting from reduced taxation, freedom from obligations to provide sick pay and pensions, and the flexibility of a workforce which could be summoned 'on tap'. Workers often found themselves at the end of a long chain of sub-contractors, with a series of intermediaries including migration agents, smugglers and gangmasters making profits on their labours. The length of the chain allowed employers to pay reduced wages or to avoid payment altogether. Meanwhile many routinely used intimidation, including threats to denounce workers' irregular status which could lead to arrest and deportation. The report noted cases of apparent collusion between employers and immigration officials, with the latter prepared to deport irregulars whom unscrupulous employers wished to release without payment. It concluded that the distinction between 'legal' and 'illegal' workers had become blurred, to the advantage of employers and agents who moved labour in and out of 'grey' areas in labour law.

By 2004 the informal market in Britain was said to be worth some US$80 billion a year (Winder 2004: 340). Although the government had still not undertaken a count of the irregular population,[32] it continued to draw attention to the problem of irregular networks and the status of those who used them:

> So whilst focusing on immigration, 'trafficking' diverts attention away from the key question of how immigration status (whether irregular or tied to a permit to an employer) contributes to vulnerability to abuse employer relations. Perversely this means that immigration controls can be presented as a solution to human rights abuses (Anderson and Rogaly 2005: 9).

Unfree labour

Some analysts of unauthorised migration maintain that controls are essentially benign. For Miller (2001), for example, they have the role of curbing exploitation of vulnerable migrants and should be implemented much more comprehensively and vigorously. It is difficult to sustain such a view. The recent history of irregular migration demonstrates that, as in the case of refugee policy, states take an instrumental approach. They are sensitive above all to the requirements of employers. As a rule, in times of economic growth employers argue for restrictions on immigration to be eased, abandoned or ignored; when demand wanes and/or political instabilities increase, employer voices become weaker, populist political campaigns become more assertive and politicians and officials inveigh against the illegal alien. There are many interests to be reconciled, however. Some employers undertake forceful lobbying to ease controls but may be opposed by others with strongly protectionist and nationalist agendas and who endorse populist movements bent upon exclusion. Both tendencies may be represented within leading political parties and within the apparatus of state. This accounts in part for the abruptness of changes in policy and the extremes of injustice vis-à-vis immigrants caught within the complexities of, on the other hand, official and semi-official amnesties and regularisations, and on the other hand, by sudden crackdowns and campaigns of exclusion. And even when the commitment to exclusion seems most complete, irregular migration continues, driven by the ceaseless search for cheap labour and the attraction of an illicit, compliant workforce.

Irregular migrants are irresistibly attractive to certain employers, especially those in industries with variable demands for labour, such as horticulture and construction, and service activities such as hotels and catering. They have much in common with the indentured workers of an earlier era, described by Miles (1987) as 'unfree wage labour'. Before industrial capitalism, labour was usually tied to the land and to specific landowners; industrialisation depended upon the uprooting of the rural population and the creation of 'free' labour – individuals who technically exercised a choice as to whom they sold their labour power. But some forms of labour remained unfree: indentured labour, for example, provided workers who were not enslaved but were restricted by arrangements which tied them to specific employers.[33] In the mid-twentieth century mass contract labour fulfilled a similar function, requiring workers to commit themselves to a specific employer for an agreed period, after which they were compelled to return to their place of origin. Technically all were aliens and entered a system which expressly limited their involvement with the host society. They did not have access to the rights claimed by local citizens and were denied education, welfare or the opportunity for family reunion. The appeal of irregular migrants to employers today is that their legal status not only makes them cheap but in the same way renders them 'disposable'. They are the object of an increasingly focused effort to create a transnational class of workers fitting the needs of a deregulated and highly exploitative labour market. It is in this context that Anderson and Rogaly (2005: 7) write of the need to consider informal migrants less in the context of smuggling and trafficking than in relations to new patterns of *forced* labour.

Demographic deficit

The irregular workforce in North America and Europe contains more and more displaced people. This is the outcome of 20 years of increasingly restrictive asylum policy. In the case of the European Union visa requirements imposed on states in the major refugee-producing regions block direct access and inhibit claims for asylum.[34] By 1997 it was estimated that half of all refugees entering Germany used irregular networks; in the Netherlands the figure was 60 to 70 per cent (Morrison and Crosland 2001: 25). The chances of official recognition were slim: in the mid-1980s about 50 per cent of applicants in the European Union had been granted refugee status, a decade later the rate had fallen to 25 per cent, and by 1998 to just over 9 per cent (Hayter 2000: 66). Most applicants were viewed as fraudulent and those unable to show proof of immigration through formal channels were liable to instant rejection on the grounds of illegal entry. By 1998 the leading countries of origin for asylum claims in the European Union were, in order of number of applicants: Yugoslavia, Iraq, Turkey, Afghanistan, Sri Lanka, Somalia, Bosnia-Herzegovina, Romania, Iran and Algeria. This represented a list of the major refugee crises worldwide – a presence in Europe of a fraction of those displaced by upheaval at a global level. Claimants from Iraq, Afghanistan and former Yugoslavia, states profoundly affected by war, were most likely to be granted recognition but were also most likely to be apprehended as illegal entrants, for the same states headed the list of detained irregular migrants.[35] Morrison and Crosland (2001: 17) suggest that most 'customers' of smugglers and traffickers offering access to Western Europe were now in fact refugees forced to use clandestine routes because of EU border policies. They conclude that it is misleading to depict the migrants as 'illegal migrants' or 'illegal aliens'; rather, they maintain, they should be seen as 'refugee[s] in need of international protection'.

Even the informal networks have not been able to meet demands for labour. In the late 1990s a series of Western European states began recruiting in Eastern Europe and the Third World. For the first time in over 30 years there was competition for imported labour, leading in 2000 to demands from the European Commission for reconsideration of the Union's immigration policy, with a final aim of putting an end to Fortress Europe. Its rationale was the reality of a huge and growing 'demographic deficit'. According to the Commission, the population of the European Union would contain a higher and higher proportion of people over 65 who were likely to be economically inactive. Unless the birth rate increased dramatically the mass of younger people required to support welfare needs of over-65s would have to be found outside the borders of the Union. To maintain a constant 'support ratio' – the number of working people for each person over 65 – the European Union would need to achieve net annual in-migration of 13 million (Stalker 2002). The Commission recognised that change would be difficult, arguing for 'strong political leadership and a clear commitment to the promotion of pluralistic societies and a condemnation of racism and xenophobia'.[36] The challenge was too much for member states, however. When in March 2001 the President of the Commission called on EU governments to respond to the proposals most ignored him or raised the spectre of a threat to national sovereignty. EU states had gone so far down the road of official exclusion that for most a public change of policy was out of the question.

The demographic crisis was most acute in countries with low or negative birthrates: Germany, Greece, Spain, Italy, Austria and Sweden.[37] In Italy, with a shrinking indigenous population, immigrants had long contributed all of the increase in the national workforce, and on one estimate by 1999 almost 570,000 workers were irregulars (Pinkerton 2004: 32). Business organisations took the lead in arguing against restrictions on entry, lobbying politicians 'not to choke the flow of workers from the Balkans, Africa and the Indian sub-continent, who

accept wages considered too low even by [the] unemployed'
(*Independent*, 9 August 2001). In Britain, which had particularly low
levels of unemployment, the leading business journal blamed excessive
bureaucracy for obstructing recruitment of foreign workers (*The
Economist*, 31 March 2001). It observed: 'The world has made
the movement of goods, money and ideas freer, but not, strangely, the
movement of people', urging 'Let the huddled masses in' (ibid). In
2005 ministers of the Scottish parliament asked the central government
in London to direct 'failed' asylum seekers to the north, in an effort to
reverse a decline in population described as the single biggest challenge
facing Scotland (*Guardian*, 13 April 2005). The British Home Office
was said to be ready to establish a new 'twin-track' immigration system
to ease the Scots' demographic crisis (ibid).

Spain, with a shrinking population and rising demand for labour in
agriculture and manufacturing, was said to require 12 million migrants
by 2030 (*Guardian*, 28 August 2000). The government nonetheless
introduced new laws to restrict immigration and to expel irregular
migrants: politicians were said to have acceded to 'conservative lobbying
and fears of a voter backlash' (ibid). At the same time it launched a new
campaign of regularisation, a further example of the contradictory
pressures and tangled motives which had already brought enormous
numbers of irregular migrants: according to Spanish trade unions by
2003 there were almost 2.5 million *indocumentados* (Pajares 2004: 3).[38]
In 2005 EU ministers criticised the Spanish government for flying
thousands of irregulars from the Canary Islands to mainland Spain,
where they were 'dumped' on the streets of major cities (*Independent*,
31 January 2005). Local authorities in Valencia described the practice
as 'inhuman', leaving immigrants vulnerable to 'marginalisation, prostitution and labour exploitation' (ibid). As demand for labour continued to increase across the European Union, it was becoming more and
more difficult to reshape immigration policy and the simplest official
response was to rely on the irregular networks, which by 2002 were
supplying up to 15 per cent of the total population of foreigners in
Europe (Stalker 2002). Forced migrants, formally reviled and rejected,
had become an indispensable part of the army of cheap labour.

Notes

1. Quoted in Zolberg 1989: 6.
2. Operations were directed by the Office of Policy Co-ordination (OPC)
   which was affiliated to the CIA. In the late 1940s it conducted clandestine
   operations 'on a massive scale': Loescher and Scanlan 1986: 35–6.

According to Bower, the British also benefited from Operation Paperclip, recruiting scientists, engineers and industrialists: see Cesarani 2001: 199.

3. Skeldon (2000: 17) notes that a number of the Chinese who arrived in the United States were from Jiudi Island in Fujian province, where most of the local population is Christian and among whom there may have been a fear, 'real or perceived', of religious persecution. Under the terms of the Geneva Convention such fear would itself be grounds for a request for asylum.

4. Quoted in Joppke 1999: 32.

5. Quoted ibid.

6. Senator Alan Simpson added: 'there is no way they can be satisfied. Their entire function in life is that when the figs are ready, the figs should be harvested and they need four thousand beings to do that'. Quoted in Joppke 1999: 36.

7. Massey comments that, 'By handing out more than 2 million green cards to former undocumented migrants Congress dramatically raised the odds that millions of other family members still in Mexico would themselves enter the United States as undocumented migrants.' Quoted in Andreas 2001: 112.

8. There is a long tradition of involvement of American officials in irregular operations and the police and Border Patrol have sometimes been integrated into the coyote networks (Spener 2000). In the case of Mexico involvement of officials became so widespread that in 2001 the incoming government of President Vicente Fox identified corruption among border guards as a key issue and proposed radical measures of control (*Washington Post*, 5 April 2001).

9. Operation Gatekeeper saw rapid expansion of manpower and equipment associated with border control. In 1994 the San Diego sector of the Border Patrol had 980 agents; three years later the number had increased to 2264. Over the same period the amount of fencing and/or walls along the border in the sector increased from 19 to 45 miles, the number of underground sensors rose from 448 to 1214, and the number of infrared scopes from 12 to 59. The number of INS inspectors responsible for working at the three official ports of entry in the sector increased from 202 to 504 (Nevins 2000: 104).

10. For eyewitness accounts of the involvement of regular troops see *In Motion* (14 September 1997), a publication produced in solidarity with cross-border migrants in the United States.

11. Inter-American Human Rights Commission report quoted by Voice of America: http://www.fas.org/irp/news/1999/02/990217-gatekeeper. In one especially tragic incident in 1996 eyewitnesses saw 10 people swept off a sandbar by currents in the Gulf of Mexico when they attempted to swim across a river at its mouth (Eschbach *et al.* 1999: 437).

12. As broadcast by Voice of America, ibid.

13. *The Economist* (31 March 2001) reached a similar conclusion, suggesting that the decision of federal authorities to allow an estimated 11 million irregulars to work unhindered lay in 'hard-nosed economics'.

14. Quoted in Collinson 1994: 44.
15. Fysh and Wolfreys 1998: 32.
16. Quoted ibid.
17. Pinkerton *et al.* 2004: 38.
18. Quoted in Collinson 1994: 49.
19. Collinson (1994: 51) quotes OECD reports of 1975 and 1976 to the effect that 'political considerations' dictated decisions by European states including Germany to halt immigration, as 'the social and political drawbacks of immigration now seem to have become greater than the economic advantages'.
20. Zimmerman calculates that during the 1960s, 4 per cent of German growth rates could be attributed to the presence of foreign workers (*Migration News*, Vol 4, No 4, 1997).
21. This has sometimes been regarded as a conundrum. Joppke (1999: 62) comments that the discrepancy between *de facto* immigration and its political denial is 'the single most enduring puzzle in the German immigration debate'.
22. Quoted in Cesarani 2001: 70.
23. See Cesarani 2001: 78.
24. Quoted in Joppke 1999: 108.
25. Conservative Party leader Sir Alec Douglas Home demanded that all irregular immigrants should be deported (Foot 1965: 130).
26. Cohen (1994: 51) shows that between 1973 and 1986 there were 6239 deportations of alleged illegal entrants, an average of 445 per year.
27. The 'Bhagwan gap', named after the winner of the *Regina* vs *Bhagwan* case (Moore and Wallace 1975: 77).
28. Quoted in Schuster and Solomos 1999: 66.
29. Former Chancellor of the Exchequer Roy Hattersley, quoted in Schuster and Solomos 1999: 68.
30. This change also applied to 'exceptional leave to remain' (ELR). In 1990, 60 per cent of applicants had been granted ELR: by 1995 the figure had dropped to 18 per cent (*Guardian*, 2 January 1996).
31. For a detailed examination of the Sri Lankans' predicament see Grenier 1997.
32. A review of research into irregular residents and workers in other states, and the implications for the United Kingdom, was conducted by Pinkerton *et al.* in 2004. Their findings, published as *Sizing the illegally resident population in the UK*, appears to be the only official attempt to approach this issue and makes only tentative proposals which might be used to investigate 'illegals' in the United Kingdom.
33. In Europe a similar system kept some domestic and agricultural workers bound to their employers: typically they were 'tied' under agreements which provided them with accommodation in exchange for token wages.
34. A 1996 agreement placed a common requirement on nationals of Afghanistan, Ethiopia, Eritrea, Ghana, Iraq, Iran, Nigeria, Somalia, Sri Lanka and Zaire (later Congo) to secure visas for entry to the European Union. These states produced most of the applications for asylum from countries of the Third World.

35. UNHCR figures quoted by Morrison and Crosland 2001: 27.
36. Quoted in *The Independent*, 23 November 2000.
37. In 2000 each of these states had a rate of natural increase below the EU average of 1.0 per 1000 of the population. In the cases of Germany, Greece, Italy and Sweden there was a negative rate (Veenkamp *et al.* 2003: 54).
38. In the case of Southern Spain large numbers of irregular workers are concentrated in areas such as Almeria, where there has been explosive growth of the horticulture industry. According to Almeria Acoge, which offers information and advice to immigrants, by 2005 there were some 40,000 irregulars in the province, with an estimated 10,000 joining the irregular workforce each year, the great majority from North Africa. (Thanks to Pedro Trespardarne for this information.)

Part III

Journeys and Destinations

Part III examines displacement, flight and the circumstances under which refugees seek asylum. It considers how inequality and gender relations affect the displaced and shape initial experiences of exile. It looks at refugees in camps and holding centres, and the attitudes of states and agencies towards them. It considers the movements of refugees through new migratory networks, and the transnational communities brought into being by recent global changes. It examines the experiences of refugees in cities of the Third World, focusing on community life. It considers the effect of regimes of terror and the impact upon forced migrants of entry into clandestine networks. Finally, it examines responses in the West to the predicaments of the displaced, focusing upon recent developments in Australia and their implications for states of Europe and North America.

9
Displacement

Human agents

The most striking feature of the contemporary discourse of the refugee is the dehumanisation of forced migrants. Refugees are routinely depicted as moving en masse in 'waves', 'tides' and 'surges' – elemental forces threatening inundation and which require containment and redirection. Their circumstances and experiences are seldom considered, for to view forced migration in this way would subvert the perspective adopted by Western states – that most refugees are rootless opportunists whose claims for asylum are illegitimate and whose presence threatens host societies. Just such a view led to tragedy in Europe in the mid-twentieth century and has since produced regimes of exclusion in which forced migrants are a new focus of racist hostility. There is a different way of viewing forced migration – as a lived experience. In this context refugees are not objects of fear or hatred but are *subjects* with specific experiences. All human beings are social agents. Our lives are constrained by structural factors but at the same time we seek to modify our circumstances by making choices and acting upon them. In the case of forced migrants the weight of constraint is overwhelming and the range of choices is often minimal: by considering refugees as human agents we can, however, examine the constraints upon them, the options available and how they experience displacement, flight and exile.

Emanuel Marx (1990: 190) suggests that the key experience affecting refugees is that of displacement. He gives a 'minimalist' definition of the refugee as 'a person whose social world has been disturbed' (ibid). The idea of 'disturbance' does not in fact accommodate compulsion and the narrowing of choice which are invariably associated with refugee crises; it does, however, focus attention upon refugees as people affected by forces which fundamentally change their circumstances, moving them physically and radically changing their accustomed relationships. Like others, forced migrants have been accustomed to reside within social networks that, until displacement, constituted their 'world'.[1] For most people such an existence is taken for granted; it is only when access to these networks is denied that their significance becomes clear. Displaced people have been forcibly separated from or – what amounts to the same thing – compelled to abandon their resources. These may be of an individual or collective nature and include: material possessions; access to land, housing and employment; kin and communal relationships; and familiar languages, traditions and institutions – the whole complex of economic, political, socio-cultural and psychological elements that make up the framework for existence of each and every human being. Loss of resources can bring what Marx (1990: 197) calls loss of 'social competence'. This does not suggest a loss of human *capacities* for thought, action and innovation – although these may be seriously damaged – but separation from pre-existing resources and a rupture in the social environment of those displaced.

Those most profoundly affected are usually the least privileged. This might seem paradoxical, for those with wealth and power might be expected to lose most – to experience the most radical change in their material circumstances and their status. In fact the experience of displacement is shaped by structures of social class, so that those who have been most disadvantaged are affected most profoundly, as their narrower range of choices is further diminished. In effect, the world of the refugee is changed in proportion to the disadvantage experienced before displacement. From the 1940s to the 1970s refugee crises were usually the outcome of particular patterns of repression or of inter-state conflicts, but they have since been linked more and more directly to increased inequality and to the associated impoverishment of large numbers of people – to the intensification of uneven development at a world level. Zolberg (1989: 210) notes that in Central America during the 1980s social conflict in Nicaragua, El Salvador and Guatemala displaced between two million and three million people 'almost entirely from the poorest sectors of the population'. This pattern has since become more general, so that by the mid-1990s the UNCHR could observe: 'Underdevelopment alone does not create refugees. But poverty, inequality and the competition for scarce resources can play an important role in creating the conditions in which mass population displacements take place' (UNHCR 1995: 154).

The very poorest may be so disadvantaged that they are not able to join movements of the displaced. This is especially clear during severe crises of food availability – 'famines' – when victims come overwhelmingly from among the most marginalised people. Dreze and Sen (1989: 48) comment that in the context of hunger and famine questions of social class are relevant 'in an obvious and elementary way'. They continue:

> Famines are always divisive phenomena. The victims typically come from the bottom layers of society – landless agricultural labourers, poor peasants and

share-croppers, pastoralist nomads, urban destitutes, and so on. Contrary to statements that are sometimes made, there does not seem to have [been] a famine in which victims came from all classes of the society. (ibid)

When hunger moves towards famine, however, the poorest rural people may be unable to participate in communal strategies to pool resources and share hardship. Lacking land or livestock, they are likely to be the first to attempt to buy food – and with little cash to pay inflated prices they are often the first to face starvation.[2] They may also be unable to participate in mass migration from affected areas, especially if this involves movements over long distances. The old, the infirm and women with children from among the very poorest social strata may be left behind when starving people finally abandon their homes. These people may be stranded – their poverty has inhibited their ability to flee.

The poor and vulnerable are not necessarily the principal intended victims of active campaigns of displacement. Inter-state conflicts may uproot whole populations and mass repression may involve entire communities without regard to status. Nazism did not distinguish between Jewish victims on the basis of their economic or social standing: it first induced all Jews to flee and later murdered as many as possible. Partition of India produced mass movements of millions of people on the basis of religious affiliation, while in Africa scores of states have been affected by conflicts and subsequent displacements which reflect the communalism favoured by colonial rule. More rarely campaigns of repression have been directed at those of a specific social status – in the 1970s the Khmer Rouge regime in Cambodia targeted hundreds of thousands of urban professionals on the basis that they enjoyed privileges vis-à-vis the rural population.

In most of these cases, however, the immediate fate of the displaced depended largely on their socio-economic status. Reviewing refugee movements across the twentieth century, Kushner and Knox (1999: 14) note the importance of assets in crises of survival: 'Resources as well as opportunities may be needed to escape. Many refugees, from the Jews in the 1930s through to the Zairians in the 1990s, have had to buy their flight to freedom.' Investigating refugee crises of the 1980s and 1990s Van Hear (2004: 28) reaches a similar conclusion: access to resources shapes migration strategies, 'the better endowed can buy a better quality of asylum'. Access to capital implies relatively wide social networks – connections at the regional, national and even international levels. Landowners, entrepreneurs, financiers, merchants and senior state functionaries are often directly associated with national power structures and may enjoy various forms of protection. They are able to buy visas and to bribe officials and border guards – often a vital consideration in countries in which such payments are routine. They may be able to use means of travel inaccessible to the mass of people, buying a less dangerous form of flight than that which others are compelled to accept. They may also have choices of destination – the possibility of selecting those further from the place of departure and which are usually safer. Those able to mobilise liquid capital may be able to transport some of their wealth and to buy sanctuary by acquiring passports and visas. Sherman (1994: 85) notes that in 1938, when the Anschluss brought Austria under Nazi control, 'a fortunate few' of the Jewish population spent enormous sums to secure air passages on flights leaving Vienna: the rest of the Jewish community of 180,000 was left to its fate. The overall pattern of flight of Jewish victims of Nazism was indeed shaped by patterns of inequality. Rubinstein (1997: 43) observes that 'the higher one was on the socio-economic and educational scale, the less trouble one had in emigrating'. Money obtained a chance of survival.

Less fortunate are those without wealth and influence: small or landless peasants, agricultural labourers, pastoralists, artisans, urban workers and the urban poor. Their social networks are more localised and most who are able to flee move shorter distances to places which are less secure. This is evident in the Palestinian experience. In the late 1940s the pattern of movement of refugee Palestinians was determined largely by their class. The Zionist militias engaged in the conflicts of 1947–48 did not distinguish between rich and poor: all Palestinians were targeted but not all endured the same experiences of flight and of exile. Smith (1984: 119) observes that access to capital shaped the trajectory of displacement. Only a small portion of capital assets held in Palestine in 1948 could be transferred by the refugees. That held in land and private homes, or invested in buildings and immovable commercial property, was lost completely: 'Nevertheless the wealth of the country was such – and the exodus of sufficient duration – to allow for the transfer of substantial sums abroad' (ibid). About a third of Palestinian Arab capital was in moveable assets: cash, deposits held abroad, government bonds, commercial stock and insured commodities. Those able to mobilise some of these resources had the choice of moving at an early stage to cities in the region – Beirut, Damascus, Amman, Cairo – where they could attempt reclamation of other assets.[3] Some of those with education and professional skills, and with social networks that extended outside Palestine, also had a chance of choosing their means of exit and destination. For the vast majority of Palestinians, however, expulsion was experienced as a sudden immediate need to flee. Most had little or no property and no opportunity to buy their way to a chosen destination. For the peasantry – the majority of the Palestinian Arab population – life changed utterly:

> Unlike those who had experienced urban life, who had received an education
> or who had business contacts abroad, they had been unable to transfer their
> possessions or to find new jobs in their places of refuge. Deprived of the land
> and consequently of their sources of livelihood, they were reduced to almost
> total dependency ... the majority became dependent on relief for their
> physical survival. (Smith 1984: 145)

For these villagers, about 750,000 people, their location in Palestinian
society before expulsion was the key factor determining their fate after
1948. Smith sums up their situation as one in which 'daily life became
consumed by the sheer struggle to survive in the face of overwhelming
odds' (ibid). They had suffered an immediate, life-altering loss of 'social
competence'. Fifty years later these refugees, their children and grand-
children were still displaced, most living within the territories to which
they had been expelled. Hence the poor peasantry of Galilee, expelled
in 1948 into Lebanon, remained in the refugee camps and quarters of
Lebanese cities, while the people of southern Palestine who fled to
Gaza were still residents of camps of the 'Gaza Strip'.

During the 1970s and 1980s mass refugee movements from Vietnam
brought similarly unequal experiences. Following the defeat of the
United States in Vietnam hundreds of thousands fled the country. The
first to leave were from among the relatively privileged – the wealthy,
senior military personnel allied to the United States, and those of
professional status. Shortly before the fall of Saigon, the United States
began Operation New Life, taking more than 120,000 people to
American bases in the Pacific. Those who could not obtain a place on
US Military Airlift Command flights used other means, so that 'boat
people' were soon arriving in Guam and other bases. More and more of
these refugees were from among the less privileged: according to
Morrison and Moos (1982: 53) those who stepped off the early flights
were 'well-dressed people of various nationalities carrying traditional
luggage and the usual accoutrements of travel including tennis rackets
and an occasional bag of golf clubs'. Later, when refugees arrived on
the beaches, 'they were more miserable than anyone had imagined'
(ibid). People unable to buy a secure means of flight were compelled to
travel through militarised border zones or to attempt dangerous journeys by sea, where they were vulnerable to unscrupulous boat-owners,
to the Vietnamese authorities and to pirates. They also faced systematic
attempts by neighbouring countries to prevent landings and claims for
asylum. In the late 1970s up to 150,000 Vietnamese may have lost their
lives at sea as a result of piracy, overcrowding of boats in bad weather
and by exclusion, as Asian states prevented landings and left refugees to

drift and to starve (Hitchcox 1990: 72). Among the more fortunate, during 1979 alone 200,000 reached one of the countries of South East Asia (Zolberg 1989: 168). Those making landfall faced new problems, however, as many states detained and confined them. Most placed in holding centres and prisons were from among the poor, ill-educated and unskilled.

More recently, displacement in Sri Lanka has provided a graphic example of the problems faced by poor people in war zones. Refugees who left the island in the 1980s were overwhelmingly from among the wealthy or from professional families, most travelling by air to North America or Europe. When conflict intensified, means of escape became more difficult and more costly: forces controlling insurgent areas demanded an exit tax, while migration agents required large payments to enter the irregular networks. McDowell (1996: 135) shows how the profile of refugees reaching Switzerland changed during this period. In the mid-1980s most possessed educational qualifications higher than the average in Sri Lanka; after a few years most were ill-educated, having been agricultural labourers. Under enormous pressure to leave, poor Tamils had borrowed large sums of money and risked increasingly dangerous routes. Many, however, had no means of raising the large sums required. Van Hear (2004: 12) quotes a woman compelled to remain in the war-affected city of Jaffna: 'It depends on money ... the people who went out are doing fine; those who stayed are suffering'.

Women migrants

Displacement strongly emphasises socio-economic difference. So too with gender: displacement not only underlines unequal relations between men and women but also places women and girls in extreme danger. Women are in general less mobile than men: both adult females and girls often have responsibilities for children and for the old, and usually have less access than men to resources which can facilitate exit. This was graphically illustrated in the 1930s by the fate of German Jews in danger from the Nazis. After years of emigration from Jewish communities in Germany those who remained were mainly women and elderly people – hence most Jewish victims of the death camps who originated in Germany were female. This pattern has not changed. The majority of all displaced people are female: by 2000 the United Nations estimated that 90 per cent of IDPs were women and children: the agency described displacement as 'a man-made problem ... men make the wars and go off to fight. The women and children are the victims'.[4] The reality is in fact more complex: over the past 30 years the pattern of female vulnerability has become more marked due both to the changing character of military conflicts and the effects of economic policies imposed worldwide.

As we have seen (Chapter 4) most casualties of war are now civilians and most are female. The implication is that more women are affected by general dislocation and by mass displacement. At the same time economic changes have affected the status of women in many parts of the Third World, especially in rural areas. Commercialisation of agriculture in Africa, Asia and Latin America has brought rapid change to local agrarian systems. Vast numbers of men and women have moved to the cities and into the urban workforce or the informal sector, while of those who remain in the countryside an increasing proportion are women. This is especially marked where there are traditions of retaining land while family members travel for seasonal work – as in Central America and Southern Africa. By the late 1990s, 70 per cent of the agricultural workforce in sub-Saharan Africa was female and many rural households were headed by women (World Bank 2000: 20). Almost invariably female-headed households were poorer and suffered more severely in times of crisis. In addition in many cultures males are fed first and more generously: this can be so marked that Dreze and Sen (1989: 55) describe gender discrimination in health and nutrition in South Asia as 'endemic'. But even in regions in which access to food has traditionally been more equal, such as sub-Saharan Africa, gender differentials in mortality have been widening. This is related to men's greater access to waged employment and so to cash. It is also the outcome of differential access to resources during crises of food availability, when the pattern of food distribution usually becomes more pro-male because men are more likely to be concentrated where food is available.

Repeated world economic crises, together with the effects of SAPs, have produced precipitous falls in state spending in most regions of the Third World, with a disproportionate impact upon women. Graham-Brown (1991) shows how in the 1980s education systems in Latin America and Africa suffered sharp falls in funding. As even basic education became less effective enrolments fell, especially among girls. Fewer women were able to take up paid employment and fewer had direct access to cash. During the 1990s education collapsed across Sub-Saharan Africa. Oxfam has estimated that on 1999 figures the number of children of school age not in education was likely to double by 2015 (*Guardian*, 3 December 1999). The proportion of illiterate women – over two-thirds in the sub-continent (as opposed to one-third of men) – was certain to increase (ibid). Women were more likely to be involved in crises of mass displacement and less likely to have material resources which might ease their predicament.

Containment

In general the displaced are regarded by governments as disorderly and as threatening – as a presence which requires regulation and containment. There can be striking differences, especially between the policies of states in the West and those of Africa, Asia and Latin America. Despite the economic impacts on poor host communities of the Third World, very large numbers of refugees have been accepted without great hostility. In the early 1990s there were some 3 million Afghan refugees each in Pakistan and Iran, a million Mozambicans in Malawi, some 500,000 Cambodians and Burmese in Thailand and an equal number of refugees of many origins in Ethiopia. Refugee communities make up a very large part of some host populations: in the case of Malawi in the early 1990s they constituted over 10 per cent of the national total while in some communities of northern Pakistan and in eastern provinces of Iran, Afghan citizens have for over 20 years been more numerous than the indigenous population. There are many similar cases in which incoming groups have found security without the hostility shown to asylum-seekers approaching states of the West. Such receptivity is not surprising. When displaced people have language, religion or ethnic affiliation in common with people across a territorial border they may be able to move without great difficulty within a common culture. Refugees nonetheless violate national frontiers, and states' overriding concern with the sanctity of borders means that most people who wish to cross them unbidden are treated with suspicion. As Zetter (1999: 75) notes: 'Refugees are perceived as an especially problematic and threatening category of migrant ... containment of refugees is the major objective of all the stakeholders, except the refugees'. Their presence may be so disturbing to states that whole refugee populations are marked out as fundamentally alien and unwelcome, a characterisation that may persist for years or even for generations. In general the greater the insecurity of state authorities the more repressive is the policy vis-à-vis refugees – and as more states have become unstable more have they proved unwelcoming to displaced people. In addition, as Human Rights Watch (2000b) has pointed out, the practice among Western states of raising barriers to refugees makes it much more likely that governments of Africa, Asia and Latin America will also become resistant to requests for asylum. The organisation has identified a number of 'traditionally generous refugee-hosting countries', including Pakistan, Thailand, Tanzania and Guinea, in which governments have refused asylum and adopted increasingly restrictive and even xenophobic policies.

Some refugee communities become permanently alienated, not only from their place of origin but from the authorities of the host society.

This has been the fate of Palestinians who entered Lebanon in 1948, and of succeeding generations born in Lebanon, who even after more than 50 years are denied basic rights enjoyed by citizens of the host state. They have remained stateless and in one sense 'rootless' – having no affiliation with an official polity they are especially vulnerable to state and to non-state forces.[5] Given the many mass displacements of the twentieth century the numbers of stateless person worldwide is small – an index of the determination of states to allocate such people to a political jurisdiction. Other stateless groups include ethnic Vietnamese in Cambodia; ethnic Chinese who fled Vietnam; and the Muslim people of Myanmar, the Rohingyas, hundreds of thousands of whom sought asylum in Bangladesh in the early 1990s. Some communities of Roma people, such as those who formerly lived in the Czech Republic, are also stateless, and vulnerable to campaigns of exclusion initiated by governments in Western Europe.

There have been more and more vigorous attempts to discourage or to prevent displaced people crossing territorial borders. In general national governments wish to contain the displaced within the state of which they are citizens, and it is only in specific circumstances that the displaced are welcomed by host authorities. In cases of mass displacement this is very rare and is usually an outcome of conflicts to which the host state is a party – hence Iran willingly accepted very large numbers of refugees from Iraq during the long war of the 1980s. The rising number of IDPs is directly related to governments' unwillingness to accept refugees 'proper' – those who have crossed international borders. The Global IDP Survey (1998: xv) observes that 'refugees are becoming less welcome, so the number of internally displaced people has been steadily growing' (ibid). According to the United Nations, by 2001 there were 25 to 30 million 'hidden' displaced people, most in Central Africa and in parts of Asia, Latin America and the Balkans: the vast majority, up to 90 per cent in some regions, were women and children.[6] The UNHCR has declined to accept the expansion of its mandate to include them: Loescher (2001: 354) identifies 'a critical weakness' in international provision for this category of migrants.

The notion of internal displacement is problematic. People who have had almost identical experiences of displacement, and who live in close proximity, may be categorised variously as refugees or IDPs. This is well illustrated by the case of Mozambique, where some five million people were displaced during the late 1980s. Very large numbers of people crossed borders to camps in neighbouring countries, especially to Malawi, where by 1991 a million were counted as refugees. At the same time some 3 million people classified as IDPs remained within Mozambique. Many Mozambicans involved in 'return' and 'ricochet' movements were classified at various times as both refugees and IDPs, and many were displaced several times from different locations, so that their identification of a national 'home' became increasingly problematic. As Mozambique became a true zone of crisis in which displacement affected the whole society a formal definition of 'refugee' became difficult to sustain and the character of mass movements could only be assessed in relation to the intentions of migrants. Wilson and Nunes (1994: 172) comment that in any attempt to understand refugee movements these intentions are crucial: 'Refugees' concerns for security, control over their lives, the desire to construct a positive and meaningful future, and the flow of information and ideas are all indeed key.'

'Havens'

Governments and agencies have been less concerned with refugees' intentions – with their status as *subjects* of the experience of displacement – than with agendas focused upon control. During the 1980s Western states' restrictions on immigration led directly to attempts to contain refugee movements from the Third World at source. The aim was to restrict displaced people within the borders of their state of origin, mainly by organising relief operations which would discourage long-distance migration. This had the immediate effect of increasing the numbers of IDPs: in effect people were forcibly prevented from entry to the formal category of the refugee. One strategy developed in the early 1990s was the 'safe area' or 'haven', ostensibly a zone within which people in danger could seek security. Creation of these zones has sometimes reflected a genuine concern among officials of relief organisations to provide protection, but it has often been difficult to distinguish this motive from a more general desire to contain the displaced. Reviewing the operation of 'open relief centres', an early form of safe haven in Sri Lanka, the UNHCR (1995: 128) commented that they improved security for civilians affected by military conflict and were able 'to limit the scale of the refugee outflow to India' – a strategic aim in itself. In Bosnia several havens were established in the mid-1990s under UN auspices, ostensibly to protect the local population from the threat of ethnic cleansing. Stubbs (1999: 16) comments

> In colloquial Bosnian parlance, these very quickly became known as 'Death Zones', a term which [soon] became chillingly true. The idea of 'protecting people where they are' can go hand in hand with preventing them from leaving and when the security element of the equation breaks down, it effectively leaves civilians at the mercy of attacking forces.

Stubbs notes that safe areas are by definition not places of asylum in which protection is offered by a host state. Rather, 'The policy of choice is to restrict these havens to within the country in conflict' (ibid): that is, to *inhibit* movement from the country of origin. In 1994 the former chief of UNHCR operations in Bosnia commented of the havens that, 'these areas are becoming more and more like detention centres, administered by the UN and assisted by UNHCR' (UNHCR 1995: 129). This was an admission that people wishing to flee to safety were held in order that they should not become refugees because a formal claim upon potential host states was undesirable. The UNHCR has recognised the difficulty this presents to an organisation which champions human rights: 'A ... danger associated with the safe haven strategy is the threat which it can pose to the principle of asylum and the right of freedom of movement' (ibid). This danger is indeed so serious that it has raised fundamental questions about the agenda of the UNHCR. Loescher (2001: 300) comments that during the Bosnian events the organisation became no more than an instrument for the West's policy of containment; in the case of Rwanda, he maintains, the involvement of Western states, the United Nations and the UNHCR was 'a colossal failure ... a major dereliction of responsibility and moral negligence' (Loescher 2001: 313). In an incisive analysis of the 'humanitarian' crises of the 1990s Rieff (2002) concludes that major agencies have taken on the priorities of states, intervening to control population movements and acting as an alibi for governments disinterested in the real causes of economic breakdown and of conflict.

Mass movements of refugees are usually seen by state authorities as destabilising and dangerous. This is evident in the best documented experience of long-term displacement – that of the Palestinians. Those expelled in 1948 found themselves in uncongenial environments – territories controlled by governments anxious to assert themselves vis-à-vis populations which had already experienced decades of anti-colonial struggle. They were determined that the refugees should not catalyse further mass activity and in the cases of Jordan and Lebanon adopted policies which aimed to erase an independent Palestinian identity. In Lebanon the refugees were concentrated into camps under the control of the police and the Deuxieme Bureau (DB), the intelligence service. Meetings of more than a few were prohibited and even visits to neighbours could bring police intervention. Residents were subject to general harassment and sometimes to beatings and imprisonment; permits were needed to visit other camps and travel to certain areas of the country was forbidden. The intention was to create a sense of fear and helplessness, a rationale set out by the head of the Palestinian section of the DB, who asserted: 'The Palestinian is like a spring. If you step on him he stays quiet but if you take your foot off, he'll hit you in the face'.[7]

The same approach was advanced by authorities in states to which Vietnamese refugees fled during the 1970s and 1980s. Some were held in 'asylum' or 'open' camps where claims for refugee status were assessed and from which large numbers were eventually resettled in the United States, Canada and Australia. Increasingly, however, refugees deemed unattractive to host states because of their lack of education or marketable skills found themselves in 'closed' camps, built both to contain them and as a means of 'humane deterrence' [*sic*] to others contemplating flight. Here the regime differed little from that in prisons everywhere: no possessions were permitted without permission of the authorities, cooking was forbidden, all were required to wash and dress according to camp regulations, letters were censored, and 'disrespectful' conduct could result in loss of privileges or confinement. Hitchcox (1990: 153) describes the process of induction into the camps as 'a lesson in submission [designed] to impress upon the Vietnamese their helplessness and dependence upon the authorities'.

'Repackaging' refugees

Until the 1960s policy towards refugees in the Third World was developed on an ad hoc basis. When a more coherent approach emerged it was driven by concern to manage the displaced on the basis that they were incapable of regulating their own affairs. Harrell-Bond (1999: 147) describes the change as the 'repackaging' of refugees. It was inseparable from policies of modernisation which during the 1960s set the agenda for world development. Following decolonisation, governments judged to be economically backward were directed by dominant states and transnational organisations to follow strategies based upon a particular vision of Western capitalist development. People of Africa, Asia and Latin America were to embrace market relations, urbanism, and specific models of government and means of administration: this would animate their societies, it was argued, bringing prosperity and self-sufficiency. Resistance to modernisation was regarded as perverse or even subversive and to be overcome, like generalised backwardness, by close regulation of processes of change. The strategy disposed of the traditions, expectations and aspirations of the mass of people worldwide.

States and agencies assumed that displaced people were incapable of self-organisation. Lacking interest in refugees' own perceptions and aspirations, officials assumed that they were an inert mass which required to be marshalled and directed towards productive activity. Here was a paradox, albeit one consistent with the contradictions in development theory. Refugees were assumed to be helpless; at the same time those who did not embrace the prescribed agenda were deemed to be dependent upon the agencies. Just as ideologues of modernisation continued to depict an energetic and progressive West vis-à-vis 'the Rest', refugees were viewed as people emptied of self-will who should be re-oriented to new methods, and failure to adapt was taken as evidence of the incapacity of these unfortunates. They were usually placed in specially constructed rural settlements close to their state of origin: in Africa the UNHCR formalised this approach as the strategy of 'zonal settlement' and over a 20-year period over 100 communities were established. Displaced people were brought together and provided with food and with tents or prefabricated housing; they also received seeds, tools and access to land, and were directed to achieve self-sufficiency. This soon became a routine means of intervention but one that, in most cases, proved a disappointment to Western planners. Reviewing the experience, Harrell-Bond (1986) shows that in only a fraction of cases were projects deemed to have achieved 'durable self-sufficiency'. Failure was attributed to what agencies termed 'dependency mentality' or 'dependency syndrome' – an alleged incapacity to achieve self-sustaining activity.

Borrowed from mental health literature, the notion of dependency suggested a pathological condition: refugees did not perform effective functions, with the result that they suffered individually and as a collective. The syndrome was associated with 'lethargy, lack of initiative, acceptance of hand-outs with little attempt at self-sufficiency, [and] frequent complaints, especially about the lack of generous outside help'.[8] The UNHCR suggested that provision of free food rations killed the aptitude for work and stifled creativity and initiative, so that many refugees were unwilling to invest their energies in work directed to self-sufficiency (Kibreab 1993: 331). Leading relief organisations such as the World Food Programme and Oxfam expressed similar views. Refugees' failure to meet the agencies' expectations was viewed as a mark of perversity, as showing lack of gratitude for external help, and often as indicator that local cultures were resistant to progress – a theme of modernisation theory and a routine explanation for the persistence of developmental problems at a world level.

'Supertankers'

Many refugees have survived initial phases of displacement thanks to emergency operations run by NGOs but many have also been forced to endure long and disabling periods of inactivity which have inhibited their own strategies for change. This is in part an outcome of assumptions made by agencies and NGOs. During the 1970s governments began to delegate major responsibilities for refugees to non-state bodies, and relationships between states and NGOs became increasingly close.

By the 1980s the position of the latter as formally unaffiliated organisations, together with their trained personnel, transnational networks and growing financial resources, made them indispensible to national governments and to new perspectives on development. Modernisation theory had been reshaped to accommodate neo-liberalism: economic and social advance now required accommodation to the world market, and states were required to reduce their role in economic affairs and to stimulate political reform. NGOs were summoned to fill some of the gaping holes which soon appeared, especially in welfare provision and in 'humanitarian assistance' in the many internal crises associated with intrastate conflicts. Bennett (1998: 22) comments that by the 1990s they had become 'the front-line arbiters of change'.

In 1978 there had been 10,000 NGOs operating internationally; 20 years later the figure had risen to 42,100.[9] By 1995 over US$10 billion of aid was passing through the NGOs – 15 per cent of all international development assistance and a much larger sum than that available through the United Nations and disbursed through governments (Bennett 1998: 21). As their number and weight grew, NGOs became more directly involved in mainstream development activity. In 1990 they had been involved in some 12 per cent of World Bank projects; by 2001 they were involved in 54 per cent of such projects.[10] Growth of the major organisations was extraordinarily rapid: Stubbs (1999: 10) suggests that by the mid-1990s agencies such as Oxfam, CARE, the International Rescue Committee (IRC), and Catholic Relief Services (CRS) had become transnational entities 'akin to TNCs': they were 'the supertankers of the NGO world'. Senior managers of leading organisations often came from among former national politicians or state functionaries and commanded large bureaucracies based mainly in the EU, where 60 per cent of international NGOs were headquartered, and in North America.[11] Although they remained non-governmental in the strict sense they had taken on quasi-state functions and adopted state-like attitudes. Rieff (2002) argues that this development is now so advanced that the major humanitarian organisations are parties to what is, in effect, a new 'humanitarian' colonialism.

By the 1990s the developmental ethic associated with refugee relief and support had been replaced by concern for swift intervention with the emphasis on emergency assistance and repatriation. As the lead agency the UNHCR responded to states anxious to cut spending on the needs of the displaced and which, formally at least, now argued that their money should be spent less on long-term support for populations in exile and more on development in countries of origin. It also complied with the wishes of its most influential state sponsors to contain and redirect refugee movements. Its first involvement in a 'safe' zone was in Iraq in 1993, in a move to satisfy the demands of Turkey and the

United States that Kurdish refugees should be held within their state of origin. This forbade displaced people the right to make a claim for refuge: within the UNHCR some viewed it as a marker of 'the end of the age of asylum'.[12] Soon afterwards the strategy came to grief in both Rwanda and Bosnia. In the latter the UNHCR and leading NGOs were active not only in relief but also in both inducing and coercing people into movement from areas in which they wished to remain. Stubbs (1999: 34) maintains that the conduct of the UNHCR damaged its reputation so seriously that it lost its claim to a lead role in co-ordinating NGOs worldwide. He maintains that attempts to manipulate population movements by disseminating false information meant that UN agencies, 'in effect, became parties to the conflict' (ibid). The UN High Commissioner later admitted that the organisation's conduct left it open to allegations of being 'an accomplice to "ethnic cleansing"'.[13] The compulsion to control forced migrants had overtaken the responsibility to protect them.

'Corrals'

Non-state bodies are focused more and more upon regulation and crisis management within the context of the *status quo ante*. This may be disagreeable to aid workers, who are often altruistic and concerned primarily for their intended beneficiaries, and who may endure difficult and dangerous conditions to fulfill their missions.[14] Refugees are allocated a subordinate role in which it is anticipated that they will accept the authority of external forces and the 'charity script' in which they have been given non-speaking parts. In fact they may be disinclined to play such roles. They may already have experienced repression and ill-treatment and may be unwilling to subordinate themselves to the authorities in camps and relief centres. These are highly institutionalised structures: Zetter (1995: 47) describes them as 'powerful symbols of the orthodox managerialist relief model'. Typically they operate on the basis of a hierarchy at the top of which are officials appointed or approved by the host government and supported by armed police, soldiers or paramilitary personnel. Management is usually in the hands of the UNHCR or of NGOs which derive their authority from the local state. Voutira and Harrell-Bond (1997: 211) observe that such regimes operate through a series of 'chains of hands' that administer aid; at the bottom of the chain is the refugee.

Camp dwellers often resist this regime, especially at times when regulations are being enforced most insistently, as during food distribution or when a camp census is under way. Skirmishes and even uprisings – usually described as riots – are commonplace. As early as 1982 the

UNHCR produced a *Handbook for Emergencies*, setting out guidelines for policing and directing staff on how to react to mass dissent. Like many NGOs the agency has since made great efforts to control 'deception' by refugees, especially ration fraud – real or imagined attempts to increase food allocations – with the result that distribution has often been organised as under a penal regime. In 1990 Oxfam produced a manual on registration of refugees in emergencies which devoted a section to 'cheating' and recommended subterfuge as a means of accurate census-taking. Some agencies have in addition built structures openly described as 'corrals' through which refugees must pass in order to get their rations. The herding metaphor reveals much: here the values expressed in mission statements and advanced by most relief workers are overwhelmed by a compulsion to administer the displaced, what Wilson terms 'concern for security and control, a need to manage a population in order to administer aid to it, and a pernicious paternalism'.[15] This approach recalls nineteenth century practices of surveillance and control of the poor in cities of Europe and North America, where paternalism was mixed with mistrust and with fear of the anarchy of the slum.

In 1995 the UNHCR produced a handbook for staff, *Working with the Military* (Wolfson and Wright 1995). This focused upon 'partnership' between the UNHCR and armed forces, and familiarity on the part of aid workers with military perspectives, structures and jargon. It did not consider the implications of such involvement for the aims, objectives and culture of the UNHCR or other non-military organisations, or for the interests of refugees.

Women in camps

States and agencies operate camps by imposing order directly and/or by mediating their control using existing structures of authority within the refugee population. Here there is a very general problem in relation to the status of women. Displacement exaggerates unequal relations of gender, and camp regimes usually further emphasise such differences, as external authorities make assumptions about gender relations which are consistent with their own expectations and with their preference for liaison with male authority figures. The effect is that customary resources are denied to women, who are often made more vulnerable. In most societies women enjoy authority in the 'private' sphere.[16] This area of activity may include food acquisition and distribution, and domestic matters focused upon kin and the community: it may also extend widely to economic and social affairs and to 'politics' in the orthodox sense. Camp structures often violate these traditions, viewing women merely as associated with males to whom they are attached as kin or as political followers. Callamard (1999: 162) suggests that the initial gender bias of international mechanisms of assistance are consolidated locally, displacing refugee women from their usual sphere of work and power, a process justified locally on the basis of women's 'biological characteristics, physical weaknesses and social backwardness'. Kibreab (1995) notes the effect in the case of Eritrean refugees encamped in Sudan. Rural women in Eritrea normally participate actively in productive activities and have control over food crops, a practice that mitigates the effect of male domination. In refugee camps in Sudan all assistance to their communities was nonetheless issued by the authorities in the name of men.[17]

Conditions in camps, holding stations and transit centres may make women particularly vulnerable, especially to sexual violence. Young men no longer associated with family groups and the influence of older relatives may focus upon women who do not have the usual kin protection. When Human Rights Watch (2000a) investigated the circumstances of Burundian refugees in camps in Tanzania it found that women were often attacked while carrying out routine daily tasks such as gathering firewood, collecting vegetables or seeking work outside the camp. It recorded all manner of abuse, including cases of mass rape. Victims often remain silent, fearful of the stigma attached to the violation itself and of the consequences of reporting the attack. Hitchcox (1990: 219) notes that among Vietnamese refugees one strategy adopted by women at risk was to marry to obtain male protection. Other refugees enter prostitution, which may become institutionalised in camp life.[18] Abuse of women by officials can become a constant threat. Nyakabwa and Lavoie (1995) describe repeated assaults and rape by officials, police and troops in the Horn of Africa. In West Africa scores of NGOs have been implicated in the abuse of girls in camps in Sierra Leone, Guinea and Liberia. An investigation by UNHCR and Save the Children in 2002 showed that aid had been withheld from young refugees and their families unless paid for by sex: staff of all major NGOs, including the UNHCR, Save the Children, Medecins Sans Frontieres, CARE and the International Rescue Committee, were involved, with the implication that senior local officials must have known of the problem (*Guardian*, 20 April 2002).

Tabula rasa

During the 1960s, 1970s and 1980s refugees encamped in the countryside were directed mainly to achieve self-sufficiency. Those who failed to conform were often viewed not merely as dependent but as malingerers or even as criminals – hence the obsessive concern of some agencies to require beneficiaries constantly to attend feeding centres and enumeration points. One effect was to lock refugees into routines which inhibited self-organisation and independent activity, the formal aims of most relief programmes. Kibreab (1993: 332) notes that schemes launched to assist displaced people in Somalia in the 1980s treated refugees less as individuals than as clients whose problems could be tackled by implementation of pre-planned programmes. Rather than assisting refugees to use their skills and capacities for innovation, mobilising those parts of family and community networks which remained intact, agencies imposed their own techniques of crisis management. Refugees were believed to have been rendered incapable of independent action, so that bureaucrats and agency staff designed, planned and implemented food and welfare programmes: 'refugees [were] treated as if they were *tabula rasa* with no history, past experience, culture, anticipation, skills [and] coping mechanisms to interpret new situations' (Kibreab 1993: 336).

All communities have their own adaptive mechanisms. Displacement brings loss of resources but does not necessarily negate the capacity to adapt and to innovate. Relief programmes in general have been based on models that assign uniform rights and duties. As a result for many years people possessing all manner of skills in animal husbandry, cultivation, craft work, manufacturing, administration, trade, transport, domestic and other activities were directed to perform identical tasks, usually to work the land. This produced frustration and rejection of agencies' agendas, often characterised by the authorities as 'idleness' and evidence of dependency. Where refugees have been provided with opportunities for self-organisation, however, outcomes have been different. Invariably people of the camps wish to establish relationships with people outside, especially with those who often accompany 'legitimate' refugees (those who have been enumerated) and who in UNHCR terms have 'spontaneously settled'. Many Somali refugees of the 1980s engaged in activities outside the camps including farming, craft work, retailing and servicing (Kibreab 1990). Refugee and non-refugee communities provided each other with opportunities – usually relationships between the two were to the advantage of non-refugees, for although the latter commanded greater resources refugees proved most innovative and most active. In a development typical among displaced people, some refugees also moved on from the camp with the intention of finding work and/or facilitating return to their place of origin. This risked loss of refugee status, as formally refugees were identified strictly as those residing in camps or attending feeding centres where they could be counted daily.

Where the authorities continue to emphasise attainment of self-sufficiency the most positive strategy for relief organisations is to direct aid to the wider community as well as to the displaced. This helps to overcome problems which may develop in communities close to camps. Here people may view the incomers as privileged: they may see food, blankets, clothes and building materials arriving; water supplies being provided; and schools, clinics and offices being constructed. Meanwhile refugees' links with agencies may be seen to provide influence which the local community does not possess. Relations between the latter and the encamped population may degenerate, so that the refugees become more and more reliant on the camp authorities. Van Damme (1999: 51) provides evidence from West Africa that refugees with freedom to develop relations with non-refugee populations attained high levels of self-sufficiency and that eventually 'their means of livelihood were intertwined with the host community'. In contrast, the minority of refugees who were segregated in formally organised camps faced serious problems and many moved out in efforts to integrate into local society.

The strategy of assisting the wider population in areas with a refugee presence has usually been resisted by governments and agencies. It suggests that differences between refugees and others might become less distinct and if this were to become general practice the particular characteristic of refugees, that of being people out of place, might be seen as less significant. Refugees continue to be seen as separate – as 'problem people' who should be isolated and who should receive specific sorts of aid directed to a narrow range of outcomes. One corollary is that those who break the rules may be punished severely. In one tragic case in 1998 over 150 Rwandan refugees and Congolese villagers were shot by the Congolese army because the latter had allowed the Rwandans to live with them, outside the refugees' designated area (Amnesty International 1999: 44).

Camps need not be run in authoritarian fashion. Hoeing (2004) shows how a flexible and participatory approach to life in the camp not only promotes productive economic activity and effective organisation of refugee communities but also contributes greatly to the latters' sense of well-being. Her research in Uganda underlines the importance of self-activity of displaced people – of understanding refugees as subjects and as people who wish to make choices and to act upon them. At the other extreme is the camp focused upon close control, with the effect that it operates as a detention centre or prison. Under these circumstances refugees may be involved in long-running conflicts. In Hong Kong, where in the 1970s and 1980s tens of thousands of Vietnamese were incarcerated in 'closed' camps, there were many protests and violent confrontations with armed guards. More recently refugees in Zimbabwe protesting over camp conditions have been attacked by the army, and in North Africa there have been prolonged and violent clashes between refugees and troops in the Spanish enclaves of Melilla and Ceuta (Gold 2000).[19] In the case of Palestinians in Lebanon resistance has gone much further. In 1969, after over 20 years of life under repression, people of the camps joined a new Palestinian resistance movement. The level of mobilisation, far higher than in other areas of the Palestinian diaspora, was widely attributed to the scale of state repression and to the regime imposed upon the camps. Sayyigh (1979: 150) comments that 'the harshness of repression added its own momentum to the building up of a revolutionary readiness among the Palestinian masses'. Armed insurrections removed the army and the police from the camps, establishing autonomous, self-governing areas within Lebanese territory. Sayyigh quotes one Palestinian sociologist's observation that, 'The most important thing was that they felt liberated from the daily persecution ... The most important benefit of the Revolution was freedom of political activity, freedom to organize and to work' (ibid).

'Warriors'

Palestinians are among those who have spent decades in camps: they have, says the USCR (2004), been 'warehoused'. This expression is being used increasingly widely to describe the circumstances of the majority of all refugees officially recognised by the UNHCR; over 7 million people who have been confined to camps or settlements for over 10 years. The USCR suggests that these refugees have been left without rights to employment, freedom of movement and of residence, and that governments and agencies are disinterested in their desire to return, to settle or seek resettlement. This is satisfactory to states which influence the policies of key agencies, and for which the presence of highly visible concentrations of migrants provides evidence both of effective control and of activity directed to refugee beneficiaries. The experience of long-term encampment may be a key factor for development of what Zolberg (1989: 275) calls 'refugee-warrior' communities. Here political activists emerge from and are sustained by large refugee populations – they fight to return to their homeland or home region, to overthrow an unsympathetic regime, to secure autonomy or a separate state. Life in the camps, argues Zolberg, is crucial to their development. The camp environment is 'dependent, degrading and fundamentally insecure' and for young people the activists' project of resistance is 'the only relevant future' (Zolberg 1989: 277). When camps are close to the battlefront or are in effect part of it, as in the Palestinian and Afghan cases, war may dominate the life of the whole community and activists appear as protectors, cementing links between themselves and the population as a whole. In the context of an international refugee regime which sustains refugee populations in exile for years, the 'warriors' can maintain a long-term project.

This analysis has been criticised on several counts. The notion of 'warriors' is itself problematic. It suggests a particular attachment of some refugee groups to violent means, although armed activity of forced migrants has often been a continuation of national struggles associated with the legacy of colonialism and which are not specific to displaced people. The idea of the warrior community may also deflect attention from the role of political currents which do not reflect the interests of the mass of the displaced. Adelman (2003: 96) describes how Rwandan Hutu militias in Zaire used refugee camps as 'safe havens' from which to launch attacks on Tutsi communities. The camps supported Hutu militias but only, Adelman argues, at the expense of the refugee population: 'They indoctrinated them [the refugees] to fear a return to Rwanda, used them as recruits for reconstructing their forces, taxed them, and took a percentage of their relief to help finance the rebuilding of their army' (ibid). The regime in the camps amounted to 'a pseudo-state of refugee warriors' (Adelman 2003: 126). Grare (2003) raises similar issues in the case of Afghan camps in Pakistan, although here external forces, states of the West, were implicated in efforts to mobilise the refugees. Zolberg's approach has a strength, however. It emphasises the importance of camps as environments in which refugee activists are open to influences associated with their experiences *as refugees*. In this context Grare (2003: 58) insists that encamped people are not merely 'a pliable population of subjects who are not actors in their own right'; rather, they have a voice and an active role in local political developments. The case of the Palestinians is instructive: camps which have housed refugees for over 50 years continue to produce new generations of activists, and the more that the camps are 'degrading and fundamentally insecure' the more likely it is that they will develop young fighters. The camps emphasise vulnerability and powerlessness; at the same time they produce specific responses to refugee predicaments – they are places in which people combine to challenge the circumstances forced upon them. They capture, perhaps in a literal sense, both the constraints upon and the creative energies of the encamped refugee. But few refugees take up arms: for most this is not a meaningful strategy and is seldom an option, and there are other pressing concerns.

Moving on

The pattern of global development means that increasingly refugees come from among the most vulnerable. The experience of displacement is one of loss of material resources – few have transferable assets – and of disruption of localised social networks. For political authorities these migrants are objects of suspicion, requiring close control and urgently in need of repatriation. For agencies and NGOs they are people whose circumstances may evoke sympathy but who need above all to be administered. Their own aspirations are seldom a matter of concern and attempts to challenge the authorities are viewed as evidence of indiscipline or perversity. The world of the refugee is one in which attempts to innovate – to 'cope' – are inhibited by institutions which exhibit deep mistrust of the displaced. It is under these circumstances that more and more refugees move away from their initial place of exile, away from camps and relief centres towards towns and cities, with their possibilities of new resources – jobs, education, new relationships, and freedom from the camp regime. For young, resourceful people who have learned how to survive this is often the only prospect of onward movement and of 'return' under circumstances of their own choosing. It is the only obvious means to establish a 'social world' which has meaning.

Notes

1. The notion of social worlds raises certain difficulties. It has associations with theories that emphasise functional relations between individuals, institutions and the wider society and within which 'worlds' can be reduced to complex individualised or even 'ego-centred' networks (Marx 1990: 193). Likewise it can suggest that under conditions of normality there is a continuity of relationships which tend towards equilibrium or even harmony. But the social network is not necessarily static, nor limited by immediate relationships or those of a specific community or a certain physical space. When considered as unbounded, the network encompasses *the whole social life* of individuals, including the experiences of change in a world of increasingly rapid transformations. In the case of refugees it assists understanding of the repeated, often sudden changes associated with displacement, flight and exile.
2. See Rahmato's account of survival strategies, quoted in Crow 2000: 20.
3. Smith (1984: 121) notes that all manner of means, including smuggling, were used to retrieve documents, safe deposit boxes, cash and valuables.
4. Denis McNamara, UN special co-ordinator for IDPs, quoted in *The Independent*, 19 December 2000.
5. In 2001 the Lebanese government introduced a new law permitting foreigners ownership of property in the country. Palestinians specifically were excluded and Palestinian men who already owned their own homes were denied the right to pass ownership to their wives or other family members on their death.

6. Denis McNamara, UN special co-ordinator for the displaced, quoted in *The Guardian,* 22 February 2001. Key countries affected, according to the United Nations were: Ethiopia, Eritrea, Burundi, Colombia, Angola, Indonesia, Sudan, Afghanistan, Congo and Sri Lanka.
7. Quoted in Sayyigh 1979: 131.
8. Clark, quoted in Kibreab 1993: 330.
9. Study by Johns Hopkins University based on data from 22 countries, quoted in *The Guardian,* 24 July 2001.
10. *The Guardian,* 24 July 2001.
11. Estimate made by the Centre for Civil Society at the London School of Economics, quoted ibid.
12. Loescher 2001: 288. See Loescher 2001: 272–86 for a discussion of the UNHCR's 'decade of repatriation'.
13. Minear quoted in Stubbs 1999: 33.
14. The physical dangers, isolation and high levels of stress associated with work in conflict zones have caused many field staff to leave front-line agencies, notably the UNHCR, in which Loescher (2001: 361) describes a major staffing crisis.
15. Wilson, quoted in Keen 1992: 64.
16. Gender matters are often discussed in the context of dichotomies – male/female, public/private and political/apolitical. This suggests distinct definitions, boundaries and oppositions, distorting the complexities of social life and its fluctuations and changes. For a discussion of some of the issues raised see Indra 1999.
17. In contrast when Eritrean refugees settled in urban areas outside the control of camp authorities women remained active economically and as 'agents of change and sources of livelihoods' (Kibreab 1995: 9). Their status in relation to men was not adversely affected.
18. Despite pressures on women there is much evidence to suggest that female refugees cope better than males. Hitchcox (1990: 219) notes that in Hong Kong most Vietnamese refugees were rendered 'inert and apathetic' by the camp regime. The effect on men who had come from a strongly patriarchal society in which they held responsibility for supporting the family and authority over its affairs was to cause deep distress and high levels of depression. Women coped better, developing traditional work in the preparation and sale of food and provision of services for the community and expanding their area of autonomous activity.
19. These including a pitched battle in Ceuta between protesters and the police in which scores of people were injured, and mass protests in Melilla in which parts of the city were destroyed (Gold 2000: 125 and 130).

10
Circuits of Migration[1]

Transnational communities

More displaced people are now long-distance migrants and more are involved in complex movements across regions and continents. Until recently, however, these experiences hardly featured in migration research. To make sense of them it is necessary to think of changed patterns of movement – of global networks within which migrants undertake multiple journeys which may involve repeat, shuttle, 'orbital', 'ricochet' and 'yo-yo' migrations, and attempts at settlement and return. Elaborate patterns of movement suggest *circuits* of migration, accommodating all manner of journeys. What accounts for their emergence and what are the experiences of those who move within them?

The scale and complexity of contemporary migrations is often attributed to globalisation. As we have seen, mainstream theories of globalisation present a false picture of changes at a world level. They amount to global determinism, imposing upon a disordered world particular models of economic and social development. One-dimensional and highly partisan, they obscure processes which precipitate crises and repeated mass displacements. But not all globalist insights should be dismissed. Of particular importance is the suggestion that movements of capital, ideas and people which pass across old borders, notably those of the nation-state, have multiple causes and require new frameworks of understanding. Papastergiadis (2000: 35) suggests that, in the context of migration, 'We ... need to think more about processes of flux and flow, rather than fixing solely on the causes or consequences of single trajectories.' These processes are associated with networks which operate across territorial boundaries – with communities that have an existence beyond societies of the nation-state.

Neither the extra-territorial entity nor the notion of transnationalism are new. Al-Ali and Koser (2002: 1) warn that the latter term is *en vogue*, that it has been overused and misused, and that in the area of migration it has been criticised as nothing novel, 'that in effect new labels are being applied to old processes'. Diasporas – 'scatterings' – do indeed have an ancient history. These networked communities of peoples residing far from real or imagined natal territories have been recorded for over 3000 years: in the case of the Jews they have been the context within which for centuries tradition has been elaborated and identity defined. But other less celebrated and less formal affiliations have been of enormous importance. For centuries before the emergence of the nation-state wide-ranging commercial networks were animated by traders who moved over vast distances. Abu-Lughod (1989) high-lights their significance for regional and global economies, and for all manner of cultural exchanges. The modern state intruded upon these networks, destroying them or, by means of colonialism, reshaping and re-directing them. It brought a new form of strictly national identification; at the same time its imposition of territorial, political and cultural borders gave a new emphasis to pre-existing linkages. In recent decades global change has facilitated growth of more such transnationalisms – networks of affiliation which have become integral to the new circuits of migration.

Three closely associated developments have been crucial to the growth of transnationalism. First, new technologies of mass transport have greatly increased temporary mobility – migrations for purposes such as business, study and tourism. In the mid-twentieth century large numbers of people in the West began to develop expectations of extended leisure time and of travel to places hitherto beyond the reach of all but the most privileged. Package holidays based on mass air transport offered huge economies of scale and the industry grew at breakneck speed: between 1950 and 1990 international tourism increased by 17 times.[2] Crash programmes of airport development transformed scores of cities into major regional transport centres and integrated hundreds of lesser provincial centres into the new networks. By the late 1990s, some 500,000 airline passengers crossed national borders every day (Rosenau 2002: 156). The human traffic was not all one-way. As the cost of air flights fell there was a new option of regular long-distance travel *from* regions which had been at the periphery of the transport systems, and of repeated movement between places sepa-rated by great physical distances. Among the first to take advantage were communities formed during the post-war era of mass labour recruitment in Europe and North America. These already maintained dense networks of exchange at the economic, social and cultural levels, now they were intensified by increased face-to-face contact.

Changes in means of communication have taken such developments to a further level. In the 1950s for the first time wide access to telephone communication offered large numbers of people the potential of almost instant dialogue. A generation later new technologies provided the opportunity for virtual communication, enormously increasing the density of contacts so that by the late 1990s an estimated 1.4 billion email messages crossed national borders every day, while hundreds of million people had access to the Internet and to satellite TV (Rosenau 2002: 154).[3] The 'compression' of space and time characteristic of these changes was especially congenial to transnational groupings – Rosenau (2002:155) describes their growth as 'an organizational explosion'. During the 1990s network organisations brought together many individuals and small groups to pool information and to maximise inputs, and diasporas which for years had been fragmented in the physical sense drew closer. Transnational networks have made use of all aspects of the cyber environment. In the case of the Palestinians the density of links developed since the uprising of September 2000, especially through web pages, has been described as a 'cyber *intifada*' (Aouragh 2003) and even as an 'Inter-fada' (Bunt 2003: 91).[4] Ellis and Khan (2002) note the importance of satellite television for the Kashmiri diaspora, and Horst (2003: 150) shows that in East Africa the radio transmitter has become a key means of communication for Somalis. This particular initiative was undertaken by Somali refugees, who adopted the device from NGOs and transformed it into a communications tool of such importance that the web of links which connects villages, camps and towns in East Africa with Somali communities worldwide is largely dependent upon transmitters.

Traditional analyses of migration are inadequate to deal with such developments. The push-pull theory long dominated migration studies. It proposed that migration was essentially a response to the demands of the marketplace, moving people from areas of surplus labour to those of labour deficiency. Migrants were entirely passive: in effect they were directed by the same 'hidden hand' that regulated market affairs. This view complemented modernisation theory: development was a linear process; so too with migration, in which mobile individuals were rewarded with improved economic status, inspiring others to follow and drawing their societies of origin towards a vision of prosperity. In the 1980s alternative analyses began to appear, focusing on migrant communities and the role of migrants themselves. Massey (1990) was among the first to emphasise the importance of both 'sending' and 'receiving' communities, of the links between them, and of their influence upon migrants' lives – the impact of the entire migratory network. Others, including Rouse (1991) and Glick Schiller *et al.* (1992) have since focused upon transnational communities as networks of social action. They suggest that the idea of community no longer implies a bounded physical presence in the territorial space of the nation-state but that the new networks themselves play a key role in shaping global movements, drawing in and re-circulating migrants as part of a process of flux and flow.

Discourse of rights

A third development of importance for the new migrations is the discourse of rights – the generalisation worldwide of ideas about human entitlements. This is a complex and contested area. On the one hand many theorists of globalisation maintain that global processes generalise awareness of rights. Waters (1995: 102) suggests that a key global development is 'institutionalization of the view that individual human beings have rights *qua* humans', and Shaw (1994: 132) identifies concepts of 'global responsibility' in which concern for human rights is a key factor. Some theorists of global cultural change go much further: Robertson (1992: 132) argues that a key feature of the contemporary world is the generalisation of ideas about 'the communal-species aspect of the global-human condition' in which notions of rights are institutionalised at a global level, so that the rights discourse is integral to a globalised society. Others see less positive developments. Brysk (2002: 1) comments that a more cosmopolitan and open international system should free individuals to pursue their rights, but that large numbers of people are suffering from both state repression and from 'new denials of rights linked to transnational forces'. She expresses fears that open markets and irregular migration present problems that are not amenable to state-based human rights regimes. As we have seen, processes associated with globalisation are contradictory: so too with claims on rights, which have in some respects been weakened but in other ways greatly strengthened.

The most important feature of the rights discourse in the contemporary world is its contested character. Ideas about rights differ radically among states, transnational organisations, political parties and communities. In the late 1980s, as neo-liberalism reset the world development agenda, the World Bank began to speak of the need for 'good governance', arguing that development was inhibited primarily by internal factors and that investment must be tied to political reform underpinned by guarantees of human rights. What was required in Africa, said the bank's president Barber Conable, was increased accountability of governments, together with 'respect for human rights and the rule of law' (George and Sabelli 1994: 156). As in the 1940s, when dominant states wrote the UDHR and later the Geneva Convention, issues of concern to the Bank were specific civil and political rights. These became central to development policy, many Third World governments being put under pressure to reform by withholding aid and by ideological offensives targeting their rights records (other states with long records of repression but friendly relations with the West were meanwhile indulged with aid and weaponry). Defence of rights soon became a rationale for Western military intervention. As Waters (1995: 103) observes, human rights became 'an important legitimizing icon' for states which wished to intervene in the internal affairs of others. The strategy had unexpected results, however, generalising at a popular level ideas which were not congenial to Western states or their associates in Third World governments. Increasingly, social and political movements across Africa, Asia and Latin America demanded guarantees of rights, and in the face of these pressures many governments established their own human rights commissions. In 1991 in all of Africa there was one such body, in Togo; ten years later half the countries in the continent had established such bodies and several others were in formation. Their credibility was in question: Human Rights Watch suggested that they were 'jumping on the human rights bandwagon' and had been formed primarily to deflect criticisms of states' own regimes of repression.[5] The commitment to human rights was indeed little more than an ideological convenience; it demonstrated, however, the extent to which discussions about rights had become a key feature of political debate.

These changes were accompanied by very rapid growth of transnational rights campaigns. By the early 1990s Amnesty International had more than 8000 local groups in over 70 countries (Amnesty International 1993: 332); by 2000 it had over a million members and subscribers (Amnesty International 2000: 273). Together with other organisations such as Human Rights Watch, it exercised an influence unwanted by dominant states and which affected the strategies of many NGOs. Organisations which had begun life in other fields of activity, such as the Red Cross and Medecins Sans Frontieres, discovered 'that speaking out on human rights [was] a necessary ancillary to their primary purpose' (Power 2001: 158). Rights-related activity had become a feature of NGOs' agendas worldwide and by the 1990s its impact was being amplified by the digital communications revolution. Weyker (2002: 118) notes the importance of new technologies for local and transnational human rights networks – in speeding up the collection and processing of information, enlarging the scale of activity and facilitating huge surges of support for victims of human rights abuses, what he calls 'global on-line cathexis'. The combined impact has been to broadcast more widely ideas about rights in general and to familiarise networks of activists with rights of special relevance to migrants and to potential migrants. NGOs have endorsed the centrality to migrant networks of the rights discourse, with its formal universalism, its critiques of the state and the state's excesses and its appeal to specific rights, notably the right to freedom of movement, the right to return, and the right to asylum. They have often played a contradictory role: charged with crisis management, containment and control; they have also facilitated the spread of ideas which encourage transnationalism and physical movement across state borders. Together with the powerful incentive to leave zones of crisis and the increasing sophistication of transport networks this has provided added encouragement to many displaced people to move on, into the circuits of migration.

Refugees 'in orbit'

Transnational networks have the potential to mobilise information and resources which can move migrants quickly over great distances. In the case of refugees, however, their development is often inhibited by the extreme disadvantage faced by many forced migrants. Their journeys are often complex and particularly circuitous, and they may be driven to the margins of marginal societies, struggling to survive and sometimes stranded far from an intended destination.

Mass long-distance movement direct to countries of asylum by means of formal, legal routes has become extremely rare. In general this takes place only when states or agencies organise an airlift from areas of conflict, as with Vietnamese in the 1970s and in the 1990s with some Bosnians and Kosovans. In the late 1980s some large refugee groups made use of direct scheduled flights: by this means several thousand Kurds found their way to Western Europe, using provincial airports in southern Turkey earlier developed to encourage tourism. European governments soon banned these arrivals and new regulations prevented such groups boarding aircraft, part of the restrictions on movement which have since driven many long-distance refugees into the irregular networks (see Chapter 11). Today few attempt to reach their desired destination by means of direct inter-continental travel; rather they make several journeys, often separated by lengthy periods of residence in temporary homes in a succession of countries or even several continents.

There is little research on such movements. The detail of specific cross-border journeys such as that from Mexico to the United States has been documented by, among others, Durand and Massey (1995) and by Annerino (1999), but the wider experience of long-distance migration is largely unrecorded. There is strong anecdotal evidence, however, to suggest that very large numbers of long-distance forced migrants undertake complex, multiple journeys. Issa, a Somali refugee now living in London, relates his experience:

> My family are from Hargeisa but we were living in Mogadishu in 1988 when the country began to collapse. We were the wrong people in the wrong place. We were in real danger and so we left for Kenya. Things were a mess there, we found enemies as well as friends. We went on to Tanzania and then to Zambia. It was clear that we couldn't go home but we didn't know where

else to go. There were Somalis all over East Africa. We went on to South Africa and there we learned how to apply for asylum in Britain. We arrived in London three years after leaving Somalia. It was a long journey but one we had to make.[6]

Anna, a Peruvian refugee, describes similar travels around Latin America:

Some of my family were connected with the guerrillas and we younger ones thought we should go into hiding. Some of us went to Bolivia, then back into Peru and on to Ecuador. We stayed there for a year and then we went to Columbia, which was more dangerous than Peru. We got papers there which allowed us to travel to Mexico and then we got the money to fly to London. We had been refugees for over five years in Latin America before we even applied to be proper refugees in England.[7]

Mohamed is an Afghan refugee living in Germany. From the early 1980s his family lived in a refugee camp in Pakistan:

I did not agree with all the ideas of the Mojahidin [the armed Afghan opposition] and it was not safe for me in the camps. I went to Iran and after a while I went on *hajj* [pilgrimage] to Mecca. I worked in Saudi Arabia for a while but I couldn't stay and I went back to Iran. Then through a friend I heard about how to go to Russia. I went to Moscow and stayed there for three years – it was very hard and difficult to get a job. I went to Poland and then at last to Berlin.[8]

Melander (1987) refers to the phenomenon of 'refugees in orbit'. Michel, a Congolese living in London, describes a series of journeys in which he became just such a 'serial' or 'orbital' traveller:

We escaped from Zaire by canoe to Angola: that was the easy part. Then we got to Luanda. It's a dangerous place, there was a war on. I decided I had to get away to safety. I took a plane to Moscow: what a shock! – it was minus 15 degrees when I arrived. I only had my clothes from Africa and I had to sleep out: I did not even have a blanket. I spent some days in the airport but I knew had to move on or freeze to death. I wanted to go to Germany but I ended up in the Czech Republic, where I was arrested and deported back to Moscow.

I flew back to Luanda and went on to Zaire. I tried to live there but it was impossible, so I went again by canoe to Angola and once more on to Luanda. The war was worse there, so this time I took a flight to Cote d'Ivoire and then to Lagos. From there I was able to fly to London. I have plenty of friends who had experiences just like mine.[9]

The further the target country the more complex and dangerous are the means which must be used. Mares (2001: 58–9) records the journey of a family of Algerians which reached Australia after a passing through Saudi Arabia, Singapore (where they were jailed for a year), Malaysia, Thailand, the United Arab Emirates, Tanzania, Zambia, and Zimbabwe. There are hosts of similar individual stories from refugees around the world, some who have secured asylum, and some of whom are marooned far from their desired destinations. What they have in common is the experience of movement through networks in which information is obtained, resources mobilised and decisions taken about further journeys. These may be part of developed transnational communities bound by regular physical contact and by elaborate electronic links. Often they are less substantial – they are marginal, transient groupings without the material resources to participate in complex electronic exchanges. They nonetheless exert a strong influence on migrants, shaping new strategies and fascilitating further journeys.

Urban refugees

The key transit points within transnational networks are located in the major cities. More and more refugees originate in cities. City-dwellers sometimes enjoy privileges vis-à-vis rural people but may also be more readily deprived of resources: they may be the first to feel the impact of shortages of food, fuel and other essentials, and of punitive measures adopted by regimes under threat. They are likely to be in the vanguard of opposition movements and are often the first to be targeted by those in power. In addition, in times of conflict, cities are often the principal targets for conflicting parties and in these situations most displaced people are likely to be urbanites. They may flee to the countryside, as in East Timor where in 1999 almost the entire population left the city of Dili. More often they move across borders to cities where familiarity with the urban environment makes for easier adjustment than for people of rural origin. In addition, many of today's urban refugees are rural people who have travelled far from centres of displacement, and from rural refugee camps and holding centres.

Cooper (1992: 5) comments that the city exerts a strong attraction:

> [W]herever forced migration takes place, certain refugees choose to move to an urban environment rather than languish in a camp, or become part of a planned settlement, or attempt to integrate with the rural population of the host country. The individuals concerned may themselves have come originally from urban environments; previous experiences abroad may have made some familiar with urban settings; news of a variety of opportunities in the 'big city' may have filtered through, including economic possibilities for moving on elsewhere, perhaps with the help of a resettlement programme; a

known community of migrants from the sending country may already exist as a network for others who have been forced to flee; life in a camp or settlement may simply seem hopeless; and for some the move to the city may in part be the result of desperation.

Growth of the new transport networks has brought big cities within reach of all but the most physically isolated communities, and urban centres worldwide now contain large refugee populations. Bogota, Colombia, is a typical example. Here migrant communities include many people displaced by conflicts in Central and South America, and who are effectively settled in the city, together with 'transit refugees' who hope to move to more desired destinations, in this case mainly to the United States. In 1997 Colombian newspapers noted the presence of large groups of refugees from Cuba, Ecuador and Peru, together with transit migrants from all over Africa and Asia – from Nigeria, Ghana, Congo, Namibia, Burundi, Mali, Senegal, Tanzania, China, India, Iran and Pakistan (*Trafficking in Migrants*, September 1997). So too in the case of Moscow. Throughout the early 1990s refugees from across Africa, Asia and the Middle East arrived in the Russian capital. By 1996 Sri Lankans, Iraqis, Afghans and Chinese were prominent among a population of at least 250,000 transit migrants.[10] The pattern is repeated for scores of regional centres, with a large and often diverse refugee presence in cities including Mexico City, Rio de Janeiro, Sao Paulo, Johannesburg, Nairobi, Cairo, Khartoum, Dakar, Istanbul, New Delhi and Bangkok. In addition numerous cities are home to large populations of specific groups of refugees. Among these are Sri Lankan Tamils in Madras; Sudanese in Cairo and Kampala; Burundians in Dar Es Salaam; Angolans in Rio de Janeiro; Haitians in Santo Domingo; Afghans in Peshawar, Lahore, New Delhi and Mashhad; Somalis in Nairobi; Sierra Leoneans in Conakry; and Palestinians in Amman, Beirut, Cairo and Damascus.

Little is known about most of these communities, described by Rogge and Akol (1989: 184) as the 'forgotten' refugees. States, agencies and researchers have been reluctant to identify forced migrants in cities as refugees, and have greatly understated numbers and problems of these communities. Hansen comments that officially recognised refugees, who are usually placed in camps in the countryside, are relatively easy to study: 'Their identity and location are known. They live in locations that are supervised and managed by the national government or by international organizations.' In contrast, he observes, urban refugees are usually dispersed, unenumerated and unmanaged.[11] Refugees as a whole are seen by states, agencies and sometimes by researchers primarily as rural people who have been displaced into camps and relief centres, while urban refugees are anomalous. This was the view advanced in the

UNHCR's first report on policy and practice in relation to urban refugees. It noted that the agency had no formal definition of the urban refugee, suggesting that the category should include 'anyone who is not a farmer or a peasant' (UNHCR 1995b: 2). It recorded 56,000 urban refugees known to the agency, and suggested that there might be some 200,000 worldwide – a gross underestimate (UNHCR 1995b: 16). Even these small numbers caused the agency great difficulty:

> Urban refugees and asylum seekers tend to include a wide variety of people, some, but by no means all, of whom have genuine asylum claims. They include opportunistic and dynamic individuals as well as those who failed to survive as part of the normal migration (or refugee) flow – the maladjusted, the social outcasts etc – a factor which can make status determination diffi-cult. Furthermore, since such movement is often stimulated, at least partially, by a desire to improve their economic potential, urban refugees and asylum seekers tend to share a culture of expectation, which, if not satisfied, often leads to frustration and violence. (UNHCR 1995b: 3)

The encamped refugee, properly contained and regulated, was the UNHCR model. Urban refugees were not to be seen as part of 'normal' migratory movements and allegedly included opportunists and dysfunctional people. In the jargon of the UNHCR and other agencies this was expressed as the belief that 'spontaneous' or 'self-settled' individuals and groups could not be considered authentic or legitimate. Some UNHCR officials also believed that urban refugees made unreasonable demands, especially over status determination, detention, demands for papers and freedom of movement (UNHCR 1995b: 6). They were seen as having an unfair advantage over camp dwellers and to present the organisation with a dilemma: 'Should the UNHCR "reward" those who have the financial and personal means to move on from a rural settlement to the city, or from one country to another, in order to seek better conditions and prospects?' (ibid). This approach borrowed much from the attitude of Western governments which by the 1990s were describing refugees in general as calculating, aggressive and undeserving. It suggested that the idea of mobile, self-directed refugees is a contradiction, violating notions that the displaced are helpless and always likely to be dependent. It negated the idea of human agency and disregarded the refugee experience.

City lives

There have been numerous criticisms of the UNHCR policy. Human Rights Watch (2002b: 1) has attacked its 'blanket assumption that most refugees should not be moving to or living in urban areas', and that communities in cities live there 'improperly'. After research in New Delhi, Cairo, Nairobi and Bangkok, the UNHCR's own policy unit argued for a new approach that recognised the scale of the refugee presence in major cities and which left 'no room for doubt that refugees in urban areas are of concern' (Obi and Crisp 2002: 1). Its research in New Delhi had given a glimpse of the problems for refugees: many, it recognised, faced immiseration, discrimination and harassment. Most lacked valid residence documents and had technically become illegal immigrants, making them liable to detention and deportation. Growing numbers survived by means of 'illicit activities' and had attempted to leave India in an irregular manner to escape from growing insecurity (Obi and Crisp 2000: 4).

In the case of cities in Africa, Human Rights Watch (2002b: 1) describes refugees as living 'hidden in plain view'. Their problems are clear to see, says the organisation, but host governments and agencies are unwilling to identify them. In Nairobi and Kampala the organisation investigated conditions of very large refugee communities which had originated in war zones of the Horn of Africa and Central Africa. It noted problems including hunger, extortion, harassment, beatings, arbitrary arrest, detention and sexual violence, mostly at the hands of the police and the army. This picture is confirmed by Horst's study of Somalis in Nairobi. Most have fled war and extreme violence: in the city they confront problems of illegality and of police harassment so severe that Horst (2003: 146) describes 'street pogroms', often associated with extortion. In Johannesburg, Landau and others (2004) have recorded similar difficulties, including systematic discrimination and police harassment. In Tanzania, Sommers has conducted detailed research on Burundian refugees. His attempts to record their lives in Dar Es Salaam, he says, brought him personal danger and an awareness of the extreme marginalisation that they experienced as 'undercover urbanites' for whom the city was 'a well of fear' (Sommers 2001a: 30 and 138). Similar problems confront Haitians living in Santo Domingo, capital of the Dominican Republic. Here, says Lee, thousands of migrants live in fear of detention and of forced repatriation.[12]

In 2001 the UNCHR revised its estimate of numbers of urban refugees to 13 per cent of the global total of refugees, some 1.9 million people in 116 countries (UNCHR 2001: 5). This figure also greatly underestimates the scale of urban refugee populations. Urban refugees are often not counted by states or agencies and many do not present themselves to the authorities, fearing arrest, deportation and/or violence. Sommers' research in Tanzania reveals typical problems: during the 1970s displaced people from Burundi began to move illegally from rural settlements as part of the general rural–urban migration that soon concentrated a third of all African refugees in cities (Sommers 2001a: 14). All of those who reached Dar Es Salaam had been born and raised in refugee camps in the west of Tanzania but moved to the capital to escape poverty and the social and political tensions of the camps. According to the Tanzanian authorities there were only a handful of Burundians; in reality, says Sommers, there were thousands. Dar Es Salaam – often known in Swahili as 'Bongo' – had achieved mythical status, as refugees in the camps learned of the prizes to be gained from a new life:

> They hear descriptions from successful returnees who re-enter the settlements bearing thousands of Tanzanian shillings and clothes, sugar, soap and other gifts for their siblings and parents. These returnees describe Dar Es Salaam as the place where buildings have 'many stories' [*sic*], vehicles clog the roadways, and no one goes barefoot. 'Bongoland' or 'Bongo' for short, translates as 'brains' in Swahili. Young men strive to get to Bongo, to prove they have what it takes to make it. (Sommers 2001a: 15)

Young Burundians run serious risks by living illegally in Dar Es Salaam but feel they have no alternative. Those studied by Sommers worked as tailors under conditions of ruthless exploitation, hardly leaving their workplaces – where they also slept – except for visits to church. As illegals they lived in constant fear of assault and robbery, and of discovery and enforced return to the camps. In a 'dangerous and alien' urban environment they were confined to limited areas and to secretive movement (ibid). Most nevertheless maintained that they had no alternative to a suffocating existence in the camps.

Cairo

In one city, Cairo, there have been studies of a number of refugee communities. During the 1980s the city became a haven for refugees from the Horn of Africa, and from Central and West Africa. In an important observation Cooper (1993a: 2) notes that it attracted people across vast distances because of the perception that the city itself might facilitate further movement: 'A magnet effect operates, and many are drawn the long distance to Egypt by news of the different resettlement possibilities from the city' (Cooper 1993a: 2). Information gathered in refugee camps and from community groups and NGOs in the zones of crisis led them towards the city – an example of the effect of incipient transnational networks among refugees and refugee-oriented organisations. In Cairo they hoped for greater security but also for access to means of further movement – primarily to the West. Efforts to organise onward movement often took years, with the result that 'transient refugee populations ... formed in Cairo essentially by default' (Cooper 1993a: 3).

By the late 1990s the number of applications for asylum made in the city was increasing very rapidly: between 1998 and 2001 it grew by over 120 per cent and UNHCR officials in the city speculated that their office received more submissions than any other of the agency's bureaux world-wide.[13] By 2002 there were several new groups of migrants from the conflict zones of Central and West Africa. In a refugee population of at least 70,000 there were refugees from 27 countries; the great majority were Sudanese, with communities of Ethiopians, Eritreans, Somalis, Congolese, Ugandans, Rwandans, Burundians, Ghanaians, Nigerians, Sierra Leonians, Liberians and a number of smaller groups from countries of the Middle East, the Balkans, Central Asia and South-East Asia.[14] By 2004 there were refugees from at least 36 countries.[15] In addition, since 1948 Cairo has been home to a large Palestinian community, usually estimated at some 75,000 (Dajani 1986: 16).

The *Needs Assessment of the Ethiopian and Eritrean Refugee Populations in Cairo*, completed in 1993, revealed that about half of the refugees interviewed had travelled directly to Egypt from their countries of origin (Cooper 1993a: 33). An almost equal number had spent time in other countries. In a large sample, 37 per cent had spent a year or more elsewhere, 22 per cent had spent five years or more elsewhere, and 13 per cent had spent ten years or more elsewhere (ibid). Among countries en route were Sudan, Saudi Arabia, Djibouti, Somalia, Lebanon, Yemen, Iraq, Kenya, Czechoslovakia, Greece and East Germany (Cooper 1992: 15).[16] Some refugees had undertaken multiple journeys, spending several years in various countries: they were ' "seasoned individuals" ... people who [had] spent a large portion of their lives searching for an acceptable solution to their predicament' (Cooper 1993a: 33). Most had reached Cairo by air but some had travelled north from Sudan by train and by boat, while an astonishing 12 per cent had walked from Sudan, following the course of the Nile through Northern Sudan and then on through Southern Egypt to Aswan (Cooper 1993a: 34). One Ethiopian refugee has since given an account of such a journey undertaken in the early 1990s:

> We had no money so we had to walk and eat what we could find on the way. My journey from Khartoum took about two months. We went up the Nile and then across the [Nubian] Desert. We didn't know if we would get to Egypt. It was hard and sometimes it was frightening, especially in the desert when we weren't sure we would be able to eat or drink, but what else could we do? There was nothing for us in Sudan, we had to go on.[17]

This corresponds with accounts provided to Cooper (1992: 15) who notes that tales abound in Cairo of refugees on the route from Sudan being robbed by some locals and receiving help from others, of attempting to find help from camel drivers, of losing their way in the desert, of splitting up with others who were never seen again, 'of forcing oneself to go on exhausted and despairing; and even on rare occasions of seeing the rotting bodies of others who had presumably been trying the same course of action, but who had clearly failed'. These journeys were feats of endurance, taking refugees through some of the most inhospitable terrain in Africa. They are testimony to the extreme pressure felt by displaced people who take every risk in order to reach places of safety. When Moorehead interviewed refugees in the city ten years later she discovered an even more complex pattern of movement. Displaced people had arrived from a swathe of African countries in conflict – from Guinea in the west to Burundi in the east. They had come 'by a hundred different paths, on foot, by ferry, in aeroplanes, on trucks and trains, by camel and horseback, believing that for all its horror, life was still worth living, that Egypt would be a gateway to a future' (Moorehead 2005: 7).

Destitution

There has been detailed research in Cairo on communities of Sudanese refugees. Moro and Lamua (1998: 21) note that most experienced a number of internal displacements before reaching Egypt, where they have faced trying circumstances. Until 1995 Sudanese nationals had rights of residence in Egypt and were therefore not usually recognised as refugees: legally they were treated as if they were IDPs. New regulations then specified that they must obtain visas to enter Egypt and must apply for asylum if they wished to remain in the country as refugees.[18] In 1998, among a very large community in Cairo only a fraction were formally refugees. Those who applied for recognition from the UNHCR, which conducts determination procedures in Egypt, were forced to wait years for interviews; if they meanwhile attempted to obtain a visa or to extend the validity of a passport they were said to be availing themselves of the protection of their state, with the result that the application to the UNHCR would be refused. Most refugees abandoned hope of recognition and remained as illegals, living in constant fear of apprehension by the police. Nonetheless pressures exerted in Sudan meant that by 2001 the community in Cairo was growing 'exponentially'.[19]

Most recent Sudanese refugees do not have the right to employment and are compelled to find work in the informal sector. Most live at the margin of survival: according to one leading support agency, they are 'increasingly more destitute ... the frustration level is mounting'.[20] Most men are unable to find work: women are more likely to be successful but almost exclusively in domestic service, where they are open to intense exploitation and abuse, including sexual abuse (Nyoka 1999: 43).

There has been great distress in Sudanese communities that some compatriots have been forced to undertake 'forbidden' practices, notably production and sale of alcohol, and prostitution. Moro and Lamua (1998: 26) conclude that 'displacement has been a painful experience to [sic] the Sudanese'. Many Sudanese arrive in Egypt as single people and find themselves without the family support networks to which they have been accustomed. Enormous efforts are made to recreate basic kin structures through which mutual support can be provided: this is the only means by which most refugees can find accommodation. By the late 1990s new arrivals from Southern Sudan were being taken into apartments which on average already had 15 to 20 residents (Nyoka 1999: 36). Lado (1996: 48) quotes a woman who lived with 18 others in a three-roomed flat: 'When someone comes to the house at night he/she cannot find a place to put his/her leg.' Other refugee communities in the city undergo much the same experience. In a study of Somali refugees Al Sharmani (1999: 25) notes that life in Cairo has proved so difficult that the clan differences and divisions which dominate socio-political life in Somalia are superseded by a form of 'continuous networking' that operates across the whole community to provide accommodation and mutual support. The outcome is 'a larger Somali identity that encompasses all the Somali refugees in Cairo' (ibid).

Eritreans and Ethiopians also face extreme pressure. Most who arrived in the late 1980s and early 1990s had urban backgrounds: typically they came from families with professional or commercial connections, and had been educated to secondary level. In Cairo they were compelled to take menial jobs, mainly as domestic cleaners: 'All of the women and most of the men confess to having cried the first time they carried out this kind of work' (Cooper 1992: 28). Many reported discrimination on the part of Egyptians – their illegal/marginal status led them to mistrust neighbours and to develop strategies of avoidance. One informant commented that, 'Everyone lives behind closed doors' (Cooper 1992: 32). Although their apartments operated as a refuge of sorts, they were also isolating, and depression was extremely common. Mikael, an Ethiopian refugee, explains: 'Most of us came on our own and met other people from home through the church or by chance. Some people live near one another but most of us are spread across Cairo and it takes a long journey to meet friends. It is a tough life here.'[21]

Recent refugees from Sudan, Central Africa and West Africa are concentrated in very poor neighbourhoods such as Arba'a wi-Nuss ('Four-and-a-Half') in the northern suburb of Nasr City. The newspaper *Ahram Weekly* describes daily life in the quarter:

> Fate dealt Arba'a-wi-noss a poor hand. There are no police stations ... Roads are unpaved – a virtual disaster when it rains. Electricity only reached parts of

the settlement last year and the supply is sporadic. A water and sewage system has been in place for nearly five years, but water has yet to run through its pipes. Absence of running water makes life particularly difficult. Residents must walk several kilometres at times to find water and bring it back in plastic containers costing anywhere from 25 to 50 piastres each ... There are no parks, no gardens, no open spaces. Garbage dumps line the southern border. (*Ahram Weekly*, 29 June 2002)

There is minimal medical care – the nearest effective facilities, which must be paid for, are in central Cairo. Malnutrition, chronic bronchial disorders and diarrhoea are common. A West African refugee who arrived in Cairo in 1999 relates his experience in the area:

It took me months to get to Egypt and now I have to live in that place. Of course I am pleased to be safe: in my country I was running from village to village to escape the army. But my life in Cairo is so hard. Me and my friends don't have money to eat, to buy shoes, even to take the bus. We walk a lot, many kilometres every day, although this can be dangerous – Downtown [Central Cairo] the refugees on the street are sometimes arrested and put in prison and we don't discover for weeks where they are. It is a hard, hard struggle. In order to survive some of my friends have to do things I cannot tell you about: it means they have lost their pride. We are living like ghosts.[22]

West Africans are not the only refugees to face harassment on the streets. The El-Nadim Centre for Rehabilitation of Victims of Violence reports widespread intimidation from police, especially if refugees are found without identification. In addition, Sudanese face a specific threat from Sudan's security services in Cairo, which appear to operate without impunity (El Nadim Centre 2004).

Co-operation and competition

During the 1980s Mexico City acted as a magnet for refugees in Latin America, paralleling the role performed by Cairo in relation to migrants from East and Central Africa. During a decade of political upheaval in Central America some 300,000 to 400,000 people fled to Mexico and very large communities of Salvadorians, Guatemalans and Nicaraguans were established, together with smaller groups from many countries further to the south (Zolberg 1989: 215–20). With the exception of specific groups of Guatemalans and Salvadoreans, none were recognised as refugees: some were given temporary asylum status, while most were categorised as economic migrants. Many wished to return to their place of origin, and during the 1990s there were several large programmes of repatriation. Others had no such prospect and wished for a secure place of asylum, usually the United States. The latter, however, enacted increasingly exclusionary policies, insisting that Mexico restrain the migrants. As more and more refugees arrived, all the city's migrant communities came under increasing pressure. Antonio is a Columbian refugee who lived in Mexico City for several years. He recalls:

> When I got there in 1994 there were refugees from all the nearby countries. Some people, like the Chileans, had been there for over 20 years. People were arriving all the time, especially from the south, countries like Peru. Those who arrived last had the toughest time. We had to start from the beginning in putting together our communities: getting jobs and homes, finding out about our rights, bringing our families. No one gave much help: actually the refugees who had been there a long time guarded important information. When you are living a refugee life, information can be more important than anything else and people protect it. This made our lives more difficult.[23]

Accounts from Africa confirm that a shared predicament does not necessarily bring co-operation among communities of the displaced. Elizabeth is a Ugandan refugee who lived for several years in Nairobi. She recalls that as new refugee groups arrived in the city, antagonisms developed:

> It got very bad when lots of Somalis came in 1990. Of course I don't blame them because we all faced the same problems. All the refugee groups had made connections with the UNHCR and with the churches and charities, and also with embassies of some countries who accepted refugees. When you are a refugee with a difficult life you learn important things about how to survive, then when new people come they have to struggle to discover the same things. Sometimes that means they fight you too.[24]

In the mid-1990s inter-communal tensions increased and there was a series of confrontations in Nairobi between groups claiming access to the same small pool of resources.[25]

Accounts from Cairo show how each incoming group struggles to establish relationships with agencies that might offer support or assist with onward movement. In order to do so they must learn basic information about survival in the city and about how to approach those who hold the keys to acceptance in resettlement programmes or other means of securing admission to a desired place of asylum such as the United States, Canada, Western Europe or Australia. This information may be closely guarded: one Sudanese refugee suggested that knowledge about such programmes was 'worth more than gold'.[26] He added: 'If we learn about new ways of leaving we tell only friends and we apply very quickly. What is the point of telling 10,000 people if there are 500 places and we want to leave? It is a race to get out.'[27]

Culture of disbelief

Refugees in the 'magnet' cities of the Third World survive as marginals, living at the edge of societies in which the mass of the local population may enjoy only a precarious existence. Their efforts to establish coherent communities, and to maintain links to home and to other places of exile are often frustrated by impermanence, by discrimination and by a pressing lack of resources. There is intense pressure to move on, but if further migration is to be accomplished through official channels, refugees must negotiate the complex world of the asylum gatekeepers – the officials at embassies, consulates and NGOs involved in adjudication of refugee status and in selection for resettlement programmes. Here they confront the reality that national frontiers are not only policed where territorial boundaries are drawn but also where migrants make their initial claims for admission. Most embassies of desired countries of asylum now maintain immigration offices which operate as advanced border posts within countries of high emigration or in which there are large refugee communities. In the case of states of North America and Western Europe such staff operate within an official culture of scepticism about applicants. A former British immigration officer who worked in an Asian capital which accommodates large numbers of refugees explains:

> Our starting-point was that refugees are economic migrants. They want to get to Britain to get a share of the good life and our job was to stop them because most made fraudulent claims. In training we were presented with all sorts of evidence to show that most asylum-seekers are just trying to use the Geneva Convention to squeeze into Britain. The training focuses on how to identify the cheats and send them away. I don't know of any other Western country whose staff think differently. It took me years to reach a different conclusion, because once you believe that the vast majority of applicants have false stories everyone is under suspicion. To my shame I have to say that I rejected hundreds of people who had no real choice but to try to leave.[28]

Extra-territorial policing of borders in most countries with large refugee populations is now reinforced by Airline Liaison Officers (ALOs). In 1996 the European Union adopted a policy by which ALOs were to be posted to consulates to advise local airline staff about the authenticity of travel documents. Britain, for example, sends ALOs to over 20 major cities including New Delhi, Colombo, Accra, Nairobi and Dakar. Morrison and Crosland (2001: 42) observe that inspection of the operations manuals used by ALOs, as well as government reports of their activities, shows no reference to possible refugee protection issues or to other human rights concerns: 'Rather, the focus is upon blanket border control against irregular migration ... Such activities do prevent refugees from leaving their country of origin or at times a neighbouring state in which they are still unsafe' (ibid).

Officials often have great difficulty visualising circumstances which have brought refugees to the city. Even the initial UNHCR report on urban refugees recognised this problem, noting that responsibility for status determination is commonly delegated to junior professional staff with little experience in refugee work who are compelled to make decisions quickly and under pressure (UNHCR 1995b: 17). In a scenario typical among major NGOs a leading transnational agency which 'processes' asylum-seekers for resettlement in the West continues to employ as case workers young men and women whose privileged lives place them a world away from those upon whom they pass life-altering judgements. One experienced official comments that she feels embarrassed and distressed that 'these youngsters' have the power to determine the fate of thousands of displaced people: 'Then they go home to their fine houses and to a good meal. The applicants they have rejected just have to pick up the pieces.'[29] Individual officials have unacknowledged influence over applications. All are bound in theory to criteria laid out in the Geneva Convention but are able to interpret Article 1, on the 'well-founded fear of being persecuted', in a host of ways. Cooper (1992: 42) notes the opinion of an immigration official in an embassy in Cairo that 'one could present almost anyone's case in such a way that the individual concerned would qualify for refugee status'. In practice this means that most claims are rejected. Refugees may have travelled thousands of miles to encounter officials who dismiss their applications and their experiences. Officials in different embassies or even in the same institution may interpret the same application in radically different ways, for 'one officer's political refugee can be another officer's economic migrant' (ibid). So too with UNHCR officials: although UNHCR offices sometimes operate under difficult circumstances, including extreme pressure from local regimes, refugees frequently relate unsympathetic, even hostile treatment at the agency. By 2001 UNHCR offices in no less than 42 cities worldwide were undertaking refugee status determination – a task far from the agency's mandate and one in which it adopts the role of the state.[30]

Evidence from Cairo suggests that UNHCR officials have adopted an extremely conservative approach: although most refugees in the city come from zones of intense conflict, in 2002 only 27 per cent were granted refugee status, leading many applicants to allege that the agency operated a quota system by arrangement with the government. The following year the total rose abruptly to 63 per cent, then fell back sharply, so that by April 2004 it was at 46 per cent.[31] By 2004 the UNHCR had recognised some 32,000 refugees in Egypt, mainly Sudanese.[32] A much larger number had been rejected, while tens of thousands had not applied for status determination: according to refugee community activists they had little confidence in the UNHCR and feared rejection and therefore disqualification from all resettlement schemes.[33]

Gatekeepers

The refugee experience of engagement with institutional gatekeepers is that of encounters with a complex, mysterious and hostile network. Applicants for visas or for resettlement often describe the experience of interview as intimidating. The level of scepticism required of officials seems to refugees to belittle the experiences they have undergone. A refugee who reached Cairo on foot from Sudan recalls his interview for resettlement in the early 1990s:

> When he [the official] asked how I arrived in Egypt I said that I had no money so I walked. He laughed, he said that nobody could walk that far and that this story would not help me. He thought I was lying and although he asked me other questions I knew that was the end of my application.[34]

Such an unsuccessful encounter with an official can have serious consequences. Mohamed, a refugee living in Cairo who requested a visa for entry to a European country, was refused and his papers stamped to indicate rejection: 'This was a disaster – the worst thing that can happen. Now I have been refused by one all the others will refuse me. How can I ever get a visa to any country? They could have put a mark on my forehead, it's the same thing.'[35]

Different treatment of those who relate similar personal experiences of displacement undermines the credibility of the asylum system as a whole. Mohamed relates that his friend Mahjoub was granted a visa by the embassy which rejected his own application, even though the two had almost identical stories to tell during their interviews.[36] Officials are often described by refugees as showing hostility towards people of certain ethnic or religious affiliation. Shanks-Riak Akuei comments of her research in Cairo within the Dinka community of Southern Sudan that religion was often cited as a problem by applicants for refugee status or for resettlement who had been rejected by local officials whom applicants believed had taken exception to their Christian affiliation.[37] Changing terms of admission to resettlement programmes, or changing requirements for visas, lead to widespread confusion about how to present applications. Successful applicants are monitored closely by other asylum-seekers who are debriefed in order to discover whether there are new rules or new interpretations of the regulations. Evidence from Cairo suggests that information is passed worldwide, with increasingly intense use of email and the Internet to exchange experiences of quota systems and resettlement schemes.[38] Refugees with specific, well-authenticated accounts of their displacement and flight may feel compelled to alter their stories in order to accommodate real or imagined changes in regulations at an embassy or NGO. Rumours about what is required spread quickly through local communities, and increasingly through the transnational networks, and may result in ill-informed refugees presenting applications which, in the eyes of officials, immediately disqualify them. Research by Currie (2004) shows that in Cairo entire kinship networks are affected by the outcome of these decisions, which not only shape family life but may determine marriage strategies and even the choice of spouses.

Part of the culture of exile among urban refugees is the establishment of relationships with specific embassies and agencies in the hope of gaining privileged access to information which may lead to onward movement. National and ethnic rivalries may develop over relations with organisations or even specific officials, making more tense the distressing lives which many refugees endure in the city. This is reflected in Elizabeth's comments about Nairobi:

> When a lot of people who had recently arrived were taken on a [resettlement] programme we were angry. Some of us had already applied to that country [of destination] and we had been refused. We asked them [the newcomers] about how they had been accepted – once they were friendly but now they would not talk to us. Our relations with them got very bad.[39]

A similar story comes from Kampala, where in the late 1990s there were outbreaks of fighting between Sudanese and Rwandan refugees after rumours spread that US resettlement programmes were giving preferential treatment to the latter.[40]

The cost of rejection by gatekeeper institutions can be high. If refugees are apprehended by the local authorities they may be identified as failed applicants and may face deportation to a state where their lives are in danger. Others may be excluded from future programmes and effectively marooned – condemned to watch new arrivals move on while they continue to live within the narrow margin permitted by the host state. A welfare worker in Cairo sums up their predicament:

> If refugees here are refused the opportunity to move on they are in trouble. Most do not have rights in Egypt and struggle to survive here. Most can't go back and they can't go on, so they are in limbo. Living in a big city like this is tough enough. Being a failed asylum-seeker can be hell.[41]

Applicants may also face problems making contact with key agencies. In Cairo some refugees speak of repeated experiences of exclusion from UNHCR offices: those unable to gain admission often believe that a payment to guards or officials would ensure a different treatment. Agency officials may be aware of the pressures and of the opportunities to exploit them. In 2001 refugees in Nairobi complained that security guards were charging them for entry to the UNHCR compound and that officials were demanding payments of up to $5000 to place applicants on schemes to settle in North America, Europe and Australia (*Guardian*, 21 February 2001). Protests at agency offices and consulates are common, and include hunger strikes and suicide attempts. In 2002 hundreds of Burmese refugees surrounded the UNHCR office in New Delhi demanding the speeding up of applications for refugee status and reviews of cases which had been rejected. Banners read 'SOS' and 'Victims of UNHCR – silent killer' (*Asia Human Rights News*, 24 October 2002).

Magnet cities are nodal points in the migration networks, sites at which people, information and resources are brought together within the wider web of transnational activity. They draw migrants across vast distances – to this extent they can be seen as exercising a 'pull' function. But insecurity and marginalisation mean that simultaneously they 'push', making forced migrants doubly displaced, or even victims of multiple displacement. For many refugees they are no more than way-stations, from which they eventually move into the informal channels of migration.

Notes

1. In this chapter I have freely made use of interviews with refugees and others conducted at various times between 1992 and 2004 in Cairo, London and Berlin. Among those interviewed are many refugees still living illegally and who requested anonymity: all names have been changed.
2. Quoted in Waters 2001: 207.
3. Less clear is the impact of global communications, especially television, upon migratory flows in general. Television broadcasts, beamed worldwide from Europe and North America, are often said to generalise aspirations among people of the Third World to secure a place in the rich West. In a detailed analysis of globalisation and migration Collinson (1999: 6) concludes, however, that there is no clear evidence for a relationship between the media and mass movement from poor to rich regions. Horst's work (2003) on Somalis in Kenya suggests that her view may need revision. This important issue requires investigation.
4. The 'cyber intifada' has spawned a counter-offensive by Israelis and others hostile to the Palestinians. For an introduction to tracking the intifada in cyberspace see The Cyber-Intifada Resource Guide: http://www.geocities. com/db8r.geo.main.html
5. Quoted in *The Guardian*, 23 February 2001.

6. Interview with Issa, London, May 1998.

7. Interview with Maria, London, May 1998.

8. Interview with Mohamed, Berlin, October 2000.

9. Interview with Michel, London, February 2001.

10. UNHCR report, 'Transit migrants and Trafficking' at http://www.unhcr. ch/cgi_bin/texis/vtxpubl/opendoc:htm?tbl=publ&page=home&id= 3b558565a

11. Foreword to Sommers 2001(a).

12. 'Haitian Political Refugees in the Dominican Republic', a paper presented by Sang Lee to the Ninth Conference of the International Association for the Study of Forced Migration, Sao Paulo, Brazil, January 2005.

13. Unpublished information obtained from the UNHCR office in Cairo, March 2002.

14. Data collected from NGOs and refugee community organisations in Cairo, April 2000. Informed estimates suggest a minimal figure of 70,000, the vast majority of whom live in Cairo. (The Nile Valley Integration Agreement of 1978 gave citizens of Egypt and Sudan rights of residence in both countries. Hence until 1995 Sudanese in Egypt were not viewed as aliens and received no protection or assistance from bodies such as the UNHCR: see note 18 below.) Some estimates run up to 250,000.

15. Information from Katarzyna Grabska of the Forced Migration and Refugee Studies Program at the American University in Cairo, January 2005.

16. When Al-Sharmani surveyed Somali refugees in Cairo ten years later she found a similar pattern: many had lived in a series of countries en route to Egypt, including Kenya, Saudi Arabia and Libya. Al Sharmani 2004: 13.

17. Interview with Tesfa, Cairo, April 1998.

18. In 1995, following an assassination attempt upon Egyptian President Mubarak in Addis Ababa (attributed by the Egyptian government to officials of the Sudanese government) borders between the two countries were closed and rights of Sudanese to enter and live in Egypt were curtailed.

19. Comments of programme leader of St Andrew's Joint Relief Ministry, one of three church-based projects which provide services to refugees in the inner city, March 2001. Because growing numbers of refugees do not apply to the UNHCR for recognition it is very difficult to calculate the refugee population in the city. Assessments by project managers are an important measure of real changes.

20. Unpublished report from St Andrew's Joint Relief Ministry, Cairo 2000.

21. Interview with Mikael, Cairo, April 1998.

22. Interview with Bukhari, Cairo, April 2002.

23. Interview with Antonio, London, May 1998.

24. Interview with Elizabeth, London, May 1998.

25. Interviews with Ethiopian refugees in Cairo, May 1995, and London, April 1996.

26. Interview with Adong, Cairo, May 1995.

27. Ibid.

28. Interview with Anne, a former senior immigration officer, London, May 2000.
29. Interviews with members of the 'processing' team at a leading migration agency in the Middle East and with an official of a local NGO, March 2000.
30. Thanks to Caroline Moorehead, who obtained this unpublished information by making repeated approaches to the UNHCR.
31. Figures from UNHCR, Cairo, April 2004.
32. Figures from Katarzyna Grabska of the Forced Migration and Refugee Studies Program at the American University in Cairo, January 2005.
33. Many refugees expressed their anger and confusion at the sharp drop in recognition rates, especially when between 2001 and 2002 the numbers accepted fell by 15 per cent. (Information from a UNHCR official, Cairo, April 2002).
34. Interview with Mikael, Cairo, 1998.
35. Interview with Mohamed, Cairo, April 1998.
36. Ibid.
37. 'Community life of Dinka refugees in Cairo': presentation by Stephanie Shanks Riak Akuei, The American University in Cairo, January 2001.
38. Interviews with Sudanese refugees, Cairo, March 2004.
39. Interview with Elizabeth, London, May 1998
40. Interview with James, Cairo, January 2001.
41. Interview with David, refugee project worker in Cairo, April 1998.

11

Cultures of Terror, Cultures of Abuse

More and more forced migrants have been victims of the culture of terror. This is developed primarily by states against real or imagined threats from below; it is also the work of nationalist and ethnically based movements. It may include terrorism and other forms of focused violence, including assassination, vigilantism, and the use of death squads.[1] It should be distinguished from these, however, as an overall strategy which aims to produce compliance and control by means of generalising fear.

Since the events of 11 September 2001 terror has been presented by Western governments and media as the work of networks of fanatics. But as Booth and Dunne (2002: 9) point out, it is states that perpetrate most acts of terror: 'As producers of terror, states remain far more significant than non-state groups.' States commit acts of barbarism that affect the lives of scores of millions of people, using the armed forces, the police, intelligence services, and sometimes 'unofficial' paramilitary groups linked to the government and/or to ruling parties and political factions. The strategy has a long history: during the twentieth century it was used by fascist and Stalinist states, colonial powers and nationalist movements. Recently it has become more general: global change has brought the spread of cultures of terror. The effloresence of nationalism which began in the 1980s has produced ethnocentric movements and ethnocracies for which the subordination of Others by means of terror is a central strategic aim. At the same time the adherence of many Third World governments to neo-liberal economics and to the rhetoric of rights has produced what Brysk (2002: 12) calls 'low-intensity democracies'. Here a formal commitment to electoralism and political pluralism is accompanied by systematic, sometimes massive campaigns of repression, in which terror is a key weapon.

The culture of terror is closely associated with mass displacement. It may be used to clear a population from areas of economic or strategic value to governments and business interests, or as part of offensives by movements for which 'cleansing' is integral to the assertion of the national or ethnic group. It may be less focused: terror as a form of control may have a cumulative effect, eroding community life so that more and more people are forced to flee or even that communities disintegrate. The pattern may vary but the outcome is certain: the more widespread is the practice of systematic terror the more there will be refugees. This is reflected in the global pattern of forced migration. By the late 1990s *most* applicants for asylum in the European Union were from areas affected by campaigns of terror. Of the ten leading countries of origin of applicants, nine – the former Yugoslavia, Iraq, Turkey, Afghanistan, Sri Lanka, Somalia, Bosnia and Herzegovina, Iran and Algeria – had been affected by long-term conflicts in which the use of terror was a key factor. EU states nonetheless continued to erect exclusionary barriers and, with rare exceptions, to treat applicants with extreme scepticism. The outcome was to force those fleeing regimes of terror into the irregular networks. Here, as we shall see, they faced dangers comparable to those from which they had fled.

'Demobilisation'

Summerfield (1995: 17) suggests that the main aim of terror is mastery of the population, and that psychological warfare is a central element: 'Atrocity, including public execution, disappearances, torture and sexual violation, is the norm' (ibid). He sets out the 'logic' of the strategy:

> A key element of modern political violence is the creation of states of terror to penetrate the entire fabric of grassroots social relations, as well as subjective mental life, as a means of social control. It is to these ends that most acts of torture are directed, rather than to the extracting of information. The mutilated bodies of those abducted by security agents, dumped in a public place, are props in a political theatre meant to render a whole society a stunned audience. Not only is there little recognition of the distinction between combatant and civilian, or of any obligation to spare women, children and the elderly, but the valued institutions and way of life of a whole population can be targeted. (Summerfield 1997: 4–5)

Sometimes this approach has been a legacy of highly centralised and repressive systems, as in the Balkans and the Caucasus, where during the conflicts of the 1990s the heritage of the Stalinist state was evident. Elsewhere, as in Iraq, Algeria, Sudan, Sri Lanka, Mianmar, India and Israel, a combination of the colonial legacy with authoritarian local nationalisms is the common factor. There has, however, been another influence at work: the use of terror as a means of political control in states associated with the West and particularly with the United States.

In the mid-1950s the Cold War strategy developed by Washington in Central America focused upon 'demobilisation', the aim of which was 'to atomize and make docile the ordinary citizenry' – to suppress movements for change which affected US interests (Booth and Walker 1993: 146).[2] Its first implementation was in Guatemala, where the CIA drew up a list of individuals they believed to be associated with political parties of the left and with peasant and labour unions. The register, known as the Black List, 'ultimately became a death list' (Booth and Walker 1993: 146). Those whose names were recorded were targets for death squads made up of plainclothes soldiers or police who carried out assassinations and kidnappings in public, often using unmarked vehicles. Oppositionists in general were labelled terrorists and campaigns of 'counter-terror' were directed against them, resulting in torture, murder and the disappearance of thousands of people, and inducing far larger numbers to flee. When rural areas were 'pacified' they came under the control of army officers who set about removing indigenous peoples, precipitating resistance which brought new campaigns of terror. During the 1960s counterinsurgency became a key element in US strategy at a global level. The aim was to identify and to neutralise internal enemies, who were defined so broadly as to encompass most sections of the population. An American military manual identified the targets: 'Every individual who in one or another manner supports the goals of the enemy must be considered a traitor and treated in that manner.'[3] Hostile elements were everywhere: they included 'labor organizations, popular movements, indigenous organizations, opposition political parties, peasant movements, intellectual sectors, religious currents, student and youth groups, [and] neighbourhood organizations'.[4] A series of official publications on counterinsurgency and low-intensity operations was produced, and the United States provided instructors and advisers for many allied governments, which were encouraged to make use of training centres such as the School of the Americas set up in Panama and later moved to Fort Benning, Georgia. In Central America the strategy became part of routine political practice. By 1988, after 20 years of repression by the US-backed state in El Salvador, the *New York Times* estimated that 70,000 people had been killed and 500,000 displaced.[5]

In the case of neighbouring Nicaragua the United States determined to overthrow the radical nationalist Sandinista government. In 1981 it established the Contras, a guerrilla force organised, trained and supplied by Washington and its allies, and which specialised in terror and sabotage to disrupt economic and social life. Contra units attacked schools, health centres, day-care clinics, government food-storage facilities, state farms and factories, and local self-help organisations. They killed local authority figures, especially those associated with the state, such as teachers, medical personnel and technicians. These activities were directed by the CIA, which produced a comic-book-style manual on sabotage for Contra foot-soldiers and a more sophisticated volume for officers, *Psychological Operations in Guerrilla Warfare*. By the mid-1980s a series of states in Central America were in the grip of campaigns that produced displacement back and forth across the borders of Nicaragua, Guatemala, El Salvador and Mexico, and stimulated major refugee movements to the United States.

Low intensity conflict

The rationale for 'demobilisation' was the need to protect American interests against the Communist threat. As the Soviet Union and its allied states weakened, however, the strategy was exported even more aggressively. US leaders declared that during the 1980s the Soviet Union had gone over to 'low-intensity warfare' across the Third World. The United States responded with its own strategy of Low Intensity Conflict (LIC), using its armed forces in new ways and combining military involvement with economic assistance, 'psychological' backup and diplomatic initiatives. When the Stalinist states finally collapsed these campaigns continued. Throughout the 1990s neo-liberalism and democratisation were exported from the United States as official paradigms for economic and political reform: they were accompanied with less fanfare by the strategy of LIC. Chomsky (2002: 132) comments that, 'Washington waged its "war on terrorism" by creating an international terror network of unprecedented scale, and employing it worldwide with lethal and longlasting effects.'

Dunn (2001: 21) identifies three key components of LIC: an emphasis on the internal defence of a nation; an emphasis on controlling targeted civilian populations; and the assumption by the military of police-like and other unconventional, typically non-military roles, along with the adoption by the police of military characteristics. Many governments in Africa, Asia and the Middle East which from the 1980s acceded to the neo-liberal model found this approach congenial. Most had roots in authoritarian nationalisms which had long operated their own regimes of control and many were based or partly based in the armed forces. They adopted without difficulty the strategy rehearsed in Latin America – a rhetoric of democracy, complete with 'free' elections and a plurality of formally free parties, together with heightened repression. Among a host of states which followed the model were Turkey, Egypt, Indonesia, the Philippines, Kenya and Peru. Turkey provides an instructive example. The United States did not introduce terror to Turkey – the state had a claim to pioneering use of mass terror in the twentieth century, having killed vast numbers of Armenians in the massacres which began in 1915. The particular forms of terror used during the 1980s and 1990s, however, owed much to the US military, which since 1940s had been closely linked to the Turkish armed forces.[6] When confronted by the Kurdish insurgency in the 1980s the latter turned to tactics tried and tested by their allies: Tirman notes that Turkish officers educated in the United States 'employed the methods familiar to peasants from Vietnam to Guatemala'.[7] Villagers in Kurdish provinces under martial law were organised to 'defend' their communities against guerrilla forces, while death squads, kidnappings, and torture became routine. In 1995 Human Rights Watch commented that the United States was 'complicit in a scorched earth campaign that violates the fundamental tenets of international law'.[8]

By the 1990s rationales for LIC had become more diverse. They included 'peacekeeping' and intervention in affairs usually regulated by civil law, notably drug-trafficking. LIC had become a generic term for measures involving military action which fell short of formal declarations of war. In Colombia the United States poured resources into campaigns formally directed against guerrilla organisations and 'narco-traffickers', making the government in Bogota the largest recipient of US aid in the western hemisphere. The US Committee for Refugees (USCR) reported on a reign of terror which, it argued, was largely the work of the state and associated paramilitary groups. These used extreme violence to depopulate areas of interest to their wealthy patrons, who included large landowners, business people and the drug cartels (USCR 1998: 12–13).[9] American counter-narcotics policy had become an open strategy of counterinsurgency in which the guerrilla opposition and its sympathisers were the target: 'What it managed to achieve was the concentration of enormous police power in the hands of the Colombian army' (Ross 2003: 33). These developments had implications for the use of terror worldwide. As the global economy proved unstable and fragile local systems fell into crisis, state forces and militias were less and less inhibited about using techniques legitimated, encouraged and often prescribed and financed by the world's dominant state. In 1999 US President Bill Clinton apologised publicly for earlier US activity in Central America. He told the people of Guatemala: 'For the United States it is important that I state clearly that support for the military forces and intelligence units which engaged in violence and widespread repression was wrong, and the United States must not repeat that mistake.'[10] But the 'mistake' had been repeated many times and had already produced many victims: according to Campbell (2002:1) since the first US-backed operations in Central America death squads alone had been responsible for the deaths of hundreds of thousands, perhaps millions of people. Many more had become forced migrants – in the case of Colombia, one in five of the rural population had been forced to flee (USCR 1998: 215). Livingstone (2003: 53–4) shows that in Colombia the state and the paramilitary forces were responsible for over half of all cases of internal displacement, with some 30 per cent of cases attributed to guerrilla forces. Children suffered disproportionately, 40 per cent of the displaced being under the age of 11 (ibid). The main reasons for communities abandoning their homes were assassinations, death threats, and 'fear' (ibid).

Regimes of terror

Campaigns of terror often begin with attacks upon political and religious leaders, and upon professionals such as teachers and doctors, with the aim of removing key resources from communities and political collectives. The intention is to weaken local solidarities and to encourage compliance by inducing a sense of defencelessness and powerlessness. The impact upon individuals is particularly destructive, for terror is often accompanied by campaigns of denial in which perpetrators insist that life is progressing as normal. Martin-Baro (1994) speaks of 'institutionalized lies' and of 'circles of silence' which forbid victims and witnesses of abuse the opportunity to give testimony and to express their anxieties and distress, a key reason why populations affected by terror, including refugee communities, suffer more often and more severely than others from mental health problems. A wider aim of those who perpetrate terror may be to precipitate mass flight. News about atrocities can clear whole regions: during the inter-communal conflicts associated with partition of India in 1947 millions of people were moved in this way across regions such as Punjab and Bengal. So too in Palestine, where the Israeli historian Benny Morris (2004: 40) makes clear that in 1948 rape and killings of Arab civilians by Zionist militias were part of an offensive which aimed 'to encourage the population to take to the roads'. The overall strategy was to project 'a message of transfer [of the Palestinians]' (ibid). Such 'cleansing' (ibid) of areas designated for Jewish settlement has since been part of the practice of many ethnically based national movements, notably those in the Balkans and in Central Africa.

The initial targets of such campaigns are usually leading male figures. The more effectively they are removed the more vulnerable becomes the community as a whole. The presence of men usually inhibits attacks upon women; by the same token communities without men, or from which important male figures have been removed, are more likely to witness systematic abuse of women and children. This is particularly important in regions in which women require the physical presence of a male relative in order to move in public spaces. McSpadden and Moussa (1993: 313) note the repeated assertion of women in the Horn of Africa that they do not feel safe unless in the company of an adult male. They quote an informant who observed, 'You have to be stuck to a man … You have to belong to a man to be safe' (ibid). During the 1990s the removal of men in several regions of the former Yugoslavia preceded ethnic cleansing and mass rape. So too in Rwanda, where the tactic was part of what Taylor (1999: 140) calls 'the cosmology of terror' embraced by militias during the genocide of 1994. In the absence of parents and/or adult family members children are also vulnerable. Those separated from their families, notes Kunder (1998: 18) 'are rarely viewed as innocents'. When militias and guerrilla groups are involved they may be seen as a useful resource – as recruits, porters and providers of sexual services. 'In short, they are prime targets for abuse' (ibid).

Terror may become a method of rule. In 1975 the Khmer Rouge regime in Cambodia initiated a national campaign of mass killing and drove millions of people from the cities into the countryside in one of the largest internal forced migrations of the twentieth century. At least 1.5 million people were killed (Pilger 1992: 408). In the same year Indonesia invaded East Timor. Over the next 15 years its army perpetrated massacres which killed over 60,000 people, some 10 per cent of the population (Cribb 2002: 181). Up to 80 per cent of males in the capital city, Dili, were murdered and most of those remaining in the towns fled to the countryside. The Indonesian state organised a programme of resettlement, compelling the displaced to live under surveillance in 'guided villages', and imposing a regime of terror under which death lists were used to identify thousands of victims, who were murdered, 'disappeared', or seized and imprisoned. There were numerous reports of rape and of women seized by Indonesian forces and associated militias being held in sexual slavery (Amnesty International 2000: 129). In advance of a ballot on autonomy organised by the government in 1999 terror was intensified and tens of thousands of people were displaced; following the ballot more than 250,000 people fled their homes, the majority to West Timor. Here they were at renewed risk of attack, especially from government-backed militias. Amnesty International (ibid) reported arbitrary killings and many cases of sexual violence against women in refugee camps.

For more than 30 years the Iraqi army and police organised kidnapping, torture, execution and mass disappearances, and co-ordinated huge population movements. In 1970 alone 300,000 Kurds were displaced; in 1973 a further 600,000 were displaced; later the Iraqi government forcibly relocated some 1400 villages and a further 300,000 people, placing them in 'strategic hamlets' (Global IDP Survey 1998: 181). During the 1980s, as part of its *Anfal* campaign, the regime killed between 50,000 and 200,000 Kurds and destroyed a further 3000 villages (ibid). During the war with Iran, Shi'a Muslim areas of the south faced similar treatment, and after the Gulf war of 1991 and the establishment of a northern 'safe haven' under UN control, Kurdish and Turkoman communities were evicted and forced into the UN zone. Those attempting to cross the international border further to the north were confronted by the Turkish state, with its own campaign of repression against the Kurds. Here terror sanctioned by a Western client state met terror initiated by a government repudiated by the West. From the viewpoint of the victims it was difficult to discriminate between the two regimes.

During the 1980s and 1990s conflicts in West Africa were characterised by extensive use of campaigns of terror. In 1989, in response to an attack on Liberian territory from guerrillas based in Cote d'Ivoire, Liberian President Samuel Doe declared that he would transform the area 'into an empty land, where ants would not live'.[11] Over the next six years more than 500,000 people were displaced by state forces and local guerrilla groups, both of which used extreme violence against the civilian population. Meanwhile in neighbouring Sierra Leone conflict between the army and guerrillas produced repeated atrocities during which, according to Amnesty International (1997: 278), it was impossible to distinguish between the conduct of the troops and that of the irregulars. Hundreds of thousands of people were displaced, fleeing attacks in which terrible injuries were inflicted purposefully upon civilians, including many children. Rape became systematic and widespread. When parts of the capital Freetown were seized by militias in 1999 several thousand civilians were abducted. Many women and girls were forced into sexual slavery and retained to cook and perform other tasks, while thousands of children were abducted and trained for military activity (Amnesty International 2000: 209–10).

Terror and the informal networks

Refugees from such conflicts are prominent among those who become long-distance migrants. There is often a desire to move far from the area of displacement, as explained by a Bosnian Muslim woman who was one of only three survivors of a large extended family:

> We come from Priador. They [Serb militias] took away all the men: my father, my uncles, my brothers and my cousins who were all boys. Everyone was removed and we never saw them again. We stayed, hoping to find them: sometimes we hid in the houses of our [Serbian] neighbours – I thank them and I will never forget them. But then they were in danger too. My mother, and my aunt and me – the only ones who remained in our family – left

quickly and we found a way to get to a safe city. Then we said: 'Let's get far from here. There is nothing for us in Bosnia except pain'.[12]

Many refugees who have experienced such offensives upon their communities have attempted to move en masse. A woman from the city of Brava in Somalia, inhabited mainly by members of a minority ethnic group, explains the predicament which confronted her community in the mid-1990s:

> When the government finally fell we became an enemy for the president's people. They threatened us. People disappeared and some were kidnapped and held to ransom. We had no guns, no army of our own like all the others, so our people who could leave, did leave. There was nowhere in Somalia where we could escape and it was dangerous for us in Kenya among other Somali refugees. We had to come a long way to be safe. Now there are thousands of us here [in London] – in a city none of us had seen before.[13]

A Sierra Leonian refugee who also found safety in Britain explains why he travelled to London:

> For a long time we hoped the war would come to an end but it just kept getting closer and closer. The stories we heard about the rebels were terrifying: how could I stay and let them do these things to my children? I got to Conakry [in Guinea] and then I used all the money I had to get my wife and children out. I decided we should get away from the whole conflict, so we left straight for England. Lots of others did the same thing. Now I tell all the members of my family and all my friends and my former colleagues back home to do as we did. At least they cannot harm us here.[14]

Such refugees have experienced more and more difficulty gaining entry to Western Europe and North America, not least because displacement by terror produces *mass* movements which are perceived as threatening by potential host countries. Under the Maastricht Treaty of 1992, EU states agreed to regulate migration through co-ordination of Justice and Home Affairs (JHA). In the late 1990s, determined not to repeat offers of temporary protection which had earlier taken many Bosnians to Western Europe, they agreed that there should be no further mass immigration of refugees. In 1998 they adopted an elaborate JHA strategy, the January Action Plan, aimed at Kurdish refugees. With full knowledge of the regimes of terror implemented over many years in Turkey and in Iraq, ministers resolved to exclude the migrants. The following year much the same policy was applied to Kosovans, also caught up in conflicts characterised by use of mass terror. The combined efforts of Europe, the United States and Turkey produced offers of temporary protection to 125,000 Kosovans – a fraction of the

800,000 who had crossed borders into neighbouring states and a much smaller proportion of the total number displaced (Koslowski 2000: 209).

As the culture of terror has become more general, regimes of exclusion have become more and more rigorous. *There is a direct association between these developments.* Global change has precipitated crises in vulnerable local economic and political structures; at the same time powerful influences have encouraged methods of political control in which terror is an instrument of choice. Meanwhile the most secure countries – preferred places of asylum – have made immigration through formal channels much more difficult. Koslowski (2000: 207) comments, 'Very simply: as more restrictive policies increase the obstacles to crossing borders, migrants increasingly turn to smugglers rather than pay the growing costs of unaided attempts that prove unsuccessful.' In the case of the European Union, Papadopolou (2004) shows how such restrictions have prompted the growth of irregular networks which offer to move migrants from the conflict zones of the Middle East through Greece into Western Europe. In fact many are marooned in Greek cities in conditions of 'vulnerability, insecurity and socio-economic marginalization': they are 'living in a state of limbo' (Papadopolou 2004: 175 and 176). This is part of a global pattern in which more forced migrants have been victims of terror and more have been compelled to put themselves at risk within the smuggling networks. They have moved from a culture of terror into a culture of abuse.

Border controls in Europe

Those who intend to make a border crossing informally may opt to buy false documents, information about how to effect entry or the services of a guide. Increasingly this is referred to by states and transnational policing organisations as 'people smuggling' – facilitation of an illegal border crossing.[15] It has been distinguished from 'trafficking', which is said to involve coercion, fraud or deception of migrants, and may result in abuse of the latter.[16] The distinction is often difficult to discern. Informal networks may contain people seized and coerced into labour or sold for purposes of sexual exploitation: they have in effect been enslaved. At the same time many forced migrants solicit the services of migration agents – they arrange to be smuggled and enter clandestine networks in which there are great dangers of abuse. The more effective are obstacles to movement of forced migrants, the more that irregular networks thrive, and the more that those within them are exploited. The relationship between controls and informal networks is sometimes recognised by state officials: according to Doris Meissner, an INS Commissioner in the United States, 'as we improve our enforcement, we increase the smuggling of aliens that occurs, because it is harder to cross and so therefore people turn more and more to smugglers'.[17] There is a corollary: as enforcement is tightened the danger of abuse within the irregular networks increases. And because most refugees who enter the networks originate in crisis zones of the Third World, far from desired countries of asylum, they are compelled to make the longest and most difficult journeys. As Ghosh (1998: 56–7) observes, it is just such people, the most desperate 'survival' migrants from areas most severely affected by conflict, terror and dislocation, who provide the most lucrative business for the irregular networks and who are forced to take the biggest risks.

In the case of those who wish for asylum in Europe measures taken by the European Union have made refugees' journeys much more complicated and hazardous. Under the Dublin Convention of 1990 the European Union agreed that a refugee's first safe country of arrival should accept responsibility for determining her/his status, establishing the concept of the 'safe third country'. Within a few years this had been extended to include states aspiring to join the Union, while specific member states had also identified neighbouring countries as safe and included them as third countries. In the mid-1990s Germany signed agreements on migration with the Czech Republic and Poland, countries through which most refugees from the east were compelled to pass in order to enter the federal republic. In 1993 Germany paid Poland DM120 million for the construction of an entire apparatus for security in frontier zones and for detention and deportation of migrants; the Czech Republic later received DM60 million for the same purpose (*Trafficking in Migrants*, September 1997). Germany went on to declare that each of the nine states bordering the federal republic was 'safe', making all refugees arriving overland ineligible for asylum and likely to face deportation. Other states, such as newly independent republics of the Baltic which aspired to membership of the EU, were also given 'incentives' to control movements across their territories. The US Committee for Refugees (USCR 1997: 3), observing developments in Europe, commented that at a stroke a refugee's route into exile, rather than the reasons for his or her flight, had become the question at issue. A policy that in legal terms could be described as presumptive *refoulement* had been introduced.

The third safe country concept was developed ostensibly to prevent the syndrome of the 'refugee in orbit'. In fact it set in motion multiple chain deportations. Most countries officially considered to be safe implemented third-country laws of their own or deported asylum seekers to other states without a review of their claims.[18] In 1995 a train containing over 100 refugees from the Middle East and Central Asia travelled across Russia, Belarus and the Baltic states for several weeks, moved back and forth across frontiers as a series of governments refused admission (*Observer*, 9 April 1995). Of the 90 Iraqis, 14 Afghans, four Palestinians and two Iranians over half were children. They had already travelled thousands of miles before their journey ended in a ritual of rejection: over a five-day period they were moved between Russia and Latvia 12 times while the authorities bickered over who should take responsibility (ibid).

During the late 1990s fortification of the eastern frontier of the European Union continued apace. Germany increased numbers of the Bundes Grenz Schutz (BGS), the border police, to 5800 (*Trafficking in Migrants*, September 1997) and introduced high technology sensors along the 450-kilometre frontier with Poland.[19] Thousands of migrants were apprehended and returned across the border: by 2001 the majority of those who attempted the crossing from Poland were Russian citizens, of whom 80 per cent were Chechens, some of whom had made a journey of 2000 miles from the Caucasus (*Guardian*, 15 March 2001). As Poland prepared to accede to the European Union it fortified its own eastern borders with Russia, Ukraine and Belarus. Hundreds of new watchtowers were constructed and 18,000 border guards recruited and provided with helicopters equipped with night-sight and thermovision. The measures were described as creating 'a new Iron Curtain' (*Independent*, 31 July 2002). Along the southern borders of the Union exclusionary measures were enacted on both sides of the Mediterranean. Spain closed the borders of Melilla and Ceuta, its enclaves in Morocco which provide the only land border between Africa and the European Union. During the 1980s the territories had attracted many migrants who became the subject of a series of restrictive immigration laws. When the enclaves continued to draw in Maghrebis and then refugees from sub-Saharan Africa more radical measures were taken. Between 1998 and 2000 each was surrounded with a 4-metre fence topped with barbed wire, thermal cameras and watch towers. Most of the cost of over US$55 million was met by the European Union (Gold 2000: 131). Among those who succeeded in entering the enclaves many were detained and later transported to 'safe' destinations. In a typical episode in 1996, 103 people from 14 African countries were flown from Melilla to Malaga in Spain and then on via the Canary Islands to Mali, Guinea-Bissau, Senegal and Cameroon. It was alleged by migrants that they had been drugged by Spanish officials and then deposited arbitrarily in the four states (Gold 2000: 126–7).

Debt bondage

The barriers which surround states of the European Union and of North America have made mass attempts at entry extremely dangerous. In the late 1990s new controls on air travel led some refugee groups to commandeer aircraft, with all the associated risks. In 1997 a Turkmenistan Airlines Boeing landed without permission at Schipol Airport, Amsterdam, with 173 Tamils who all claimed asylum (*Trafficking in Migrants*, March 1997). In February 2000 an Ariana Airlines flight was hijacked in Afghanistan and flown from Kabul to the provincial city of Mazar-e Sharif, then to Tashkent in Uzbekistan, to Moscow, and eventually to Stansted Airport near London. In Britain all the passengers were detained and most returned to Afghanistan. Nine men who identified themselves as members of a dissenting group of Afghan intellectuals were tried by a British court and imprisoned for hijacking.

Most journeys into Western Europe and North America are now undertaken by small groups of refugees who travel overland and/or by sea, often crossing many borders. A minority have developed their own strategies to elude police and border guards but most use migration agents – 'facilitators'. As we have seen, displacement and flight accentuate differences of social status. Nowhere is this clearer than in the informal networks, where the safety of migrants is determined by the resources they can mobilise to pay for the journey. Koslowski (2000: 212) gives the example of two routes across the Adriatic Sea from Albania to Italy: in 1999 US$4000 bought an airline ticket, a passport with a valid visa, and the co-operation of airport officials; for US$600 the same agent provided only a place on a speedboat and a dangerous landfall. Long-distance travel is much more expensive: even in the mid-1990s people seeking passage from South Asia to Europe via the Mediterranean were charged US$8,000 each, a sum far beyond the immediate reach of all but a small minority of potential migrants (Ghosh 1998: 31). In a study of Sri Lankan and Tamil refugees Van Hear (2004) makes clear that the poorest refugees have to surmount the greatest obstacles in their search for security. They may be forced to violate obligations to kin, such as marriage arrangements, using resources accumulated for bridewealth or dowry as a downpayment to migration agents, or mortgaging themselves and their families by entering debt relations.

There is an assumption among politicians, officials and media people in the West that the sums involved prove that migrants have ample resources and that, in effect, they are an investment in journeys which will bring personal advancement in the country of destination. Migrants' testimonies suggest otherwise. When a ship containing Kurdish refugees from Iraq was wrecked on the French coast in 2001, those aboard revealed that each had paid US$4,000 for the journey. Their families had sold everything they possessed – all their belongings, livestock and land. They had surrendered a lifetime's resources in order to reach Europe (*Observer*, 25 February 2001). In many cases refugees give up passports and other identification papers which are used as 'collateral' until the cost of the passage is repaid. They may enter commitments to work in the destination country, often at high levels of exploitation little different from the indentured labour of an earlier age. Debt bondage may be enforced by threats of injury to families in the countries of origin and/or by threats to the migrants themselves, whose informal status makes them highly vulnerable. Ghosh (1998: 22) makes an important point about such debt relationships: 'payments for trafficking are not a simple and straightforward transaction in cash at the beginning or even at the end of the journey; often it is a long, complex and tortuous process ... involving several parties'. The outcome is that the poorest and most desperate people not only face the greatest risks by undertaking hazardous journeys but that they, their families and communities may be locked into relationships in which they all face long-term insecurity and danger.

Death at sea

Most migrants now face danger en route long before they reach the intended country of destination. This is especially clear in the case of the European Union, where closure of the eastern borders has led more migrants to attempt clandestine entry from the south, necessitating a journey by sea. Since the mid-1990s there have been a host of tragedies in which migrants have died attempting to cross the Mediterranean, and according to maritime authorities many more migrants have been fortunate to escape disasters in ships which are invariably old, overcrowded and unseaworthy. Pugh (2004: 56) suggests that many thousands of migrants die in such tragedies – perhaps as many as a third of all irregular migrants travelling by sea. Many failed to reach Spain from Morocco across the Straits of Gibraltar, the world's busiest shipping lane. Here the most commonly used vessels are *pateras*, small wooden boats which lie low in the water and are difficult to detect but which are also vulnerable to bad weather, especially when overloaded by their operators. During the 1990s the number of drownings increased rapidly: between 1998 and 2001 some 3000 people were said to have died in efforts to reach Spain, making the Straits 'the largest mass grave in Europe' (*Observer*, 15 April 2001). Many *pateras*, inflatable boats and rafts have been hit by ocean-going vessels in unrecorded incidents. In Morocco stories abound of these tragedies and of migration agents who have sold their customers unseaworthy craft or who have abandoned them in mid-channel, escaping into other vessels. Despite these tragedies by 2001 Spanish police detained 1000 people a week as they attempted the crossing, with the implication that thousands more crossed undetected (*Financial Times*, 20 February 2002). The Spanish government has installed a system of radars and night vision cameras forming a 350-mile electronic 'wall' across the Mediterranean that detects all vessels in the Straits. Migration agents have responded by opening other routes, like that from North-West Africa to the Canaries, a perilous trip across open ocean. In February 2001 at least 15 African migrants drowned attempting to reach the Canaries from El Aioun in Western Sahara (*Guardian*, 2 June 2001); in 2002 Spanish police estimated that 8000 migrants would reach the islands during the year – a 400 per cent increase on 2001 (*Guardian*, 25 May 2002).

A new generation of boat people has attempted to reach countries of the European Union across the seas of Northern Europe. From the mid-1990s efforts began to reach Sweden, Denmark and Germany from Russia and the Baltic states, using the Baltic Sea, and to reach England across the English Channel. In addition many have attempted the Channel route by means of the rail tunnel.[20] Thousands have put their lives at risk by paying migration agents to accommodate them in trucks and containers in which they run the risk of suffocation or abandonment. In July 2000 the corpses of 58 Chinese migrants were discovered in a refrigerated lorry in Dover, England – the biggest deathtoll in a single incident of its kind. Despite widespread publicity numbers attempting to cross the Channel later increased.[21]

Criminal or functionary?

The agents who bring migrants to such frontiers, secrete them in trucks and containers or supply them with boats are reviled by politicians and officials. In 1999 ministers of the G8 countries meeting in Moscow declared that the growth of smuggling/trafficking constituted 'the dark side of globalisation'[22] and in 2001 a joint statement from the prime ministers of Britain and Italy attacked traffickers for 'a catalogue of death' (*Guardian*, 5 February 2001). Most academics and NGOs pass similar judgements.[23] Such unanimity about the informal networks can be contrasted with the lack of detailed research and of knowledge about the dynamics of smuggling/trafficking. In a review of literature on the networks Salt (2000: 32) notes enormous interest in the issue among states and NGOs but little research and coherent analysis: 'many of the mechanisms in the trafficking process and empirical knowledge of their effects remain in the realm of (variously informed) speculation'. The paucity of material is indeed very striking, especially for an activity that by 2000 was estimated to be worth US$10 billion a year (*Financial Times*, 17 March 2001), that was facilitating movement of 500,000 people annually into Europe, and by the late 1990s had delivered up to

15 million informal migrants to the United States (Ghosh 1998: 10). There is a widespread assumption that 'gangs' and 'syndicates' have entered the migration business but significantly there have been few accounts of how irregular networks have been brought into being and of the human relationships which sustain them.

In one of the few accounts of human smuggling worldwide Kyle and Dale (2001: 49) conclude that irregular networks often arise as responses of local entrepreneurs to uneven development: that the networks represent 'a sort of grassroots development project' which provides services for a mass of people seeking release from the pressures caused by global crises. Andreas (2001: 111) proposes a similar analysis: he notes that during the 1970s coyotes came to prominence in Mexico to provide for 'special needs' – the movement to the United States of women, children, the elderly and non-Mexican nationals, their expertise reducing the risk of assault by bandits or of abuse by officials. Harding (2000) also concludes that refugees and migration agents have developed a mutually beneficial relationship. While researching irregular routes to Italy he says that he became suspicious of the idea that traffickers are 'a modern embodiment of evil' (Harding 2000: 19). The *scafisti* (boatmen) who carry migrants across the Adriatic to Southern Italy take risks, he suggests, and sometimes save lives. Their ability to evade the police and immigration authorities is important to their clients. Although they are driven by the search for profit, they have a function:

> [W]hen they set out to extort from their clients, when they cheat them or despatch them to their deaths, they are only acting an entrepreneurial version of the disdain which asylum seekers suffer at the hands of far more powerful enemies – those who terrorise them and who are determined to keep them at arm's length ... In the end the question of good or bad intentions is less important than the fact that the *scafisti* and others like them provide a service for desperate people, to whom most other avenues have been closed. (Harding 2000: 20)

Pugh (2004: 58) takes a similar view. *Scafisti* do not create demand for services they provide, he maintains, and may even demonstrate altruism vis-à-vis their clients. These comments point up the hypocrisy of politicians who have erected barriers which migrants are compelled to evade in the search for sanctuary and security. The same politicians and officials may also tacitly encourage irregular entry to maintain flows of labour, sustaining migration networks and feeding the appetite of migration agents for easy money.

In the case of Chinese migrants to the United States the effect of regularisation by the American state of millions of undocumented aliens has given an enormous boost to the informal networks. In the 1970s market reforms in China greatly increased pressure to migrate

(Liang and Ye 2001). Social inequalities widened very rapidly and China soon became an exceptionally unequal society by world standards. By the early 1990s internal migration was accelerating at an extraordinary pace, with 60 million *yuming* – 'floating people' – searching the country for jobs (Kwong 1997: 55). In China's southern cities, which attracted most of the migrants, the effect was to drive down wages, putting intense pressure on 'people at the bottom', whose experience of relative deprivation caused them to leave China, mainly for other states of East Asia and South-East Asia, and for North America (Liang and Ye 2001: 197). These pressures were intensified by the relentless oppression of a regime which favoured both market reform and continued authoritarian control – the combination which was producing higher levels of mass displacement worldwide. Old traditions of migration to the United States were soon reasserted and with the aid of smugglers many Chinese reached American cities. Here the amnesty of 1986, regularising millions of irregulars, had already prompted what Kwong (2001: 237) calls a further 'mad rush' from China.

These developments were encouraged by the violent repression which followed the 1989 Tiananmen massacre in Beijing. At first, activists of the Democracy Movement were warmly received in the West, US President George Bush issuing an executive order which gave shelter to Chinese nationals in the United States and unilaterally extended rights to what he called 'political asylum' by offering refuge to anyone who opposed the one-child policy of the Chinese state (Kwong 1997: 164). It was only later, when the Clinton administration moved against immigration in general, that movements from China came to public attention. In 1993, as the United States launched high-profile campaigns against irregular entry from Mexico, the *Golden Venture* – a ship with hundreds of Chinese aboard – ran aground off a New York City beach. Some of the passengers drowned and most of the others were detained amid a media panic about mass migration from the East. Journeys from China now became much more risky but the irregular networks still had plenty of business: millions of Chinese were desperate to leave and American employers were eager to import them. Recalling events of the mid-nineteenth century, Kwong (2001: 246–7) points out that 'desperate, undocumented aliens' of Chinese origin have once more become a target for American employers. They are 'modern-day coolies', highly prized as workers in the textile industry and in catering, and so vulnerable to employers that withholding of wages in sweatshops in New York has reached epidemic proportions.[24] Their presence, he suggests, aids efforts to drive down wages and to break collective resistance, including unionisation of the local workforce.[25] But employers are not the only ones to profit. In the United States top officials of the INS have been implicated in smuggling,[26] while in

China involvement reaches up to the most senior level, even to vice premier: Kwong (1997: 63) comments that the Chinese government itself has operated as a 'snakehead'.

Those moved successfully through the networks to the United States may suffer in other ways. Extreme overwork may cause life-threatening illnesses, undiagnosed and untreated because immigrants' clandestine status inhibits their access to medical services. Under constant pressure from employers, and from smugglers prepared to use all means to enforce debt repayment, they enter a spiral of decline which can have fatal outcomes. Even this does not inhibit potential migrants, many of whom continue to leave China after committing huge sums to the smugglers. Between 1991 and 1994 migrants from one city in Fujian, Fuzhou, paid some US$3 billion to be moved to the United States. Most arrived indebted and worked for years to pay labour agents, often under threat of torture, kidnapping and rape. Anderson and Rogaly (2005: 10) have identified the same practices in Britain. Here, they report, migrants are not only under constant threat but may be kept in isolated accommodation with the aim of maintaining ignorance of their rights and of inhibiting collective action to assert them. They conclude that relations between migration agents and employers on the one hand, and migrants on the other, result in the exercise of control over 'the whole personhood' of the latter (ibid).

Deception

Transnational networks are sometimes depicted as functional, harmonious webs of migrant activity. As the China–US example demonstrates they can in fact be dominated by small numbers of people whose agendas differ radically from those of their compatriots or 'co-ethnics'. Do these networks serve migrants? Koslowski (2000) suggests not only that they do but that they are an outcome of the latters' own creative emerges. He maintains that contemporary debates about migration are defined largely in terms of the state as a strong border-enforcer confronted by individuals who attempt to defy controls: 'the contest is framed in terms of the state against the migrant' (Koslowski 2000: 205). This is inadequate, he maintains, primarily because the unwanted migrant is not simply an object of state control, nor merely pursues her/his own interests, but is an active force in the creation of social networks within which migration agents play a key role. As we have seen in the case of Europe, however (Chapter 8) informal networks have in general not been initiated by migrants, nor do they express a relationship of mutual benefit between 'facilitators' and their clients. In a formal sense, migrants voluntarily agree a transaction with agents, exchanging money for expertise in evading migration controls.

But as Ghosh (1998: 23) comments, migrants' recourse to traffickers is 'less a matter of free choice than of compulsion'. The agents trade upon their clients' vulnerability and, once the latter have entered the networks, most fall under their control. As Koser (2001) shows in the case of Iranians attempting to enter Europe, it is agents who decide who will travel, and when and how the journey is to be accomplished.

Many migrants are deceived as to their destinations. One refugee now living in the Netherlands relates his story:

> I went from Afghanistan to Iran and then to Turkey. We paid a lot of money to go to Germany. With some others we went on a long journey by truck into Eastern Europe. Until now I don't know the route we took. When they let us out they said we were in Germany. They drove off and left us and we soon knew it was not Germany it was Poland. We went back from Poland to Russia, where we had nothing. Only from there, and after a long time, could we get to Germany.[27]

A refugee from Sri Lanka had a similar experience:

> I went to Saudi Arabia where I worked for a while. But I had no work documents and it became dangerous when the government removed people like me. So I paid to go to Italy and I hoped that I could go on to England because I speak English. I flew to Turkey and then we went further in a boat and we were put into the sea and told to swim to the shore. It wasn't Italy – it was Greece! The last we saw of the people who took us there was their boat on the horizon.[28]

Such deception on a far bigger scale was reported in 1995 when almost 1000 Africans paid US$750 each to be taken by sea to Italy. On arrival they found they were in Yugoslavia. For a further payment they were promised transport to Austria: in the event they were abandoned in Hungary (*Economist*, 5–11 August 1995). This was also the fate of the Sri Lankans whose tragic story began this book.

It is migration agents who pack their clients into ships, trucks and containers, often without food or water or even an adequate air supply. In February 2001 the *East Sea*, a rusting freighter which had set out for France from Turkey with 908 Iraqi Kurds on board, was steered onto rocks near the Mediterranean resort of Frejus. The crew had destroyed all the ship's documentation before abandoning the vessel. Refugees told French police that they had not seen the faces of the crew, who were hooded and appeared only occasionally during the eight-day voyage to throw inadequate supplies of food and water into two small airless and unlit holds which contained all the human cargo. 'There was excrement everywhere. The stench was pestilential', said a police officer who boarded the ship (*Independent*, 19 February 2001). In October 2001 a court in France was told about two German smugglers who secreted 10 migrants in a steel box welded into a van which they attempted to drive to England (*Daily Telegraph*, 8 October 2001). The migrants had no water and when found were suffering from dehydration. The French public prosecutor commented: 'I can't help thinking of the old slave ships, where it didn't matter if half the cargo died as long as there was a profit at the end' (ibid). The 58 Chinese migrants found dead at Dover, England, in June 2000 had undergone a similar journey. They had first travelled from Fujian to Peking. Here, although promised a flight to Europe, they had boarded a train which took seven days to travel across Siberia to Moscow, where their documents and luggage were confiscated by the smugglers. They were then put aboard trains, trucks and even horse-drawn carts to pass through the Czech Republic, Germany and Holland before dying on the Channel crossing to Britain (*Independent*, 23 June 2000). Most evidence from the networks suggests that agents show little compunction about misleading or abandoning their clients. Hein (2000: 139) notes, contrary to Harding, that during the crisis in Kosovo in 1999 many refugees were killed or injured during boat trips across the Adriatic to Italy, and that there were many incidents in which smugglers threw their clients overboard.

Sexual abuse is systematic on many routes. Almost all those involved in smuggling/trafficking are male: drivers, boat crews, messengers, guards, police, soldiers and officials. Their control over migrants means that they have almost unparalleled opportunities for abuse, especially of women and children. The danger is greatly increased by other uses of the networks, especially for movement of women and children who are to be exploited commercially for sex. According to the *Financial Times* (17 March 2001) by 2000 some 700,000 women and children were being moved through the informal networks each year, many to be sold into sexual slavery.[29] Some women begin their journeys convinced that they are to work in regular employment abroad with opportunities to repatriate their earnings. They pay large sums to migration agents or sign promissory notes for air fares and recruitment fees. At their destinations they are made to surrender their passports: largely helpless and vulnerable to threats from the agents and from their new 'employers' they are made to work as prostitutes, or for clubs or procurement agencies, and may be sold by brothels, even to operators in other countries. The threat of AIDS has contributed to increasing demand for young women and children as prostitutes: even more vulnerable, they can be lost within the international networks.

Where sexual violation is general and unremarked, refugee women and children are easily targeted. Abuse may be an integral part of the system, as when migration agents use access to female migrants as part of the bribe by which they evade border controls, so that rape by border guards, police or immigration officials may be commonplace. A Kurdish woman from Iraq relates her experience:

> I was lucky, they didn't touch me. But before I left I heard what happens to many women. Since I got to Europe I have met women, including some who were just girls when they left, who were raped and sometimes they were beaten. Can you imagine what this means in a culture like ours? It means you can never, never talk about it openly. You just take it with you all your life. It is part of the price that our women pay to become refugees.[30]

The same informant comments on the significance of such abuse for families and communities:

> Everyone in a family in which women are raped is affected by what has happened. It is not a new thing to us. In Iraq soldiers and police and the *mukhabarat* [intelligence services] do it all the time. They torture the men and rape the women – and they torture the men by raping the women. These are reasons to escape but sometimes the escape is as dangerous as staying at home. What should we do?[31]

In 2001 a report to the German government from its intelligence services warned that smugglers and traffickers were becoming more violent in their treatment of asylum-seekers.[32] This added to a mass of evidence available to Western states which had established the close connection between exclusionary policies and the dangers faced by refugees. There has been no sign, however, that European states are prepared to break the link; rather the relationship appeared to be confirmed, part of a pattern of relations worldwide in which the poor and the powerless are penalised again and again.

Notes

1. Campbell (2002: 2) provides a typology of these closely related practices.
2. Chomsky (1994: 41) suggests that this had its origins a decade earlier when the victorious powers of the Second World War initiated programmes of 'counterinsurgency' for the purpose of dispersing the anti-fascist resistance in Southern Europe.
3. Quoted in Chomsky 1994: 57.
4. The European–Latin-American *State Terror* enquiry, quoted ibid.
5. Quoted in Booth and Walker 1993: 148.

6. For three decades the United States had sent aid and arms to Turkey. During the 1950s alone military supplies amounted to almost US$1.5 billion (Berberoglu 1982: 73).
7. Quoted in Chomsky 1999: 53.
8. Quoted in Chomsky 1999: 55.
9. In 1999 Amnesty International (2000: 76) recorded over 3500 political killings and many disappearances; in that year alone over 250,000 people were displaced.
10. Quoted in Human Rights Watch 1999: 133.
11. Quoted in Van Damme 1999: 37.
12. Interview with Yasmin, London, September 1997.
13. Interview with Fatimah, London, May 2001.
14. Interview with Leslie, London, September 2000.
15. Morrison and Crosland (2001: 5) point out that as more organisations and agencies have become involved there has been much confusion about definition of informal movements. See definitions of smuggling provided by the International Organisation for Migration (IOM) and the International Centre for Migration Policy Development (ICPMD) in Morrison and Crosland (2001: 5–6).
16. In December 2000 a UN Convention and Protocol was agreed in Palermo, Italy. The *Convention Against Transnational Organized Crime, and Protocol to Prevent, Suppress and Punish Trafficking in Persons, especially Women and Children* defined trafficking as:

    > The recruitment, transportation, transfer, harbouring or receipt of persons, by means of the threat of the use of force or other forms of coercion, of abduction, of fraud, of deception, of power or of a position of vulnerability, or of giving or receiving of payments or benefits to achieve the consent of a person having control over another person, for the purpose of exploitation. Exploitation shall include, at a minimum, the exploitation of the prostitution of others or other forms of sexual exploitation, forced labour or services, slavery or practices similar to slavery, servitude or the removal or organs.

17. Quoted in Andreas 2001: 117.
18. See the report on the 'safe third country' concept by the United States Committee for Refugees (USCR 1997: 6).
19. These thermographic devices were originally designed for military purposes – to spot tanks in night-time battles (*Guardian*, 15 March 2001).
20. Many migrants have attempted to cross the Channel without boats. In April 2001 a group clung to the side of a ferry for 20 miles before being removed; in July 2001 a group tried to paddle to England on children's inflatable mattresses (*Guardian*, 31 July 2001).
21. During the first six months of 2001 several migrants were crushed to death by trains as they attempted to walk through the Channel Tunnel (*Guardian*, 31 July 2001). In March 2001 several were lucky to escape

alive after hiding in the external luggage compartment of a train travelling through the Tunnel. In August almost 50 migrants walked several miles along railway tracks in the Tunnel – a disaster was narrowly averted (*The Times*, 31 August 2001). In December 2000, 500 migrants attempted to enter the tunnel on foot before being removed by French police (*Times*, 27 December 2000).

22. Quoted in Morrison 2001: 71.
23. Reviewing irregular movements to Europe, Morrison and Crosland (2001: 1) assert that agents abuse the human rights of migrants and 'deserve the full [attention] of international law and criminal justice'. Analysing Chinese irregular migration Skelton describes a 'trade in human aspirations and human misery' and concludes that trafficking is an evil that must be eradicated (Skeldon 2000: 21 and 28). So too with movements from Central America to North America: The Binational Study on Migration between Mexico and the United States identifies coyotes as exploitative and criminal (*Binational Study*, 2000: 50).
24. By 1997 Chinese workers in New York had filed hundreds of complaints about employers with the state Labor Department: there had been two prosecutions (Kwong 1997: 104).
25. A similar situation obtains in Europe: recent Chinese migrants to Britain who find work in the catering industry have typically been employed at half the standard wage (*Independent*, 21 June 2000).
26. The INS's top investigator into Chinese human smuggling was arrested in 1996 in Hong Kong with passports he intended to sell to prospective migrants (Kwong 1997: 63).
27. Interview with Ahmed, London, May 1998.
28. Interview with Neelan, London, June 2000.
29. In a draft report produced in 1998 the United Nations suggested that the figure might be as high as 1 to 2 million. Quoted in Ghosh 1998: 26, n. 78.
30. Interview with Dina, London, June 2000.
31. Ibid.
32. Report of Agence France Presse, 28 April 2001.

12

Conclusion: Racism without End?

Refugees and crime

Migrants offer a host of benefits to politicians and officials of the modern state. They not only provide a cheap and often compliant work-force but also, when required, a ready target for campaigns which seek enemies: enemies of the people, enemies of the nation, and 'global' ene-mies. They are readily criminalised. There are elaborate legal frameworks for controlling entry to the territories of states: systems of passports, entry permits, visas, refusals, detentions and deportations. These are supported by bureaucracies which patrol borders in the physical sense and which maintain principles of cultural differentiation. They dis-tinguish between citizen and alien – in practice they define membership of the nation. Those who attempt to evade these barriers violate princi-ples which are at the heart of national identification. They are not only seen as manifestly illegal but as threatening to the essential values of national life.

The link between nation and migration goes back centuries. Nation-states have always required the presence of aliens, without and within: imagined communities are intimately associated with the imagined threat of the stranger. In this sense the modern state exists only within the context of migration, and unwanted immigration – or the prospect of such immigration – can be functional to the state itself. Those who dominate states have changing agendas, however, and so the status of migrants must also change. For long periods governments may encour-age all forms of immigration, including irregular entry; at times of general instability, and/or when elections, referendums or other tests of mass opinion loom, migrants in general and irregulars in particular once more become the menacing presence of the national myth. This is the context in which, in the case of the United States, politicians and officials have developed fantasies of alien invasion – the 'Yellow Peril' of

263

the late nineteenth century and, 100 years later, new visions of inundation from the East.

The notions of nation and alien are opposite and complementary: they are a dualism at the heart of the modern political order. Changes in the character of one must affect the other, and so changes at a world level which bear upon the nation-state have their implications for the treatment of migrants. Global processes, including economic changes and innovations in transport and communications, have stimulated anxieties among those in authority that all nation-states are becoming weaker. Although the impacts on dominant states are often exaggerated there is a widespread belief that the state is under threat because the capacity to regulate movement of people is being undermined. Dauvergne (2003: 91) comments

> In this era when the capacity of a nation to control its borders and make them meaningful is being questioned in many fora, moving to reinforce them against 'outsiders' is an assertion to the contrary. Through [new immigration controls], nations reassert their sovereignty ... By moving to reinforce the borderline between us and them, nations seek to bolster their self-identity, their way of being nations.

During the 1990s the legal status of migrants became, publicly at least, a central concern of governments in Europe and North America. Irregular migration was presented as a threat to global order and an influence which subverted the integrity of every state, requiring demonstrations of authority which reaffirmed borders and border control. It was also associated with another global problem – that of organised crime. Since the 1980s global crime networks have become a key issue on the security agendas of the major Western powers, part of a matrix of threats which have replaced old Cold War enemies (Ali 2002, Marfleet 2003). Grewcock (2003: 116) comments that within the law enforcement discourse irregular migration is threatening by definition: 'it is illegal, clandestine, well-organised, beyond official scrutiny and control. It has a shadowy and dangerous character and the capacity to threaten national security, social integration and racial harmony'. The increased pace of activity within irregular channels has been taken as evidence of a growing threat posed not merely by the networks but by those compelled to use them. This has been amplified by the determination of the United States and its allies, since 11 September 2001, to present certain migrants as the most active agents of a new threat – that of global terror.

The work of Huntington, Kaplan, Pipes and others ensured that demonisation of people of the Third World, and in particular of Islamic regions, was already well advanced when the events of 9/11 refocused attention of the US state on irregular migration networks. These were seen as facilitating movement of terrorists: notwithstanding that they had been encouraged by the state itself, they were identified with criminality in general and with political violence in particular. At the same time the asylum system came under suspicion as a means by which hostile political activists gained access to states of the West. Crime, terror, Islam, migration and asylum were made to converge as a nexus of dangers, with the effect that forced migrants – already marked historically as a special category of alien – were again constructed as malign outsiders bearing the imminent threat of violence and subversion. They were now designated among the chief enemies of the US administration's 'war on terror'. As if to confirm Kaplan's warnings of the mid-1990s, they had re-emerged as bearers of instability and insecurity: 'carriers of the disease that had wracked their own societies' (Gibney 2002: 41).

Detention

It is against this background that many Western governments have intensified campaigns of arrest, detention and deportation. These were already well advanced: for decades very large numbers of irregular migrants have been absorbed into unofficial or 'grey' areas of the economy while a minority has been targeted as part of the criminal networks. New laws, such as the IIRAIRA passed in the United States in 1996, have been accompanied by high-profile campaigns to seize illegals, encouraging popular hostility towards migrants, including vigilantism.[1] Critics of the policy suggest that 'the battle for the border' is in fact less an assault on irregular migration than an attempt to demonstrate the authority of the American state (Spener 2000: 116). The 'battle' has been less concerned with the actual exercise of physical control over cross-border movements 'and much more to do with the *symbolic* assertion of the ability and will to exercise control' (ibid: emphasis in original).

Detention is one of the most important means of asserting state authority. In Europe the number of irregular migrants held in prisons, or in prison-like conditions, has increased rapidly. As we have seen (Chapter 8), many are refugees detained as illegal entrants and/or as 'failed' applicants for asylum. Some are migrants seized at sea or while attempting landfall: in Italy thousands held in this way have been imprisoned in camps known coyly as 'permanent temporary centres'. At the same time the policy of isolating refugees within the country of application for asylum has become widespread. There is no official list of centres: the Jesuit Refugee Service (JRS-Europe 2004: n.72) points out that neither the UNHCR nor The European Committee for the Prevention of Torture and Inhuman or Degrading Treatment or Punishment (CPT) compiles such a record. The

JRS offers a 'preliminary inventory'. According to the organisation by October 2004 there were centres in the following states:

States	Number of detention centres
Austria	1
Belgium	6
Croatia	2
Czech Republic	8
Denmark	2
France	20
Germany	45
Greece	19
Hungary	8
Ireland	6
Italy	16
Luxemburg	1
Malta	3
Netherlands	8
Poland	24
Romania	2
Russian Federation	6
Spain	13
Slovakia	2
Slovenia	4
Sweden	5
Turkey	2
Ukraine	1
United Kingdom	12
Total	216

Note: A number of states are omitted. In many states refugees are also held in prisons and police stations.

Source: JRS-Europe 2004.

Such an extensive network is a novel feature of EU migration policy. Not since the 1940s have such large numbers of aliens been isolated in this way: then fascist and Stalinist regimes detained all manner of internal and external enemies, while all parties to the Second World War held 'enemy' citizens and others said to threaten the war effort. The character of the new network is illustrated by developments in Belgium. The *opvangcentra* (reception centre) at Steenokkerzeel in Flanders is one of a series of detention sites for applicants for asylum. When opened in 1994 then minister of interior affairs Louis Tobback asserted that it was not a prison: 'here there are no criminals', he declared, 'only illegal aliens' (Blommaert and Verschueren 1998: 187) But Blommaert and Verschueren describe 'a complex with searchlights and two rows of barbed wire, four metres high. Inside, fifty guards, aided by a system of video surveillance, keep everything under control'. Inmates are forbidden to leave: Blommaert and Verschueren attest that it has 'all the appearances of the prison system' (ibid). By using such centres to isolate migrants the state emphasises not only their legal standing but also their distinct socio-cultural status. This practice has a disturbing history: in the 1980s refugees in Germany were forbidden to work, given provision only in kind, and restricted to 'encampments', a policy that stigmatised them and targeted them for special attention. Joppke (1999: 89) comments that 'creation of enclaves of idle, foreign-looking [*sic*] asylum seekers living on social welfare reinforced the public image of the parasitic "bogus asylum seekers" and provided easy targets for public hostility'. People in many villages and towns protested against the establishment of camps, so that across Germany anti-alien sentiment was intensified. The government's programme, Joppke suggests, 'laid the ground for the violent outbursts of xenophobia that would sweep the country a few years later' (ibid.). By the early 1990s refugee hostels were coming under attack and there was a string of murders, most notoriously in Hoyerswerda in 1991 and in Rostock in 1992.

Governments across Europe have pursued not only the policy of detention but also wider strategies of isolation of refugees. The British government has introduced the policy of 'dispersal'. Ignoring the advice of refugee groups and support organisations, it has distributed newly arrived refugees nationwide, including to areas of extreme social deprivation in which they have often been compelled to live in sub-standard accommodation judged unacceptable for other people. This has had the outcome its many critics had feared, exposing refugees to both informal and organised racist pressures, including hostile campaigns in the media, and to physical assaults which in several cases have been fatal. After a spate of attacks in 2001 the UNHCR alleged that some British politicians and newspapers had contributed to these tragedies. It described the killings as predictable, given the 'climate of vilification of asylum seekers' that had taken hold in the United Kingdom (*Guardian*, 11 August 2001). In 2004 police in several cities told the Home Office that dispersal should be halted because the policy was 'creating racial tension and violence' (*Daily Telegraph*, 14 November 2004). Notwithstanding these urgent warnings, the programme has continued.

The Australian option

Like imprisonment, these assertions of state authority have the effect of segregating migrants – in effect the latter are quarantined, publicly restrained from importing illegality and other undesired and threatening influences. The policy has been developed most fully in Australia. Here every informal migrant is detained. Although only a few thousand people enter illicitly each year, a fraction of the numbers arriving in Europe and North America, the Australian government maintains that its approach is essential if immigration is to be controlled. A nation-state which began as a penal colony, populated forcibly by means of transportation, has become the only liberal democracy to impose detention upon all uninvited migrants, including children. Since the declaration of a global war on terror its policies have been canvassed worldwide.

The policy was implemented in 1992 after attempts by refugees from South East Asia to land on the remote north-west coast. The numbers were modest: between 1989 and 2000 there were 7532 recorded illegal arrivals (Pickering 2001: 172). Most came from zones of acute crisis in Asia and the Middle East: by 1999 two-thirds were from Iraq and Afghanistan, with smaller groups from Algeria, Iran, Palestine and Sri Lanka.[2] Eighty per cent were eventually granted refugee status, leading critics of the system to point out that the state imprisoned thousands of people in the knowledge that most could show a case for admission, even under the limitations imposed by international and Australian law. By March 2000 there were 3622 people in detention centres (*Guardian*, 27 July 2001). An investigation by the government ombudsman concluded that they had fewer rights than criminals held in Australia's prisons, while UN reports found that mandatory detention breached Australia's human rights obligations (ibid.).

Several detention centres were extremely isolated – the largest, at Woomera in South Australia, was 700 kilometres north of the city of Adelaide in a bleak desert environment, and was described by a former Australian prime minister as 'a hell-hole'.[3] Psychological distress among the inmates was reflected in high levels of depression, and in hunger strikes and suicide attempts, some of which were successful.[4] In 2002 a report by the Australian Human Rights and Equal Opportunity Commission said there was a 'culture of despair' in the camps (*Melbourne Age*, 6 February 2002). The regime of incarceration has been accompanied by an aggressive strategy of exclusion, in which refugees have been intercepted at sea and transported to islands outside Australian territory – what the Australian government has called the 'Pacific solution'. When in September 2001 some 500 Afghans, Iraqis and Palestinians were taken from sinking ships in the Java Sea they were transported to the Pacific island of Nauru, the world's smallest republic, over 3000 kilometres from Australia. Migrants were also held on Christmas Island, the Cocos Islands, Papua New Guinea and Manus Island; the states of East Timor, Fiji, Palau and Kiribati refused requests to set up similar centres.[5] There were numerous reports that migrants had been forced to enter the camps: in the case of Manus Island, Iraqis said that they had been promised they would land in Australia but were subsequently driven into the centre at gunpoint (*Sydney Morning Herald*, 6 February 2002).[6]

Australia is a state large enough to be identified as a continent. It is sparsely peopled: population density in 2000 was 2 per square kilometre (World Bank 2000: 230). In 2001 Australian politicians nevertheless claimed that the boatpeople threatened to overwhelm the country, and transported them to states which were a fraction the size of Australia but with population densities which dwarfed that of the continent.[7] In the case of Nauru the first 500 boatpeople increased the island's population of 12,000 by 4.3 per cent – the equivalent of Australia admitting 500,000 refugees. These states were induced to accept the migrants by pressure from their powerful neighbour and by large payments: over three months in 2001 they received US$100 million from the Australian government (*Guardian*, 26 November).[8] There was fierce criticism from across the Pacific, including accusations that Australia's whole aid programme for the region had been distorted (*Melbourne Age*, 4 February 2002). Pacific churches and regional NGOs issued a joint statement condemning the Australian government and rejecting the use of the region as 'a dumping ground for everything industrialised countries reject'.[9] Oxfam pointed out that at a time when the government was championing policies of good governance, accountability, transparency and equity as the key principles for states in the region, it had effectively imposed its refugee policy on former colonies (ibid.).[10] The Edmund Rice Centre, a Catholic charity, said the policy was morally indefensible. It involved 'a bunch of white fellas running around the Pacific asking a bunch of brown fellas from impoverished third-world nations to take over our responsibilities with regard to asylum seekers'.[11]

'Boundless Plains'

These events present in an especially stark form the contradictions within immigration policies of all Western states. Like the United States, Australia has been peopled by migrants who at an early stage displaced the indigenous inhabitants. Its national anthem, Advance Australia Fair, echoes Emily Lazarus' welcome to America:

> For those who've come across the sea
> We've boundless plains to share
> With courage let us all combine
> To advance Australia fair.

For over a century immigration has been a highly charged issue in Australia's domestic politics. Waxman (2000: 53) notes tersely that 'Australia's immigration policy prior and subsequent to Federation [in 1901] was based on racist exclusion'. The first law passed by the federal government was to confirm a White Australia policy which barred non-European immigration and over the next 40 years political parties aligned with British imperial interests, with labour and with nationalisms across the political spectrum variously championed and opposed immigration – or at least selected immigration, for the migrants concerned were almost always from Britain. The economic boom which followed the Second World War increased the pace of immigration. Under the slogan 'populate or perish' many European refugees officially designated as Displaced People were accepted and later the assisted passage scheme, long in place for British emigrants, was extended to some Southern European and Middle Eastern countries. When the White Australia policy formally came to an end in 1973, Australian governments eager to expand their influence into East Asia and South East Asia allowed limited immigration from these regions, including that of refugees such as boatpeople from Vietnam, and in the early 1980s, 20,000 visas were issued each year to overseas applicants who could cite humanitarian grounds for admission. But by the 1990s repeated world recessions had taken their effect and Australian governments were developing more parochial concerns. Supporters of the 1989 Democracy Movement in China were the last refugees to be admitted in numbers and in 1992 mandatory detention, which had been implicit in a law of 1958, was enforced by the Migration Amendment Act. This required that a 'designated person' who was a non-citizen should be kept in custody until receipt of an entry permit. By the mid-1990s the population in detention was increasing steadily.

The Australian government has argued that informal migration violates principles which underlie its scheme for settlement of 'offshore' applicants for asylum. In fact this scheme has been structured in such a way as to discriminate against refugees from zones of crisis who have the most pressing need for sanctuary. In 2000, of 7500 places for offshore applicants, 45 per cent were allocated to Europeans, leaving 2206 places for the whole Middle East and 1738 for all of Africa (Mares 2001: 20). The Australian High Commission in Nairobi, which deals with asylum applications for 34 African countries, had 8000 cases on its books, with a further 2000 to be registered; there was an even bigger backlog in Islamabad, which served all of Western Asia (ibid). On average, applications took 18 months to be processed but in many countries those wishing to apply had no means to approach the Australian authorities: in Iraq and Afghanistan, which produced the largest numbers of boatpeople, Australia had no diplomatic representation.[12] In addition, applications were more likely to be successful if refugees had friends or family in Australia, possessed certain skills and spoke English. The overall effect was to disadvantage those most urgently seeking asylum.

As in Europe and North America increased official hostility to refugees was associated with resurgence of the political right. During the 1990s the One Nation Party grew in influence, articulating explicit anti-Asian racism focused upon a threat of invasion from the north, and calling for repatriation of refugees. Its increased prominence prompted a move by both major parties, Liberal and Labor, towards more restrictive immigration policies. In 1998 a minister in the coalition government warned of the dangers of One Nation's policy: deportations, he said, would 'continue the suffering of refugees who have been tortured and could well complete the work that torture began' (ibid). Mares (2001: 27) identifies the influence of One Nation and its leader Pauline Hanson upon both major parties. He is particularly critical of the adaptation of the Australian Labor Party (ALP) to Hanson's strident nationalism:

> The APL's lack of spine is a symptom of the Hansonite poison that continues to course through the Australian body politic; its debilitating effect being further exaggerated by breathing in an atmosphere of panic, and being fed a diet of animosity. By playing on deeply rooted popular fears, the government has engendered a mood of crisis around the issue of boat-arrivals and promoted an attitude of hostility towards asylum seekers and refugees. Previous Labor governments did the same thing and the media has gone along for the ride. (ibid)

The effect of One Nation on the conservative Liberal Party, which led the coalition government of the late 1990s, was of equal importance. Anxious to recapture electors lost to Hanson the party adjusted its position on immigration to absorb much of her policy. According to a senior Australian official, the Liberal-led Coalition Government of the late 1990s found 'rich pickings' in the area of immigration in general and in relation to refugees in particular.[13] In February 2001 Labor nevertheless won a landslide victory in state elections in Queensland when the Liberal vote collapsed in the face of attacks from One Nation during which Hanson made immigration the theme of her campaign, attacking refugees as 'queue jumpers' who were 'bringing diseases' into Australia (*Guardian*, 19 February 2001).

Playing politics with refugees

The Pacific solution announced a few months later was a response by Liberal leader John Howard to the prospect of defeat in a federal election. *The Economist*, an enthusiastic backer of Howard's neo-liberal agenda, saw exclusion of the boatpeople as a populist gesture crucial to his fortunes. It noted that with the Liberal Party trailing in the polls its leader had seized upon the refugee issue. Under the headline 'Election ahoy' it commented: 'Mr Howard saw an opportunity to beat the drum about his government's determination to stop the human tide supposedly invading Australia's northern coast' (*Economist*, 6 September 2001). With government encouragement, interceptions at sea were given high-profile treatment in the media; at the same time officials were instructed to discourage public sympathy for the refugees: one tactic was to ensure that press and television did not have access to 'personalizing or human images' of asylum seekers.[14] Meanwhile false information was presented by ministers and officials in a calculated attempt to persuade the public of the cynicism and immorality of the refugees.[15] The polls showed a sharp swing towards the Liberals and soon afterwards Howard won an election in which immigration had become the key issue.

Andreas (2001: 112) notes how, in the 1990s, recession and political instability in the United States prompted similar campaigns, as politicians 'rushed to outdo one another' in proposing tougher immigration controls. But as in Australia new measures of exclusion did not necessarily mean that all migrants, even all informal migrants, were to be excluded. Rather *some* migrants, those most readily identified as different, were featured as threatening and illegitimate, while others were accommodated. The Howard government in Australia followed this approach to the letter, for while boatpeople were imprisoned much larger numbers of applicants for asylum continued to arrive, attracting little attention. The Australian press struggled to resolve the apparent contradiction: *The Australian* (6 February 2002) noted that boatpeople were greatly outnumbered by 'planepeople' who arrived on student or tourist visas and applied for refugee status in-country. Government policy embraced a paradox, suggested the newspaper: 'These ["plane"] people lied to the authorities yet we let them remain free in the community while their applications were processed' (ibid). In addition to the planepeople, by 2001 'overstayers' easily outnumbered boatpeople, with Britain and the United States heading the list of visa violators (Dauvergne 2004: 97).

Many informal migrants have in effect been amnestied in Australia. Under conditions of relative stability such transgressors are 'forgiven' but when circumstances change some are transformed into the malign opportunists of the dominant refugee discourse. It is in this context that the boatpeople were identified for mass detention. They were an easy target. Almost without exception they originated in countries afflicted by decades of conflict in which local regimes and/or competing political factions had routinely used terror as a political weapon – hence they were prepared to travel thousands of miles in the hope of finding security, undeterred by extreme risks.[16] Many were ill-educated and impoverished, having sold all their possessions and/or having borrowed heavily to pay migration agents. All were non-Europeans from countries in which the dominant cultural identification was with Islam, an important marker of difference in all Western societies, and one which after the events of 11 September 2001 was specifically associated with terrorism by the Australian government. Its campaign was a calculated attempt to mobilise national sentiment against alien Others. The effect was to intensify racism in general and to direct attention to particular groups within Australian society, with potentially dangerous consequences. In January 2002 one of the government's most senior advisers on immigration, the Chair of the Council for Multicultural Australia, resigned 'in disgust' at the policy (*Sydney Morning Herald*, 23 January 2002). Neville Roach said that identification of refugees' 'deviousness and even criminal intent' had serious implications for the whole society, alleging that the Government had not only given 'comfort to the prejudicial side of human nature' but also encouraged hostility towards certain groups of Australians. He added: 'The greater tragedy is that the vilification, abuse and even violence that has resulted has not been directed exclusively towards asylum seekers but to the wider Islamic community and others of Middle Eastern appearance' (ibid). Many others opposed Howard's policy and his claim to speak on behalf of all Australians, and in March 2002 demonstrators at the Woomera detention centre cut and scaled razor-wire fences, freeing scores of detainees.

Acts of war

During the 1990s the threat conjured by the One Nation Party had been that of the 'Asianisation' of White Australia. As the pattern of informal migration changed, bringing people from the Middle East, the Howard government seized the opportunity to identify them too as different and as especially dangerous. Placing Australian policy in the context of the newly declared war on terror, Immigration Minister Philip Ruddock asserted that the boatpeople, overwhelmingly Muslims, should be viewed as potential criminals 'who could be murderers, could be terrorists'.[17] This encouraged a popular discourse which combined anti-refugee and anti-Islamic sentiment. The position of successive Australian governments during the 1990s had already encouraged generalised suspicion of refugees: Pickering and Lambert (2002: 65) describe an 'incessant background hum' of official hostility.

Pickering (2001) suggests that the Press was instrumental in disseminating negative images of the migrants. She has analysed the content of two leading newspapers, both 'quality' broadsheets, in relation to refugee issues during this period. She found that the *Sydney Morning Herald* and *Brisbane Courier Mail*, owned by rival publishers, took a similar approach to the migrants. Their editorials, news reports, features and commentaries saw an elemental confrontation of Australians and unwelcome outsiders. According to the two titles,

> 'we' are soon to be 'awash', 'swamped', 'weathering the influx', of 'waves', 'latest waves', 'more waves', 'tides', 'floods', 'migratory flood', 'mass exodus' of 'aliens', 'queue jumpers', 'illegal immigrants', 'people smugglers', 'boat people', 'jumbo people', 'jetloads of illegals', 'illegal foreigners', 'bogus' and 'phoney' applicants and 'hungry Asians' upon 'our shores', 'isolated coast-lines' and 'deserted beaches' that make up the 'promised land', the 'land of hope', the 'lucky country', 'heaven', 'the good life', 'dream destination', and they continue to 'slip through', 'sneak in', 'gathering to the north', 'invade' with 'false papers', or 'no papers', 'exotic diseases', 'sicknesses', as part of 'gangs', 'criminal gangs', 'triads', 'organized crime', and 'Asian crime'. (Pickering 2001: 172)

This dramatic imagery was mobilised as part of what Pugh (2004: 55) calls 'hate speech', a discourse which appears to have special intensity when mobilised in relation to those who arrive by sea: 'menacing, quasi-natural forces of migrants "washing out" a homeland and national identity'. The appropriate response to the immigrants, suggested Australian newspapers, was 'closed doors'; Australia should 'deter', 'lock up' and 'detain' (Pickering 2001: 172).

Military metaphors were in constant use: refugees approaching Australia were an 'invasion', an 'incursion' requiring a 'defence plan'; immigration controls were a matter of national security requiring 'full deployment' of the country's military resources (Pickering 2001: 173–4). Australia was at war, party to a conflict which would be either won or lost, and which required that the contending sides should be demarcated and boundaries drawn to identify 'ours' and 'theirs'. With the launch of global war against a shadowy new enemy Australian policy could be vindicated and re-asserted.

The official discourse of the refugee suggests a dual threat: the menace of those likely to violate territorial boundaries *and* the presence of aliens within. Policies of exclusion therefore usually attempt a parallel strategy, containing migrants at the border or in extra-territorial locations, and at the same time isolating certain groups within the borders of the state. In the case of Australia irregular migrants who succeeded in making a landfall were associated with crime and with disease. Newspapers repeatedly demanded medical checks – the incomers were said to be a health threat, contaminating Australian society merely by their presence. Like those who compromise general well-being they should be quarantined – hence the importance of detention camps far from centres of population. These views had implications for all manner of people who could be identified as Other. Australian national identity has long been constructed against the idea of threats from the Orient, first from China, later from South-East Asia, and by the 1990s from the Middle East. Poynting (2002) shows how during and after the Gulf War of 1990–91 Arab and Muslim Australians became objects of hostility in the media and were victims of widespread racist attacks. By the late 1990s the focus had moved to refugees, presented by the media as an 'endless and unstoppable flow ... invariably described as "Middle-Eastern" ' (Poynting 2002: 46). The events of 11 September 2001, together with the national panic about refugees, intensified these sentiments: Poynting suggests that refugees were now directly associated with calculated violence: ' "Boat people" = Middle Eastern = Arab = Criminal and Terrorist' (Poynting 2002: 53). Raids by police and intelligence organisations targeted homes of Arab and Asian Australians as the threat of transnational crime and terrorism was identified locally in workplaces and even suburban households. Australia's asylum panic became inextricably linked with 'interior' racisms, so that boatpeople could not be separated from the traditional demons of local bigotry and Australians of many origins became targets of official and unofficial attacks. Poynting (2002: 59) concludes that this was the outcome of a clear relationship – a symbiosis which embraced populist xenophobia, a 'manipulated and largely supine' media, and the repressive arms of the state.

Encampment

The Howard government has used its relationship with former colonies to establish extraterritorial prison camps which recall the penal settlements of European colonial powers (notably those established in Australia). In 2004 a number of European states proposed a similar strategy, canvassing Howard's 'Pacific solution' as a 'Mediterranean solution' in which states of North Africa would be rewarded for policing the strategy of exclusion. As in Australia this approach has been associated with intensification of 'internal' racisms. This is particularly clear in the case of Britain. Here leading politicians had made repeated commitments to multiculturalism, a perceived mutual acceptance and co-existence of people of diverse cultures and traditions. Successive governments formally opposed racism, notably after a high-profile report into racial discrimination among the police in London.[18]

At the same time, however, racism was being fuelled by more and more restrictive asylum policies. The government announced that it would deport more 'failed' applicants, setting in train a process of administrative exclusion which had the effect of increasing hostility to refugees. The media intensified its demands: during one particularly frenetic asylum panic in February 2001 *The Daily Mail* (1 February 2001) declared that Britain was 'a soft touch' and an 'asylum magnet', urging much harsher action against migrants, while *The Sun* (14 February 2001) declared the country 'Lunatic Asylum' and argued for mass expulsions.

The policy of dispersal of refugees to provincial centres continued. In 2001 a report from the organisation Refugee Action concluded that it had serious effects on migrants' well-being. It observed that they were compelled to live far from their communities and language groups, that many were unable to get employment or proper access to medical care, and were liable to be detained and isolated, often without knowing why. The result, said the agency, was that some refugees fell into advanced states of depression, thinking that the only solution was to return to their countries of origin, even when these were unstable and dangerous (*Guardian*, 22 October 2001). Despite such warnings, the government brought forward plans to confine more refugees in reception centres where inmates would be under curfew and if found to be absent would forfeit claims for refugee status. All services, including legal advice, health and education, were to be provided on site, minimalising contact with local communities. More recent proposals include plans for comprehensive health checks on all applicants for asylum, with the implication – echoing many earlier episodes of state hostility to refugees – that as bearers of disease they require isolation and remedial treatment. As in Australia, refugees in Britain are to be quarantined – identified as alien and undesirable and set aside from society at large.

A report on centres elsewhere in Europe had earlier warned specifically against these measures. In 1986 Caritas concluded that isolation of refugees in Germany had had serious consequences, producing 'instability, depressions, total apathy, persecution mania, pyscho-somatic diseases, aggression against other persons, things [*sic*] and auto-aggression … [and] suicidal intentions' (Joppke 1999: 89). The organisation also suggested that after long periods of isolation refugees found great difficulty adapting to normal social life. Ten years later a British mental health trust reported in almost exactly the same terms on refugees detained in the West Midlands. It described 'a beleaguered group of people', many of whom had experienced detention, torture and persecution in their country of origin and now presented with symptoms of mental illness, including depression, anxiety, psychosis and deliberate self-harm (Pourgourides 1998: 200). The British government nonetheless proceeded with plans for 15 new centres which would eventually hold tens of thousands of refugees. It seemed determined to transform migrants into people with problems – isolated, troubled and dependent upon welfare – the very figures that it had warned against.

Official racism

During the 1990s hostility to refugees became a common currency of politicians across Western Europe. According to Andrew Lansley, a strategist for the British Conservative Party, campaigns which focused on immigration 'played particularly well' in the media and were effective in damaging rivals' electoral prospects (*Observer*, 3 September 1995). Both major parties in Britain identified immigration in general with refugees, whom they described in pejorative terms. This practice reached such a pitch that in April 2000 the Labour government, fearful of losing support among Black and Asian voters, instructed its own ministers to moderate their comments.[19] At the same time the UN committee on the elimination of racial discrimination criticised the British government for its record, pointing out that there was a connection between official attitudes to refugees and increasing levels of harassment of minority communities (*Guardian*, 23 August 2001). Despite these warnings refugees featured more and more prominently in political propaganda in Britain and throughout Western Europe. In 2002 parties of the right in France, Belgium, the Netherlands, Denmark and Norway each campaigned aggressively against asylum rights.[20] In the case of Denmark, which had boasted a particularly liberal asylum regime, the populist People's Party joined a new government which immediately introduced the most restrictive immigration rules in Western Europe. Critics described these as racist and likely to turn the country into 'a fortress'; the UNHCR questioned the status of the plans under international law.[21] In 2003, 53 per cent of those applying for asylum in Denmark had been granted refugee status: by 2004 the figure was 9 per cent.[22]

What is the relationship between such policies and the spread of popular prejudice? For some writers on migration, fear and hatred of Others is ubiquitous. This is the implication of Weiner's comment on people's 'visceral anxieties' about those unfamiliar to them (Weiner 1995: 14), of Harris's reference to 'the predisposition to xenophobia among people at large' (Harris 2002: 45),[23] and the observation by Hollifield (2000: 139) that 'xenophobia could be considered a basic human instinct'. Although racism may gain a purchase within any area of society the notion that it has an atavistic basis is not an explanation for changing ideas about difference and exclusion. Discourses of race and specific racisms are in a constant state of flux: like all social constructions they are made and unmade, demonstrating certain continuities but also showing rapid modification. In the United States in the nineteenth century vast numbers of people, many of them immigrants, interacted and collaborated without difficulty;[24] at the same time exclusionary campaigns successively targeted people of African origin and indigenous Americans, and later Irish, Chinese, Jewish and Japanese migrants. The character of these campaigns varied widely, providing a range of rationales for discrimination, and with a range of impacts upon different areas of society. Similar patterns of change were evident in Europe a century later. In the 1940s and 1950s millions of people from Eastern and Southern Europe moved to states of Northern Europe, where at first they were widely considered racially and culturally inferior. Less than a generation later they had become 'Europeans' whose presence excited little interest: targets of racist hostility were more likely to be people of African or Asian origin, or to be refugees, soon to be constructed as a threat to the whole continent.

A key factor in the development of specific racisms is the relationship with influential political actors. Those with power and authority, who are most directly involved with the structures of the state, play a central role in shaping and generalising ideas about difference and exclusion, and in encouraging popular attachment to them. This is especially significant at times of instability, when those in power often choose to *promote* racist discourses, using the resources of the state itself to disseminate them. These resources are of great significance: Balibar (1991: 15) notes the ubiquitous presence of the state in the lives of its citizens, 'right down to the organization of everyday relations between individuals', and the impact of state institutions upon 'mass thinking'. He continues

> Modern racism is never simply a '*relationship to the Other*' based upon a perversion of cultural or social significance; it is a relationship to the Other *mediated by the intervention of the state* … In fact it is the state qua nation-state which actually produces national or pseudo-national 'minorities' (ethnic, cultural, occupational). Were it not for its juridical and political intervention, these would remain merely potential. Minorities only exist in actuality from the moment when they are codified and controlled (emphasis in original).

Measures for codification and control are the work of those in authority. As we have seen, politicians and officials may confirm and elaborate ideas about difference and measures of control – or challenge them and relax or even remove restrictions on movement. In the late seventeenth century enormous efforts were made by the British state to ease admission and integration of refugees from France. This involved a campaign of mass education about the Huguenots and their well-being, about notions of rights and religious obligations, and about the benefits of the migrant presence. There have since been similar episodes in Britain and elsewhere, but these are exceptions to a pattern which demonstrates that those in authority usually emphasise the idea of national and/or communal differentiation. Although they do not necessarily originate theories of difference, and some among them may find racism irrational or distasteful, they also find that these ideologies are of instrumental value. They make concessions to such views or incorporate them in official policy, encouraging prejudice and demands for more exclusionary measures. MacMaster (2001: 8) contends that in Europe racist practice should be understood in this context: it has been essentially 'a top-down process through which elites have played the greatest role in initiating action or forming a wider public opinion'. Reviewing the last 150 years of racist ideology and practice he concludes that although popular racisms may have a dynamic of their own they are driven from above, often directly through the machinery of state: 'Through the mobilization of prejudice, either from the level of the central or local state apparatus, elites can create and then harness racism as a political resource and source of power' (MacMaster 2001: 9).

Systematic migration control dates from the 1870s. It was at this period that ideas about exclusionary racism became widespread in North America and Europe – a development associated with imperialist competition and conflict, heightened nationalism, and fear among those in power of movements from below. In the United States the anti-alien lobby grew with remarkable speed, drawing support from many sources – the wealthy and powerful of the East Coast establishment, academics and writers, religious currents and leaders of organised labour.[25] The stimulus for exclusion, however, came from above, driven by industrial and commercial interests anxious about the instability of post-Civil War society and intent upon generalising ideas of nation and of national belonging. Zolberg (1997: 297) observes that the exclusionary campaign was 'initiated by traditional social elites' which succeeded in constructing a new migration regime in which exclusionary measures were directed first against Asians, later against Latinos and selected Europeans. This episode marked a decisive moment in the development of the official discourse of American identity, one at which for the first time laws on exclusion were mobilised to shape new notions of national community.

At the same time exclusionary campaigns emerged in Europe. In the case of Britain these also engaged coalitions across the political spectrum, involving leading figures in government; parties of the right, including the anti-Semitic British Brothers League; and representatives of the trade union movement. They drew on strong traditions of 'internal' differentiation, notably of hostility to Irish people, but the driving force came from above, in particular from Conservative politicians concerned at the growing strength of labour and its perceived threat, in an age of high imperialism, to the integrity of nation and of a state now associated with ideas of a global racial mission. Throughout the 1890s the conservative press attacked Jewish refugees in Britain, intensifying their offensive during the Boer War when Jews were accused of subverting the British military effort in South Africa, and the British imperial and national projects as a whole. The outcome was the Aliens Act of 1905, the first formal legislation against refugees, and a precedent for later sweeping laws against immigrants in general.[26] World War took these developments a stage further. In Britain the state armed itself with powers against all non-citizens, with the result that some 50,000 people were incarcerated and/or deported. For the next 30 years hostility towards foreigners was maintained at a high pitch by continued deportations, and by a series of punitive laws aimed at ethnic minorities. There was a similar pattern of active state racism in France: MacMaster concludes that in both countries the authorities worked systematically to racialise certain groups. Such purposive action, he argues, should be distinguished from the essentially reactive development of popular prejudice: 'The origins of both racist propaganda, as well as institutional racist practices, can be traced to elites, rather than to any initiatives or antipathy arising from the British or French working class' (MacMaster 2001: 124).

State racism

Politicians and state officials often justify their policies as responses to mass opinion: the state is innocent, merely reflecting the concerns of its citizens. In this context Hollifield (2000: 170) writes of the impact of 'postindustrial society' in Western Europe and North America. Feelings of failure, alienation, and resentment become widespread, he notes, 'especially among workers in the most industrial societies, many of whom see immigrants as the cause of their problems'. All that is required to spread prejudice 'is some entrepreneurial (usually right-wing) politician to trigger feelings of xenophobia and racism in these segments of the population' (ibid). He might have added that those within the state who encourage such ideas and formalise them as government policy imbue such notions with legitimacy. They undertake a double displacement of responsibility, identifying Others as the source of economic, social or cultural tensions, and deflecting onto the mass of the population the state's own interest in stimulating prejudice. The history of exclusionary racism has been marked by these disingenuous and cynical efforts, which have recently focused upon refugees. In the case of Germany in the 1990s, Erb (1997: 215) suggests that hostility towards asylum-seekers and foreigners was 'politically instrumentalized by mainstream democratic parties', part of a practice of xenophobia and ethnocentrism which, he maintains, is a habitual resort of establishment parties focused on electoral success. In the case of Britain, Kundnani (2001: 43) traces the means by which government attitudes towards refugees have been transmitted to homes and workplaces, becoming 'a complementary popular racism on the ground'. British immigration officials have been trained to view refugees with suspicion, to see applicants for asylum as dissemblers aiming to exploit the host community: 'This mindset migrates from the corridors of the Home Office to the streets, the schools, the pubs; carried there by tabloid newspapers eager to play up fears of an "influx" ' (Kundnani 2001: 42). The media is often deeply implicated. In Britain the tabloids have played a particularly active role, operating as an interface between state and popular racisms, a form of managed populism which claims to speak for the mass of people while disseminating the perspective of the state. They attack refugees as a menacing presence and a threat to national integrity; at the same time they silence refugees, making them 'a screen on to which all manner of evils can be projected' (Kundnani 2001: 48). In 2004 the National Centre for Social Research reported that public opinion against immigration had hardened since the advent of New Labour governments in 1997. It attributed the change to 'increasingly hard-line statements on asylum from Home Office ministers', and to a policy of soliciting the media to cover cases of detention and deportation (*Guardian*, 7 December 2004). The report suggested that traditions of tolerance 'seemed to come under sustained attack from the Labour government, aided and abetted by the Conservative opposition' (ibid).

European governments and establishment parties have long used the threat of the extreme Right as an alibi for their own offensives on migrants. They suggest that popular opinion is always likely to accommodate racism and that the intervention of the state is required to protect community integrity. Blommaert and Verschueren (1998: 188) identify just such practices in Belgium, where the government justifies its asylum and detention policies by reference to the alleged fears of the public:

> A favourite strategy [of the government] is the recourse to public opinion. It is the ordinary citizen who is opposed to the presence of foreigners. It is the ordinary citizen who could become the victim of violent conduct – or who could start voting for the [far right] Vlaams Blok. Thus a repressive admittance [*sic*] policy and a repressive attitude towards illegal aliens, in the hand of socialist ministers, become instruments of democracy.

Invariably this practice has a different outcome. Nick Griffin, leader of the neo-fascist British National Party (BNP), has spelt out how during the 1990s the attitudes of successive British governments towards refugees encouraged and consolidated racist ideas and parties of the extreme Right:

> The asylum seeker issue has been great for us [the BNP]. We have had phenomenal growth in membership. It's been quite fun to watch government ministers and the Tories play the race card in far cruder terms than we would use, but pretend not to. This issue legitimises us. (*Guardian*, 20 May 2000)

From prejudice to solidarity

Poynting's observations on the Australian experience could be applied more widely. At the core of each generalisation of racism vis-à-vis refugees is a focused effort to promote difference, involving the state and the media, and with the effect of generating 'populist xenophobia'. Such campaigns are not always successful, however, or they produce contradictory outcomes, a development clear since the first attempts to formalise policies of exclusion. This is evident in the case of Britain, the state which pioneered exclusionary laws. When in the nineteenth century British politicians began to revise their attitude to European exiles, refugees were strongly defended by the Chartist movement. Later those campaigning for exclusion met strong resistance, to the extent that the Aliens Act of 1905 was a much weaker version of the law they had intended. In 1914 the British government was overwhelmed by offers of help from the public for refugees from Belgium to whom it offered sanctuary in the face of German military offensives. In the 1930s official hostility towards refugees from Europe was challenged by large numbers of people whose understanding of the plight of victims of fascism was the key factor producing a change in policy. The National Joint Committee for Spanish Relief co-ordinated hundreds of support groups for Basque refugees: it was part of a movement of solidarity for Republican Spain that Fyrth describes as 'the most widespread and representative mass movement in Britain since the mid-nineteenth century days of Chartism ... and the most outstanding example of international solidarity in British history'.[27] When the government eventually agreed to accept Basque children, and then Jewish children from Germany and Czechoslavakia, it was in response to a public mood of solidarity that could no longer be ignored. What makes these examples particularly important is the resolve of campaigners, who created movements of support for refugees at a time when state discourses of exclusionary nationalism were at their most intense.

When hostility to a different generation of refugees began to spread across Europe in the 1980s new movements of solidarity with migrants came into being. Erb (1997: 214) traces the development of the German movement: a series of grass-roots campaigns 'dedicated to tolerance, protection of refugees, and fighting racism'. Similar backing for *sans-papiers* in France in the 1990s demonstrated the scale of opposition to official discrimination and helped to stimulate a wider European move-ment of support for migrants in general and refugees in particular. And in 2005 over 200,000 people in the Netherlands signed a request for a royal pardon for 26,000 refugees threatened with deportation. There are in addition countless examples of localised opposition to official anti-refugee sentiment, involving demonstrations of solidarity, physical protection of refugees, and campaigns against imprisonment and deportation. Some are at the level of individual protest: across Europe there have been incidents in which witnesses to deportations have objected to the violence used by police and private security forces on aircraft, with the result that pilots have insisted on removal of deportees and their escorts.[28] In Britain there has been a host of campaigns against deportation: Weller (1987) records the emergence during the 1980s of solidarity actions he describes as a new sanctuary movement, and Cohen (2003) examines the impact of campaigns in the north of England in the 1970s and 1980s, based upon what he calls 'a culture of resistance' to racism and to state controls (Cohen 2003: 224). Between 2000 and 2005 a different form of resistance emerged, with thousands of children involved in school-based campaigns to prevent deportation of refugee pupils and their families.[29] Similar developments have taken place in Germany, the Netherlands, Italy and Spain, with local activists taking responsibility for refugees within their own communities, and with mounting support from organised labour. Meanwhile networks of activists have provided shelter for migrants. In the United States during the 1980s the Sanctuary Movement, organised mainly through reli-gious networks, offered protection to refugees attempting to cross the US–Mexico border by illicit means: it claimed the involvement of 300 congregations and over 70,000 supporters, with more than 20 towns declared 'sanctuary cities' (Cohen 1994: 132). The tradition is main-tained by a series of organisations such as the Scalabrini Order, which continues to shelter people on the move to the United States from the south.

These developments constitute a long and largely unrecorded history of solidarity: a rejection of the politics of exclusion and an assertion of positive engagement between citizens and Others. They should be meas-ured against the widespread view that public opinion in Western states does not identify with migrants and their predicaments. Gibney, for example, maintains that public criticism of state responses to outsiders is 'relatively rare' and that popular pressures are almost invariably exerted to demand exclusionary measures (Gibney 2004: 207). What is true is that identification with migrants is initially a form of dissidence. It contests dominant ideas about the state, the nation, citizens and Others, and as such is treated with scepticism and usually hostility by those in power and with the influence which shapes media coverage and everyday political discourse. This makes recent developments even more striking, for solidarity movements have not only contested states and their nation-centred agendas but have organised energetically across national borders. In an important expression of 'alter globalisation', support for refugees has become a key concern of radical movements that have spread world-wide since the late 1990s. The World Social Forum (WSF), a collaboration of NGOs and campaigns against global capital which links millions of activists, has placed problems of exclusion high on its agenda, and the European Social Forum (ESF) has engaged large numbers of refugees alongside trade unionists, peace campaigners and anti-war activists in challenges to Fortress Europe. Klein, a leading figure within these movements, describes them as an expression of the 'lived reality' of globalisation, collaborations of 'the rabble of the real world' which interrogate the wealthy and powerful (Klein 2002: xv and xviii). She sets out their agenda for contesting neo-liberalism: 'to challenge homelessness, wage stagnation, rent escalation, police violence, prison explosion, criminalisation of immigrants and refugees, the erosion of public schools, and imperilling of the water supply' (Klein 2002: 244).

Here refugees are placed *within* a project for global change, their involvement challenging the priorities of dominant states and the long history of state exclusion. This development is in part an outcome of over 50 years of discussion about asylum rights, including debates among states and agencies about their responsibilities towards forced migrants. To this extent it can be argued that official discourses have stimulated positive interest in the circumstances of refugees. But today's discussions in forums such as the WSF also throw into relief the inadequacy of the international refugee regime and the self-serving conduct of states, especially their complicity in the refugee tragedies of the twentieth century. There is a sharp contrast, for example, between today's transnational forums of activists and the international collaborations which discussed refugee issues in the 1930s. In 1938 the United States summoned states to the Evian Conference to discuss the plight of the Jews of Germany and Austria. Their decision, records Sherman, was to abandon the migrants:

> no country, in any part of the world, wanted to add to its population desti-
> tute and demoralised outcasts. For such many of the refugees had become.
> Expelled from their countries of long residence, and labelled with the
> by-now pejorative collective title of 'refugees', the fugitives wandered aim-
> lessly on a planet which appeared quite simply to have no room for their
> kind. (Sherman 1994: 111)

The experience of Nazi persecution and of its fearful conclusion might have revised ideas about the effects of economic and political crisis and the need for places of sanctuary. It did not. When the first formal legal regime on asylum was developed in the 1940s it was designed to serve specific interests: the Geneva Convention was a partisan document, defining refugees so narrowly that most forced migrants were excluded. Within a few decades its provisions were under threat from states which wished to ignore even these limited commitments. Rubinstein comments that little has changed since the pre-war era. The contemporary refugee regime, he suggests, has a more humane face but is 'surprisingly similar' to that of the 1930s: 'The policies of the democracies in [the 1930s] were not so different from the policies of the democracies towards the world's refugees today' (Rubinstein 1997: 42–3). This is a sobering judgement from a historian who has examined the events of the 1930s in fine detail. It is essentially correct, for both the conditions which precipitate mass displacement and the policies of states are largely unchanged. Economic and political crisis accompanied by heightened nationalism in desired countries of asylum remain the contexts for regimes of exclusion which leave millions without sanctuary. The world's wealthiest, most powerful and stable states are intent, formally at least, upon a policy of 'no room' and the term refugee has again taken on a strong pejorative connotation. In this context the approach of transnational movements such as the WSF is a development of immense importance. It demonstrates that there is an alternative to the long tradition of high scepticism by states towards refugees, and places the latter at the centre of a network of solidarity.

'Designer migrants'

The refugee policies of most Western states are increasingly narrow and self-serving. On rare occasions groups of forced migrants who can be mobilised for specific ideological purposes are admitted; most others are excluded, with the result that many desperate survival migrants enter the irregular networks. Some are accepted informally on the basis that they will satisfy the demands of employers; others are selected for special treatment. These rejects come from among those whose cultural markers – physical appearance, language, religion, traditions – make them amenable to the particular task of identification of the alien. They are incarcerated and/or deported, sometimes as part of anti-immigrant campaigns conducted at such a pitch of intensity that they take the form of mobilisations for war. In the United States, control of movements along the border with Mexico has for many years been conducted in the context of Low Intensity Conflict, with whole populations in the border region placed within the theatre of confrontation. Here, says Falcon (2001: 43), border guards, troops and officials are encouraged to 'see the enemy' – to view some migrants as antagonists who must be confronted in the interests of national integrity. Since 9/11 this approach has been projected worldwide, driving migrants deeper into the irregular networks, with predictable consequences for their well-being.

In this scenario refugees are, paradoxically, made integral to national/ nationalist agendas. They are the principal focus of fears and insecurities which have little obvious connection to immigration as such, and are made to carry the historic burden of racism associated with the nation-state. They are not the only victims however. Offensives against refugees have implications for the whole society, for when refugees are racialised all are affected: economic and social problems are displaced onto Others; surveillance is intensified; communities, workplaces and collective organisations are divided; and individuals are targeted, as all are invited to 'see the enemy'. In 2004 the British government directed immigration officers to patrol the public transport system in London with the aim of identifying people who looked or sounded 'foreign', and to demand proof of their right to residence – an approach that echoes state strategies against enemy aliens in time of war. The human rights organisation Liberty commented on 'the clear racist implications'.[30] The involvement of the state in these initiatives is explicit: in the name of society at large it amplifies and generalises ideas about difference, exciting fear and mistrust. To paraphrase Mares' comments on Australia, state-led discrimination spreads a poison that takes its effect on society as a whole.

A number of writers have challenged the detail of official representations of the refugee. In the case of Britain, Hayter (2000), Cohen, Humphries and Mynott (2002), Lynn and Lea (2003), and Winder (2004) have examined myths of the asylum-seeker, including fantasies of inundation; allegations of opportunism, dissimulation and welfare 'tourism'; and the identification of refugees with crime and criminal networks. These ideas are dangerous in the hands of the extreme Right but when they become rationales for state policy they are immensely damaging to social relations at every level: Winder (2004: 338) describes them as reference points for debates that are 'rancid and polarised'. There has been somewhat less attention to the material costs of exclusionary policies. In the early 1990s European governments were said to be spending US$7–8 billion on refugee control and assessment (Harris 1996: 130). A decade later the cost of maintaining one detainee in custody for one day in Europe was Euro60–100 (Jesuit Refugee Service 2004: 118). With scores of thousands of refugees confined across the continent the total cost is vast – billions of Euros are being directed to the imprisonment of people among whom many will be released and promptly absorbed into the workforce.[31] The European Union nonetheless proposes to extend the system beyond the borders of the Union, establishing asylum 'processing centres' in North Africa, with the aim, says the President of the European Commission, of preventing migrants 'swamping' [*sic*] the Union (Human Rights Watch 2004). This strategy raises the prospect that dominant states are to attempt a more general reshaping of global movements, directing migrants to a series of regional holding units, dubbed 'international transit centres' (ITCs). According to the British think-tank Demos, these should be located close to sites of displacement and upheaval (Veenkamp 2003: 14). Here European states will select workers for priority projects – designer migrants who will become the *Gastarbeiter* of a new era. Those judged unsuitable will be detained or shipped back to their places of origin; according to Demos they will be assisted with 'redirection or return' (ibid). The costs will be enormous: between 2001 and 2003 the Australian government spent some US$500 million on its Pacific solution (Moorehead 2005: 111); the cost to the European Union of ITCs in Eastern Europe and the Mediterranean is certain to dwarf this figure. Meanwhile rejected migrants and others who avoid ITCs will be diverted onto irregular routes where agents will continue relentlessly to exploit their human cargo.

European governments are aware not only that the strategy of containment is undesired by influential business lobbies but also that it is futile. A report commissioned by the British government concluded it should be 'realistic' about deterrence. It noted a growing consensus that migration of asylum seekers 'has a momentum of its own which is hard to stop' and that dissemination of information about conditions in Britain would be unlikely to inhibit applicants for asylum (Koser and Pinkerton 2002: 32 and 34). Similar evidence came from reactions to a video shown in 2002 to thousands of refugees in France believed to be en route to Britain. The film, described as a 'video nasty', portrayed the hardships of life in Britain and the dangers of trying to cross the Channel and explained that those who joined a special programme would be paid to return home. The scheme was abandoned after only 17 people applied (*Independent*, 7 January 2002). These propaganda efforts are developed largely for a domestic audience: they are part of the attempt to pursue populist policies while satisfying urgent demands for more migrants. The observation of Calavita and Suarez-Navaz (2003: 111) on policy in Spain could be applied to the European Union as a whole: 'instead of controlling *immigration* [the policy] controls *immigrants*, ensuring their marginalization and their contribution to the economy as "flexible" workers' (emphasis in original). The idea of regulation is in fact inextricably linked with social control *in general* – with the anxiety of those in power to assert authority in the face of global and local instabilities.

Open borders

It is in the interests of the majority of people to find alternatives to such policies. Carens (1987) and Dummett and Nichol (1990) were among the first to set out arguments for open borders.[32] There was a negative response from many academics and researchers, especially from 'realist' analysts in political science, migration studies and international relations. In 1995 Weiner commented that the proposals were 'extreme', adding: 'To any realist, a safe and prosperous country that declared its borders open risks being overwhelmed by a massive influx from poor or violent countries', opening the possibility of rising xenophobia, violence and social disorder (Weiner 1995: 75). With neo-liberal and realist ideas dominant during much of the 1990s there were few further examinations of the case for free movement. By the end of the decade, however, with many assumptions about world development in doubt, a new literature appeared. Hayter (2000) and Harris (2002) argued strongly for unhindered movement, and Dummett made the case for open borders except in 'rare cases'.[33] Debate has since intensified: Meilaender (2001: 177) calls for a modification of refugee law, so that all who are 'truly desperate' will be admitted to states in which they seek security. This would allow for the accommodation of victims of famine and similar disasters, he suggests, but should not be taken to imply that states should surrender control of immigration. Gibney (2004: 83) makes a similar argument, maintaining that a 'humanitarian' approach to asylum will allow the accommodation of needy migrants while retaining controls essential to protect the institutions and values of the liberal democratic state. The case for open borders, he maintains, is 'unworldly': it is an abstract position without an obvious audience which can act in the real world (Gibney 2004: 260). This is mistaken: the case for free movement is being discussed more and more openly: in academic literature, in think-tanks and research organisations, and most importantly in the new activist movements.[34]

The alarmist suggestion that open borders will produce a surge of immigrants likely to overwhelm receiving states has not been borne out by recent experience in Europe. Enlargement of the EU in 2004 was accompanied by repeated warnings that destination states would be 'swamped' by migrants from the east. The tide of incomers has not materialised, rather the main concern of many Western European governments has been to stimulate *more* immigration, with most content to allow millions to enter through irregular networks. Rather than easing restrictions on entry, and investing in the education of those sceptical about the necessity and value of immigration, they have accelerated programmes of detention and deportation for a minority of migrants, encouraging popular hostility towards them through ideological offensives which embrace dissimulation and outright deceit. Here the state itself perpetuates prejudice and heightens fears of inundation which affect the well-being of migrants and of the 'host' society alike. It is in this sense that the study of migration, and particularly of forced migration, raises awkward questions about the character of the liberal state.

Immigration control, racism and exclusion are inseparable. Like the case against war, the argument against controls maintains that hostility towards Others is not a feature of the human condition and that, when people combine against the drive to social conflict, divisive consequences can be avoided. Arguments against war-making and against migration control are indeed more and more closely linked, especially since the declaration of a war on terror in which migrants are centrally implicated. War has an impact upon the population at large: it mobilises 'us' against 'them', focusing popular sentiment against enemies abroad and at home; it encourages the identification and persecution of aliens; it brings onto the agenda the prospect of mass repression; and it wastes public resources. The case against war as military conflict is well understood and, like arguments against poverty, global inequality and disease, it has become part of the discourse of current affairs. We should subject immigration controls to the same critical examination.

Leaders of the G8 have referred to irregular migration networks as the 'dark [*sic*] side of globalisation'. The truly negative aspect of a globalising world is the agenda of dominant states, of transnational agencies and financial organisations. They drive forward the neo-liberal project, promoting more inequality and inequity, more environmental degradation, more conflict and displacement, and – at the same time – more hostility to forced migrants, with the outcome that irregular networks are encouraged, together with increased aggression towards those who make use of them. This formula offers racism without end. A better world *is* possible, one in which people move freely and are able to prosper through the embrace of diversity and difference. Arendt (1986: 267) described the refugees of the 1930s as homeless, stateless and rightless: they were, she says, 'the scum of the earth'. Today, the 'rabble of the world' has put onto the agenda a prospect of global order without racism and war.

This is the right time to advance the argument for open borders. Meanwhile it is important to look at other dimensions of forced migration. The discourse of the refugee sees forced migrants as mere ciphers and much of the literature on displacement views them as people characterised by deficits. In fact refugee lives usually speak of energy, resilience and imagination, qualities highly prized in other contexts. The journeys of the displaced often require great determination, while life in exile is a challenge to innovate, to resolve relations with the host society, and to create new communities that may have an unprecedented diasporic character. It is such communities that generate projects of return, visions of home, and reflections on exile that are productive not only of social and political activism but of great literature and visual art. These activities do not take place in isolation from the wider society but as part of it. Despite the efforts of many states to impose regimes of isolation refugees are not without friends in host societies, although these seldom come from those who enjoy wealth, power and privilege. The achievements of refugees and those with whom they interact are a key part of the story of forced migration – but they are the subject for a different book.

Notes

1. These moves excited a tradition of vigilantism which goes back to the years of the Depression. Watkins (1999: 407) notes attacks on Mexicans and other immigrant workers during the early 1930s that consciously imitated racist assaults on African-Americans.
2. Of 3737 boatpeople who landed in Australia in 1999, 2300 were from Iraq and Afghanistan (Amnesty International 2000: 37).
3. Malcolm Fraser, quoted in the *Guardian*, 27 July 2001.
4. In January 2002 a large group of Afghan detainees at Woomera tried to kill themselves in protest against the government's decision to stop processing their asylum applications.
5. Kiribati had earlier unsuccessfully requested that Australia accept as environmental refugees some of its citizens who had been displaced by the effects of climatic change.
6. In these centres refugees came under the authority of Australian officials – in effect the camps became sovereign Australian territory. One effect was to reshape the regional refugee regime. By imposing new arrangements within Pacific states Australia exported mandatory detention, a policy expressly opposed by the UNHCR.
7. In Papua New Guinea population density is 10 per square kilometre, five times that of Australia, and income per capita a tenth of that in Australia (World Bank 2000, 230–1). Fiji and Kiribati have population densities of 45 and 117 per square kilometre respectively – over 20 times and 50 times greater than that of Australia. In each the per capita income is about one sixth that enjoyed by Australians (World Bank 2000: 272).
8. Nauru alone received US$15 million – a sum greater than all Australian aid provided to the state between 1993 and 2001 and almost a fifth of all that allocated for the Pacific Islands for 2001–2 (*Guardian*, 26 November).
9. Hilda Lini, Director of the Pacific Concerns Resource Group, quoted in a submission by the National Council of Churches in Australia to the Australian Senate Select Committee Inquiry into *A Certain Maritime*

Incident, at: http://www.aph.gov.au/Senate/committee/martime_incident_ctte/submission/sub18.pdf

10. Nauru was under Australian administration until 1968 and Papua New Guinea was an Australian colony until 1975.

11. Phil Glendinning, director of the Centre (*Guardian*, 26 November 2001).

12. In the case of the former Yugoslavia during the crises of the 1990s Australia like Britain demanded that all applicants make a formal approach to the embassy in Belgrade, unreachable from Bosnia and Kosovo where most applicants were located.

13. Chris Conybeare, quoted in Mares 2001: 155–6.

14. See evidence given by the Director General of Communication Strategies in the Government's Public Affairs and Corporate Communication unit, quoted in Poynting 2002: 48.

15. During the height of the election campaign in October 2001 the Australian Defence Minister declared that refugees had thrown their children overboard in attempts to encourage rescue. This was later shown to be false, as was a video which had been modified to add weight to the story (see Marr and Wilkinson 2003). In October 2002 a formal report from the Australian Senate concluded that the minister had 'engaged in the deliberate misleading of the Australian public concerning a matter of intense political interest during an election period' (*Guardian*, 24 October 2002).

16. In October 2001, 350 people from Iraq, Afghanistan, Algeria and Palestine drowned when their boat sank in the Java Sea. The Refugee Council of Australia commented that they were typical of migrants so desperate for security that they could not wait to pass through official immigration channels (*Guardian*, 24 October 2001).

17. Speaking in June 2000, Ruddock commented that detainees at Woomera were 'people who may have substantial criminal records, who could be murderers, could be terrorists' (Mares 2001: 153).

18. The McPherson Report into police investigations of the murder of Stephen Lawrence, a Black teenager murdered by racists in South London.

19. After a warning from trade union leaders that Labour ministers' comments on refugees were 'giving life to the racists' and risked alienating many of the party's supporters, ministers were told to find new terms for describing asylum-seekers: in particular the word 'bogus' was not to be used (*Independent*, 17 April 2000).

20. These developments are closely related to harmonisation of asylum policy across the European Union, part of a general climate of hostility towards Europe's internal and external 'enemies' (Marfleet 1999, 2000, 2003).

21. *The Guardian*, 10 April 2002.

22. Figures from the Danish Refugee Council at: www.flygtning.dk/Fakta_om_flygtninge.1625.97.html

23. Harris, while arguing against border controls, repeats this assertion in various forms, including the suggestion that campaigns of exclusion awaken 'ancient paranoid fantasies' of invasion (Harris 2002: 22).

24. This is not to suggest that American society was free of conflict: on the contrary, it was in a state of continuing disturbance in which issues of class, race and cultural difference were all significant. Gilje (1996: 142) comments that it was often difficult to distinguish between labour, ethnic and political strife, against a background of racism shaped by centuries of slavery. Tens of millions of people nonetheless continued to enter from Europe, settling mainly in the cities of the East, the Mid-West and the Pacific Coast, and entering into collaborative relations with hosts of others in probably the greatest multicultural interaction of modern times.

25. The movement was opposed by an equally diverse range of groups, notably employers habituated to very cheap labour, the Catholic church, and Jewish organisations. See Zolberg 1997.

26. Cohen (2003: 81) has argued that the involvement of trade union organisations in the exclusionary movement was decisive and the key factor in securing the Aliens Act of 1905. This greatly understates the influence of conservative nationalism generated within the British ruling class, of sustained anti-alienism within the press and among influential establishment figures, and the role of Conservative politicians in driving through the legislation. Cohen wrongly suggests that a continuous history of anti-Semitism dating from medieval times had in effect contaminated the labour movement in general. MacMaster (2001: 110) provides a corrective, noting that throughout the period from 1870 to 1914, political anti-Semitism 'remained a marginal issue, one that barely found a [popular] purchase outside the East End of London'.

27. Quoted in Kusher and Knox 1999: 105–6.

28. For details of a number of high-profile cases see Fekete 2005, chapter 2. One result of 'countless' protests is that European governments have turned to the use of chartered private aircraft for large-scale deportations. Fekete (2005: 20) cites the case of the Netherlands government, which in 2002 organised 25 charter flights to carry 1384 escorts and 1404 deportees.

29. See the Schools Against Deportations campaign at:
www.schoolsagainstdeportations.org

30. Report of Liberty at: http://www.liberty-human-rights.org.uk/issues/are-you-british-.shtml

31. Meanwhile large sums are being allocated for deportation: in January 2004 the European Union allocated Euro30 million to finance joint deportations (Schuster 2004: 8).

   Payne, who has conducted unique research on patterns of detention in Europe and the United States, asks whether such a pattern of waste is driven in part by the transnational prisons corporations, which exert an increasingly powerful influence over the 'corrections industry' and which operate many detention centres and escort services in Australia and on both sides of the Atlantic. Payne, R., *Cashing in on Asylum*, unpublished MA thesis, University of East London.

32. I exclude from consideration the conservative libertarians for whom the demand for free movement is part of a campaign against the state as a perceived interference in the operation of open markets.

33. For Dummett (2001: 73) all migrants should be able to cross borders freely, except when a population 'is in genuine danger of being submerged' or the number entering would bring about serious overpopulation. These reservations are matters for debate: the case for open borders should be examined less as a utopian formula and more as an agenda to free societies in sending and receiving regions from the destructive effects of regimes of control.

34. See the books by Cohen, Humphries and Mynott (2002) and Cohen (2003), and the debate on open borders organised by Open Democracy and involving leading academics in the field of Refugee Studies: www.opendemocracy.net/debates/article-10-96-1657.jsp

Bibliography

Abdel-Malik, A. (1968) *Egypt, Military Society: The army regime, the left, and social change under Nasser* (New York: Vintage Books).

Abu-Lughod, J. (1989) *Before European Hegemony: The world system AD1250–1350* (Oxford: Oxford University Press).

Adelman, H. (1999) 'Modernity, globalization, refugees and displacement', in Ager, A. (ed.) *Refugees: Perspectives on the Experience of Forced Migration* (London: Continuum).

Adelman, H. (2003) 'The uses and abuses of refugees in Zaire', in Stedman, S. J. and Tanner, F. (eds) *Refugee Manipulation: War, Politics and the Abuse of Human Suffering* (Washington DC: Brookings Institution Press).

African Development Bank (1997) *African Development Report 1997* (Oxford: Oxford University Press).

Al-Ali, N. and Koser, K. (2002) *New Approaches to Migration? Transnational communities and the transformation of home* (London: Routledge).

Al-Khalil (1989) *Republic of Fear* (London: Hutchinson Radius).

Al-Sharmani, M. (1999) *The Somali refugees in Cairo: Issues of survival, culture and identity* (unpublished MA thesis, The American University in Cairo).

Al-Sharmani, M. (2004) *Refugee Livelihoods: Livelihood and diasporic identity constructions of Somali refugees in Cairo*, New Issues in Refugee Research, Working Paper No 104 (Geneva: UNHCR).

Ali, T. (2002) *The Clash of Fundamentalisms: Crusades, Jihad and Modernity* (London: Verso).

Amnesty International (1993) *Amnesty International Report 1993* (London: Amnesty International).

Amnesty International (1997) *Amnesty International Report 1997* (London: Amnesty International).

Amnesty International (1998) *Amnesty International Report 1998* (London: Amnesty International).

Amnesty International (1999) *Amnesty International Report 1999* (London: Amnesty International).

Amnesty International (2000) *Amnesty International Report 2000* (London: Amnesty International).

Anderson, B. (1983) *Imagined Communities: Reflections on the Origin and Spread of Nationalism* (London: Verso).

Anderson, B. and Rogaly, B. (2005) *Forced Labour and Migration to the UK* (Oxford: COMPAS, at: www.compas.ox.ac.uk/publications/papers/forced%20labour%20TUC%20report.pdf).

Andor, L. and Summers, M. (1998) *Market Failure: A Guide to the Eastern European 'Economic Miracle'* (London: Pluto).

Andreas, P. (2001) 'The transformation of migrant smuggling across the US–Mexico border', in Kyle, D. and Koslowski, R. (eds) *Global Human Smuggling: Comparative Perspectives* (Baltimore: Johns Hopkins).

Annerino, J. (1999) *Dead in the Tracks: Crossing America's Desert Borderlands* (New York: Four Walls Eight Windows).

Aouragh, M. (2003) 'Cyber intifada and Palestinian identity', in *ISIM Newsletter* 12.

Arendt, H. [1951] (1986) *The Origins of Totalitarianism* (New York: Harvest).

Arnaout, G. M. (1988) Asylum in the Arab-Islamic tradition (Geneva: UNHCR).

Bairoch, P. (1975) *The Economic Development of the Third World Since 1900* (London: Methuen).

Balibar, E. (1991) '*Es Gibt Keinen Staat in Europa*: Racism and politics in Europe today', *New Left Review* 186, March/April 1991.

Ballard, R. (1987) 'The political economy of migration: Pakistan, Britain and the Middle East', in Eades, J. *Migrants, Workers and the Social Order* (London: Tavistock).

Ballard, R. (2001) 'The Impact of Kinship on the Economic Dynamics of Transnational Networks: Reflections on some South Asian Developments'. Paper presented to the Workshop on Transnational Migration, Princeton University, June 2001, at: http://www.transcomm.ox.ac.uk/working%20papers/Ballard.pdf

Barraclough, S. L. (1991) *An End to Hunger: The Social Origins of Food Strategies* (London: Zed).

Berberoglu, B. (1982) *Turkey in Crisis* (London: Zed).

Behr, E. (1961) *The Algerian Problem* (London: Penguin).

Bennett, J. (1998) 'Internal displacement in context: The emergence of a new politics', in Davies, W. (ed.) *Rights Have No Borders: Worldwide Internal Displacement* (Oslo: Norwegian Refugee Council/Global IDP Survey).

Biersteker, T. (2000) 'Globalization as a mode of thinking in major institutional actors', in Woods, N. (ed.) *The Political Economy of Globalization* (Basingstoke: Macmillan).

Binational Study on Migration (2000) *Migration Between Mexico and the United States*, at: http://utexas.edu/lbj/uscir/binational.html

Blommaert, J. and Verschueren, J. (1998) *Debating Diversity: Analysing the discourse of tolerance* (London: Routledge).

Bloxham, D. and Kushner, T. (2005) *The Holocaust: Critical Historical Approaches* (Manchester: Manchester University Press).

Booth, J. A. and Walker, T. W. (1993) *Understanding Central America* (Boulder: Westview).

Booth, K. and Dunne, T. (2002) *Worlds in Collision: Terror and the Future of Global Order* (Basingstoke: Palgrave).

Bosswick, W. (2000) 'Development of asylum policy in germany', *Journal of Refugee Studies* Vol. 13, No. 1.

Braudel, F. (1972) *The Mediterranean and the Mediterranean World in the Age of Philip II, Vol. 1* (London: William Collins).

Braudel, F. (1974) *Capitalism and Material Life 1400–1800* (London: William Collins).

Breitman, R. (2000) *Official Secrets* (London: Penguin).

Brettell (2000), 'Theorizing migration in anthropology' in Brettell, C. B. and Hollifield, J. F. (eds) *Migration Theory: Talking Across Disciplines* (London: Routledge).

Brysk, A. (ed.) (2002) *Globalization and Human Rights* (Berkeley: University of California Press).

Bunt, G. R. (2003) *Islam and the Digital Age: E-Jihad, Online Fatwas and Cyber Islamic Environments* (London: Pluto).

Burgess, A. (1997) *Divided Europe: The New Domination of the East* (London: Pluto).

Bustamente, A. R. (1998) 'As guilty as hell: Mexican copper miners and their communities in Arizona 1920–1950', in Hart. J. M. (ed.) *Border Crossings* (Wilmington: Scholarly Resources).

Calavita, K. and Suraez-Navaz, L. (2003) 'Spanish Immigration Law and the construction of difference: Citizens and "illegals" on Europe's southern border' in Perry, W. P. and Maurer, B. (eds) *Globalization Under Construction* (Minneapolis: University of Minnesota Press).

Callamard, A. (1999) 'Refugee women: a gendered and political analysis of the refugee experience', in Ager, A. (ed.) *Refugees: Perspectives on the Experience of Forced Migration* (London: Continuum).

Campbell, B. B. (2002) 'Death squads: Definitions, problems and historical contexts', in Campbell, B. B. and Brenner, A. D. (eds) *Death Squads in Global Perspective: Murder with Deniability* (Basingstoke: Macmillan).

Carens, J. H. (1987) 'Aliens and citizens: The case for open borders', *Review of Politics*, Spring 1987.

Carrasco, G. P. (1997) 'Latinos in the United States: Imitation and Exile', in Perea, J. F. (ed.) *Immigrants Out!* (New York: New York University Press).

Castles, S. (1993) 'Migrations and minorities in Europe. Perspectives for the 1990s: eleven hypotheses', in Wrench, J. and Solomos, J. (eds) *Racism and Migration in Western Europe* (Oxford: Berg).

Castles, S. (2004) 'Why migration policies fail', *Ethnic and Racial Studies* Vol. 27, No. 2, March 2004.

Castles, S. and Davidson, A. (2000) *Citizenship and Migration* (Basingstoke: Macmillan).

Castles, S. and Miller, M. J. (1993) *The Age of Migration: International Population Movements in the Modern World* (Basingstoke: Macmillan).

Castles, S. and Miller, M. J. (2003) *The Age of Migration: International Population Movements in the Modern World* [Third Edition] (Basingstoke: Macmillan).

Carter, A. C. (1975) *Getting, Sending and Investing in Early Modern Times* (Assen: Van Gorcum).

Caufield, C. (1998) *Masters of Illusion: The World Bank and the Poverty of Nations* (London: Pan).

Cerny, P. (1993) 'The political economy of international finance', in Cerny, P. (ed.) *Finance and World Politics: markets, regimes and states in the post-hegemonic era* (Aldershot: E. Elgar).

Cesarani, D. (2001) *Justice Delayed: How Britain Became a Refugee for Nazi War Criminals* (London: Phoenix).

Chester, E. T. (1995) *Covert Network: Progressives, the International Rescue Committee and the CIA* (Armonk, NY: M. E. Sharpe).

Chomsky, N. (1989) *The Culture of Terrorism* (London: Pluto).

Chomsky, N. (1994) *World Orders Old and New* (Cairo: The American University in Cairo Press).

Chomsky, N. (1999) *The New Military Humanism: Lessons from Kosovo* (London: Pluto).

Chomsky, N. (2002) 'Who are the global terrorists?', in Booth, K. and Dunne, T. (eds) *Worlds in Collision: Terror and the Future of Global Order* (Basingstoke: Palgrave).

Chossudovsky, M. (1997) *The Globalisation of Poverty: Impacts of IMF and World Bank Reforms* (London: Zed).

Claassen, J. -M. (1999) *Displaced Persons: The Literature of Exile from Cicero to Boethius* (Madison: University of Wisconsin Press).

Clegg, A. (1971) *Workers Self-Management in Algeria* (London: Allen Lane).

Cohen, R. (1994) *Frontiers of Identity: The British and Others* (London: Longman).

Cohen, R. (1997a) *Global Diasporas: An Introduction* (London: UCL Press).

Cohen, R. (1997b) 'Diasporas, the nation-state, and globalization', in Gungwu, W. (ed.) *Global History and Migrations* (Boulder: Westview).

Cohen, R. and Joly, D. (1989) 'The 'New' Refugees of Europe', in Cohen, R. and Joly, D. (eds) *Reluctant Hosts: Europe and its Refugees* (Aldershot: Avebury).

Cohen, S. (2002) 'In and against the state of immigration controls: Strategies for resistance', Cohen, S. Humphries, B., and Mynott, E. (eds) *From Welfare Controls to Immigration Controls*, (Stoke-on-Trent: Trentham).

Cohen, S. (2003) *No One Is Illegal: Asylum and immigration control past and present* (Stoke-on-Trent: Trentham).

Cohen, S. Humphries, B., and Mynott, E. (2002) *From Welfare Controls to Immigration Controls* (Stoke-on-Trent: Trentham).

Collinson, S. (1994) *Europe and International Migration* (London: Pinter).

Collinson, S. (1999) *Globalisation and the dynamics of international migration: implications for the refugee regime*, New Issues in Refugee Research, Working Paper No. 1 (Geneva: UNHCR).

Cooper, D. (1992) 'Urban refugees: Ethiopians and Eritreans in Cairo', *Cairo Papers in Social Science*, Vol. 15, Monograph 2.

Cooper, D. (1993a) 'A needs assessment of the Ethiopian and Eritrean refugee populations in Cairo' (Report to the Ford Foundation, Cairo).

Cooper, D. (1993b) *Waiting for a chance: The social construction of the refugee world in Cairo*, unpublished manuscript.

Copeland, E. (1998) 'Reshaping the international refugee regime: Industrialized states' responses to post-Cold War refugee flows', *International Politics* Vol. 35, No. 4, December 1998.

Cottret, B. (1991) *The Huguenots in England* (Cambridge: Cambridge University Press).

Cox, R. (1995) 'Critical political economy', in Hettne, B. (ed.) *International Political Economy: Understanding Global Order* (London: Zed).

Cribb, R. (2002) 'From *Petrus* to Ninja: Death squads in indonesia', in Campbell, B. B. and Brenner, A. D. (eds) *Death Squads in Global Perspective: Murder with Deniability* (Basingstoke: Macmillan).

Crisp, J. (1999) *Policy challenges of the new diasporas: migrant networks and their impact on asylum flows and regimes* (Geneva: UNHCR).

Crow, B. (2000) 'Understanding famine and hunger', in Allen, T. and Thomas, A. (eds) *Poverty and Development into the 21st Century* (Oxford: Oxford University Press).

Currie, L. (2004) *Who can be added: The effects of UNHCR's refugee status determination process and Third Country resettlement on the marital strategies, rites and customs of the Southern Sudanese refugee community living in Cairo, Egypt* (unpublished MA thesis, University of East London).

Dajani, M.A. 'The institutionalization of Palestinian identity in Egypt', *Cairo Papers in Social Science*, Vol. 9, Monograph 3, Fall 1986.

Dale, G. (1999) 'Germany: Nation and immigration', in Dale, G. and Cole, M. (eds) *The European Union and Migrant Labour* (Oxford: Berg).

Dauvergne, C. (2004) 'Making people illegal', in Fitzpatrick, P. and Tuitt, P. (eds) *Critical Beings: Law Nation and the Global Subject* (Aldershot: Ashgate).

Delanty, G. (1995) *Inventing Europe: Idea, Identity, Reality* (Basingstoke: Macmillan).

Delouvin, P. (2000) 'The evolution of asylum in france', *Journal of Refugee Studies* Vol. 13, No. 1.

Deng, F. M. (1993) *Protecting the Dispossessed: A Challenge for the International Community* (Washington DC: Brookings Institution).

Diner, H. R. (2000) 'History and the study of immigration', in Brettell, C. B. and Hollifield, J. F. (eds) *Migration Theory: Talking Across Disciplines* (London: Routledge).

Dinnerstein, L., Nichols, R. L. and D. M. Riemers (1979) *Natives and Strangers: Ethnic groups and the building of America* (New York: Oxford University Press).

Divine, R. A. (1957) *American Immigration Policy 1924–1952* (New Haven, CT: Yale University Press).

Dreze, J. and Sen, A. (1989) *Hunger and Public Action* (Oxford: Clarendon Press).

Dummett, A. and Nicol, A. (1990) *Subjects, Citizens, Aliens and Others* (London: Weidenfeld & Nicolson).

Dummett, M. (2001) *On Immigration and Refugees* (London: Routledge).

Dunn, T. J. (2001) 'Border militarization via drug and immigration enforcement: Human rights implications', *Social Justice* Vol. 28, No. 2.

Durand, J. and Massey, S. M. (1995) *Miracles on the Border: Retablos of Mexican Migrants to the United States* (Tucson: University of Arizona Press).

Edmonston, B., Passel, J. S. and Bean, F. D. (1990) 'Perceptions and estimates of undocumented migration to the United States', in Bean, F. D., Edmonston, B. and Passel, J. S. (eds) *Undocumented Migration to the United States: IRCA and the Experience of the 1980s* (Santa Monica, CA: Rand Corporation/Washington, DC: The Urban Institute).

Edsforth, R. (2000) *The New Deal: America's Response to the Great Depression* (Oxford: Blackwell).

Edwards, C. (1992) 'Industrialization in South Korea', in Hewitt, T., Johnson, H. and Wield, D. (eds) *Industrialization and Development* (Oxford: Oxford University Press/Open University).

Eickelman, D. and Piscatori, J. (1990) *Muslim Travellers* (Berkeley: University of California).

El-Ghonemy, R. (1998) *Affluence and Poverty in the Middle East* (London: Routledge).

El Nadim Centre (2004) *Torture in Sudan: Facts and Testimonies* [Arabic] (Cairo: El Nadim Centre).

Ellis, P. and Khan, Z. (2002) 'The Kashmiri diaspora: Influences in Kashmir', in Al-Ali, N. and Koser, K. (eds), *New Approaches to Migration? Transnational Communities and the Transformation of Home* (London: Routledge).

Erb, R. (1997) 'Public responses to antisemitism and Right-Wing extremism', in Kurthern, H., Bergmann, W. and Erb, R. (eds) *Antisemitism and Xenophobia in Germany After Unification* (Oxford: Oxford University Press).

Eschbach, K., Hagan, J. and Rodriguez, N. (1999) 'Death at the Border', *International Migration Review* Vol. 33, No. 2.

Escobar, A., Gonzalez, M. and Roberts, B. (1987) 'Migration, labour markets and the international economy', in Eades, J. (ed.) *Migrants, Workers and the Social Order* (London: Tavistock).

Evans, M. (1996) 'Languages of racism within contemporary Europe', in Jenkins, B. and Sofos, S. A. (eds) *Nation and Identity in Contemporary Europe* (London: Routledge).

Evans, T. (2001) *The Politics of Human Rights* (London: Pluto).

Falcon, S. M. (2001) 'Rape as a weapon of war: Advancing human rights for women at the US–Mexico border', *Social Justice* Vol. 28, No. 2.

Falk, R. (2002) 'Interpreting the interaction of global markets and human rights,' in Brysk, A. (ed.) *Globalization and Human Rights* (Berkeley: University of California Press).

Feingold, H. (1980) *The Politics of Rescue, The Roosevelt Administration and the Holocaust 1938–1945* (New York: Holocaust Library).

Fekete, L. (2005) *The Deportation Machine: Europe, asylum and human rights* (London: Institute of Race Relations).

Fermont, C. (1998) 'Indonesia: The inferno of revolution', *International Socialism* Vol. 2, No. 80.

Ferro, M. (1997) *Colonization: A global history* (London: Routledge).

Fitzgerald, N. (1997) 'Harnessing Globalization: challenges for government and business', *International Affairs* Vol. 73, No. 4, October 1977.

Fontaine, J. (1852) [1712] *Memoirs of a Huguenot Family* (New York: G. P. Putnams).

Foot, P. (1965) *Immigration and Race in British Politics* (London: Penguin).

Fox, J. P. (1988) 'German and European Jewish refugees 1933–1945: Reflections on the Jewish condition under Hitler and the Western World's response to their expulsion and flight', in Bramwell, A. C. *Refugees in the Age of Total War* (London: Unwin Hyman).

Freeman, G. (1998) 'The decline of sovereignty? Politics and immigration restriction in liberal states', in Joppke, C. (ed.) *Challenge to the Nation-State: Immigration in Western Europe and the United States* (Oxford: Oxford University Press).

Friedlander, S. (1997) *Nazi Germany and the Jews Vol. 1: The Years of Persecution, 1933–39* (London: Phoenix).

Fryer, P. (1984) *Staying Power: Black people in Britain since 1504* (London: Pluto).

Fukuyama, F. (1989) 'The End of History', *The National Interest* 16.

Fysh, P. and Wolfreys, J. (1998) *The Politics of Racism in France* (New York: St. Martins Press).

Garrett, G. (2000) 'Globalization and national autonomy', in Woods, N. (ed.) *The Political Economy of Globalization* (Basingstoke: Macmillan).

Gellner, E. (1983) *Nations and Nationalism* (Oxford: Blackwell).

George, S. and Sabelli, F. (1994) *Faith and Credit: The World Bank's secular empire* (London: Penguin).

Ghai, Y. (1997) 'Migrant workers, markets and the law', in Gungwu, W. (ed.) *Global History and Migrations* (Boulder: Westview).

Ghosh, B. (1998) *Huddled Masses and Uncertain Shores: Insights into irregular migration* (The Hague: Martinus Nijhof).

Gibney, M. J. (2002) 'Security and the ethics of asylum', *Forced Migration Review* No. 13.

Gibney, M. J. (2004) *The Ethics and Politics of Asylum: Liberal democracy and the response to refugees* (Cambridge: Cambridge University Press).

Giddens, A. (1999) *Runaway World: How globalisation is shaping our world* (London: Profile Books).

Gilje, P. A. (1996) *Rioting in America* (Bloomington: Indiana University Press).

Glick Schiller, N., Basch, N. and Blanc, C. S. (1992) 'Transnationalism: A new analytical framework for understanding migration', in Glick Schiller, N., Basch, N. and Blanc, C. S. (eds) *Towards a Transnational Perspective on*

Migration: Race, Class, Ethnicity and Nationalism Reconsidered (New York: New York Academy of Sciences).

Global IDP Survey (1998) *Internally Displaced People: A global survey* (London: Earthscan).

Gluckstein, G. (1999) *The Nazis, Capitalism and the Working Class* (London: Bookmarks).

Gold, P. (2000) *Europe or Africa? A Contemporary Study of the Spanish North African Enclaves of Melilla and Ceuta* (Liverpool: Liverpool University Press).

Gorman, R. (1994) 'Poets, playwrights, and the politics of exile and asylum in ancient Greece and Rome', *International Journal of Refugee Law* Vol. 6, No. 3.

Graham-Brown, S. (1991) *Education in the Developing World: Conflict and crisis* (London: Longman).

Grare, F. (2003) 'The geopolitics of Afghan refugees in Pakistan', in Stedman, S. J. and Tanner, F. (eds) *Refugee Manipulation: War, politics and the abuse of human suffering* (Washington DC: Brookings Institution Press).

Gray, J. (1998) *False Dawn: The Delusions of Global Capitalism* (London: Granta).

Green, P. (1983) 'Debt, the banks and Latin America', *International Socialism* Vol. 2, No. 21.

Green, P. and Grewcock, M. (2002) 'The war against illegal immigration: State crime and the construction of a European identity', *Current Issues In Criminal Justice* Vol. 14, No. 1.

Grewcock, M. (2003) 'Irregular migration, identity and the state – the challenge for criminology', *Current Issues In Criminal Justice* Vol. 15, No. 2.

Grenier, M. (1997) *Sri Lankan Tamils, the Home Office and the Forgotten Civil War* (London: Refugee Council).

Gungwu, W. (ed.) *Global History and Migrations* (Boulder, CO: Westview).

Gutierrez, C. G. (1993) 'Limits and possibilities for the Mexican government', in Lowenthal, A. F. and Burgess, K. (eds) *The California–Mexico Connection* (Stanford, CA: Stanford University Press).

Gwynn, R. D. (1985) *Huguenot Heritage* (London: Routledge and Kegan Paul).

Hadari, Z. V. and Tsahor, Z. (1985) *Voyage to Freedom: An episode in the illegal immigration to Palestine* (London: Valentine, Mitchell).

Harding, J. (2000) *The Uninvited: Refugees at the rich man's gate* (London: Profile).

Harman, C. (1984) *Explaining the Crisis* (London: Bookmarks).

Harman, C. (1991) 'The state and capitalism today', *International Socialism* Vol. 2, No. 51.

Harman, C. (1996) 'Globalisation: A critique of a new orthodoxy', *International Socialism* Vol. 2, No. 73.

Harper, M. (2003) *Adventurers and Exiles: The great Scottish exodus* (London: Profile).

Harrell-Bond, B. (1986) *Imposing Aid: Emergency assistance to refugees* (Oxford: Oxford University Press).

Harrell-Bond, B. (1999) 'The experience of refugees as recipients of aid', in Ager, A. (ed.) *Refugees: Perspectives on the Experience of Forced Migration* (London: Continuum).

Harris, N. (1983) *Of Bread and Guns: The world economy in crisis* (London: Penguin).

Harris, N. (1990) *National Liberation* (London: Penguin).

Harris, N. (1995) *The New Untouchables: Immigration and the New World worker* (London: Penguin).

Harris, N. (2002) *Thinking the Unthinkable: The immigration myth exposed* (London: I. B. Tauris).

Harris, N. (2003) *The Return of Cosmopolitan Capital: Globalisation, the state and war* (London: I. B. Tauris).

Harrison, P. (1993) *Inside the Third World* (London: Penguin).

Hayter, T. (2000) *Open Borders: The case against immigration controls* (London: Pluto).

Hein, C. (2000) 'Italy: Gateway to Europe, but not the gatekeeper?', in Van Selm, J. (ed.) *Kosovo's Refugees in the European Union* (London: Pinter).

Hewison, K. (1996) 'Emerging social forces in Thailand: new political and economic roles', in Robison, R. and Goodman, D. S. G. (eds) *The New Rich in Asia: Mobile phones, McDonalds and middle-class revolution* (London: Routledge).

Higashide, S. (2000) *Adios to Tears: The memoirs of a Japanese-Peruvian internee in US concentration camps* (Washington: University of Washington Press).

Hill, C. (1967) *Reformation to Industrial Revolution* (London: Penguin).

Hill, C. (1972) *God's Englishman: Oliver Cromwell and the English Revolution* (London: Penguin).

Hing, B. O. (1993) *Making and Remaking Asian America Through Immigration Policy, 1850–1990* (Stanford, CA: Stanford University Press).

Hinnebusch, R. (1985) *Egyptian Politics Under Sadat* (Cambridge: Cambridge University Press).

Hippler, J. (1994) *Pax America? Hegemony or Decline* (London: Pluto).

Hirst, P. Q. and Thompson, G. (1996) *Globalization in Question: The international economy and the possibilities of governance* (Cambridge: Polity).

Hitchcox, L. (1990) *Vietnamese Refugees in Southeast Asian Camps* (Basingstoke: Macmillan).

Hitler, A. (1972) *Mein Kampf* (London: Radius/Hutchinson).

Hobsbawn, E. J. (1962) *The Age of Revolution 1789–1848* (New York: Mentor).

Hobsbawm, E. J. (1990) *Nations and Nationalism Since 1780: Programme, myth, reality* (Cambridge: Cambridge University Press).

Hobsbawm, E. J. and Ranger, T. (1983) *The Invention of Tradition* (Cambridge: Cambridge University Press).

Hoeing, W. (2004) *Self-image and the well-being of refugees in Rhino Camp, Uganda*, New Issues in Refugee Research, Working Paper No. 103 (Geneva: UNHCR).

Hollifield, J. F. (2000), 'The politics of international migration: How can we "Bring the state back in?",' in Brettell, C. B. and Hollifield, J. F. (eds) *Migration Theory: Talking Across Disciplines* (London: Routledge).

Hoogvelt, A. (1997) *Globalisation and the Postcolonial World: The new political economy of development* (Basingstoke: Macmillan).

Horne, A. (1979) *A Savage War of Peace: Algeria 1954–1962* (London: Penguin).

Horsmann, M. and Marshall, A. (1994) *After the Nation State: Citizens, tribalism and the New World disorder* (London: Harper Collins).

Horst, C. (2003) *Transnational nomads: How Somalis cope with refugee life in the Dadaab camps of Kenya*, PhD thesis, University of Amsterdam.

Hudson, K. (2003) *Breaking the South Slav Dream: The rise and fall of Yugoslavia* (London: Pluto).

Hughes, R. (1987) *The Fatal Shore: a history of the transportation of convicts to Australia, 1787–1868* (London: Collins Harvill).

Human Rights Watch (1999) *World Report 1999* (New York: Human Rights Watch).

Human Rights Watch (2000a) *Seeking Protection: Addressing sexual and domestic violence in Tanzania's refugee camps* (New York: Human Rights Watch).

Human Rights Watch (2000b) *World Report 2000* (New York: Human Rights Watch).

Human Rights Watch (2002a) www.hrw.org/reports/2002/spain/Spain0202.htm

Human Rights Watch (2002b) *Hidden In Plain View: Refugees living without protection in Nairobi* (New York: Human Rights Watch) at: www.hrw.org/reports/2002/kenyugan

Human Rights Watch (2004) 'Closed-door immigration policy is shameful vision', www.hrw.org/english/docs/2004/06/16/eu9351.htm

Humphries, B. (2002) 'From welfare to authoritarianism: The role of social work in welfare controls', Cohen, S., Humphries, B. and Mynott, E. (eds) *From Welfare Contolsl to Immigration Controls* (Stoke-on-Trent: Trentham).

Hunt, L. (2000) 'The paradoxical origins of human rights' in Wasserstrom, J. N., Hunt, L. and Young, M. B. (eds) Human Rights and Revolutions (Lanham: Rowman & Littlefield).

Huntington, S. P. (1993) 'The clash of civilizations?' *Foreign Affairs*, Summer 1993.

Huntington, S. P. (1998) *The Clash of Civilizations and the Re-Making of World Order* (London: Simon & Schuster).

Ibrahim, S. E. (1982) *The New Arab Social Order: A study of the social impact of oil wealth* (Boulder: Westview).

Indra, D. (ed.) (1999) *Engendering Forced Migration: Theory and Practice* (New York: Berghahn Books).

International Monetary Fund (1992) *World Economic Outlook May 1992* (Washington DC: International Monetary Fund).

Issawi, C. (1982) *An Economic History of the Middle East and North Africa* (London: Methuen).

Jacobson, D. (1996) *Rights Across Borders: Immigration and the decline of citizenship* (Baltimore: Johns Hopkins University Press).

Jesuit Refugee Service (JRS) – Europe (2004) *Detention in Europe: Administrative detention of asylum-seekers and irregular migrants* (Brussels: JRS, at: www.irr.org.uk/pdf/JRS_european_detention.pdf).

Johnson, H. J. M. (1972) *British Immigration Policy 1815–1830: 'Shovelling out paupers'* (Oxford: Clarendon).

Joly, D. (1996) *Haven or Hell? Asylum Policies and Refugees in Europe* (Basingstoke: Macmillan).

Joppke, C. (1998) 'Asylum and state sovereignty: A comparison of the United States, Germany and Britain', in Joppke, C. (ed.) *Challenge to the Nation-State: Immigration in Western Europe and the United States* (Oxford: Oxford University Press).

Joppke, C. (1999) *Immigration and the Nation-State: The United States, Germany and Britain* (Oxford: Oxford University Press).

Kaldor, M. and Vashee, B. (1997) (eds) *New Wars: Restructuring the Global Military Sector* (London: Pinter).

Kaplan, R. (1994) 'The coming anarchy', [*Atlantic Monthly* 1994] reprinted 2000 in O'Meara, P., Melinger, H. D. and M. Krain (eds) *Globalization and the Challenges of a New Century* (Bloomington: Indiana University Press).

Kay, D. and Miles, R. (1992) *Refugees or Migrant Workers? European Voluntary Workers in Britain 1946–1951* (London: Routledge).

Keen, D. (1992) *Refugees: Rationing the Right to Life: The emergency crisis in relief* (London: Zed).

Kegley, C. W. Jr. and Wittkopf, E. R. (1995) *World Politics: Trend and Transformation* (New York: St Martin's Press).

Kenrick, D. (1998) 'Selective memory', *Jewish Socialist* No. 39.

Kershen, A. K. (1997) 'Huguenots, Jews and Bangladeshis in Spitalfields and the spirit of Capitalism', in Kershen, A. K. (ed.) *London: The promised land? The migrant experience in a capital city* (Aldershot: Avebury).

Kibreab, G. (1990) *Refugees in Somalia: A burden, an opportunity and a challenge* (Nairobi: IDRC).

Kibreab, G. (1993) 'The myth of dependency among camp refugees in Somalia 1979–1989', *Journal of Refugee Studies* Vol. 6, No. 4.

Kibreab, G. (1995) 'Eritrean women refugees in Khartoum, Sudan, 1970–1990', *Journal of Refugee Studies* Vol. 8, No. 1.

Kiely, R. (1995) *Sociology and Development: The impasse and beyond* (London: UCL Press).

Kiely, R. (1998) 'Globalization, post-Fordism and the contemporary context of development,' *International Sociology* Vol. 13, No. 1.

Kiernan, V. G. (1998) *Colonial Empires and Armies 1815–1960* (Stroud: Sutton).

King, R. (1993) (ed.) *Mass Migration in Europe: The legacy and the future* (Chichester: Wiley).

King, R. (1995) 'Migrations, globalization and place', in Massey, D. and Jess, P. (eds) A *Place in the World* (Oxford: Oxford University Press/Open University).

Kingston, B. (1988) *The Oxford History of Australia Volume 3, 1860–1900: Glad, Confident Morning* (Melbourne: Oxford University Press).

Kiray, M. M. (1976) 'The family of the immigrant worker', in Abadan-Unat, N. (ed.) *Turkish Workers in Europe 1960–1975* (Leiden: E. J. Brill).

Kirk, G. E. (1948) *A Short History of the Middle East* (London: Methuen).

Klein, M. (2002) *Fences and Windows: Dispatches from the front lines of the globalization debate* (London: Flamingo).

Kochavi, A. J. (2001) *Post-Holocaust Politics: Britain, the United States and Jewish Refugees, 1945–1948* (Chapel Hill: University North Carolina Press).

Kocturk, T. (1992) *A Matter of Honour: Experiences of Turkish women migrants* (London: Zed).

Kolinsky, E. (1996) 'Non-German minorities in German society', in Horrocks, D. and Kolinsky, E. (eds) *Turkish Culture in German Society Today* (Providence, RI: Berghahn).

Korac, M. (1998) *Linking Arms: Women and war in post-Yugoslav states* (Uppsala: Life and Peace Institute).

Koser, K. (2001) 'The smuggling of asylum seekers into Western Europe: Contradictions, conundrums and dilemmas', in Kyle, D. and Koslowski, R. (eds) *Global Human Smuggling: Comparative Perspectives* (Baltimore, MD: Johns Hopkins).

Koser, K. (2002) 'From Refugees to transnational communities?', in Al-Ali, N. and Koser, K. (2002) *New Approaches to Migration? Transnational Communities and the Transformation of Home* (London: Routledge).

Koser, K. and Pinkerton, C. (2002) *The Social Networks of Asylum Seekers and the Dissemination of Information about Countries of Origin* [Home Office] at: http://www.homeoffice.gov.uk/rds/pdfs2/socialnetwork/pdf

Koslowski, R. (2000) 'The mobility money can buy: Human smuggling and border control in the European Union', in Andreas, P. and Snyder, T. (eds) *The Wall Around the West: State Borders and Immigration Controls in North America and Europe* (Lanham: Rowman & Littlefield).

Koslowski, R. (2001) 'Economic globalization, human smuggling, and global governance', in Kyle, D. and Koslowski, R. (eds) *Global Human Smuggling: Comparative Perspectives* (Baltimore: Johns Hopkins).

Kushner, T. and Knox, K. (1999) *Refugees in an Age of Genocide* (London: Frank Cass).

Kulischer, E. (1943) *Europe on the Move: War and Population Changes 1917–1943* (New York: Colombia University Press).

Kunder, J. (1998) 'Internally Displaced Children: Just scratching the surface', in global IDP survey, *Internally Displaced People: A global survey* (London: Earthscan).

Kundnani, A. (2001) 'In a foreign land: the new popular racism', *Race and Class* Vol. 43, No. 2.

Kwong, P. (1997) *Forbidden Workers: Illegal Chinese immigrants and American labor* (New York: New Press).

Kwong, P. (2001) 'Impact of Chinese human smuggling on the American labor market', in Kyle, D. and Koslowski, R. (eds) *Global Human Smuggling: Comparative Perspectives* (Baltimore: Johns Hopkins).

Kyle, D. and Dale, J. (2001) 'Smuggling the state back in: Agents of human smuggling reconsidered', in Kyle, D. and Koslowski, R. (eds) *Global Human Smuggling: Comparative perspectives* (Baltimore: Johns Hopkins University Press).

Kyle, D. and Koslowski, R. (2001) 'Introduction', in Kyle, D. and Koslowski, R. (eds) *Global Human Smuggling: Comparative perspectives* (Baltimore: Johns Hopkins University Press).

Lado, J. K. E. (1996) *Women as refugees: Change through displacement among southern Sudanese women in Cairo* (unpublished MA thesis, The American University in Cairo).

Laitin, D. D. and Samater, S. S. (1984) 'Somalia and the World Economy', *Review of African Political Economy* Vol. 11, No. 30.

Landau, L. B. (ed.) (nd) *Forced Migrants in the New Johannesburg: Towards a local government response* (Johannesburg: Forced Migration Studies Programme, University of the Witwatersrand).

Lapati, A. E. (1993) 'Changing socioeconomic conditions and migration patterns', in Lowenthal, A. F. and Burgess, K. (eds) *The California-Mexico Connection* (Stanford, CA: Stanford University Press).

Lee, G. L. (1936) *The Huguenot Settlements in Ireland* (London: Longmans Green).

Leontidou, I. and Afouxenidis, A. (1999) 'Boundaries of social exclusion in Europe', in Hudson, R. and Williams, A. M., *Divided Europe* (London: Sage).

Lesch, A. (1990) 'Egyptian labor migration', in Oweiss, I. O. (ed.) *The Political Economy of Contemporary Egypt* (Washington, DC: Centre for Contemporary Arab Studies, Georgetown University).

Levenstein, A. (1983) *Escape to Freedom: The story of the international rescue committee.*

Levy, M. L. (2004) *We Are Millions: Neo-liberalism and new forms of political activism in Argentina* (London: Latin America Bureau).

Liang, Z. and Ye, W. (2001), 'From Fujian to New York: Understanding the new Chinese immigration', in Kyle, D. and Koslowski, R. (eds) *Global Human Smuggling: Comparative perspectives* (Baltimore, MD: Johns Hopkins).

Lievens, J. (1999) 'Family-forming migration from Turkey and Morocco to Belgium: The demand for marriage partners from the countries of origin', *International Migration Review* Vol. 33, No. 3.

Lipstadt, D. (1994) *Denying The Holocaust: The growing assault on truth and memory* (London: Penguin).

Litvinoff, B. (1989) *The Burning Bush: Antisemitism and world history* (London: William Collins).

Livingstone, G. (2003) *Inside Colombia: Drugs, democracy and war* (London: Latin America Bureau).

Loescher, G. (1993) *Beyond Charity: International cooperation and the global refugee crisis* (Oxford: Oxford University Press).

Loescher, G. (1999) 'Refugees: a global human rights and security crisis', in Dunne, T. and Wheeler, N. J. (eds) *Human Rights in Global Politics* (Cambridge: Cambridge University Press).

Loescher, G. (2001) *The UNHCR and World Politics: A perilous path* (Oxford: Oxford University Press).

Loescher, G. and Scanlan, J. A. (1986) *Calculated Kindness: Refugees and America's Half-Open Door, 1945 to the present* (New York: Free Press).

London, L. (2000) *Whitehall and the Jews 1933–1946: British immigration policy and the Holocaust* (Cambridge: Cambridge University Press).

Lynn, N. and Lea, S. (2003) ' "A phantom menace and the new Apartheid": The social construction of asylum seekers in the United Kingdom', *Discourse and Society* Vol. 44, No. 4.

Macmaster, N. (2001) *Racism in Europe 1870–2000* (Basingstoke: Palgrave).

Maher, K. H. (2002) 'Who has a right to rights? Citizenship's exclusions in an age of migration', in Brysk, A. (ed.) *Globalization and Human Rights* (Berkeley: University of California Press).

Mandel, P. (1998) 'Foreigners in the Fatherland: Turkish immigrant workers in Germany', in Guerin-Gonzales, C. and Strikwerda, C. (eds) *The Politics of Immigrant Workers: Labor activism and migration in the world economy since 1930* (New York: Holmes and Meier).

Mares, P. (2001) *Borderline: Australia's treatment of refugees and asylum seekers* (Sydney: University of New South Wales Press).

Marfleet, P. (1999) 'Europe's civilizing mission', in Cohen, P. (ed.) *New Ethnicities, Old Racisms* (London: Zed).

Marfleet, P. (2000) 'A new orientalism: Europe confronts the Middle East', in Ismael, T. Q. (ed.) *The International Relations of the Middle East in the 21st Century* (Aldershot: Ashgate).

Marfleet, P. (2003) 'The clash thesis: War and ethnic boundaries in Europe', in *Arab Studies Quarterly* Vol. 25, Nos. 1 and 2, Winter/Spring 2003.

Marr, D. and Wilkinson, M. (2003) *Dark Victory* (Sydney: Allen and Unwin).

Marrus, M. R. (1985) *The Unwanted: European refugees in the twentieth century* (Oxford: Oxford University Press).

Marrus, M. R. (1989) *The Holocaust in History* (London: Penguin).

Marshall, B. (2000) *The New Germany and Migration in Europe* (Manchester: Manchester University Press).

Martin, P. L. (1999) 'Guest worker policies: an international survey', in Bernstein, A. and Weiner, M. (eds) *Migration and Refugee Policies: An overview* (London: Pinter).

Martin-Baro, I. (1994) *Writings for a Liberation Psychology* (Cambridge, MA: Harvard University Press).

Marx, E. (1990) 'The social world of refugees: A conceptual framework', *Journal of Refugee Studies* Vol. 3, No. 3.

Marx, K. (1957) *Capital, Vol. 2* (London: J.M.Dent).

Massey, D. (1990) 'Social structure, household strategies, and the cumulative causation of migration', *Population Index* Vol. 56, No. 1.

Massey, D., Arango, J. Hugo, G. Kouaouci, A. Pellegrino, A. and Taylor, J. (1993) 'Theories of international migration: A review and appraisal', *Population and Development Review* Vol. 19, No. 3.

Masud-Piloto, F. R. (1996) *From Welcomed Exiles to Illegal Immigrants: Cuban Migration to the US, 1959–1995* (Lanham: Rowman & Littlefield).

Mazur (2000) 'Labour's new internationalism', *Foreign Affairs* 79.

McDowell, C. (1996) *A Tamil Asylum Diaspora: Sri Lankan migration, settlement and politics in Switzerland* (Providence, RI: Berghahn).

McGrew, A. (2000) 'Sustainable globalization? The global politics of development and exclusion in the new world order', in Allen, T. and Thomas, A. (eds) *Poverty and Development into the 21st Century* (Oxford: Oxford University Press/Open University).

McSpadden, L. and Mousa, H. (1993) 'I have a name: The gender dynamics in asylum and resettlement of Ethiopian and Eritrean refugees in North America', *Journal of Refugee Studies* Vol. 6, No. 3.

Melander, G. (1987) 'Refugees with no country of asylum: Strategies for third country resettlement', in Rogge, J. (ed.) *Refugees: A Third World dilemma* (Lanham: Rowan and Littlefield).

Meilaender, P. C. (2001) *Toward a Theory of Immigration* (Basingstoke: Palgrave).

Mertus, J. A. (2000) *Women's Offensive on Women* (Bloomfield: Kumarian).

Miall, H., Ramsbotham, O. and Woodhouse, T. (1999) *Contemporary Conflict Resolution* (Cambridge: Polity).

Milanovic, B. (2002) 'True world income distribution, 1988 and 1993: First calculations based on household surveys alone', *Economic Journal* Vol. 112.

Miles, R. (1983) *Racism and Migrant Labour* (London: Kegan Paul).

Miles, R. and Cleary, P. (1993) 'Migration to Britain: State regulation and employment', in Robinson, V. (ed.) *The International Refugee Crisis* (Basingstoke: Macmillan).

Miller, M. (1999) 'The prevention of unauthorized migration' in Bernstein, A. and Weiner, M. (eds) *Migration and Refugee Policies: An overview* (London: Pinter).

Miller, M. J. (2001) 'The sanctioning of unauthorized migration and alien unemployment', in Kyle, D. and Koslowski, R. (eds) *Global Human Smuggling: Comparative perspectives* (Baltimore: Johns Hopkins).

Mittelman, J. H. (2004) *Whither Globalization? The Vortex of Knowledge and Technology* (London: Routledge).

Moghadam, V. M. (1994) *Gender and National Identity: Women and politics in muslim societies* (London: Zed).

Moorehead, C. (2005) *Human Cargo: A journey among refugees* (London: Chatto & Windus).

Moore, R. and Wallace, T. (1975) *Slamming the Door: The administration of immigration control* (London: Martin Robertson).

Moro, N. L. and Lamua, L. S. (1998) 'Economic Situation', in Sudan Cultural Digest Project, *Coping with Dynamics of Culture and Change: The Case of the*

Displaced Sudanese in Egypt (Cairo: Office of African Studies, The American University in Cairo).

Morris, B. (2004) 'On ethnic cleansing', *New Left Review*, Second Series, Vol. 26, March–April 2004.

Morris, L. (2002) *Managing Migration* (London: Routledge).

Morrison, G. S. and Moos, F. (1982) 'Halfway to nowhere: Vietnamese refugees on Guam', in Hansen, A. and Oliver-Smith, A. (eds) *Involuntary Migration and Resettlement: The problems and responses of dislocated people* (Boulder: Westview).

Morrison, J. (2001) ' "The dark side of globalisation": the criminalisation of refugees', *Race and Class* Vol. 43, No. 1.

Morrison, J. and Crosland, B. (2001) *The trafficking and smuggling of refugees: the end game in European asylum policy?* New Issues in Refugee Research, Working Paper No. 39 (Geneva: UNHCR).

Nadig, A. (2002) 'Human smuggling, national security, and refugee protection', *Journal of Refugee Studies* Vol. 15, No. 1.

Nafziger, E. W. (1988) *Inequality in Africa: Political elites, proletariat, peasants and the poor* (Cambridge: Cambridge University Press).

Nevins, J. (2000) 'The remaking of the California–Mexico boundary in the age of NAFTA', in Andreas, P. and Snyder, T. (eds) *The Wall Around the West: State borders and immigration controls in North America and Europe* (Lanham: Rowman & Littlefield).

Nordstrom, C. (1997) *Girls and Warzones: Troubling questions* (Uppsala: Life and Peace Institute).

Nowrojee, B. (1998) 'Displaced people: A Kenya case Study', in Davies, W. (ed.) *Rights Have No Borders: Worldwide internal displacement* (Oslo: Norwegian Refugee Council/Global IDP Survey).

Nugent, W. (1992) *Crossings: The great transatlantic migrations, 1870–1915* (Bloomington: Indiana University Press).

Nyakabwa, K. and Lavoie, C. (1995) 'Sexual violence against women refugees in the Horn of Africa', *African Women* Vol. 10.

Nyoka, C. M. (1999) *Southern Sudanese women in refuge: Experiences in Egypt* (unpublished MA thesis, The American University in Cairo).

Obi, N. and Crisp, J. (2000) 'Evaluation of UNHCR's policy on refugees in urban areas: A case study review of New Delhi' (Geneva: UNHCR Evaluation and Policy Unit).

Obi, N. and Crisp, J. (2002) 'UNHCR policy on refugees in urban areas: report of a UNHCR/NGO workshop' (Geneva: UNHCR Evaluation and Policy Unit).

O'Hagan, J. (1995) 'Civilizational conflict? Looking for cultural enemies', *Third World Quarterly* Vol. 18, No. 1.

Ohmae, K. (1990) *The Borderless World: Power and strategy in the interlinked economy* (New York: Harper).

Ohmae, K. (1995) *The End of the Nation-State: The rise of regional economies* (New York: Free Press).

Pajares, M. (2004) *Immigracion Irregular En Cataluna: Analisis y propuestas* (Barcelona: CERES).

Papademitriou, D. (1993) 'Confronting the challenge of transnational migration: domestic and international responses', in OECD, *The Changing Course of International Migration* (Paris: OECD).

Papadopolou, A. (2004) 'Smuggling into Europe: Transit migrants in Greece', *Journal of Refugee Studies* Vol. 17, No. 2.

Papastergiadis, N. (2000) *The Turbulence of Migration* (Cambridge: Polity).

Parmet, R. D. (1981) *Labour and Immigration in Industrial America* (Boston: Twayne).

Pastor, R. A. (1985) *Migration and Development in the Caribbean: The unexplored Connection* (Boulder: Westview Press).

Patterson, T. C. (1997) *Inventing Western Civilization* (New York: Monthly Review Press).

Payne, R. (2002) *Cashing in on asylum: An investigation into the multinational companies operating immigration detention centres for the Home Office* (unpublished MA thesis, University of East London).

Pickering, S. (2001) 'Common sense and original deviancy: News discourses and asylum seekers in Australia', *Journal of Refugee Studies* Vol. 14, No. 2.

Pickering, S. and Lambert, C. (2002) 'Deterrence: Australia's refugee policy', in *Current Issues In Criminal Justice*, Vol. 14, No. 1.

Pilger, J. (1986) *Heroes* (London: Pan).

Pilger, J. (1992) *Distant Voices* (London: Vintage).

Pinkerton, C. McLaughlan, G. and Salt, J. (2004) *Sizing the illegally resident population in the UK* (London: Home Office).

Pirenne, H. (1936) *Economic and Social History of Medieval Europe* (London: Routledge and Kegan Paul).

Porter, B. (1975) *The Lion's Share: A short history of British Imperialism 1850–1970* (London: Longman).

Porter, B. (1979) *The Refugee Question in mid-Victorian Politics* (Cambridge: Cambridge University Press).

Porter, B. (1984) 'The British Government and Political Refugees, 1880–1914', in Slatter, J. (ed.) *From the Other Shore* (London: Frank Cass).

Potts, L. (1990) *The World Labour Market: A History of Migration* (London: Zed).

Pourgourides, C. (1998) 'The mental health implications of detention of asylum seekers', in Hughes, J. and Liebaut, F. (eds) *Detention of Asylum Seekers in Europe: Analysis and Perspectives* (The Hague: Martinus Nijhoff).

Poynting, S (2002) ' "Bin laden in the suburbs": Attacks on Arab and Muslim Australians before and after 11 September', in *Current Issues In Criminal Justice* Vol. 14, No. 1.

Power, J. (2001) *Like Water on Stone: The story of Amnesty International* (London: Allen Lane).

Pugh, M. (2004) 'Drowning not waving: Boat people and humanitarianism at sea', *Journal of Refugee Studies* Vol. 17, No. 1.

Raudzens, G. (1999) *Empires: Europe and Globalization 1492–1788* (Stroud: Sutton).

Reaman, G. E. (1964) *The Trail of the Huguenots* (London: Frederick Muller).

Rees, J. (1999) 'The socialist revolution and the democratic revolution', *International Socialism* Vol. 2, No. 83, Summer 1999.

Refugee Council (1999) *Unwanted Journey* (London: Refugee Council).

Reno, W. (1998) *Warlord Politics and African States* (Boulder: Lynne Rienner).

Richmond, A. (1993) 'Reactive migration: Sociological perspectives on refugee movements', *Journal of Refugee Studies* Vol. 6, No. 1.

Richmond, A. (1994) *Global Apartheid: Refugees, racism and the new world order* (Oxford: Oxford University Press).

Rieff, D. (2002) *A Bed for the Night: Humanitarism in crisis* (London: Vintage).

Rietbergen, P. (1998) *Europe: A Cultural History* (London: Routledge).

Roberts, S. (2003) 'Global strategic vision: Managing the world', in Perry, W. P. and Maurer, B. (eds) *Globalization Under Construction* (Minneapolis: University of Minnesota Press).

Robertson, R. (1992) *Globalization: Social Theory and Global Culture* (London: Sage).

Robinson, W. I. (1996) 'Globalisation: nine theses on our epoch', *Race and Class* Vol. 38, No. 2, October–December 1996.

Robison, R. (1996) 'The middle class and the bourgeoisie in Indonesia' in Robison, R. and Goodman, D. S. G. (eds) *The New Rich in Asia: Mobile phones, McDonalds and middle-class revolution* (London: Routledge).

Rodrigez, N. P. (1997) 'The social construction of the US–Mexico border', in Perea, J. F. (ed.) *Immigrants Out!* (New York: New York University Press).

Rogge, J. and Akol, J. (1989) 'Repatriation: Its role in solving Africa's refugee dilemma', *International Migration Review* No. 23.

Rose, N. (1994) *Put to Work: Relief Programmes in the great depression* (New York: Monthly Review Press).

Rosenau, J. N. (2002) 'The drama of human rights in a turbulent, globalized world', in Brysk, A. (ed) *Globalization and Human Rights* (Berkeley: University of California Press).

Ross, E. B. (2003) *Modernisation, clearance and the continuum of violence in Colombia*, Institute of Social Science Working Papers Series, No. 383 (The Hague: Institute of Social Studies).

Rouse, R. (1991) 'Mexican migration and the social space of postmodernism', *Diaspora* No. 1.

Rubinstein, W. D. (1997) *The Myth of Rescue* (London: Routledge).

Rudge, P. (1992) 'The asylum dilemma – Crisis in the modern world: A European perspective', in Loescher, G. (ed.) *Refugees and the Asylum Dilemma in the West* (University Park, PA: Pennsylvania University Press).

Ruigrok, W. and van Tulder, R. (1995) *The Logic of International Restructuring* (London: Routledge).

Ryan, W. C. (1987) 'The historical case for the right of sanctuary', *Journal of Church and State* Vol. 29, Spring 1987.

Sala-i-Martin, X. (2002) *The disturbing 'rise' in global income inequality*, NBER Working Papers at: http://www.papers.nber.org/papers/w8904.

Salomon, K. (1990) 'The Cold War heritage: UNRRA and the IRO as predecessors of UNHCR', in Rystad, G. (ed.) *The Uprooted* (Lund: Lund University Press).

Salt, J. (2000) 'Trafficking and human smuggling: A European perspective', *Perspectives on Trafficking of Migrants* (Geneva: International Organization for Migration/United Nations).

Salt, J. and Stein, J. (1997) 'Migration as a business: The case of trafficking', *International Migration* Vol. 35, No. 4.

Sampson, A. (1981) *The Money Lenders: Bankers and a World in Turmoil* (New York: Viking).

Sassen, S. (1998) *Globalization and its Discontents* (New York: New Press).

Sassen, S. (1999) *Guests and Aliens* (New York: New Press).

Sayigh, R. (1979) *Palestinians: From Peasants to Revolutionaries* (London: Zed).

Schechtman, J. E. (1963) *The Refugee in the World: Displacement of Integration?* (New York: A. S. Barnes).

Schmeidl, S. (2001) 'Conflict and forced migration: A quantative review, 1964–1995', in Zolberg, A. R. and Benda, P. M. (eds) *Global Migrants, Global Refugees* (New York: Berghahn).

Schwartz, B. (1996) 'The expansion and contraction of England', in Schwartz, B. (ed.) *The Expansion of England* (London: Routledge).

Schwartz, H. (1980) *The French Prophets* (Berkeley: University of California Press).

Schonwalder, K. (1999) ' "Persons persecuted on political grounds shall enjoy the right of asylum – but not in our country" – asylum policy and debates about refugees in the Federal Republic of Germany', in Bloch, A. and Levy, C. (eds) *Refugees, Citizenship and Social Policy in Europe* (Basingstoke: Macmillan).

Schuster, L. and Solomos, J. (1999) 'The politics of refugee and asylum policies in Britain: Historical patterns and contemporary realities', in Bloch, A. and Levy, C. (eds) *Refugees, Citizenship and Social Policy in Europe* (Basingstoke: Macmillan).

Schechtman, J. B. (1963) *The Refugee in the World: Displacement and integration* (New York: A. S. Barnes).

Seddon, D. (1989) 'Riot and rebellion in the North Africa: Political responses to economic crisis in Tunisia, Morocco and Sudan', in Berberoglu, B. (ed.) *Power and Stability in the Middle East* (London: Pluto).

Sen, A. (1993) 'Capability and well-being', in Nussbaum, M.C. and Sen, A. (eds) *The Quality of Life* (Oxford: Clarendon).

Shacknove, A. (1993) 'From asylum to containment', *International Journal of Refugee Law* Vol. 5, No. 4.

Shafer, B. C. (1972) *Faces of Nationalism: New realities and old myths* (New York: Harcourt Brace Jovanovich)

Shah, N. (2001) *Contagious Divides: Epidemics and race in San Francisco's Chinatown* (Berkeley: University of California).

Shaw, M. (1994) *Global Society and International Relations* (Oxford: Blackwell).

Sherman, A. J. (1994) *Island Refuge: Britain and refugees from the Third Reich 1933–1939* (London: Frank Cass).

Simons, A. (1995) *Networks of Dissolution: Somalia undone* (Boulder: Westview).

Simpson, J. S. (1939) *Refugees: A review of the situation since September 1938* (London: Royal Institute of International Affairs).

Singer, A. and Massey, D. (1998) 'The social process of undocumented border crossing among Mexican migrants', *International Migration Review* Vol. XXXIII, No. 3, Fall 1998.

Sivanandan, A. (1998) 'Globalisation and the Left', *Race and Class* Vol. 40, Nos. 2/3.

Sjoberg, T. (1991) *The Powers and the Persecuted: The refugee problem and the Intergovernmental Committee on Refugees (IGCR) 1938–1947* (Lund: Lund University Press).

Skeldon, R. (2000) *Myths and Realities of Chinese Irregular Migration* (Geneva: International Organization for Migration).

Smith, A. (1993) *An Inquiry into the Nature and Causes of the Wealth of Nations* (Oxford: Oxford University Press).

Smith, P. A. (1984) *Palestine and the Palestinians 1876–1983* (London: Croom Helm).

Smiles, S. (1868) *The Huguenots* (London: John Murray).

Solomos, J. and Back, L. (1996) *Racism and Society* (Basingstoke: Macmillan).

Sommers, M. (2001a) *Fear in Bongoland: Burundi refugees in Tanzania* (Oxford: Berghahn).

Sommers, M. (2001b) 'Young, male and Pentecostal: Urban refugees in Dar es Salaam, Tanzania', *Journal of Refugee Studies* Vol. 14, No. 4.

Sorensen, N. N., Van Hear, N. and Engberg-Pedersen, P. (2002) *The Migration–Development Nexus: Evidence and policy decisions* (Copenhagen: Centre for Development Research)

Spener, D. (2000) 'The logic and contradictions of intensified border enforcement in Texas', in Andreas, P. and Snyder, T. (eds) *The Wall Around the West: State borders and immigration controls in North America and Europe* (Lanham: Rowman & Littlefield).

Spener, D. (2001) 'Smuggling migrants through south Texas: Challenges poses by operation Rio Grande', in Kyle, D. and Koslowski, R. (eds) *Global Human Smuggling: Comparative perspectives* (Baltimore, MD: Johns Hopkins).

Spero, J. E. and Hart, J. A. (1997) *The Politics of International Relations* (London: Routledge).

Spybey, T. (1996) *Globalization and World Society* (Cambridge: Polity).

Stalker, P. (2000) *Workers without Frontiers: The impact of globalization on international migration* (Boulder: Lynne Reinner).

Stalker, P. (2001) *The No-Nonsense Guide to International Migration* (Oxford: New Internationalist Publications).

Stalker, J. (2002) *Migration Trends and Migration Policy in Europe* (Copenhagen: Centre for Development Research).

Stedman, S. J. and Tanner, F. (eds) (2003) *Refugee Manipulation: War, Politics and the Abuse of Human Suffering* (Washington, DC: Brookings Institution Press).

Stent, R. (1980) *A Bespotted Page* (London: Andre Deutsch).

Stiglitz, J. (2002) *Globalization and its Discontents* (London: Penguin).

Stopford, J., Strange, S. and J. S. Henley (1991) *Rival States, Rival Firms: Competition for world market shares* (Cambridge: Cambridge University Press).

Strawson, J. (ed.) (2002) *Law After Ground Zero* (London: Cavendish).

Stubbs, P. (1999) *Displaced Promises: Forced migration, refuge and return in Croatia and Bosnia-Herzegovina* (Uppsala: Life and Peace Institute).

Suhrke, A. (1997) 'Uncertain globalization: Refugee movements in the second half of the twentieth century', in Gungwu, W. (ed.) *Global History and Migrations* (Boulder: Westview).

Summerfield, D. (1995) 'Addressing human response to war and atrocity', in Kleber, R. J., Figley, C. R., and Gersons, B. P. R. (eds) *Beyond Trauma* (New York: Plenum Press).

Summerfield, D. (1997) 'The social, cultural and political dimensions of contemporary war', *Medicine, Conflict and Survival* Vol. 13, Nos 3–25.

Summerfield, D. (1999) 'Sociocultural dimensions of war, conflict and displacement', in Ager, A. (ed.) *Refugees: Perspectives on the experience of forced migration* (London: Continuum).

Swierenga, R. P. (1986) 'Dutch International Migration and Occupational Change: A Structural Analysis of Multinational Linked Files', in Glazier, I. A. and De Rosa, L. (eds) *Migration Across Time and Nations* (New York: Holmes and Meier).

Taylor, C. C. (1999) *Sacrifice as Terror: The Rwandan genocide of 1994* (Oxford: Berg).

Taylor, P. (1971) *The Distant Magnet: European emigration to the USA* (London: Eyre and Spottiswode).

Thomas, H. (1998) *The Slave Trade* (London: Papermac).

Thomas, J. J. (1995) *Surviving in the City: The urban informal sector in Latin America* (London: Pluto).

Thompson, E. P. (1968) *The Making of the English Working Class* (London: Penguin).

Timberlake, L. (1985) *Africa in Crisis: The causes, the cures of environmental bankruptcy* (London: Earthscan).

Torpey, J. (2000) 'States and the regulation of migration in the twentieth-century North Atlantic world', in Andreas, P. and Snyder, T. (eds) *The Wall Around the West: State borders and immigration controls in North America and Europe* (Lanham: Rowman & Littlefield).

Tuitt, P. (1996) *False Images: Law's construction of the refugee* (London: Pluto).

Tussie, D. and Woods, N. (2000), 'Trade, regionalism and the threat to multilateralism', in Woods, N. (ed.) *The Political Economy of Globalization* (Basingstoke: Macmillan).

UNCTAD [United Nations Conference on Trade and Development] (2001) *World Investment Report* (Geneva: UNCTAD).

UNCTAD [United Nations Conference on Trade and Development] (2004) *Development and Globalization: Facts and figures* (Geneva: UNCTAD).

UNDP [United Nations Development Programme] (1998) *Human Development Report 2000* (New York: Oxford University Press).

UNDP [United Nations Development Programme] (2000a) *Human Development Report 2000* (New York: Oxford University Press).

UNDP [United Nations Development Programme] (2000b) *Poverty Report 2000: Overcoming human poverty* (New York: UNDP).

UNDP [United Nations Development Programme] (2003) *Human Development Report 2003* (UNDP: New York).

UNHCR [United Nations High Commissioner for Refugees] (1995a) *The State of the World's Refugees* (Oxford: Oxford University Press).

UNHCR [United Nations High Commissioner for Refugees] (1995b) *UNHCR's Policy and Practice Regarding Urban Refugees, A Discussion Paper* (Geneva: UNHCR).

UNHCR [United Nations High Commissioner for Refugees] (2000) *The State of the World's Refugees* (Oxford: Oxford University Press).

UNHCR [United Nations High Commissioner for Refugees] *UNHCR Statistical Year book 2001* (Geneva: UNHCR).

UNHCR [United Nations High Commissioner for Refugees] (2003) *Global Report* (Geneva: UNHCR).

UNHCR [United Nations High Commissioner for Refugees] (2004) *Asylum Levels and Trends in Industrialized Countries, Third Quarter, 2004* (Geneva: UNHCR).

USCR [US Committee for Refugees] (1997) *At Fortress Europe's Moat: The 'Safe Third County' Concept* (Washington: US Committee for Refugees).

USCR [US Committee for Refugees] (1998) *Colombia's Silent Crisis: One million displaced by violence* (Washington: US Committee for Refugees).

USCR [US Committee for Refugees] (2004) *Refugee Reports*: special issue on refugee warehousing, Vol. 24, No. 3.

Vachudova, M. A. (2000) 'Eastern Europe as gatekeeper: The immigration and asylum policies of an enlarging European Union', in Andreas, P. and Snyder, T. (eds) *The Wall Around the West: State Borders and Immigration Controls in North America and Europe* (Lanham: Rowman & Littlefield).

Van Damme, W. (1999) 'Do Refugees belong in camps? Experiences from Goma and Guinea', *Journal of Refugee Studies* Vol. 12, No. 1.

Van Hear, N. (1998) *New Diasporas: the mass exodus, dispersal and regrouping of migrant communities* (London: UCL Press).

Van Hear, N. (2004) '*I went as far as my money would take me': Conflict, forced migration and class*, Centre of Migration, Policy and Society Working Paper No. 6 (Oxford: University of Oxford).

Van Selm, J. (ed.) (2000) 'Conclusion' in Van Selm, J. (ed.) *Kosovo's Refugees in the European Union* (London: Pinter).

Veenkamp, T., Bentley, T. and Buonfino, A. (2003) *People Flow: Managing Migration in a New European Commonwealth* (London: Demos).

Vernez, G. (1993) 'From rapid growth to likely stability', in Lowenthal, A. F. and Burgess, K. (eds) *The California–Mexico Connection* (Stanford, CA: Stanford University Press).

Voutira, E. and Harrell-Bond, B. (1995) 'In search of the locus of trust: The social world of the refugee camp', in Daniel, E.V. and Knudsen, J. C. *Mistrusting Refugees* (Berkeley: University of California Press).

Wade, R. H. (2004) 'Is globalization reducing poverty and inequality?', *World Development* Vol. 32, No. 4.

Wain, B. (1981) *The Refusal: The agony of the Indochina refugees* (New York: Simon and Schuster).

Walton, J. and Seddon, D. (1994) *Free Markets and Food Riots: The politics of global adjustment* (Oxford: Blackwell).

Warren, B. (1980) *Imperialism: Pioneer of capitalism* (London: Verso).

Wasserstein B. (1988) *Britain and the Jews of Europe 1939–1945* (Oxford: Institute of Jewish Affairs/Oxford University Press).

Waters, M. (1995) *Globalization* (London: Routledge).

Waters, M. (2001) *Globalization* (second edition) (London: Routledge).

Watkins, T. H. (1999) *The Hungry Years: A Narrative History of the Great Depression in America* (New York: Henry Holt).

Waxman, P. (2000) 'The shaping of Australia's immigration and refugee policy', *Immigrants and Minorities* Vol. 19, No. 1.

Weller, P. (1987) *Sanctuary: The beginning of a movement?* (London: Runnymede Trust).

Werbner, P. (1990) *The Migration Process: Capital, gifts and offerings among British Pakistanis* (Oxford: Berg).

Weiner, M. (1995) *The Global Migration Crisis: Challenge to states and to human rights* (New York: HarperCollins).

Weiner, M. (1997) 'The global migration crisis', in Gungwu, W. (ed.) *Global History and Migrations* (Boulder: Westview).

Weiss, L. (1998) *The Myth of the Powerless State: Governing the economy in a global era* (Cambridge: Polity).

Westin, C. (1999) 'Regional analysis of refugee movements: origins and response', in Ager, A. (ed.) *Refugees: Perspectives on the Experience of Forced Migration* (London: Continuum).

Weyker, S. (2002) 'The ironies of information technology', in Brysk, A. (ed.) *Globalization and Human Rights* (Berkeley: University of California Press).

White, J. (1997) 'Turks in the New Germany', *American Anthropologist* Vol. 99, No. 4.

Williams, E. (1964) *Capitalism and Slavery* (London: Andre Deutsch).

Wilson, K. B. and Nunes, J. (1994) 'Repatriation to Mozambique', in Allen, T. and Morsink, H. (eds) *When Refugees Go Home* (London: James Currey).

Winder, R. (2004) *Bloody Foreigners: The story of immigration to Britain* (London: Little, Brown).

Wolf, M. (2005) Why *Globalization Works* (New Haven, CT: Yale University Press).

Wolfson, S. and Wright, N. (1995) *Working With The Military* (Geneva: UNHCR).

Woods, N. (2000) 'The political economy of globalization', in Woods, N. (ed.) *The Political Economy of Globalization* (Basingstoke: Macmillan).

World Bank (1989) *World Development Report 1989* (New York: Oxford University Press).

World Bank (2000) *World Development Report 1999–2000* (New York: Oxford University Press).

Yuval-Davis, N. (1997) *Gender and Nation* (London: Sage).

Zaret, D. (2000) 'Tradition, human rights and the English Revolution' in Wasserstrom, J. N., Hunt, L. and Young, M. B. (eds) *Human Rights and Revolutions* (Lanham: Rowman & Littlefield).

Zertal, I. (1998) *From Catastrophe to Power: Holocaust survivors and the Emergence of Israel* (Berkeley: University of California Press).

Zetter, R. (1991) 'Labelling refugees: Forming and transforming a bureaucratic identity', *Journal of Refugee Studies* Vol. 4, No. 1.

Zetter, R. (1995) 'Shelter provision and settlement policies for refugees', in Zetter, R. and Baker, J. *Studies on Emergencies and Disaster Relief Report No. 2* (Uppsala: Nordiska Africainstitutet).

Zetter, R. (1999) 'International perspectives on refugee assistance', in Ager, A. (ed.) *Refugees: Perspectives on the experience of forced migration* (London: Continuum).

Zolberg, A. (1983) 'International migrations in political perspectives', in Kritz, M. M., Keeley, C. B. and Tomasi, S. M. (eds) *Global Trends in Migration: Theory and research on international population movements* (New York: Centre for Migration Studies).

Zolberg, A. (1997) 'Global movements, global walls: Responses to migration, 1885–1925', in Gungwu, W. (ed.) *Global History and Migrations* (Boulder: Westview).

Zolberg, A. R. (2001) 'Introduction: Beyond the crisis', in Zolberg, A. R. and Benda, P. M. (eds) *Global Migrants, Global Refugees* (New York: Berghahn).

Zolberg, A., Suhrke, A. and Aguayo, S. (1989) *Escape from Violence: Conflict and the Refugee Crisis in the Developing World* (Oxford: Oxford University Press).

Zuckert, M. (2000) 'Natural rights in the American Revolution: The American amalgam', in Wasserstrom, J. N., Hunt, L. and Young, M. B. (eds) *Human Rights and Revolutions* (Lanham: Rowman & Littlefield).

Index